DESIGNING INTERVENTIONS FOR PRESCHOOL LEARNING AND BEHAVIOR PROBLEMS

David W. Barnett
and
Karen T. Carey

DESIGNING INTERVENTIONS FOR PRESCHOOL LEARNING AND BEHAVIOR PROBLEMS

 Jossey-Bass Publishers
San Francisco

For sales outside the United States contact Maxwell/Macmillan
International Publishing Group, 866 Third Avenue, New York,
New York 10022

Manufactured in the United States of America

 The paper used in this book is acid-free and meets the
State of California requirements for recycled paper
(50 percent recycled waste, including 10 percent
postconsumer waste), which are the strictest guidelines
for recycled paper currently in use in the United States.

Library of Congress Cataloging-in-Publication Data

Barnett, David W., date
   Designing interventions for preschool learning and behavior
problems / David W. Barnett, Karen T. Carey.
     p.   cm. — (The Jossey-Bass social and behavioral science
series) (The Jossey-Bass education series)
   Includes bibliographical references (p.   ) and index.
   ISBN 1-55542-409-0
   1. Problem children — Education (Preschool). 2. Behavior disorders
in children. 3. Behavior modification. 4. Socialization.
I. Carey, Karen T., date. II. Title. III. Series. IV. Series:
The Jossey-Bass education series.
LC4801.B36 1992
371.93 — dc20   91-38009
                                                            CIP

FIRST EDITION
HB Printing   10 9 8 7 6 5 4 3 2 1   *Code 9214*

A joint publication in
The Jossey-Bass Social and Behavioral Science Series
and
The Jossey-Bass Education Series

Psychoeducational Interventions:
Guidebooks for School Practitioners

Consulting Editors

Charles A. Maher
Rutgers University
Joseph E. Zins
University of Cincinnati

Contents

Preface

THIS BOOK HAS ONE OVERALL PURPOSE: TO HELP EDUCATORS AND psychologists develop interventions for preschool children with learning and behavior problems. Assessment and intervention design should be based on a theoretical model directly related to psychosocial change. Steps to achieve interventions should be guided by a scientist-practitioner model that integrates research and deals effectively with the realities of practice.

Most major intervention efforts have focused on serving groups of children and have been demonstration or research programs such as Head Start and Abecedarian. This book looks at case studies of specific interventions supported by research. The studies were done with individuals and small groups of young children described as normal, high risk, or disabled.

We highlight intervention design for enhancing roles of parents and teachers of young children. Many interventions are based on studies of competence and on what parents and teachers do in teaching children, enhancing developmental skills, or resolving the challenges that children present. Thus, we emphasize a theory of psychosocial change rather than developmental theories and have organized the book by intervention design and by the possible roles of caregivers in the natural settings of family and school.

Rather than identifying children as disabled, we stress *problem situations*. Early intervention is important for children who present instructional or parenting difficulties and children who have limited positive experiences with peers. That is, this book is for young children who are difficult to parent, teach, or befriend. While some children traditionally characterized as disabled, handicapped, or at risk may fit this focus, others do not. In certain places, we have used traditional descriptors to help the reader when the discussion is embedded in tradition, for example, integrating disabled children into regular classrooms.

Who Should Use This Book

Designing Interventions for Preschool Learning and Behavior Problems will appeal to professionals and graduate students in psychology. Much of the book, if not all, will also be of interest to early childhood specialists.

The book is written for readers with prior training in social cognitive interventions, applied behavior analysis, behavioral research methods, parent and teacher consultation, and legal and ethical issues related to assessment and intervention. Introductory knowledge of measurement is helpful for Chapter Two.

Throughout, we try to identify sound interventions and useful ideas contained in a technical body of research. Of necessity, some details of the studies have been omitted. In every case, we risk oversimplifying the complexities of intervention design for those readers not well versed in those areas mentioned above.

How to Use This Book

The professional judgments involved in the delivery of preschool services are considerable. The most important safeguards involve collaborative problem solving, ecobehavioral and functional assessment methods, systematic consideration of valid intervention alternatives, and evaluation. This book will be useful for examining assessment and intervention plans related to children's problem behaviors or learning difficulties.

Interventions should be based on reflective and research-based strategies and on a coherent model of service delivery. Thus, throughout the book we attempt to find practical and creative ways to intervene with children and to specify interventions based on research.

Some of the situations and problem behaviors described in this book are potentially dangerous. While we have tried our best to present reasonable approaches to challenging problems, the ambiguities and unknowns are too great for guarantees or promises. The ultimate responsibility for decision making rests with individuals: knowledgeable professionals and well-informed parents.

The Ethnic Validity of Early Intervention Efforts

The issue of cultural diversity requires our attention. We agree with Gibbs and Huang (1989, p. 11): "Developmental, ecological, and cross-cultural perspectives overlap considerably and may be conceived . . . parsimoniously as three interacting dimensions of the child's experience."

Selecting assessment procedures and interventions for young children is difficult enough; doing so in the context of different cultural groups is formidable indeed. One must allow for many cross-cultural variables: language, cognitive style, opportunities and experiences, adaptive and coping methods, mistrust, and prejudice. Furthermore, it is not always clear how directly the specific problems are linked to complex interactions of social, economic, political, situational, and individual factors. When problems stem from profound economic or social concerns, individual interventions may not be adequate.

Despite these complexities, we believe that many techniques in this book will fit children and families of different cultural and ethnic origins if guidelines are followed to establish, borrowing from Savage and Adair (1980), *ethnic validity* of the intervention efforts. This is a collaborative process using team members of the same ethnic background as the child and family to establish and "anchor" the cultural appropriateness of assessments and interventions. Steps for achieving ethnic validity are founded in ecobehavioral analysis (Vincent, Salisbury, Strain, McCormick, & Tessier, 1990) and in collaborative problem solving and decision making.

We do not want to minimize the challenges. However, those who wish to address the individual needs of culturally different children and families can take several important steps: (1) establish an advocacy role; (2) understand and accept cultural differences related to the population being served; (3) involve professionals and other community members of the same background in the process; and (4) use consultative and behavioral approaches to intervention design.

Training Preschool Professionals

This book originated with David W. Barnett's experiences preparing psychologists to work with young children, their families, and teachers. The overall context of the training is important. At the University of Cincinnati, practicum experiences are three quarters during the second year of graduate study. Most important, in addition to foundation courses in child development and assessment, the training in preschool service delivery has been supported by many other applied courses: social cognitive interventions, applied behavior analysis, behavioral research and accountability methods and practicum (with an emphasis on single-case experimental designs), psychoeducational interventions, family interventions, and consultation (at present, three courses).

An Overview of the Contents

Chapter One provides a framework for assessment and intervention. We consider the limits of knowledge about early intervention and focus on understanding the processes of change. For this reason, the emphasis is on the scientist-practitioner model and the importance of both creative and reflective practice, collaborative problem solving, naturalistic intervention design, and empirical and accountable practice.

Chapter Two may bring some surprises. Many professionals and students are familiar with the challenges of assessing young children, but the difficulties of using traditional developmental scales are even more troublesome than commonly thought. Many of the diagnostic "tools of the trade" produce error rates that would be unacceptable to most professionals. Moreover, they produce results unrelated to the information needed for intervention design. Thus, Chapter Two encourages the reader to think critically about the contributions of assessment practices. Rather than test or instrument reliability and validity, the most important aspects to consider are *decision* reliability and validity linked to personal, social, and educational outcomes.

Chapter Three introduces consultation-based service delivery and ecobehavioral and functional assessment that lead to intervention. First, assessment and intervention should occur within a *system of service delivery*. We present parent and teacher consultation as a framework for preschool psychological services. While not perfect, parent-teacher consultation offers a viable way to help assess the adequacy of decisions and to organize and guide assessments related to intervention design. We describe three ecobehavioral interviews — eco-maps, waking day (and sleep), and problem-solving interviews — and discuss their technical adequacy.

Chapter Four presents observation techniques as foundations of intervention design. Planning an observation means deciding what, where, who, when, and how to observe. Strategies of direct observation by consultants, participant observation by parents and teachers, and self-observation by caregivers and children are discussed. We also introduce the basic principles of curriculum-based measurement, another foundation of early intervention efforts. The chapter ends with a discussion of technical adequacy related to observation.

Chapter Five deals with selecting target behaviors and strategies for change. The necessary frameworks are conceptual, empirical, and practical, and the end results are best considered as plans that need to be evaluated. The professional judgment required is considerable. Because children frequently present more than one behavior that is of concern to parents or teachers, prioritization is important. Also, the most obvious behaviors may not be the ones best suited for change. Settings, caregivers' behaviors, and steps in the intervention process must be considered. The chapter closes with a discussion of evaluating interventions, emphasizing accountability.

Chapters Six and Seven are organized around basic interventions. We have extensively reviewed interventions found in the literature where at least some compelling evidence was offered for validity and usefulness. These interventions are elaborated in Chapters Eight through Eleven.

Chapter Twelve elaborates on the scientist-practitioner theme and reviews legal, ethical, and professional principles related to intervention decisions and accountability. We think scientist-practitioners are valued by parents and teachers and that their ideals should be at least approximated in practice. However, many real-world barriers stand in the way.

More Research Is Necessary

In every study we reviewed, researchers could have concluded with the statement that more systematic research was necessary. Most often, they raised questions (or could have) about long-term effects, generalization, relative cost effectiveness, and basic elements of design. In addition, since many studies appeared, more stringent research standards have been set, and include such matters as procedural reliability and treatment integrity. We have decided to focus on creative and systematic efforts of researchers. For this reason, we also have emphasized the scientist-practitioner role, which includes evaluating intervention efforts on a case-by-case basis.

Acknowledgments

We extend our gratitude to Northern Kentucky Head Start in Newport, Kentucky. This center has served as a training site for school psychology students at the University of Cincinnati (UC) since 1978. For many years, Madhavi Parikh, director of the center, encouraged innovation. More recently, Joan Menning has served as director in an exemplary way. Both directors helped create expectations for excellence and gave critical support for research and training. All UC students had opportunities to design, implement, and evaluate a wide range of interventions for children, teachers, and parents. They conducted many studies that helped alter the ways that services were provided. We also would like to thank Maxine Walker, the Head Start secretary for all those years, for her assistance on countless occasions. We wish we could list all the teachers. Laurie Wolsing, education coordinator, gets special thanks.

Doctoral students Ron Bramlett, Scott Grow, John Hall, Nancy Hampel, Antoinette Miranda, Charlene Ponti, Rita Poth, and Stacy Vedder Dubocq all helped define and develop preschool psychological services and training experiences. Karen Carey worked in this capacity for two years. Special appreciation is extended to Marcia Madden, who helped with the first stages of the computer search for preschool interventions, and to Scott Grow, who helped in organizing the vast amount of research.

In training students in preschool services, we have benefited from the perspectives of respected colleagues in the field of school psychology: Michael Curtis (consultation, organizational development), Janet Graden (family interventions), and Ed Lentz (applied behavior analysis and psychoeducational interventions).

The end result was greatly aided by Mark Wolery's magnificent critique. Thanks to Ed Lentz and Michael Forcade for numerous discussions and valuable comments, and to Lisa Barnhouse for helpful insights into professional practice.

During the summer of 1990, the following students critiqued an earlier draft of the text, and we thank them for their many suggestions: Katherine Bofinger, Emily Brown Cabezudo, Michelle Buchan, John Dorger, Elizabeth Fishbach, Jane Gallagher, Sharon Goskoski, Gerald Guild, Jane Ruwet Hopson, Linda Reifin, Janice Singerman, Michelle Smock, Amy Storer, Lori Strengholt, and Kent Youngman. Carmen Barnett and Dana Matsuzaka helped with references. In spite of all this help, all problems that remain in the text are our own.

February 1992   David W. Barnett
                                                  Cincinnati, Ohio

                                                  Karen T. Carey
                                                  Fresno, California

*This book is dedicated
to the teachers, parents, and children
at Northern Kentucky Head Start.*

The Authors

DAVID W. BARNETT is professor of school psychology at the University of Cincinnati. He received his B.A. degree (1969) from the University of Delaware in psychology, his M.A. degree (1971) from Fairleigh Dickinson University in psychology, and his Ph.D. degree (1974) from Indiana State University in school psychology. He has written extensively in areas related to professional practices and school psychological services. Since 1978, he has concentrated on preschool psychological and educational services and research through associations with Head Start, other preschool programs, and as a co-chair of the preschool interest group of the National Association of School Psychologists. Barnett has received state and local awards for research, service, and innovation related to preschool services. His books include *The Personal and Social Assessment of Children: An Analysis of Current Status and Professional Practice Issues* (1990, with K. Zucker) and *Nondiscriminatory Multifactored Assessment: A Sourcebook* (1983). He is a Fellow of Division 16 of the American Psychological Association.

KAREN T. CAREY is assistant professor of school psychology at California State University, Fresno. She received her B.S. degree (1974) from San Diego State University in psychology, her M.S. degree (1979) from the University of Nevada, Las Vegas, in school psychology, and her Ph.D. degree (1989) from the University of Cincinnati in school psychology. She has been involved with the National Association of School Psychologists at many levels, including as chair of the children's services committee and coordinator of the preschool interest group. Carey has also been involved in several state associations for school psychologists and has received awards for assessment and intervention practices.

DESIGNING INTERVENTIONS FOR PRESCHOOL LEARNING AND BEHAVIOR PROBLEMS

1

Critical Issues
in Preschool Intervention

PSYCHOLOGISTS AND EDUCATORS, EVEN THOSE WITH VERY DIFFERENT theoretical and practical orientations, believe the preschool years, broadly defined as ages two to five, are the most significant period for development. "It is unquestionably the period during which the foundation is laid for the complex behavioral structures that are built in a child's lifetime" (Bijou, 1975, p. 829).

Federal legislation passed in 1986 (PL 99-457, amended by PL 101-476) testifies to our understanding of the importance of early intervention. In the legislation, educational services for children with disabilities are extended to children between three and five years old. The act also enables states to serve infants and toddlers.

However, despite the much-needed attention to early intervention, many questions remain about how to identify children requiring services and how the interventions should be carried out. Concerns with labeling and placing children in special programs now have reached a critical stage. Questions include the appropriateness of labels and the effectiveness of special programs. For younger children, these concerns are intensified. For a variety of reasons, many traditional assessment methods used to diagnose preschool children have come under increasing attack.

One of the most significant issues is who should be served. Based on substantial research in applied developmental psy-

1

chology, our response is that intensified efforts should be dedicated to young children who are difficult to parent, teach, or befriend. These children may or may not be the same as those traditionally classified as "at risk" or mildly "handicapped." The focus is on problem *situations,* and not necessarily developmental characteristics of children.

A second issue is *how* children should be served. Assessment and intervention should be based on theory directly related to psychosocial change, should be supported by research, and should deal effectively with the realities of practice through collaborative problem solving with caregivers. One outcome of using a problem-solving framework is that alternative methods for providing services will be generated.

Frameworks for Assessment and Intervention

The frameworks for assessment and intervention design are based on theory, a comprehensive review of interventions found in the literature, and a coherent system for providing psychological and educational services. Here we discuss social cognitive theory, reflective and research-based practices, principles of "naturalistic" intervention design, and alternative educational systems that emphasize expanding educational opportunities in mainstream settings.

Social Cognitive Theory as a Guide

What factors guide professionals who must make decisions about assessment and intervention in ambiguous and complex real-life situations? Whether obvious or not, decisions are guided by theory. Many developmental theories remain viable in the minds of professionals and caregivers. Practitioner theories may be deliberate and formal; they may be a personalized adaptation of a venerable theory, they may be allegedly atheoretical, or they may be eclectic, accidental, ad hoc, or out of awareness. When theories remain unspecified, the intervention process remains blurred.

Theories warrant ongoing appraisal. Bandura's criterion is pertinent: "The value of a theory is ultimately judged by its usefulness as evidenced by the power of the methods it yields to effect psychological changes" (1986, p. 4). Some theories lead to less effective strategies. Often, they are not sufficiently evaluated.

Our focus here is on designing assessments and interventions. Strategies are needed to frame the problem, to plan and implement the interventions, and to analyze the changes that occur over time. Our approach is built on social cognitive theory, which represents a consensus position and focuses on behavioral change. One of the significant aspects of social cognitive theory is the concept of the "reciprocal influence process" as the basic unit of analysis. Interactions of person and cognitive variables, overt behaviors, and environmental factors can all be important in the assessment-intervention process. Bandura (1986) argued that "behavior, cognitive and other personal factors, and environmental influences all operate interactively as determinants of each other" (p. 23). The relative influence of specific factors will vary with persons, situations, and behaviors (Bandura, 1985).

Social cognitive theory has several aspects that are critically important in assessment and intervention design: the roles that cognitive processes play in decision making and actual performance; the stress on self-regulatory processes; the emphasis on the analysis of life events, including those that are accidental; the self-efficacy of the child, caregivers, and consultant when faced with difficult tasks; and the criterion of behavior change to test the value of theory, including the personal theories of caregivers and consultants. In sum, an important application of social cognitive theory is to help analyze planning strategies: the appraisal of current systems resources, potential resources, modifiable behaviors across numerous settings, implicit or explicit causal theories, the use of research on a case-by-case basis, and the determination of results.

Developmental versus Behavioral Perspectives

Personal and social development is the broadest context for assessment and intervention design. Achenbach wrote that *change* is the major characteristic of childhood: "Children are biologically and cognitively designed for adaptation and change" (1982, p. 655). Unfortunately, understanding and especially altering the developmental trajectories of children have special difficulties, both theoretical and practical. The theoretical issues generally deal with the continuity and discontinuity of personal and social development; the practical challenges involve understanding the processes of psychosocial change.

The developmental perspective is based on the premise that "children generally perform similarly across many skill areas and [that] a major discrepancy between skill levels is indicative of developmental problems" (Bailey & Wolery, 1989, p. 369). When children do not keep up with their peers they are viewed as "immature" or "delayed." Sometimes a waiting game is played by parents or professionals to see if a child will catch up.

The following guidelines for evaluating developmental psychopathology were adapted from Wenar (1982, pp. 194–197):

1. Behavior, once age-appropriate, continues to be manifest at a later age and is no longer appropriate.
2. A child has progressed in development but reverts to behavior appropriate at an earlier age.
3. Age-appropriate behavior may be exaggerated, deficient, or absent.
4. A behavior may appear to be without a counterpart in normal development.
5. The growth curves may have different rates and shapes.
6. Variability may be exaggerated.
7. The sequences of development may be altered.

Our concern is not with the study of development but with how developmental analyses translate into professional practice. Two issues stand out. First, for many children it may not be reasonable to design interventions around apparent skill deficits as measured by traditional developmental scales. Second, many of the developmental techniques used to establish discrepancies between normal and deficit behavior are quite error prone.

Conceptual and methodological changes since the 1960s

have made behavioral principles less susceptible to criticisms such as the apparent lack of emphasis on maturational processes or the narrowness of change efforts. Behaviorism does not ignore maturational processes, but its focus is different. In the way it is applied here, it is concerned with identifying behavior and learning problems of children, and enhancing the *natural* roles of caregivers (parents and teachers) as a way of ameliorating those difficulties or helping children cope successfully with long-term problems. Behaviorism has been directly influenced by ecological, social, and cognitive research. Behavioral approaches also have been applied to major developmental issues (Bijou, 1975).

Many converging lines of evidence suggest that behavioral interventions have great utility but are underused in practice. Behavioral interventions have been applied in creative ways to diverse problems with young children. One major advantage of behavioral interventions is that the focus on observable behaviors makes it possible to describe elements of the interventions very specifically.

There are no insurmountable differences between behavioral and developmental approaches to early intervention. The two approaches share three important foundations for early intervention:

1. A nurturing caregiver is available.
2. The curriculum is developmentally appropriate.
3. The goal is functional environmental adaptation.

Naturalistic Interventions

Interventions may be viewed on a continuum of intrusiveness. At one extreme, radical changes may be suggested for teachers, parents, or children. At the other extreme, interventions may fit into, or be adapted to, existing styles of parenting or teaching. A basic premise is that, whenever possible, we should use the least intrusive intervention that will accomplish the goals of change. Using principles founded in developmental psychology, naturalistic intervention design stresses the analysis of actual roles, routines, skills, and interests of children and caregivers.

We think that naturalistic intervention constitutes a fundamental approach to intervention design. Naturalistic interventions are a form of environmental intervention (Hart, 1985) and are founded on developmental studies of competent caregivers (Sigel, 1982; White, Kaban, & Attanucci, 1979). They are interventions revealed by the natural teaching styles of successful caregivers. When viewed broadly, they incorporate behavioral and developmental principles.

. Learning builds on direct and incidental experiences within the context of a caring relationship. The caregiver selects learning events, focuses the child's attention on those that are important, and also, following the child's lead, encourages curiosity and skill development. Learning events may be both pleasant and unpleasant; caregivers intentionally provide some experiences, but also frame serendipitous events. Perhaps most events provide the opportunity to teach cognitive, behavioral, language, and affective skills to some extent.

Personal and social learning cannot be readily separated from early cognitive and language learning and mastery of a broad range of skills. Attitudes toward oneself, social competence, and social responsibility (attitudes and acts toward others) are taught, modeled, and valued. They also arise out of interactions with others. Therefore, one task of an early intervention consultant is to help caregivers explore an expanded and deliberate role in cognitive and social modeling. Behaviors of caregivers that elicit and mediate children's responses are also targets of assessment and intervention. Based on longitudinal research related to risk factors, Werner concluded that interventions for children may be conceived "either by decreasing their exposure to biological factors and cumulative life stresses, or by increasing the number of protective factors (competencies, sources of support) that they can rely on within themselves or their caregiving environment" (1986, p. 25). In sum, many successful interventions are based on ensuring that a caregiver is accessible to a child and on planned changes in caregiver behavior.

An example of naturalistic intervention is the use of incidental teaching in facilitating language development (Hart,

1985). In normally developing children, incidental teaching capitalizes on natural routines and on brief but important exchanges between child and caregiver. We risk trivializing the process through an example. Picture a parent and child walking down the street. The child points to a truck. The parent says, "What's that? [pause] Can you say truck? Yes! That's a red [or broken, etc.] truck." In contrast, imagine a different caregiver who frequently ignores the child's gestures. The value of these experiences is the profound cumulative effect; from many types of salient and subtle situations, caregivers capitalize on opportunities to learn, expand, and practice affective, social, cognitive, and language skills.

Thus, naturalistic interventions include those that may be incorporated easily into caregivers' routines, or those that extend or modify experiences that occur within settings important to children. Exhibit 1.1 includes some of the core features of naturalistic interventions.

Exhibit 1.1. Characteristics of Naturalistic Interventions.

- Naturalistic interventions constitute a fundamental conceptual and research-based approach to treatment design.
- Naturalistic interventions are founded on developmental studies of competent caregivers and the intervention implications of settings.
- Prototypic examples are based on facilitating language development.
- Important characteristics of settings include opportunities for learning skills or alternative responses for maladaptive behaviors, and the behavioral strategies of caregivers and peers.
- Naturalistic approaches stress the need for assessment and intervention to occur within significant settings, and with caregivers and peers having the greatest opportunity to interact with the child.
- Plans for naturalistic interventions are based on the collaborative analysis of actual roles, skills, and interests of caregivers, and children's behavior.
- Beyond the research basis, there are two important reasons for examining naturalistic interventions.
  1. The acceptability and overall effectiveness of an intervention may be directly associated with the degree that it fits the caregiver's current situation and plans.
  2. When interventions are accomplished in specific training environments, techniques used in natural settings should parallel those used in training settings in order to facilitate generalization and maintenance of behavioral change.
- Assessment plans can be directed to the identification of:

Exhibit 1.1. Characteristics of Naturalistic Interventions, Cont'd.

1. A range of treatment options based on research.
2. Interventions that may be adapted to evident styles of parenting or teaching, those that may be incorporated into the routines of caregivers, and those that may be extended to the child's home, school, and community settings.
3. Important environmental barriers that maintain problems or prevent resolution.
4. Behavior deficits related to failures to meet environmental expectations.

For many reasons, naturalistic interventions are of critical importance. Naturalistic strategies stress the need for assessment and intervention to occur within significant settings and with caregivers who have the greatest opportunity to interact with the child. Natural settings typically hold the greatest potential for providing frequent opportunities for learning new skills or alternative responses for maladaptive behaviors. In addition, naturalistic interventions may help establish the generality of behavioral change.

In naturalistic intervention decisions for children, identifying functional objectives is especially important. A *functional* model is based on "the acquisition of those skills that will immediately or in the future improve a child's ability to interact with the environment and to become more self-sufficient and independent" (Bricker, 1986, p. 190). To accomplish these goals, principles of parent and teacher consultation are stressed because the caregiver's concerns are central, including objectives, problems, and actual interactive strategies. For many children, the emphasis should be on language competence, cognitive skills, and preacademic skills (e.g., Odom & Karnes, 1988). Furthermore, interpersonal problem solving and other skills associated with social competence can be directly taught, guided, prompted, and practiced.

The Scientist-Practitioner

A significant foundation for practice is based on the scientist-practitioner tradition (Barlow, Hayes, & Nelson, 1984; Bloom

& Fischer, 1982). The scientist-practitioner uses problem-solving methods that stem from the scientific method and research to guide practice. The end result also leads to accountability.

Reflective Practice. Reflective practice is built on problem-focused and creative steps. Reflective approaches are necessary because of the uniqueness of child and caregiver situations. The major techniques are encompassed by ecobehavioral consultation and problem solving appropriate to the situation. The stages of problem solving generally include (1) problem identification and clarification, (2) ecological and behavioral assessment, (3) solution generation, (4) selection of intervention strategies, (5) planning and implementation, and (6) evaluation. In sum, reflective practices include strategies for problem structuring and problem solving.

Research-Based Practice. Empirical practices provide accountability. These practices include using research to guide assessment and intervention plans, and using practitioner-oriented methods to evaluate intervention outcomes. Research may guide assessment and intervention plans in several ways.

One practice is to consider interventions that have some evidence of effectiveness for specific classes of problem behaviors. Barlow, Hayes, and Nelson have asked, "Where do practitioners get their techniques?" (1984, p. 33). From a scientist-practitioner perspective, the response would be: "From studies where interventions are well defined, carefully executed, and adequately evaluated." Thus, a critical component of practice is the ability to generalize from intervention research.

Research-based syndromes or constellations of behavior (for example, conduct disorders and autism) facilitate communication between researchers and practitioners. Reliable and valid syndromes can aid practice by identifying key or prototypic behaviors, enabling predictions about the etiology and course of a disorder, and establishing a range of intervention alternatives. At the same time, using syndromes can be harmful; they can produce outcomes similar to other labels and may lack validity.

Within the scientist-practitioner tradition, intervention effectiveness must be ascertained. Functional assessments, time-series methods, and practitioner-oriented single-case experimental designs are suitable for this purpose. The basic strategy underlying time-series methods is the repeated measurement of behavior under conditions that enable researchers to evaluate the effects of interventions (Barlow, Hayes, & Nelson, 1984).

Alternative Service Delivery

The characteristics of alternative services include three important concepts. First, *normalization* is the guiding principle. Normalization refers to the "utilization of means which are as culturally normative as possible, in order to establish and/or maintain personal behaviors and characteristics which are as culturally normative as possible" (Wolfensberger, 1972, p. 28). An important premise is that more serious behavior problems can be prevented through early intervention (see Dunlap, Johnson, & Robbins, 1990). Second, to meet children's and parents' needs, a range of alternatives usually is required. Alternatives include various school-based and home-based programs for parents and children. Third, intervention decisions are based on the analysis of (a) current situations of children and caregivers, (b) developmentally appropriate and functional objectives that stem from mutual problem-solving and intervention-based assessments, and (c) evaluation. In addition, one of the propositions of the National Association of School Psychologists Position Statement on Early Intervention Services in the Schools (1987) is that service delivery should be provided without unnecessary diagnostic labels. *Inclusion* should be a fundamental policy.

Research in Early Intervention

The effectiveness of early intervention has been discussed extensively. The central issues of early intervention are avoiding the consequences of biological or social adversities, minimizing the impact of such adversities, and enhancing the development of children with identified disabilities through early intervention. It is a surprisingly small, inconclusive, but complex literature.

Typically, evaluations of large-scale projects such as Head Start (Zigler & Valentine, 1979), Abecedarian (Ramey & Campbell, 1987), and High/Scope (Berreuta-Clement, Schweinhart, Barnett, Epstein, & Weikart, 1984) suggested that early intervention holds considerable *promise* of effectiveness. Overall, early intervention programs may be quite cost effective, but generalizations are based on only a few carefully designed and executed studies (Barnett & Escobar, 1988, 1990; Farran, 1990). The research also suggests the need to evaluate multiple outcomes over long time periods, to evaluate outcomes for specific populations of children (such as children raised in poverty, hearing impaired, and so on), and to evaluate specific methods and programs.

Programs for children characterized as *high risk* have been studied (Bryant & Ramey, 1987; Consortium for Longitudinal Studies, 1983; Head Start Evaluation, Synthesis, and Utilization Project, 1983), with these findings: Children may in these programs be less likely to repeat grades or be referred for special education; they may be more achievement oriented, more likely to complete high school and enroll in postsecondary educational programs; cognitive and academic gains may be documented; and program participants may be more likely to be employed, less likely to commit crimes, and may have fewer teenage pregnancies. Also, parents may have higher educational and career aspirations for these children. It is important to note that these results are not guaranteed, and may not generalize across different samples of children, especially those with different characteristics or in different early intervention programs.

In comparing curricular models, Schweinhart, Weikart, and Larner (1986) found differential effects on social outcomes. Members of one of the three experimental groups (Distar) were reported to be involved in twice as many delinquent acts as the other groups. Distar is a program based on direct instruction and operant learning theory (Bereiter & Englemann, 1966). Schweinhart, Weikart, and Larner stressed the importance of "child-initiated learning activities" and planning for "social-behavior consequences" (p. 43). In contrast to their finding of negative social outcomes for the group receiving direct instruction, other reviews suggest important long-term academic and personal gains based on direct instruction techniques (Gersten, Carnine, & White, 1984), and there may be methodological weaknesses in the Schweinhart study (Farran, 1990). Also, direct instruction can be combined with plans for learning social problem-solving skills to help prevent negative outcomes.

These research projects illustrate design components for major facilities and programs. In fact, minor variations on well-developed educational methods may not be very important if the basics are in place. Some generalizations are possible (Dunst, Snyder, & Mankinen, 1989). Early intervention programs must be well designed, coherent, and should continuously monitor progress. They need to address a wide range of personal and social competencies, and persist beyond the preschool years. Systematic interventions within educational programs for at-risk populations and children with disabilities are important because the needs of these children will vary in significant ways. Most important, major efforts also should include interventions within normal preschool settings. The programs should meet parental needs as well; an examination of the family ecology is an important step.

Evaluating Early Intervention Findings

Despite the optimism for early intervention, numerous questions remain, and many research problems plague the field. Programs are difficult to replicate because the efforts and resources needed for planning, program execution, and evaluation are great, and because the early excitement of program innovation may not last or transfer to replications by others. Samples of children sometimes have not been well defined. Descriptions of interventions often have lacked the detail necessary for replication or sufficient measures of treatment integrity to determine if the intervention was actually executed as planned. Measures of treatment integrity are essential to evaluating program effectiveness.

Also, control groups are difficult to establish, especially for certain disabling conditions. The developmental trajectories of children with seemingly similar conditions and circumstances may vary substantially because of unknown but important differences in children or in caregivers' behaviors. Other unknowns involve ideal levels of program intensity (that is, the frequency or duration of parental or teacher contacts).

In summary, the empirical foundations for preschool intervention design include the promising effects shown by large-scale demonstration projects. Preschool program personnel must ensure that key organizational components are in place, that instructional objectives are developmentally appropriate and functional, and that progress is continually monitored. Overall, the effectiveness of early intervention is based on outcomes for individual children and families. Since the topic of this text is on planning individual interventions for young children, we focus next on intervention research for specific problem behaviors.

Importance of Single-Case Designs

Behavioral approaches follow a general model. First, targets for intervention are carefully selected, based on multiple rationales. One of the most compelling is that behavioral changes lead to improvements in independent functioning in normal settings. Second, repeated measures of behavior are taken. Third, an intervention is introduced while holding measurement conditions constant. Fourth, intervention outcomes are examined over substantial periods of time, and changes are made when necessary.

Single-case designs are important for several reasons. Children with unusual learning and behavior problems, children with disabilities, and children at risk have diverse needs. The diversity necessitates at least some degree of individual programming. Also, single-case designs add to our base of knowledge. The current literature reveals many effective interventions for learning and behavior problems. It also reveals many gaps. Single-case designs provide methods for accountability to evaluate and to make necessary changes in interventions.

The Complexity of Developmental Changes

Personal and Social Change

The course of personal and social development is complexly determined by psychological, social, biological, and accidental events. The task of the professional is to identify and modify factors that have the potential for enhancing development and altering maladaptive behaviors.

There is impressive evidence that personality and social behaviors are determined early, and also that substantial change occurs through adulthood. Many behaviors that may be detected in the preschool years have links to difficulties experienced in adulthood. The concept of continuity relates early characteristics of personality and behavior to adult qualities. Examples include children identified as conduct disordered (Robins, 1986), and those who experience early learning difficulties, social withdrawal, isolation, and rejection (Achenbach & McConaughy, 1987). Frequently, these problem behaviors may exist in combination (Macmann et al., in press). Perhaps the most reasonable view is Rutter's: "The concept of continuity implies meaningful links over the course of development — not a lack of change" (1984, p. 62).

In the literature we increasingly find successful interventions that may help with these problem behaviors. Early intervention has also shown substantial promise with more severe syndromes of developmental psychopathology such as autism (Lovaas, 1987).

When the focus is on changing behaviors, the emphasis shifts from child variables to specific interactions between the child and family members, peers, and caregivers. Sroufe and Rutter suggested that "disordered behavior generally does not simply spring forth without connection to previous quality of adaptation, or without changing environmental supports or altered environmental challenges" (1984, p. 22). Some children seem to adjust well despite quite threatening early environments and experiences, but even their development can be facilitated by a range of environmental supports (Garmezy, 1985; Werner, 1986; Werner & Smith, 1982).

Another issue has been the debate over the relative importance of situational versus personal determinants of behavior. The focus points have been the obvious control that situations exert on behavior, and the relatively modest predictive power of measured "person" or trait variables. Most researchers assume an interactionist position on the question.

In summary, personal and social development results from many sources. It may be impossible to account for all of the variables. Given the complexities, intervention should be guided, at least initially, by factors that enhance the child's adaptation to natural, well-functioning groups. As a practical matter, this means supporting and expanding the caregivers' role in both families and preschools.

Cognitive Change

Historically, a major focal point of early intervention efforts was increasing cognitive skills. IQ tests have traditionally been used to measure cognitive skills and developmental changes over time, but there are limitations. IQ tests measure an individual's position in relationship to a normative group. They do not necessarily elucidate a child's thinking or problem-solving strategies. Many cognitive skills are untapped by standard measures, and the skills that are measured vary considerably by developmental period.

Because of their omnibus nature, IQ scales can be insensitive to meaningful changes that could be attributable to interventions. Thus, the focus on IQ may not lead to the most useful outcomes for early intervention. For very young children, cognitive development cannot be easily separated from other aspects of development. Another important limitation is that IQ measures do not lead to useful and reliable educational decision making for individual children.

However, despite these limitations, IQ tests are among the most reliable techniques available to researchers, and the validity evidence is not easy to dismiss. Several generalizations can be made about IQ changes for children. IQs may fluctuate considerably over time. From ages three to five the median absolute change in one study was about eight IQ points (Hindley & Owen, 1978). Between ages five and seventeen, IQs for half the children are likely to change by more than ten IQ points, 25 percent will change by twenty-two points or more, and 6 percent by thirty points or more (Hindley & Owen, 1978). In some cases, the change may be even more dramatic (Honzik, Macfarlane,

& Allen, 1948; McCall, Appelbaum, & Hogarty, 1973): changes of as much as fifty to seventy IQ points have been documented.

Meaningful changes are not likely to be abrupt, but tend to happen over long time periods. IQs stabilize to a degree at approximately age six, but important individual changes may be noted later. Thus, while there is overall evidence for the stability of IQ measures, substantial changes occur for individual children. For some children, IQ changes may be on an upward or downward trend. The specific reasons for individual changes may never become clear, but evidence suggests a range of possible factors, including personality as well as environmental influences (Wohlwill, 1980).

The degree of cognitive change is instructive for at least two reasons. First, the extent of change highlights some of the inherent difficulties in early labeling. Second, and more positively, the variability provides at least a crude estimate of potential change.

A second and more controversial context for the analysis of IQ changes has been the effects of specific early interventions. Fortunately, much of this complicated topic has recently been reviewed in an edited work by Gallagher and Ramey (1987). Among the most notable of these intervention efforts have been the Perry Preschool Project, Head Start, Abecedarian, and the Milwaukee Project (Bryant & Ramey, 1987). Overall, IQ changes based on participation in experimental programs have been more difficult to achieve than originally hoped for. Typically, programs have been able to boost IQ performance immediately following the interventions (the median change is about .5 standard deviation across studies, with a range from three to thirty-two IQ points), but the gains have proven difficult to sustain. More intensive programs have yielded more impressive results, but still the IQ gains seem to fade over time. Scarr and Arnett summarize their analysis: "Intelligence can be said to be malleable, then, but only within certain limits" (1987, p. 82).

Overall, the preliminary results of early intervention are encouraging. Meaningful social and academic benefits have been documented but should not be viewed as givens. We must remember that intervention design is in its infancy and that many innovations lie ahead. Furthermore, intervention design across developmental areas is not restricted to qualities of children, but implicates the skills and motivation of caregivers, and their relationships with children, over long time periods.

Challenges of Preschool Psychological Services

To actualize the potential of early intervention efforts, those providing preschool services face many challenges. For each challenge, the opportunities associated with preschool psychological services are great.

Preschools are typically the first settings where developmental difficulties that have social and educational significance have the chance to surface. If young children are initially evaluated in clinic settings, observations that include social interactions, complex adaptations required by classrooms, and the outcomes of instruction are often neglected. Thus, the challenge is to give preschool personnel the instructional and intervention skills they need to successfully integrate children with various learning and behavioral problems and disabling conditions.

Second, the range of preschool educational philosophies and corresponding objectives and teaching strategies is considerable. There is no clear consensus about curricula for preschool children. Furthermore, the formal preparation of preschool personnel varies greatly, with corresponding differences in theories about child development and teaching strategies. Theories can either facilitate or hinder assessment plans and intervention strategies. In this book, we stress the need for a developmental and functional curriculum.

Third, the challenges of parental involvement need to be reconciled on a practical level. The significance of parental behavior and family environment for early development is well known. Furthermore, specific parent-child links for various maladaptive behaviors have been fairly well established as, for example, with conduct-disordered behavior. At the same time, the increasing complexity of family life, and trends of single parents and working mothers make parental intervention components quite vulnerable.

Despite the possible challenges, family members should be included in early intervention efforts. Family assessment related to early intervention encompasses the following (adapted from Bailey & Simeonsson, 1988, pp. 9–18): (1) child characteristics, parent-child interactions, family needs, critical personal or family events, and family strengths; (2) family values, traditions, and routines; (3) goals and services based on family priorities; (4) considerations for parents based on type of preschool program (home-based or center-based); and (5) periodic evaluation of outcomes.

Fourth, diagnosis and classification are difficult for those working with young children. While classification in one form or another may be unavoidable, established tests and classification schemes do not answer service delivery issues for young children. Thus, our focus is on naturalistic assessment and intervention design.

Potential Risks of Early Intervention

The potential benefits of early intervention are clear, but there are some risks.

First, there is the risk of ineffective interventions or interventions resulting in inconsequential gains. Placement in special education programs should be considered a type of intervention. Given the frequently undocumented success of placements for school age children classified as mildly disabled, it may be detrimental to await the evaluation of outcomes of the recent preschool legislation unless substantial innovations and programmatic changes are made. To help with this potential risk, professional practice should emphasize providing alternative services, integrating children with disabilities, and identifying robust interventions for parents and teachers.

Second, there may be psychological costs associated with interventions, even those that have some measure of success — for example, an intervention so intrusive and exhaustive that a parent is reluctant to continue it or a teacher is unwilling to use it later with other children. Intervention outcomes need to benefit all participants. This is one reason we stress naturalistic interventions.

Third, interventions may involve stigma. One obvious example involves early labeling associated with special classes. In addition, parents or teachers may be concerned with the effects of individualizing programs that make some children seem more different than necessary. These are further reasons for the emphasis on alternative and integrated services, and on naturalistic interventions.

Fourth, there are risks in not applying what is known about early intervention. This is why we emphasize in subsequent chapters the research basis for early intervention efforts.

Summary and Conclusions

This chapter reviewed a wide range of considerations that professionals must face when designing and conducting interventions for learning and behavior problems of young children. The frameworks for these decisions are based on theories of psychosocial change, reflective practices related to problem solving, and research. Our emphasis is on identifying intervention strategies that can be used effectively in natural settings.

There are numerous reviews of the potential benefits of early intervention. Perhaps the most significant context for early intervention efforts is research on the malleability of developmental trajectories. Overall, early intervention may be characterized as promising, but methodological questions prevent many further generalizations. Throughout the following chapters, many examples of successful interventions are described for a wide range of problem behaviors.

Early intervention efforts pose many challenges, even risks. For many reasons related to these challenges and risks, we stress naturalistic intervention design, and the basics of parent and teacher consultation. The core elements of intervention design include the analysis of problem situations, the roles of caregivers and peers, and the experiences provided to children.

PART ONE

ASSESSMENT FOR INTERVENTION DESIGN

2

The Need for Change
in Assessment Practices

ASSESSMENT IS THE FOUNDATION FOR INTERVENTION, BUT PROFES-
sionals who assess and intervene with young children face many
challenges. The problems are interrelated: (a) different approaches
to assessment lead to different decisions concerning children,
(b) diagnostic profiles based on available developmental measures or behavior ratings may not lead to defensible psychological and educational interventions, and (c) traditional measures
thought to improve decision making actually may produce errors concerning risk or diagnostic status.

Most sources that address assessment issues warn professionals that these problems exist. Furthermore, professional judgment is frequently offered as a panacea to overcome the problems
in test usage. We contend that problems of both measurement
and professional judgment have been greatly *underestimated*.

Recognizing these difficulties, many assessment sources
stress the need for *idiographic assessment*. Idiographic assessment
involves discovering factors that guide individual behavior. In
contrast, the term *nomothetic* is used to describe laws that pertain to people in general. While there are no inherent safeguards
for idiographic assessment practices, they should result in hypotheses or plans that are subsequently evaluated. An integration of nomothetic and idiographic approaches may be achieved
by basing plans on research related to specific learning or behavior problems and interventions. A model incorporating both
approaches is presented in Chapter Three.

A Critique of Traditional Approaches to Assessment

Traditional approaches to the assessment of children's learning, behavior, and emotional problems have long been the center of controversy.

Conceptual Issues

The potential purposes of assessment are many: screening, diagnosis, classification or determination of program eligibility, intervention planning, monitoring, evaluation, and research. Measurement should be related to specific purposes of assessment; therefore the measurement procedures may vary considerably, depending on the purpose.

The dominant model has been referred to as *multifactored* assessment. It was developed as a way of providing the broad-based information necessary for educational decisions and for intervention planning. Multifactored evaluation was part of the solution to the requirement of a "full and fair" evaluation for children with suspected handicaps (Martin, 1979). The following areas have traditionally been used to define the needs of most young children with mild disabilities: emotional and social functioning, cognitive and intellectual functioning, language and communication skills, adaptive behavior, visual and gross motor skills, and preacademic skills.

Despite the attractiveness of the multifactored assessment model, as commonly carried out, it has many limitations. It has led to a reliance on test batteries, regardless of the reason for conducting an assessment, and the outcomes have been primarily child centered. However, assessment must take into account the nature of the problem, the situation, the developmental level and needs of the child, and the needs of the caregiver. The skills of caregivers, especially with young children, are of critical importance. Furthermore, the adult caregiver is often the client, and the desired outcomes frequently pertain to changes in environment, interactions, or instruction.

Our interest is with the design, implementation, and evaluation of interventions for children and their caregivers. As professionals, our ultimate goal should be positive outcomes for children and caregivers. We rarely have seen this occur when the emphasis is on traditional assessment practices. This is due primarily to the greatest conceptual limitation of the multifactored assessment model: the procedures are not guided by the theory and concepts that underlie intervention design.

The central constructs used in facilitating change are different from those typically associated with developmental theories or those measured by traditional developmental scales. The foundation for intervention design rests not only on research associated with normal development, but also on mechanisms of learning and changing the predicted course of maladaptive behavior. When the focus is on intervention design, major emphasis is placed on environmental experiences, contingencies, and available models for learning appropriate behavior. The implications of *applied* developmental psychology for professional practice and change theory are examined in Barnett and Zucker (1990).

Finally, although we have been critical of the multifactored assessment model, we do agree that assessments for children with suspected disabilities should be interdisciplinary and based on effective teaming strategies. Throughout this book we assume that professionals from many disciplines may contribute to effective service delivery.

Technical Issues

There are many technical problems with the instruments commonly used to screen, diagnose, and classify children. In addition to a wide range of differences in philosophies that guide scale development, large gaps exist in the psychometric data available on preschool instruments. Most important, few validity studies examine key facets of the problem: (a) whether the constructs that underlie the scales are adequately measured in a way that supports necessary professional-practice decisions; (b) whether the scales can be interpreted with confidence for *individual* children; (c) whether there are significant benefits over alternative measurement procedures; and (d) whether the results

have clear utility for intervention design. Discussions of reliability and validity issues can be found in many standard texts;
our concern is with certain issues that have not received sufficient
attention.

The Problems of Profile Reliability and Validity. Profile interpretation has been the foundation of many techniques, and of the
diagnostic process itself. Profile interpretation is commonly
defined in two ways: (1) the meaning that can be attributed to
an individual's pattern of scores, and (2) the question of whether
a child's profile is similar to a profile of a defined group, such
as those used for special education classifications or other diagnostic purposes (for example, *DSM-III-R*). Three dimensions
of profiles are important: (1) the level or elevation of scores,
(2) the dispersion or "scatter" of scores, and (3) the shape or features of the pattern.

   In practice, profiles for individual children are discussed
in two interrelated ways. Most individual developmental scales
result in a profile of supposed strengths and weaknesses across
specific domains (cognitive skills, language skills, or adaptive
behavior, for example). Different tests may be combined into
a battery used to develop a profile of skills across different measures or domains of functioning.

   Barnett and Zucker (1990) identified twelve problems associated with profile interpretations:

   1. The reliability of subscales, the validity of subscales,
and the reliability and validity of patterns are likely to vary *within*
a scale. While some profiles or patterns ultimately may be useful, research has not been encouraging.

   2. If there is an important general factor in scales, peaks
and valleys in the profile may connote relatively trivial differences. This has been a common finding in many preschool scales
as well as scales for older children.

   3. The reliability of the *difference* between two correlated
scales or subscales is lower than the reliability of either scale
or subscale. The difference is influenced by errors present in

both scales. The higher the intercorrelations across scales that are being compared, the more likely that observed differences are due to chance. (The equation for determining the reliability of differences is presented in a subsequent example of profile interpretation.)

4. The reliability of the overall profile necessarily will be considerably less than the reliability of individual scales or subscales that comprise the profiles, but for practical purposes it should be treated as an unknown. Due to all the above factors, the overall pattern may be quite unstable.

5. As the number of comparisons increases, differences due to chance are more likely to occur. Furthermore, most comparisons are unplanned. Thus, profile interpretations for individual children capitalize on chance occurrences of behaviors.

6. Extreme scores are most often "interpreted," and these have the most error. A score that is two standard deviations from the mean has twice as much absolute error as one that is one standard deviation from the mean.

7. Subscales themselves may have very different meanings at different elevations, within different or unique profiles, or for different populations of children. For developmental scales, differences in the processes used in solving problems and content at different scale levels create difficulties in interpretation.

8. Unusual patterns may not be represented in taxonomies or classification schemes.

9. Meaningful patterns may not be detected even if they do exist, depending on the scale that is used. Nonsignificant statistical results are difficult to interpret for this reason.

10. Research support for the utility of profiles in intervention decisions should be evaluated. The usefulness of developmental profiles for intervention design has not been demonstrated.

11. Profile classification must also be understood in terms of error rates. Important facets for studying decision outcomes include convergence in decisions across alternative instruments and different test occasions. In a series of studies across various methods and populations, the ratio of inconsistent-to-consistent classifications of diagnostic status was approximately 5:1 (Hall & Barnett, 1991; Macmann & Barnett, 1985; Macmann et al., 1989).

12. The "criterion problem" is evident in establishing profile validity. Criterion measures necessary for estimates of profile validity must be evaluated for reliability and validity. At the same time this has created circularity in selecting and using instruments as criterion measures. Profiles generally lack strong validity support given the goals of professional practices.

One of the most straightforward methods to examine profile reliability and validity issues is through the use of a multitrait-multimethod (MTMM) analysis (Campbell & Fiske, 1959). The MTMM analysis provides an important conceptual model because it allows for many different assessment instruments to be used, depending on professional preferences. In an MTMM analysis, at least two constructs need to be measured by at least two different methods. For example, social and adaptive behavior could be assessed by teacher and parent ratings, or cognitive, language, and motor skills could be assessed by different developmental tests.

Two sources of validity evidence are considered. First it is necessary to examine *convergent validity*. Logically, the methods intended to measure the same trait should converge or be higher than those developed to measure different traits. Second, *discriminant validity* indicates the predicted divergence of the traits. Dissimilar traits should have a lower intercorrelation than those found for similar traits.

For professional practices, the concern is with the confidence in *conclusions* that can be drawn from alternative scales, raters, and assessment procedures. In practice, developmental profiles are the basis of statements of strengths and weaknesses, such as "The child was weak in motor skills but strong in language." The similarities in conclusions that can be made from different instruments yield an upper bound of confidence for the particular construct being assessed.

In a series of investigations with common preschool scales using the multitrait-multimethod technique, the following problems were noted (Barnett, Faust, & Sarmir, 1988; Hall & Barnett, 1991; Macmann & Barnett, 1984; Poth & Barnett, 1988).

1. The convergent validity coefficients, even when statistically significant, were usually in the low to moderate range.
2. Discriminant validity also was difficult to establish; scales measuring different constructs often were significantly correlated.
3. The subscales within measures were often moderately to highly correlated. This means that the measures functioned in a global way in estimating developmental performance, rather than contributing to a profile of discrete skills for a child.

In sum, professionals make decisions based on the confidence they place on various techniques. Profile analyses of traditional developmental measures have revealed a very disappointing picture and a very unsound framework for professional practices. Thus, confidence in various techniques is seriously limited. Furthermore, the criteria of meeting both convergent and discriminant validity are not particularly stringent (e.g., Fiske, 1982), even apart from other considerations such as cost and utility.

Decision Reliability. Assessment strategies need to be analyzed with respect to the core issues of decision reliability and validity. We view these dimensions as fundamental aspects of technical adequacy which delimit the use of assessment information for the design and evaluation of interventions (Barnett & Macmann, in press).

Decision reliability refers to the consistency of outcomes across such factors as alternative instruments or methods, raters,

and assessment occasions. The requirement of decision reliability is implicit in many parts of the *Standards for Educational
and Psychological Testing* (AERA, APA, & NCME, 1985). Simply, the question of reliability is not with the scales per se, but
with the *outcomes of decisions*. To examine the reliability of professional decisions, important choices or outcomes need to be
represented: the child fits a classification or does not; the child
would benefit from intervention or would not; the child is deficient in motor skills or is not. Procedures for analyzing the
reliability of decisions must necessarily be flexible. Different
scales, raters, test occasions, observational systems, and decisions implied by test outcomes can be compared (for example,
parent versus teacher ratings; parent versus clinician ratings;
two different developmental scales) with the outcomes dichoto-
mized (for example, eligible versus not eligible for services).

     In sum, it is reasonable to require decision reliability
criterion levels that are equal to other criteria for reliability levels
(.90 to .95 for individual decisions), but the results of studies
have been disappointing. Alternative methods of screening are
likely to identify *different* children as "at risk" in a relatively large
number of cases. Diagnostic outcomes are often specific to the
instrument and time of testing. Different methods should converge on outcomes. However, outcomes are likely to differ because of the natural variability of behavior, the variability introduced by raters, differences in instruments that purportedly
can be used for the same function (to assess a domain such as
cognitive skills, communication skills, or social skills), and for
unknown reasons termed "errors of measurement." When evaluating assessment procedures, decision reliability is critical, but
it has been surprisingly low even with techniques that meet established conventions for reliability and validity.

Decision Validity and Treatment Utility. Validity focuses on what
a test measures and the generalizations that are possible from
test results. Validity of assessment techniques has been widely
studied; the validity of decision outcomes is less well developed.
Decision validity represents the appropriateness of using assessment data for specific decision purposes (Messick, 1989).

Hayes, Nelson, and Jarrett (1986, 1987) discuss treatment utility, which is a subset of decision validity. Treatment utility focuses on the outcomes of assessment methods based on their contributions to intervention effectiveness. The authors suggest that "many of the most central questions in clinical assessment are of this type, and yet often the field has generated virtually no data directly relevant to them" (1987, p. 965).

Perhaps the most important issue is that untested scales or instruments need to be compared to techniques with demonstrated value to intervention design. For example, an essential technique that professional psychologists use for intervention design is the problem-solving interview. In two separate group studies, the overall robustness of intervention plans developed through problem-solving interviews has been demonstrated with parents of high-risk preschool children. The studies evaluated the potential treatment utility of the eco-map (Carey, 1989) and the Parenting Stress Index (Vedder-Dubocq, 1990). (The interview format and eco-map are described in Chapter Three.) Although these two techniques may be useful for individual parents, the results of studies by Carey and Vedder-Dubocq found that problem-solving interviews overall were strongly related to intervention plans. Messick (1989) and Hayes, Nelson, and Jarrett (1986, 1987) stretch the analysis further, pointing to the need to evaluate assessment activities in relation to long-term therapeutic and social outcomes of intervention plans. The discussion of validity related to target behavior assessment is resumed in Chapter Five.

The Requirement for Professional Judgment. Professional judgment is the pervasive term used to describe a personal process that guides practitioners in controversial and ambiguous circumstances. Professional judgment supposedly bridges the gap between the knowledge base and actual strategies used to solve real-life problems. Some view it as a professional strength, or as a process that enables the professional to overcome the weaknesses of formal measures. However, we believe that professional judgment should be treated as an *unknown* — at best. Given the ambiguous and unreliable outcomes associated with various assessment techniques, including interpretations of observations, rating scales, developmental tests, and interviews, the potential exists for significant judgmental differences. Choices between instruments, raters, and even sequences of assessment events can have profound effects on interpretations. Sources of error and ways to reduce professional judgment error are reviewed in Barnett and Zucker (1990).

Examples of Technical Problems of Test Interpretation. There are other problems associated with test and profile interpretation based on common preschool assessment instruments.

1. The statistical significance of scores is determined based on deviations from the mean. However, the obtained score may not be the best estimate to use for certain educational and psychological decisions. "Obtained scores are biased estimates of true scores" (Nunnally, 1978, p. 217). Extreme scores need to be "regressed" to identify a child's probable range of scores. That is, high scores and low scores are expected to be less extreme on subsequent test occasions. The obtained scores are typically adjusted by a small amount given the reliabilities of most developmental scales. However, these amounts can be critical when specific cut scores are used for decision making—which is a common practice.

$$\text{Estimated True Score} = \bar{x} + (r_{xx})(x - \bar{x})$$
Where:
$\bar{x}$ = mean of test
x = obtained score
r_{xx} = reliability

2. Three "standard error" statistics are used to evaluate the effects of test reliability and the dispersion of scores on decision making. The standard error of *prediction* is the standard deviation of expected scores across retest occasions. It results in the most conservative approach to decision making and enables a norm-referenced interpretation of a confidence interval (Schulte & Borich, 1988).

$$\text{Standard Error} = \text{Standard Deviation} \sqrt{(1 - r_{xx}^2)}$$
Where:
r_{xx} = reliability

A *confidence interval* indicates the probability that an individual's score lies within a specified range. Thus, confidence intervals are used to establish a likely range of scores for an individual, given the error associated with a measurement procedure. We believe that consumers of psychological and educational services will understand and accept the notion of "errors of measurement." For example, rather than stating that a child received a development quotient of 113, or that a child *has* an IQ of 83, a range of scores is communicated in test interpretation based on the likelihood of the "true score" falling within a specified range. It is important to remember, however, that the true score always remains unknown. All we have to work with are obtained scores. True score theory has been widely challenged.

Exact confidence intervals are easy to calculate based on desired change probability levels. Confidence intervals typically are developed based on one or two standard errors, where the "true score" is expected to lie within a specified range of scores on approximately 68 percent or 95 percent of retest occasions. For example, given a standard error (of prediction) of 5.00 and retest reliability of .90, the confidence interval at the 68 percent level for an obtained IQ of 83 would be 84.7 +/− 5.00 or 80 to 90 (rounded). Notice that we built the confidence interval not on the obtained score (83), but on the estimated true score (84.7). Upon retesting, a child's score is expected to be closer (regressed) to the mean. However, the 68 percent level is far too risky (32 percent chance of error) for many professional-practice situations. At the 95 percent level, the confidence interval would be approximately 75 to 95.

While the use of estimated true scores for the purpose of setting confidence intervals has generated some controversy (debated in [1988] *Journal of Special Education, 22*[3]), it does demonstrate vividly the potential frailties of the use of cut scores for individual decision making. For individual children, the confidence intervals may suggest little in the way of confidence, particularly when multiple sources of assessment error are considered.

3. If a statistically significant difference is found for an obtained score, the reliability of the difference should be determined. The reliability of a difference is related to (a) the reliability of each measure or scale, (b) the intercorrelation between the measures, and (c) other factors such as differences in norming procedures. The equation below represents the traditional method of determining the reliability of difference scores (from Thorndike & Hagen, 1961).

$$r_{diff} = \frac{[\,\frac{1}{2}(r_{xx} + r_{yy})\,] - r_{xy}}{1 - r_{xy}}$$

Where:

r_{xx}, r_{yy} = reliabilities of x and y

r_{xy} = correlation between x and y

For example, a clinician may want to make statements about potential strengths and weaknesses in the child's profile. It is compelling to analyze profiles: to state that the child has a relative strength in language, for example, as compared to motor or cognitive skills.

However, even differences between scales within a given instrument may not lead to reliable conclusions. We give an example from the *DIAL-R* for a child who was three years and ten months old. The *DIAL-R (Mardell-Czudnowski & Goldenberg, 1983/1990)* is considered a screening instrument, and is not recommended for diagnostic purposes; we selected it to simplify the discussion. It is one of the best examples of a preschool assessment device, and it includes traditional "developmental domains" that lead to hypotheses about what areas to assess in depth (the title stands for Developmental Indicators for the Assessment of Learning). Most significantly, screening devices are used for decision making with huge numbers of children. For more complex developmental scales with additional subtests, such as the *K-ABC, WPPSI-R,* and McCarthy Scales, the errors related to individual profiles are compounded. Even though subtest reliabilities may be higher than those found on screening instruments like the *DIAL-R,* high intercorrelations within the scales, as well as other reasons identified earlier, defeat the ability to establish reliable and interpretable profiles for individual children.

In the manual, these coefficient alpha reliabilities are given: motor (r=.68), concepts (r=.81), and language (r=.70). The correlations between the scales are as follows: motor × concepts=.85, motor × language=.77, concepts × language=.79. If a child received a motor scaled score of 8 and a language score of 12, the *reliability of the difference* would be − .35. In other words, the difference cannot be interpreted as reliable. In cases where the correlations between scales or subscales are higher than test reliabilities, it is impossible to derive profiles of skills.

4. Estimates of decision reliability are necessary. The concept is of critical importance. Decision reliability requires that professionals analyze the stability of decisions across test occasions and any other assessment procedures that may be used. We focus on two prototypic uses of developmental scales that include decision outcomes.

Again, using the *DIAL-R* as an example, several studies have revealed potential difficulties concerning decisions for the *DIAL-R* total score and profiles. A study by Hall and Barnett (1991) found that the correlation between the *DIAL-R* and *SCREEN* (Hresko & colleagues, 1988) total scores was a modest .54 (N = 84). However, the proportion of specific agreement between children screened as "at risk" by both measures was .34. The finding has an important implication: a strong possibility exists that if another screening instrument is used, children will change classifications.

Second, with regard to strengths and weaknesses, the clinician would need to consider estimates based on alternative instruments that purport to measure similar constructs. In the study by Hall and Barnett (1991), the correlation between the *DIAL-R* language scale and the *SCREEN* language quotient was .31. While statistically significant, this correlation does not instill much confidence that a child's normative functioning will be described in a similar way (the standard error of prediction is quite large). In another study (Barnett, Faust, & Sarmir, 1988), the correlation between the *DIAL-R* language scale and the *LAP-D* (LeMay, Griffin, & Sunford, 1981) language scale was found to be .74 (*N* = 114). While this is much more impressive, the same correlation (.74) was found between the *DIAL-R* language scale and the *LAP-D motor* scale. A strong general factor may contribute to convergence across developmental domains.

5. The determination of clinical versus statistical significance should be made. *Clinical significance* has to do with the actual psychological or social importance of the findings for the child and caregivers. A related term is *social validity*. The topic is examined in a special issue of *Behavioral Assessment* (1988, *10*) with regard to intervention outcomes. In contrast, *statistical significance* reveals only that the results or findings were unusual to the degree that their probability of chance occurrence was remote. Statistical significance is far easier to determine than clinical significance, but it is not sufficient if the findings do not have practical importance. In most cases of actual practice, the clinical significance of the findings remains unknown.

In sum, professionals need evidence that the construct has been adequately measured, that the finding is reliable, that the finding has psychological or educational importance, and that the outcomes are useful for designing interventions. Using traditional instruments has led to profiles that cannot be interpreted with confidence and decisions that may be quite error prone. Ironically, tests that were designed to improve decision making may be untenable as aids to achieving reliable and valid *outcomes* for children.

The Use of Behavior Rating Scales

Numerous scales have been developed to rate children on personal and social characteristics or adjustment. These ratings usually attempt to assess relatively stable attributes. Frequently, rating scales are recommended for various assessment purposes, especially concerning psychopathology, personality, social skills, and adaptive behavior. We will not review individual scales; we are concerned with core issues that affect how professionals use behavior rating scales in their practices.

There are limitations to how accurately the rater responds. Cairns and Green wrote: "The distinguishing characteristic of rating scales is that they involve a social judgment on the part of the observer, or 'rater,' with regard to the placement of an individual on some psychological dimension" (1979, p. 210). Thus, interpretations *"begin* with the complex information-processing capabilities of the rater" (p. 211). Furthermore, the rater must understand the quality being rated and specific behaviors that reflect the quality in the same way as the person who developed the rating scale. The relevant information needs to be detected within the stream of everyday activities, settings, and events. Last, the rater is assumed to have the same underlying framework as other raters.

Other limitations include the effects of potential embarrassment, desire to convey a particular impression, possible indifference, or degree of conscious awareness of behaviors. Tolerances for behaviors may influence the behaviors of parents and teachers. Considerable differences between raters with regard to insightfulness and observational skills are likely. These factors must be treated as unknowns.

The convergence between different raters will probably be limited. The results of the meta-analysis by Achenbach, McConaughy, and Howell (1987) suggest that systematic as well as unknown factors contribute to the low to moderate relationships between different raters. While the correlations between raters achieved statistical significance, important differences were found between various raters. Similar raters (such as both parents) reached the highest level of agreement (mean $r = .60$). Agreement between different raters was much lower (between parent and teacher, mean $r = .28$; between subjects and raters, mean $r = .22$). Achenbach, Edelbrock, and Howell (1987) found mean interparent ratings to vary from .47 at age two to .58 at age four for the Child Behavior Checklist (CBCL). The low correlations may mean that each rater contributes different information; they also imply considerable error. For these and other reasons, Achenbach and co-workers have described a multiaxial empirically based assessment system (Achenbach & McConaughy, 1987), but the decision outcomes and contributions to assessment design have not yet been evaluated.

There is likely to be limited convergence between different methods of analysis. Numerous studies have evaluated the convergence of various rating scales and the correspondence between rating scales, other developmental techniques, and direct observations. The result is a confusing array of findings. Hoge, Meginbir, Khan, and Weatherall (1985) found that convergent validity coefficients for the Preschool Behavior Questionnaire ranged from .13 to .46, based on comparisons of teacher ratings with observer ratings and direct observations. Keenan and Lachar (1988) found statistically significant convergence between the Personality Inventory for Children (PIC) as rated by the child's mother, and teacher ratings on a behavior checklist. However, the highest correlation achieved between the adjustment scale on the PIC and the ratings of school disturbance was .69. Most of the correlations were in the .40s, demonstrating statistical significance but at best limited clinical significance. A reanalysis of the factor structure of one of the major tools for empirically based syndromal assessments based on behavioral ratings (Child Behavior Checklist, Achenbach & Edelbrock, 1983) suggests severe limitations in the discriminant validity of both the broad and narrow band scales (Macmann et al., in press).

Most scales have an intentional bias toward identifying psychopathology. Most behavior rating scales that have been developed to assess preschool children are designed to facilitate the assessment and classification of psychopathology. Unfortunately, this may occur at the expense of assessing factors associated with psychosocial change. Other potential vulnerabilities are evident in pressures to diagnose, inconsistencies between alternative diagnostic categories, and unintended results of labeling through the use of the constructs or syndromes. Most important, questions about reliability, validity, and treatment utility can be raised concerning the syndromes.

Appropriate Use of Behavior Rating Scales

Decisions about the use of rating scales should be based on the match between the validity of the scale, the problem behavior of the child, and the expected utility of the ratings. Overall, the potential uses of behavior rating scales may be highly overrated.

One appropriate application of rating scales is to help with the evaluation of research-based constellations of behaviors (Kazdin, 1985). The normative information provided by behavior rating scales may be useful for clarifying the problem and estimating its severity.

An emerging procedure involves making comparisons of the similarities between a child's profile and the *prototypic* or distinctive features of empirically based syndromes (Achenbach, 1988). On the positive side, the greatest potential contribution is that the adequacy of assessment and intervention plans can be tested logically. Surprisingly, the correlations between internalizing and externalizing disorders are quite high (for boys age four to five, $r = .74$). This finding, apart from other psychometric problems discussed earlier, means that syndromes and individual profiles for children will be difficult to interpret — if not impossible.

In sum, syndromal diagnosis (appraising the degree to which empirically based syndromes or constructs might fit an individual child) is an important point of assessment. However, we view it as only one step in the process. When working with children referred for various learning and behavior problems, perhaps the greatest benefit will be to help in making *logical generalizations* about interventions described in research.

When Testing Is Unavoidable

We recognize the potential for dissonance created by our discussions of fallible assessment techniques. Unfortunately, practitioners are often pressed to determine children's eligibility for special services under state and federal mandates and are required to do so by testing. However, for children traditionally labeled as mildly handicapped, many traditional testing practices result in dead ends. What could be more descriptive than Galagan's (1985) title: "Psychoeducational Testing: Turn Out the Lights, the Party's Over."

Many tests and procedures in common use have been widely criticized (IQ tests); others should be (developmental scales, adaptive or other behavior rating scales). Nonetheless, professionals are often required to use them. In these circumstances, we offer the following considerations for their use.

Testing is an accepted professional function. Despite the controversies, testing is a well-accepted method for determining eligibility for special services. The most important points are that while global performance measures such as IQ, developmental scales, and behavior ratings do have some general predictive and descriptive value, they do not provide a foundation for early intervention and are error prone for individual children. We must work toward long-term changes to help reduce inappropriate referrals for testing and to establish intervention assistance programs.

Use the scales in a reasonable manner. The controversies should be well known by those who use various scales and by consumers of educational and psychological services. "Although the test developer and publisher should provide information on the strengths and weaknesses of the test, the ultimate responsibility for appropriate test use lies with the test user" (AERA, APA, & NCME, 1985, p. 41). Perhaps the most important point is to follow existing guidelines for technical adequacy standards and professional practices and report only what can be said with confidence. Unfortunately, the dilemmas are considerable, and often very little can be stated with confidence. It is better to communicate uncertainty than misinformation.

Do not test unless you have to. The most important recommendation is to be oriented by the referral question. If parents or teachers are asking questions that will not pertain directly to the results obtained from tests, testing need not be offered. If parents or teachers do ask specifically that a child be tested, it may be valuable to discuss possible misunderstandings related to tests and associated outcomes, and alternative assessment procedures that will provide information that is needed. Sometimes, without careful explanation, consumers of services may think that appropriate services are being denied if tests are not given.

Consider alternative assessment frameworks. The alternatives include adaptive testing, testing of limits procedures, and comparisons of results across test occasions and different measures. Estimates can be derived about three facets of performance: (a) skills mastered by the child independent of assistance and evident across different types of measurement procedures, (b) skills the child is close to mastering, and (c) skills that become manifest through aided performance — conditions under which the highest levels of performance will be maintained at a specific time.

Vygotsky defined the zone of proximal development as "the distance between the actual developmental level as determined by independent problem solving and the level of potential development as determined through problem solving under adult guidance or in collaboration with more capable peers" (1978, p. 86). While it is a disservice to place Vygotsky's work under the rubric of "testing," he made critical points that fit well. "The state of a child's mental development can be determined only by clarifying its two levels: the actual developmental level and the zone of proximal development" (p. 87). He added that "the only 'good learning' is that which is in advance of development" (p. 89). For discussion of various alternative assessment strategies see Sattler (1988) and Schwebel and Maher (1986). Overall, these approaches to testing are not well developed and technical adequacy questions apply, but they may yield a better overall understanding of performance.

Consider intervention-based questions. Even when traditional tests are used, intervention-based questions help guide interpretations and recommendations and thus help orient the overall process to goals related to change. We offer the following:

> What is the range of skill development?
>
> What component skills did the child demonstrate?
>
> What skills are necessary in solving inadequately performed tasks?
>
> What problem-solving steps or knowledge did the child seem to be missing?
>
> How could these be adequately assessed?
>
> How do children acquire those skills?
>
> What learning difficulties seem to exist (attentional, retentional, productive, motivational)?
>
> Are there deficits in related skills (such as language) that affect the level of performance?

> How did the performance in testing compare with the
> child's performance with other materials, test questions,
> in other environments, or at other times?
> What are the child's current optimal performance levels?

The greatest problem with this approach is that test-based deficits
may not be the most beneficial targets for change.

Consider aids for decision making. Strategies other than
tests are needed for determining program eligibility and needed
services. One way is to structure parent and professional *opinions* about the child and needed services. An example is the System to Plan Early Childhood Services (SPECS) (Bagnato &
Neisworth, 1990). SPECS involves several components, including Developmental SPECS, Team SPECS, and Program
SPECS.

Developmental SPECS involves team ratings on developmental skills in the following dimensions: communication, sen-
sorimotor, physical, self-regulation, cognition, and self-social.
Team SPECS is used to structure and facilitate interdisciplinary team meetings. The individual team members' ratings from
Developmental SPECS are recorded on a team summary form.
The form enables a profile of potential needs based on perceptions by team members across developmental domains. Judgments also are made about service options (special education,
behavior therapy, speech/language therapy, and so on) and a
consensus of perceptions of functional status across the developmental dimensions. Program SPECS is used to plan a program
based on team discussions of ratings of needed services.

We offer several considerations. First, judgments by professionals and parents should not be considered as strengths but
as unknowns. The results of judgments should be treated as hypotheses that need to be evaluated, even if reached by consensus.
Second, the fundamental aspects of intervention design are relevant to SPECS regardless of eligibility and placement outcomes.
Third, the technical qualities of SPECS are similar to those of
scales producing the error rates discussed earlier. In comparing child status from records and SPECS ratings, the overall
classification agreement for various childhood disabilities ranged

from a low of 75 percent agreement for developmental delay to a high of 93 percent for hearing impairment. However, the chance-corrected agreement may be considerably lower (kappa for the status of developmental delay is .46.)

The end result of determining eligibility for special services is an Individual Educational Plan (IEP) to meet federal requirements. The IEP is based on parent and professional team decision making and includes at least the following: a description of current levels of performance, annual and short-term goals, services to be provided, dates of the initiation and the duration of services, setting in which the child will receive services (including participation in regular programs), evaluation procedures, and procedures and schedules for at least an annual review. The overriding concern with the process has been the efficacy of special programs for children with mild disabilities.

Plan procedures to "exit" from special services and for normalization as carefully and deliberately as entry into special services. There are compelling legal, philosophical, social, and educational reasons for integrating children with disabilities into regular programs. However, the educational and social benefits of integration are not guaranteed; the quality of plans to achieve integration is critical.

Summary and Conclusions

The multifactored assessment model has led to a reliance on test batteries and child-centered skills. The inherent problems with traditional techniques are much worse than imagined and greater than warnings in screening and diagnostic manuals would suggest. In contrast, assessment for intervention design is founded on ecological and behavioral principles, factors facilitating change, and sequential rather than diagnostic decisions — not by available tests or techniques. We now return our attention to this emphasis.

3

Consulting with Parents and Teachers

THE LAST CHAPTER LEFT US WITH A BROADER APPRECIATION OF THE complexity of the assessment problem but with no solutions. This chapter and the next present alternative assessment techniques related to designing interventions for young children. The central theme is that assessment should lead to a better understanding of the problem situation. Assessment strategies also are used to help develop treatment goals and intervention plans, and to monitor intervention outcomes.

Parent and Teacher Consultation

Assessment and intervention practices require ongoing problem solving rather than explicit responses to a set of "given" questions (Schön, 1983). Consultation is a systematic way to guide the problem-solving process. The stages of ecobehavioral consultation generally follow this sequence: (1) problem identification, (2) problem analysis, (3) plan development, (4) plan implementation, and (5) evaluation.

    School and parent consultation is based on systems theory. Applications of systems theory are pervasive. The topics generally deal with issues of "wholeness" and purposive behavior, and such related factors as the analysis of complex interactions, orderliness of behavior, and system regulation. Comprehensive intervention-based services require a systematic appraisal of the systems within which the child interacts, and a mutual and reciprocal partnership with the child, parents, and school personnel. In addition, consultation helps practitioners deal with complex legal and ethical considerations because the focus is on mutual decision making.

Core Features of Consultation

A primary underlying assumption of consultation-based service is the importance of providing assistance to caregivers rather than direct services to children (Gutkin & Curtis, 1990). It is founded on team members' mutual respect for one another. A collaborative atmosphere of openness and trust between participants is essential. Parents, school personnel, and other professionals are considered experts in their knowledge about a child; the consultant demonstrates expertise in problem solving and intervention design. Thus, the consultant is able to provide structure and organization to the problem-solving process. The active involvement of caregivers is important for successful outcomes, although involvement alone does not guarantee success. Another important premise is that the caregivers' problem-solving skills can be enhanced by the experience of working with a skilled consultant (Curtis & Watson, 1980).

Witt and Martens (1988) critiqued consultation-based methods from an ecobehavioral viewpoint. They stressed the need to assess prerequisites such as environmental variables and teacher skills before implementing behavioral change programs, and to build on existing strengths. Their concerns are addressed by naturalistic intervention design and strategies described in Chapter Five.

Teaming Strategies

A team perspective underlies consultation. For children with severe learning or behavior problems, team members include parents, teachers, and specialized consultants. Teams can be composed and function in different ways. They can be *multidisciplinary* (team members function independently), *interdiscipli-*

nary (members work together in a coordinated effort), or *trans-disciplinary* (members share roles and responsibilities) (Bagnato & Neisworth, 1990).

Some may perceive consultation as different from teaming; they believe that a consultant provides the "answers" for others, who then implement the consultant's recommendations. Rather, conjoint, problem-solving methods are used throughout the assessment-intervention steps, and *consultation* is the term used to describe this process. Thus, teams may comprise parents and a range of professionals in different combinations, but the core element is interactive problem solving between team members.

Problem-Centered and Developmental Consultation

Kratochwill and Bergan (1990) distinguished between two types of behavioral consultation; both have important implications for relationships with parents and teachers. *Problem-centered consultation* refers to situations where the problems are limited to "specific behaviors of immediate concern to the consultee" (p. 37). Examples would be specific conduct problems in the classroom or home. *Developmental consultation* refers to situations where the focus is one or more long-range objectives. An example they give is improving a child's social interactions, a process that may require considerable planning and time. "Developmental consultation requires repeated application of the problem-solving model" (p. 38), combinations of interventions, and different change agents.

Component Strategies for Preschool Assessment Design

The component assessment strategies for intervention design are identified in Exhibit 3.1. They are used in an iterative fashion, based on a problem-solving model. *Iterative* means that steps are repeated as necessary, and with progressive refinement. For example, questions about changes in child systems are pertinent throughout the assessment-intervention process. Also, the entire process is *idiographic,* which means that individual "laws" or factors that guide behavior are of immediate interest. *Nomothetic* principles (general laws or more universal variables) are

Exhibit 3.1. Component Strategies: Assessment for Intervention Design.

Idiographic Assessment: Initial constructs used as targets of assessment have meaning for the client or significant others. All components listed below are based on idiographic practices, although there are direct links to nomothetic data.

1. *Ecological Assessment.* Family, school, and community systems should be assessed for contributions to the understanding of adjustment, system problems, and system strengths.
2. *Behavior Assessment and Person Variables.* Pathological descriptors should be redefined in terms of desired outcomes, specific objectives, and barriers to adjustment. Adult (parental, teacher) and child behaviors may be included.
3. *Research-based Constructs.* The correspondence between constructs that evolve from descriptions of the client and those that should have research support should be determined. Kazdin (1985) refers to the understanding of research-based "constellations of behavior."
4. *Formal Assessment Techniques.* Decisions about formal techniques should be based on the match between problem behavior and test validity, technical adequacy, and, especially, expected utility.
5. *Applications of Change Theory and Research.* Target behaviors and treatment options should be examined systematically based in part on a review of validated interventions for specific problem behaviors, functional analysis, and acceptability. The end results are plans that should be evaluated.

From David W. Barnett & Karl B. Zucker, *The Personal and Social Assessment of Children: An Analysis of Current Status and Professional Practice Issues.* Copyright © 1990 by Allyn & Bacon. Reprinted with permission.

considered through the evaluation of research-based constructs, assessment techniques, and change theory and research.

The components, as interrelated steps, serve as an outline or template that professionals may follow. Both reflective and research-based strategies are necessary for each component of the process.

Ecobehavioral Interviews

Ecological theory is based on the tenet that problems do not reside within individuals but instead are shared by members of pertinent systems (peer, family, school, community) and even broader influences as well. Interviews are useful for understanding ecological factors that affect behaviors, since parents, teachers, and other caregivers describe behaviors in context.

An ecobehavioral approach provides alternatives for resolving problems: (a) modifying the problem behavior; (b) altering or clarifying the expectations of persons encountering the problem behavior; or (c) changing situations or environments. In addition, system strengths such as healthy adaptive mechanisms and coping strategies can be analyzed.

Ecological interviews involve "mapping" the world the family lives in, including the networks of parental work, family and social relationships, community involvement, and preschool and day-care settings. We discuss three interrelated ecobehavioral interview techniques: the eco-map, the waking day interview, and the problem-solving interview.

The Eco-map

The eco-map (Hartman, 1978; Hobbs, 1966) has been used to describe family and community systems. It may be developed with family and community members or by the professional. The primary value of the eco-map is its visual impact. The map can portray complex networks and stresses of contemporary families that result from divorce, separation, shared custody, foster care, adoption, or alienation from traditional community life.

An eco-map is depicted in Figure 3.1. Squares represent males, circles represent females. Ages may be placed in these shapes. Relationships are depicted with different connecting lines: solid lines for strong, positive relationships; dashed lines for tenuous relationships; X's for conflicted or stressful relationships. The child has had a difficult adjustment to both preschool and day care. Furthermore, the relationship between the child and mother is characterized by stress. The mother is working and going to school, and has limited support systems, as indicated by the dashed line between mother and grandmother and the absence of other relationships. Additional symbols may be added to represent agencies, friends, and other significant forces.

The eco-map may be used as an assessment tool (jointly by professional and client), a thinking tool to examine problems and resources, a recording and communication tool, and a measure of change. However, very little research has been

Figure 3.1. An Example of an Eco-Map.

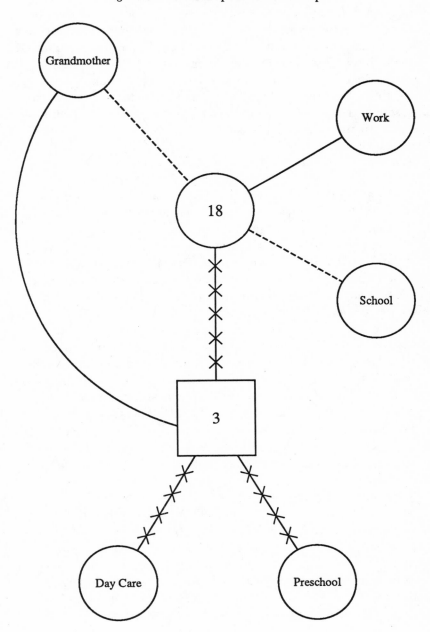

done with the technique. One study (Carey, 1989) found no contributions of the eco-map to intervention design beyond those obtained through a semistructured problem-solving interview for parents of high-risk children (although benefits were found for individual parents). Since technical adequacy remains undetermined, use of eco-maps is a matter of judgment. However, we think that the eco-map is fundamental for depicting child systems, decisions in intervention design, and changes that are made in intervention plans.

Waking Day (and Sleep) Interview

The waking day interview involves a detailed description of behaviors. It can be used to help select target behaviors and environments to support interventions.

In the interview, the parent is asked to describe the child's typical day by focusing on events, routines, and behavior from awakening until bedtime. Preschool teachers are asked to describe behavior during transportation to and from school, entering school, specific class activities, transitions, lunch, and other events. Behaviors of greatest concern to the caregiver often are revealed during the interview. The waking day interview may also be used to help select equivalent conditions needed to establish baseline information (discussed in Chapter Five).

A typical waking day interview is shown in Exhibit 3.2. The interview was suggested by Wahler and Cormier (1970). We have added questions about sleep disturbances because of their importance to child and family functioning. The interview typically takes between twenty and forty minutes for each caregiver.

One study found high procedural reliability and acceptability with teachers (Hampel, 1991). Because caregivers perceive the interview as relevant, it also has been useful for rapport building. In sum, we consider the waking day interview basic to parent and teacher consultation because the information it provides is significant for intervention decisions. Also, the interview is used to examine successful settings for children that may provide ideas for naturalistic interventions.

Exhibit 3.2. Waking Day (and Sleep) Interview.

Home Setting	*Problems*

Describe your child's behavior in the following settings or situations.

Sleep patterns?
Waking up time?
Breakfast?
Dressing?
To school?
After school?
Dinnertime?
After dinner?
Bath time?
Bedtime?
In the car?
Play?
  With siblings?
  Peers?
  Alone?
Discipline techniques?
Chores?
Shopping?
Other community settings?
With visitors?

School Setting	*Problems*

On the bus?
Entry in classroom?
Organizational activities?
Transition times?
Lunchroom?
Bathroom?
Large group activities?
Freeplay time?
Individual activities?
Small group activities?
Out of classroom activities (i.e., gym, walks, special events or trips)?
Relationships with parents (e.g., home-school communication)?

Problem-Solving Interviews

Problem-solving interviews have two functions: scanning problem behaviors and circumstances, and analyzing problem situations in depth (Peterson, 1968). The basic interview with modifications is used throughout the assessment, intervention, and evaluation phases.

A twelve-point framework for the guided interview, developed by Carey (1989) and Vedder-Dubocq (1990), is presented in this section. It is based on the work of several authors: Alessi and Kaye (1983); Kanfer and Grimm (1977); and Peterson (1968). With modification, the interview format may be used with various caregivers such as parents or teachers.

Effective communication — both verbal and nonverbal — is basic to interviews. Some of the important factors include genuineness, listening and encouraging consultee verbalizations, empathy, questioning skills, clarification, summarization, and, at times, confrontation (Gutkin & Curtis, 1982).

1. *Explain the problem-solving interview and its purpose.* It is best to set the tone and establish guidelines for the interview by giving an overview of what is to be accomplished.

    Example: The purpose of this interview will be to talk about problems related to parenting [or teaching] so we can develop goals to make parenting easier or more enjoyable. In order to accomplish this, we need to discuss the areas of difficulty which bother you most, when they occur, how often they occur, and what you think might influence these behaviors.

2. *Define problem behavior.* Question and probe as needed to determine the caregiver's view of the problem: what the child is doing, or not doing, and whether others see this as a problem. If the caregiver responds in generalities such as "my child is hyper," ask the caregiver to describe the behavior more explicitly.

    Examples: Please describe your greatest areas of difficulty related to your role as a parent. What exactly does [*child's name*] do when [he or she] is acting this way?

3. *Prioritize multiple problems.* If the caregiver identifies multi-

ple concerns, guide him or her in prioritizing these behaviors. It may be helpful to have the caregiver's perceptions about which behavior the intervention process might
reasonably start with.

> *Examples:* Which bothers you the most? Which of these
> concerns are most pressing to you? Tell me which of these
> problems you think you could learn to manage most eas-
> ily or successfully?

4. *Define severity of the problem.* Try to link estimates of severity
    with specific examples and trends of actual occurrences. This
    may require probing (Peterson, 1968, p. 121).

    > *Examples:* How often do you, or does your child . . . ?
    > About how many times a day, week, etc., does this prob-
    > lem occur? Would you say this problem behavior is start-
    > ing to happen more often, less often, or is it staying about
    > the same? (adapted from Alessi & Kaye, 1983, Appen-
    > dix B).

5. *Define "generality of the problem."* Question and probe to de-
    termine the length of time the behavior has been a prob-
    lem, and the situations in which it is observed (Peterson,
    1968, p. 121).

    > *Examples:* How long has this been going on? Where does
    > the problem behavior usually come up? Do you observe
    > the behavior at home? How about when visiting friends
    > or family, or shopping? (adapted from Peterson, 1968,
    > pp. 121–122)

6. *Explore determinants of the problem behavior* (Peterson, 1968, p.
    122). This aspect of the interview is based on a functional
    analysis of behavior. In addition, beliefs about causality may
    be important in considering motivational issues and inter-
    vention alternatives.

    (a). *Conditions that intensify the problem. Example:* I want you
          to think about the times when [the problem] is worst.
          What sort of things are going on then? (adapted from
          Peterson, 1968, p. 122)

    (b). *Conditions that alleviate the problem. Example:* What about
          the times when [the problem] gets better? What kinds
          of things are happening then? (adapted from Peter-
          son, 1968, p. 122)

(c). *Caregiver's perception of the origin of the problem.* The causes should be accepted as stated, but when necessary, reframe the interpretation in order to discuss intervention implications. For example, "hyperactivity" is reframed as "frequent activity changes," "doesn't complete tasks," "difficulty with sustained play," or "difficulty with self-regulation." Some perceived causes may require considerable attention, for they may reduce motivation for the intervention process (for example, if the caregiver thinks that inherited qualities are responsible for aggressive behaviors). *Example:* What do you think is causing [the problem]? (Peterson, 1968, p. 122).

(d). *Antecedents, personal, and social influences. Examples:* Think back to the last time [the problem occurred]. What was going on at the time? Where were you? Were there any other people around? Who? What were they doing? What were you thinking about at that time? How did you feel? (adapted from Peterson, 1968, p. 122).

(e). *Consequences. Examples:* What usually happens after [the problem] occurs? Does this happen consistently? *For social consequences:* What did [significant others] do? *For personal consequences:* How did that make you feel? What were you thinking about then? (adapted from Peterson, 1968, p. 122).

7. *Determine modification attempts.* This topic may reveal information related to naturalistic interventions and self-efficacy. *Examples:* What things have you tried to stop this problem behavior? How long have you tried that? How well did it work? Have you tried anything else? (adapted from Alessi & Kaye, 1983, Appendix B).

8. *Identify expectancies for improved behavior.* It is important to determine desired levels of performance or changes in roles and behaviors. These also help determine goals for intervention. *Examples:* In this kind of situation, what would you like [your child, yourself, spouse] to do instead of the problem behavior? If [child] were to improve, what would you notice first? What is the desired behavior you would

like to see [your child, yourself] accomplish? (Alessi & Kaye, 1983, Appendix B).

9. *Summarize caregiver's concerns* (Alessi & Kaye, 1983, Appendix B). Give a rationale for the summary and briefly summarize parent or teacher concerns, confirm caregiver's definition of the problem behavior, priorities, and goals for treatment. Summarization is used to integrate information and to facilitate continued exploration of a problem area.

10. *Explore the caregiver's commitment and motivation to work on the problem.*

    Examples: How would solving this problem make your day easier? Were this problem to go away, how would this change your day? If this problem were to get worse, how would this affect your parenting/teaching? What do you think the chances are of resolving this problem? (adapted from Alessi & Kaye, 1983, Appendix B).

11. *Have caregiver summarize problems, treatment goals, and plans.* At different phases of the assessment and intervention process, caregivers may be asked to summarize the exchange of information. Having the caregiver summarize meeting events gives an immediate and powerful check for communication effectiveness and areas that may need clarification. It also may give caregivers an important opportunity to "own" plans. The consultant may facilitate summarization through careful wording of the request.

    Example: In order to make sure I understand your concerns and goals, I would like you to summarize them for me. Please describe your impression or understanding of how the intervention will work.

12. *Discuss and mutually arrive at plans for the next steps.* The subsequent steps may include further consultation to review uncertainties about information revealed in the interview, plans for observation, referral to another agency, or a wide range of other mutually agreed upon outcomes.

    In sum, the problem-solving interview is a basic technique for uncovering and clarifying caregiver concerns, problem settings, and possible contributions of individuals to intervention plans.

Other Interview Techniques

In addition to these three ecobehavioral interview techniques, there are many other approaches to interviews. In this section, we review general considerations in interviewing preschool children and other interview approaches with parents.

Interviewing Children

Many factors influence child interviews: the child's motivation, developmental level, and communication skills; specific problem areas; and interviewer characteristics. Because of all these variables, it is difficult to study the interviews. Thus generalizations are limited, and results should be considered cautiously.

At the same time, there are many compelling reasons for conducting child interviews. First, even very young children can participate in the intervention process. Second, interviews may reveal information that is impossible to gain from other sources.

One of the classic descriptions of child interviews is by Yarrow (1960), and we borrow from this analysis. Although developmental ages may be misleading for generalization, some guidelines can be offered. Between the ages of four and five, children become interested in exchanging information and describing people, objects, and events. Also, at this age, they may be able to describe causes and the emotions of others. However, young children may have difficulties in understanding temporal relationships.

While direct interpretations of interviews often are difficult, the information does not necessarily need to be treated as factual to be of value. From the child's point of view, perceptions can be significant. Yarrow stressed that the interview may be important in "uncovering subjective definitions of experiences," assessing children's perceptions of significant people and events, and studying conceptualizations of life experiences (1960, p. 561; see also Bierman, 1983).

Especially with young children, the motivation to communicate with an adult is "developed during the course of the interview" (Yarrow, 1960, p. 568). If information is not revealed under one set of circumstances, it may be offered at other times or to other individuals. Yarrow described many adaptations (such as toy phone and doll play) that may help with rapport, or accommodate for expressive language development. Many strategies may be used to help with anxiety, such as having the children bring pictures that they have drawn.

One of the most extensive recent discussions of interviewing children is by Garbarino and Stott (1989). We refer childcare professionals who must interview children to their guidelines. They emphasize using familiar language and terms that the child will understand, and conducting interviews in everyday settings when possible. Another example is having the child try to repeat what is said instead of asking perfunctorily, "Do you understand?" Garbarino and Stott also review interview techniques related to specific problem areas such as sexual abuse. They conclude: "What we learn from children in interviews will necessarily depend on the communicative competence of the child, the professional qualities and personal characteristics of the interviewer, the purposes for which the information is sought, and the specific interview techniques, including the context of the interview" (p. 202).

Other Family-Based Interviews

Approaches to family assessment are numerous. We described three ecobehavioral techniques, stressing functional outcomes for children specifically related to intervention design. We think that in general ecobehavioral interview techniques adequately address "the core dimensions of family assessment," given the realities of most professional practice situations (Krauss & Jacobs, 1990, p. 312). These core dimensions are parental and family events, needs, stressors, coping strategies, resources, and the family environment as they interact with or influence child behavior. However, based on the interview findings, professionals may want to examine these areas in more depth. Barriers to family functioning and family needs may preclude approaches to intervention design.

While many scales and techniques are currently available to measure facets of family or parental functioning, issues concerning technical adequacy, especially decision reliability, decision validity, and treatment utility, are prevalent. Also, the potential benefits of adding assessment procedures need to be weighed. Sechrest (1963) introduced the term *incremental validity* to emphasize the importance of evaluating the contributions of assessment procedures beyond the information that is readily available or already known.

Our recommendation is to structure ecobehavioral interviews and observations around core concerns in ways that lead to intervention decisions. Ecobehavioral interviews are flexible and powerful in this regard. For example, parents may reveal that they have poor health and a lack of support systems. Ecobehavioral interviews and observations can reveal the extent of parental functioning vis-à-vis child-care responsibilities, possible sources of support, and a range of intervention alternatives within actual parental capabilities. The periodicity of a disorder may be significant for a parent (as with sickle cell), and ecobehavioral interviews can help examine parental coping in crisis situations. Other limitations in caregivers' ability or motivation to perform childrearing duties may be examined. Many questions have been raised about the effects of a child with disabilities on the family, and this may be examined functionally through ecobehavioral interviews and observations.

Discussions of alternative interviews and other assessment techniques for those who disagree with our recommendation can be found in Bailey and Simeonsson (1988), Dunst, Trivette, and Deal (1988), and throughout the edited book by Meisels and Shonkoff (1990). A special issue of *Journal of Early Intervention* (*14*[3], 1991) was dedicated to families.

Telephone Contacts

In some situations, a professional's only feasible ongoing access to parents may be through the telephone. It can also be used as an adjunctive source of information sharing throughout the assessment-intervention process. Phone contacts may be relatively nonintrusive and may result in minimal reactivity. While further research is necessary, the research that does exist is promising.

One of the best examples is described by Patterson and others (1975); telephone contacts with parents were used to obtain information on low-rate or infrequent problems. This feature is important because low-rate behaviors are more likely to be missed in direct home observations. They used a thirty-four-item "Parent Daily Report" (PDR), a relatively simple structured interview, to collect data on specific behaviors. Because it deals with behaviors of concern to parents, another potential benefit of a PDR target behavior score is its sensitivity to intervention outcomes. It is important to note that they do not recommend its use for therapeutic purposes.

To use the Parent Daily Report (PDR), the professional reviews the items at an orientation session and parents indicate the problems relevant to their child. During scheduled telephone calls, parents report the occurrence or nonoccurrence of the specific events during the past twenty-four hours. The phone contacts take about five minutes each. The PDR is reproduced in Exhibit 3.3.

Chamberlain and Reid (1987) described the PDR and reviewed its technical characteristics. The PDR yields two scores related to total problem behavior and targeted behaviors. Interrater agreement (obtained through the use of an extension phone) was good (85 percent entry by entry agreement). Agreement between parents was marginal, similar to other interrater findings. Comparisons with direct home observations support the validity of the measure. Chamberlain and Reid noted the possibility of a "first-day effect," in which the total behavior scores may be inflated for the first day. They suggest that seven telephone calls over a two-week period will give adequate estimates of problem behavior if the first-day interview is discarded.

Other examples of phone use related to early assessment and intervention are provided by Brown, Cunningham, and Birkimer (1983) and Frankel and Weiner (1990).

Technical Adequacy of Interviews

Alternative assessment techniques such as interviews and observations are not immune to questions of technical adequacy. The technical qualities of interviews have received insufficient

Exhibit 3.3. The Parent Daily Report Checklist.

Phase: baseline, intervention, termination, follow-up
Week beginning: (Mon) _____ /_____ (Sun)

Behavior	M	T	W	Th	F	Behavior	M	T	W	Th	F
Aggressiveness						Noncomplying					
Arguing						Not eating meals					
Bedwetting						Pants wetting					
Competitiveness						Pouting					
Complaining						Running around					
Crying						Running away					
Defiance						Sadness					
Destructiveness						Soiling					
Fearfulness						Stealing					
Fighting w/sibs						Talking back-Adult					
Firesetting						Teasing					
Hitting others						Temper tantrums					
Hyperactiveness						Whining					
Irritableness						Yelling					
Lying						Police contact					
Negativism						School contact					
Noisiness						Parents spank					

Source: Reprinted with permission from *Behavioral Assessment, 9,* P. Chamberlain and J. B. Reid, "Parent Observation and Report of Child Symptoms," Copyright 1987, Pergamon Press plc.

study. In describing a prototypic behavioral interview, Peterson (1968) warned that interviews should not necessarily be "regarded as the 'truth' about the individual and his environment, but as another form of data whose reliability, validity and decisional utility must be subjected to the same kinds of scrutiny required for other modes of data collection" (p. 13). One of the greatest problems with interviews is the reliance on self-report information. In addition, important factors may be "out of awareness" (Bowers & Meichenbaum, 1984).

Earlier, we described parents and teachers as full participants in consultation and as "experts" in their observations of children and behavior contexts. We now begin to raise questions about this facet of the assessment process. The most important factor is that many of the problem areas are pertinent not only for caregivers, but potentially influence all participants who are engaged in problem solving. There are differences in roles between consultants and consultees, but there are commonalities: both are subject to normal difficulties that surround inference and judgment. It is not surprising that a wide range of consultant and consultee variables may influence the outcomes.

In sum, the interview contributes to the formulation of an overall plan and to its evaluation. The iterative nature of the process is the best safeguard for developing workable plans and reducing errors of judgment.

The Relationship Between Interviews and Observations

Ecobehavioral interviews are used to clarify a wide range of issues pertaining to intervention design: problem behaviors and circumstances, settings, key persons, likely change agents, and significant time periods. Interviews also are used to examine intervention alternatives and possible barriers to the intervention processes, and to help evaluate intervention outcomes. Defining the problem situation by its physical and social characteristics is one of the first steps in problem solving, and interviews are essential in this regard.

Interviews also provide incomplete information. The results of interviews are dependent on the skills of the consultants and the caregivers' observations. There are three potential problem areas for "participant" observers — parents and teachers. Certain types of observations, such as those pertaining to broad ecological variables, participant-child interactions, and child-child interactions out of the caregiver's purview, are problematic. Second, interviews typically stress the "verbal behavior" of the teacher or parent and not actual child, teacher, and peer behaviors in specific contexts. Last, caregivers may serve as "untrained" observers (Kratochwill, 1985), and the data may be variable or hard to interpret. Consultation may be needed to pinpoint what to observe and which strategies of observation to use.

Only through direct observation is it possible to closely examine the relationship between environment and behavior. Reliable observations are necessary for the analysis of home and classroom environments, specific skills, behaviors, interactions between persons, and sequences of interactions. In addition, observations are used to monitor interventions and to help determine their effectiveness.

Summary and Conclusions

This chapter introduced assessment for intervention design. Defining the purpose of assessment is critical. From ecobehavioral theory, a central purpose is to restore or improve the functioning of groups for the well-being of all group members. Thus, ecobehavioral analysis focuses on natural systems such as families and schools. Children are described as hard to teach, parent, or befriend because they are not participating satisfactorily in school, family, or peer groups.

A second consideration is "what is the service delivery system?" There are countless possibilities. We presented the core features of parent and teacher consultation as a service delivery system that is adaptable to many different programs, practices, and philosophies. The central process is mutual problem solving.

Ecobehavioral interviews help elucidate which environments and behaviors will be the subject of analysis. They enable consultants to consider a range of intervention alternatives, possible barriers to interventions, and potential resources.

4

Principles and Techniques for Observations

THIS CHAPTER REVIEWS PRINCIPLES AND STRATEGIES FOR OBSERVING children referred for learning and behavior problems. To conduct observations, basic decisions are necessary: *what* and *where* to observe, *who* is to observe, *when* to observe, and *how*. The answers to these interrelated questions are linked directly to interviews and the results of parent and teacher consultations.

Planning Observations

Two general strategies are recommended for developing observational systems for individual children. First, ecobehavioral interviews and preliminary observations are used to help define important situations and target behaviors. Situations are defined in terms of physical and social settings and the observable events that occur within the setting (Bijou, Peterson, & Ault, 1968; Bijou, Peterson, Harris, Allen, & Johnston, 1969).

Second, structured observations are conducted, based on the problem identification and clarification stages of consultation, preliminary observations, and an analysis of relevant research. The selection of behaviors for observation requires conceptual, research-based, practical, and ethical frameworks that are discussed in later chapters.

While many sources state that "informal" observations may be used as an assessment strategy, we do not think that they will produce effective results. To reduce sources of error, initial observations should be as "hypothesis free" as possible. Hypotheses about the child's behavior are then formed based on the integration of the preliminary observations with interview results, or the child may be observed further before hypotheses are formed. Theory and research also guide the development of hypotheses as discussed in Chapter Three (Exhibit 3.1).

What to Observe

Practically speaking, it is impossible to record all that is occurring in most preschool situations or family environments, even through the use of video recordings. Naturalistic observation is so complex that observers must use "filters." The observer's decisions about what behaviors to focus on constitute one kind of filter. Filters also involve human capabilities in selective attention and perception — "key elements in observational recording" (Cairns & Green, 1979, p. 215) — and vigilance. Filters should be planned. When unplanned or not noticed as such, they result in observations that are difficult to evaluate.

It is not possible to observe everything. At the same time, it is frequently necessary to measure several different facets of behavior. For example, the play behavior of socially isolated children requires measuring frequency of interactions and, later, duration and quality. Different types of play interactions between children may be observed, and a variety of play behaviors may be targeted for intervention.

Perhaps the best guideline is that there should be a natural basis for behaviors that are observed and recorded. The natural units should meet at least the following criteria: (a) they should have unequivocal validity for describing significant interactions between the child and environment, (b) they should be capable of reflecting planned changes that result from interventions, and (c) they should be countable or repeatable (Johnston & Pennypacker, 1980). Determinations of validity are based on the importance of the behavior for the child's adaptation; we expand this discussion in the following chapter.

Where to Observe: School, Home, and Clinic

School Observations. For practical reasons, most observations will be conducted in preschool settings. As general strategies, we recommend the following steps: (a) waking day followed by problem-solving interviews with teachers, (b) preliminary observations, and (c) depending on the outcomes of interviews and preliminary observations, constructing an observation plan. The plan includes times and conditions for observations, the length of observations, and strategies. The Preschool Observation Code (Bramlett, 1990), as well as other useful strategies, are discussed in the section "Observing and Recording Behavior."

Home Observations. There are many significant reasons for conducting home observations. Observations in clinic settings may be too limited to be of value. Drotar and Crawford (1987) commented that home observations can be a positive factor for parents because they demonstrate professional commitment and facilitate productive communication. For understanding ecological and cultural influences, home observations are essential.

Many techniques described in this chapter may be adapted to home observations. Drotar and Crawford discussed practical issues. The HOME assessment by Caldwell and Bradley (1979) is perhaps the most widely researched assessment technique under this topic, but it does not lend itself to the types of intervention decisions that form the basis of the book.

We offer the following practical considerations:

1. We recommend the use of parent consultations, waking day interviews, and problem-solving interviews to structure observations around specific concerns or events, settings, and times for observation sessions. Problem-solving interviews are useful for prioritizing target behaviors and determining specific observational techniques. Preliminary observations (real time) may be used to further define classes of behaviors that may be useful for structured observations. Legal and ethical guidelines are discussed in the final chapter.

2. A detailed rationale for home observations is important. Drotar and Crawford (1987, p. 343) offer the following:

> In our work with other children who have problems similar to those of your child, we have often found that a home visit can provide important information which can be used to understand and help your child. The purpose of this visit is to observe how your child behaves and interacts with you and your family at home. Because children are generally more comfortable interacting with their family in their home setting, this is often a good way to evaluate your child's problem in order to determine the best way of helping you and your child. In addition, we have found that the entire family is important to your child's development and that it is often helpful for us to work together to find ways to help him or her. For this reason, we would like to have you and other family members participate in the home visit.

3. It is necessary to observe the behaviors under natural conditions, or to structure observations in a way to facilitate specific interactions between family members without interruptions. Ground rules need to be covered carefully. Key family members should be present, guests should be discouraged, activities should be restricted to one or two rooms, distractions such as television should be eliminated, and telephone calls should be limited to brief responses to incoming calls. Rules, such as no talking with the observers during the session, also should be considered.

4. Given the complexities of interactions, the strategy used by Dishion and others (1984) is instructive. Their Family Observation Code is made up of "coding segments" or "trials"; for each trial, one family member is selected as the focal subject (child, mother, father, siblings). Coding is restricted to the interactions of the focal subject with other family members.

The potential difficulties in home observations are numerous. Home observations will not be readily accepted by many parents, and may be difficult in some communities. Reliability and validity issues may be difficult to evaluate. The observations may be influenced by the presence of the observer (termed *reactivity;* see Kazdin, 1982) or unknown distortions. However, Thibodeaux, Gardner, Forgatch, and Reid summarized research this way: "Though parents might be prone to attempt a 'look good' impression, the ability to effectively achieve that result is uncommon, especially in problematic families. . . . Habitual modes of acting exert a much stronger force on behavior than any attempt to 'fake good' or 'bad'" (1984, pp. 1-2). In sum, home observations provide an *estimate* of behavior that would occur under natural or structured conditions.

Extreme poverty and family stress will be likely to induce stress on the professional. Drotar and Crawford wrote: "In some instances, naturalistic observation yields discouraging information concerning family constraints that interfere with a family's capacity to implement intervention" (1987, p. 346). Safety concerns — for family members and for professionals — may exist. We recommend that teams be used, for reasons of safety and for estimating agreement in fast-paced and stressful situations. The economics of home observations may be the greatest perceived drawback; cost-benefit analyses are necessary (see suggestions by Drotar & Crawford, 1987).

Overall, we think that the use of home observations of young children is a significant strategy, especially in cases of severe behavioral problems, abuse, or neglect. Other likely applications include facilitating the natural teaching role of parents in situations associated with risk or children's developmental problems, and for programming the generalization of skills taught in preschools.

Clinic and Analogue Measures. Many interventions reported in the literature involve observations in clinic or *analogue* settings. Analogue settings simulate natural conditions and are used when direct observation is not possible. The analogue conditions can include a wide range of structured events, role play, or "free" behavior (Cone, 1978). Direct measurement is used in analogue settings, and thus similar reliability and validity considerations apply — with one important exception. Analogue measurement is not likely to directly predict natural occurrences for many behaviors.

Analogue and clinic observations lend themselves to the use of equipment such as audio and video recording, one-way mirrors, and "bug-in-the-ear" communication devices to give private instructions or prompts to participants.

Who Is to Observe?

Three strategies may be used to observe behavior: direct observation by a consultant, participant observation by a caregiver, and self-observation or self-monitoring. They may also be used advantageously in various combinations. We describe the different approaches briefly.

Consultant Observation. This refers to a trained observer who has no specific instructional responsibilities with the target child. The amount of time dedicated to the observations is usually brief.

Participant Observation. This strategy has been widely used in ethnographic research, where the observer has two roles: "(1) to engage in activities appropriate to the situation and (2) to observe the activities, people, and physical aspects of the situation" (Spradley, 1980, p. 54). In anthropological studies, the participant observer is also the scientist. However, the term has been applied to a range of caregivers (Hay, Nelson, & Hay, 1980).

Participant observation with caregivers is widely used, and the range of techniques is quite broad. It is generally necessary for consultants to help structure participant observations to reduce the complexities and to improve the usefulness of the data. It is especially important to ensure that observations will be sensitive to intervention outcomes.

Overall, participant observation is likely to have side effects or unique outcomes, some of which may be beneficial.

When parents and teachers are observers, their behavior may change as well as the children's behavior. If the procedures are too burdensome, they will be ignored or errors will be substantial.

Self-Observation or Monitoring. Self-observation is similar to direct and participant observation in methodology. In self-monitoring, clients both observe themselves and record their own behaviors. The two are best viewed as separate processes, since each requires attention and effort. Especially for children, motivation or the presence of external contingencies or feedback may be critical.

Self-monitoring procedures may involve recording the frequency, duration, or intensity of behaviors, and they are amenable to time-sampling procedures discussed later in the chapter. They can be used across the various functions of assessment and intervention, both with caregivers and children.

When to Observe?

Continuous observation is usually not possible, so the question becomes how to *sample* behaviors across periods of time.

Intersession sampling has to do with deciding which "chunks of time" are used as observation sessions. Observation sessions represent only a small part of the time period of interest. Researchers or practitioners generalize from baseline sessions to the "time prior to intervention"; observation sessions during and after interventions are used to generalize about intervention effectiveness (Suen & Ary, 1989, p. 95).

In selecting times to observe in order to determine intervention effects, two conditions must be met: (1) the sessions must be equivalent in opportunities for the occurrence or nonoccurrence of behavior; and (2) conditions must be the same for all observation sessions (Cooper, Heron, & Heward, 1987). Usually, time periods are selected through waking day interviews; for example, group instructional time, transitions between activities, free play, or lunchtime may be chosen as the focal points of observations. This makes it possible to select comparable *sessions* for the observations.

Ideally, based on interviews, all possible observation sessions within the defined period of interest should be identified, to create a pool of observation times that would meet the criteria of comparability. From the pool, an observer can randomly select a sample of sessions. However, because of schedule practicalities, systematic selection is more common. In sum, the core issue regarding intersession sampling is that data collected within observation sessions "must be representative of the behavior of interest throughout the period of time" for which generalizations are desired (Suen & Ary, 1989, p. 96).

How Long and How Often

First, it is important to select an adequate observation length. Considerations are based on the results of ecobehavioral interviews and the qualities of the behavior to be observed. For example, behaviors with low frequency have to be observed during longer time periods. Highly variable behavior suggests the need to extend observations.

A related question is, how often should the observations be conducted? Again, the solution is based on the qualities of the behavior being observed.

For both decisions, the guiding factors are that the samples are representative and the observations are accurate. In sum, the length of observation sessions and the number of occasions must be determined for each situation. The overall considerations are based on the confidence in the resulting data and the generalizations that are desired.

Observing and Recording Behavior

This section deals with methods of observing and recording behavior: *how to* observe. Observation includes "recording the stream of behavior, dividing it into units, and analyzing the units" (Wright, 1967, p. 10). The record of observation is a "detailed, sequential, narrative account of behavior and its immediate environmental context as seen by skilled observers" (Wright, 1967, p. 32). Observations also are structured for instructional and intervention purposes. In these cases, observation methods are guided by specific questions related to behaviors, skills, tasks or demands, environmental conditions and manipulations, and teaching strategies (Wolery, 1989).

Real-Time Observation

Observations conducted in natural environments provide an on-going record of behavior as it actually occurs. We recommend that *preliminary observations* be done using real-time methods, to help determine the features of behavior and environment that are important to record.

In conducting real-time observations, it is important to focus on the child's situation as well as the behavior. Actions of others (peers, teacher) toward the child should also be noted. Each line (or sentence) should contain one molar (meaningful and complete) unit of behavior. Behaviors should be mutually exclusive (one activity is recorded) and exhaustive (all the time is accounted for by recorded behaviors) (Sackett, 1978; Suen & Ary, 1989). Time notations are made at prespecified intervals. Wright (1967) suggests one minute; Bijou and colleagues (1969) suggest two minutes; we present a variation.

The procedure depicted in Exhibit 4.1 requires recording the exact times for the initiation and termination of behavior. The child's activity changes are recorded by the time notations. In the figure, arrows are used to incorporate the observer's judgments of the appropriateness or maladaptive nature of the behavior. Arrows (up/down) indicate judgments (appropriate/inappropriate) about behavior. Brackets can be used to record notes or interpretations. Bijou and associates (1969) also recorded antecedent, response, and consequent events. An antecedent-behavior-consequence (ABC) analysis based on this strategy is described in a subsequent section. Preestablished behavioral codes may also be used.

From real-time observations, the following data may be derived (Suen & Ary, 1989).

1. *Frequency.* This is also known as event recording. The frequency equals the number of times behavior occurs in a session. Frequency may be useful to describe behaviors such as hitting or swearing or activity changes.

Exhibit 4.1. An Example of Real-Time Recording.

Setting: Preschool Classroom/Freeplay   *Date:*
Time: 2:25 to 2:45   *Child:* J

2:25   Child is observed in play area with two peers (boys). *J* is fighting with another child over trains.

2:26   *J* hit peer. Teacher intervenes: "Why did you hit *M*?" *J*: "That is my motor. I don't want to play with him." Teacher: "What if he hit you, would you like that?" *J*: "I wouldn't care."

2:28   *J* leaves trains and moves to dollhouse. Plays with *A* (girl).

2:29   *J* tries to take doll from *A*.

2:30   *J* begins moving the furniture in the dollhouse that *A* has set up.

2:31   *J* to *A*: "Can we trade places?" *A* says ok.

2:32   *J* begins knocking furniture around. *A* says "No." *J* continues to knock down furniture, then stops.

2:34   Playing better.

2:35   Leaves dollhouse. Says to another child, "Hey, big butt!" Other child appears not to have heard *J*.

2:36   Moves to puzzle area with three peers (two girls, one boy). Sits down and begins putting puzzle together.

2:38   Other children left area. *J* working alone. Trying to put clock puzzle together.

2:40   Gets another child to work with him. Another child comes. Both leave.

2:41   Works on puzzle. Chewing on sleeve of his shirt.

2:42   Leaves puzzle area. Did not clean up. Moves to sandbox. Tries to get *T* to leave. "How much time have you been in? I'll be your friend if you get out." *T* leaves sandbox. *J* gets in sandbox and plays.

2:44   Playing alone in sandbox.

Adapted from observations by Lori Strengholt.

2. *Rate of occurrence.* The rate of behavior is the frequency of behavior divided by the length of the observation session. Using the rate of behavior enables comparisons of frequency across sessions of different lengths.

3. *Bout duration.* Bout duration is the length of time that the behavior occurs. (A *bout* is one occurrence of behavior.) Duration may be useful for states (such as crying), on-task behavior during instructional periods, or activity engagement (such as play). A state is a stable pattern of behavior that occurs over time.

4. *Prevalence.* Prevalence is the proportion of time that a bout is found within a session. Bout durations are summed and then divided by the session length (expressed in the same time units), and the result is multiplied by 100 percent. It is used to compare states of behavior across observation sessions of different lengths.

5. *Interresponse time (IRT).* This is defined as the time between bouts and is calculated by recording the time period from the end of a behavior to the initiation of the next behavior. The mean IRT may be calculated by dividing the sum of all interresponse time durations by the number of nonoccurrences of behavior. One practical use of IRT is to help set the time span for an intervention based on Differential Reinforcement of Other Behavior (DRO), described in Chapter Seven. The IRT also is used to help set observation intervals, discussed in the section on time sampling.

Advantages and Disadvantages of Real-Time Observations

The most important advantage is that many classes of behaviors and characteristics of the setting can be recorded. Real-time observations are useful in provisionally determining the behaviors of interest and in clarifying problem behaviors that are difficult to define. Real-time observations serve as an important criterion for other assessment methods, such as behavioral ratings by parents and teachers, and for judging the adequacy of observational methods in general.

For young children, the technique may provide a recording of the stream of behavior including (a) play activities; (b) peer relationships; (c) relationships with adults; (d) responses to learning tasks, demands, and rules; (e) antecedent and consequent events for specific behaviors; and (f) language samples. Real-time observations may be used to analyze sequential or conditional behaviors (discussed in a later section). Another dimension—intensity—is infrequently used, primarily because of measurement problems.

Real-time observations can be quite demanding; the

method is ill suited for participant observers. Also, the results may vary greatly by setting characteristics, behaviors, and skills of observers. Accuracy may be difficult to determine, and the results may be subjective. The salience of certain behaviors may lead to others being ignored. Despite these disadvantages, we view it as a fundamental technique.

ABC Analysis

ABC stands for *Antecedent-Behavior-Consequence*. Antecedents are events or stimuli that precede a behavior of interest and that may increase or decrease the behavior. Examples include a teacher asking the class (or child) to clean up materials or to stand quietly in line. Consequences may be either reinforcing, punishing, or neutral; for example, praising for compliance or repeating a command ("I told everyone to be quiet").

The ABC method of recording behavior was described by Bijou (Bijou, Peterson, & Ault, 1968; Bijou et al., 1969) and has similarities to real-time observation. First, the setting is described (lunch or snack periods, free play). Second, observations are recorded on a three-column form (Exhibit 4.2). A column for time notations also is included. Recording time notations can create ambiguities. Two systematic ways are to make a notation at preestablished intervals, such as every two minutes, or to record the times associated with activity changes.

Advantages and Disadvantages of ABC Analysis

ABC recording is a basic strategy for the functional analysis of behavior. Functional analyses are used to test hypotheses about control of behavior and behavioral change. A functional analysis of behavior requires three outcomes: (1) the operational description of undesirable behaviors, (2) "prediction of the times and situations when the undesirable behavior(s) will and will not be performed across the full range of typical daily routines," and (3) "definitions of the function(s) (maintaining reinforcers) that the undesirable behavior(s) produces for the individual" (O'Neill, Horner, Albin, Storey, & Sprague, 1990, p. 3). Func-

Exhibit 4.2. An Example of ABC Analysis.

Date: _____   Behavior of Concern: _____

Time	What was going on before	What was the behavior	What happened after

tions of misbehavior may be classified in two ways: "to *obtain* something desirable and to *avoid* or *escape* something undesirable" (p. 12).

Many of the advantages and disadvantages of ABC analysis are the same as those described for real-time observation. Judgments of technical adequacy must be determined on a case-by-case basis. Identifying antecedents and functional consequent events may be difficult in complex settings. Reinforcement intrinsic to the behavior (such as self-stimulating) will not be detected through ABC analysis because the behavior is performed without observable consequences. Also, behavior may be a function of general conditions, not discrete antecedents or consequences. Furthermore, functional relationships are not necessarily revealed through observations of natural events; experimental procedures may be necessary (Iwata, Vollmer, & Zarcone, 1990). Finally, behaviors may be associated with multiple functions, or the child may be without other alternative behaviors appropriate for the situation.

Frequency (or Event) Recording

This method is based on real-time or continuous observations during a specified period of time, but it is much simpler: only certain predefined behaviors or events are recorded. Frequency recording involves tallying the number of times the behavior of interest occurs in an observation session. Behaviors that may be successfully recorded this way are discrete behaviors of brief and stable durations: for example, activity changes, swearing or calling out, aggressive acts, and specific teacher-child or parent-child interactions. Rates of behavior are used to compare observation sessions of unequal duration.

Duration (or State) Recording

Duration recording — the elapsed time for each occurrence, and the total duration or prevalence of the behavior — may be used when the focus is on the length of time a child engages in a specific behavior. For some behaviors such as tantrums and play, it may be important to record both frequency and duration. Also, the *latency* of a response may be of interest. Latency is defined as the amount of time before beginning a task or initiating a behavior, such as the length of time it takes a child to comply with instructions. It is measured much the same way as duration.

Advantages and Disadvantages of Frequency and Duration Recording

A major advantage is simplicity. Also, these measures may be interpretable as basic dimensions of behavior. For low-rate behaviors, participant observers may be able to provide accurate records. The disadvantages are that behaviors have to be discrete (having clear beginnings and ends). Also, obtaining satisfactory measures of agreement requires that specific time intervals be recorded for the observation sessions. Recording multiple behaviors or bursts of behavior may be difficult.

Time-Sampling Techniques

Time sampling is an alternative to continuous observation of behavior. Professionals must decide when to conduct observation sessions (discussed earlier) and how to sample behaviors within observation sessions (termed *intrasession* sampling). Time sampling also enables practical and systematic observations of several children or multiple behaviors, and facilitates assessment of observer agreement. Two strategies — momentary time sampling and interval sampling — have been widely used.

Momentary Time Sampling. Momentary time sampling is most useful with continuous behaviors, when duration is of primary interest, and when behaviors have no clear beginnings or ends (Hartmann, 1984). These characteristics may be described as states of behavior. Momentary time sampling also is useful with behaviors having high rates.

To use momentary time sampling, an observation session is divided into smaller intervals. The occurrence or nonoccurrence of a defined behavior is recorded at the specific moment of an observation. Thus, within each session, at a prespecified interval (i.e., fifteen or thirty seconds), the observer records whether or not the child is engaged in the behavior. The interval of interest is the time between discrete observations. For this reason it is also referred to as "instantaneous time sampling" or "discontinuous probe time sampling."

Advantages and Disadvantages of Momentary Time Sampling. Studies have demonstrated that momentary time sampling yields an unbiased estimate of prevalence (Suen & Ary, 1989). Depending on the interval length and behavior of interest, momentary time sampling may be time efficient and convenient (Hartmann, 1984). Relatedly, with very prevalent or high-rate behaviors, it may be acceptable for use by participant observers such as teachers because the time span can be set at long intervals. For accurate frequency estimates, Suen and Ary recommend that the interval length be less than both the shortest bout in a session and the shortest interresponse time. They also provide equations to estimate duration.

Momentary time sampling is not useful for brief, low-rate behaviors. The amount of error may be large if the interval size is great. Frequency is likely to be underestimated (Suen & Ary, 1989) in such cases. As with other methods of time sampling, the coherence of behavior may be lost if interval lengths are long.

Interval Recording. Interval recording has been used to record both events and states of behaviors. As with momentary time sampling, the observation session is divided into smaller time intervals (such as ten seconds). However, here the observer records the occurrence or nonoccurrence of behavior within each interval instead of at one precise moment. Observers must decide how to record behaviors within the interval and how to determine the length of the interval.

Two strategies are used primarily. With *partial-interval sampling,* an occurrence is defined by the presence of the target behavior during any part of the interval. Each occurrence is scored only once even though behaviors may be repeated during the interval. Partial-interval recording may be useful for behaviors of brief duration and when the goal is behavioral reduction (Cooper, Heron, & Heward, 1987; Hall & Van Houten, 1983; Wolery, 1989a).

Whole-interval sampling requires that the behavior occur for the duration of the interval. Whole-interval recording may be most helpful for behaviors of relatively long duration and when the goal is to increase behaviors (Cooper, Heron, & Heward, 1987; Wolery, 1989).

In interval recording, observers use a score sheet consisting of small numbered boxes representing the intervals. For partial interval recording, the observer puts a check or slash mark in the appropriate box, if the behavior occurs during an interval; a zero represents an absence of the behavior. For whole interval recording, a mark indicates the behavior was present during the entire interval. For both, percent of occurrence across intervals is used to summarize the sessions.

Advantages and Disadvantages of Interval Recording. Interval sampling and recording has been widely used in behavioral studies because it is applicable to a broad range of responses. It facilitates observation of several children or multiple behaviors. It also aids in estimating agreement between observers. A practical strategy is to alternate observing with brief recording intervals.

A primary disadvantage of interval sampling is that estimates of frequency and duration are confounded. Also, systematic biases exist in estimating these dimensions. Partial-interval sampling tends to overestimate prevalence and underestimate frequency of behavior; whole-interval sampling is likely to underestimate both prevalence and frequency (Suen & Ary, 1989).

For accurate frequency estimates with partial-interval recording, Suen and Ary recommend that the interval length be less than the shortest bout and also less than half of the shortest interresponse time. For accurate frequency estimates with whole-interval recording, they recommend that the interval length be less than half of the shortest bout and also less than the shortest interresponse time. They also provide an equation to estimate duration.

Other Methods of Collecting and Analyzing Data

Many other observational strategies may be useful for preschool assessments. Some of these overlap with methods described earlier.

1. *Discrete skill sequences* are frequently used to record behaviors. Examples include problem-solving, social, dressing, and bathroom skills. Task analysis, discussed in a later section, is a method to derive skill sequences.

2. *Category sampling* is used for behaviors that can be descriptively analyzed or categorized (Wolery, 1989). Examples include recording on-task or play engagement or types of play. The categories should be mutually exclusive and exhaustive, so that observed behavior fits only one category and the categories together account for all the behavior in the session. Occurrences of behaviors represented by the categories may be recorded through real-time, event, or time-sampling procedures.

3. *"Permanent" products* result from tangible effects of behaviors. Examples include work or puzzle completion, coloring, bedwetting. Also, audio and video recordings are classified in this way.

4. *Trials to criterion* involve maintaining a record of how many times a "response opportunity" is presented before a child performs at a specified criterion (Cooper, Heron, & Heward, 1987, p. 74). This measure is helpful for comparing alternative teaching techniques for the same skills.

5. *Levels of assistance* is a method of recording the level of support needed for participation in activities and, alternatively, the support that must be ultimately removed before the child can function independently (Wolery, 1989). The occurrence-nonoccurrence of behavior is recorded on different levels of assistance provided to the child.

6. A *probe* is defined as a "brief, structured presentation of a task for the purpose of collecting data" (Wolery, Bailey, & Sugai, 1988, pp. 77–78). Probes are useful when continuous observation is not feasible or desirable, and when assumptions can be made with confidence that a behavior is relatively stable. They also may be useful when repeated measures result in reactivity. Carefully planned probes may help avoid "ritualistic" data collection, where the performance level can be predicted accurately (Cooper, Heron, & Heward, 1987).

Preintervention probe *trials* may be conducted intermittently on behaviors that will be subsequently trained, and probes

can be conducted later to measure outcomes of the intervention, including maintenance and generalization. Most probes
have dealt with preacademic skills. James and Egel (1986) used
them in evaluating sibling play skills; they conducted freeplay,
generalization, stimulus control, and follow-up probes. For the
freeplay probes, siblings were brought to a play area and were
instructed to play together while observers recorded their behavior for five minutes. Data were collected an average of four
times per week. Probes also may be used to record brief samples of behavior in different time periods, conditions, or settings.
When they are used to evaluate interventions, the criteria for
consistent conditions apply.

7. *Discriminated (or restricted) operants* result when the opportunity for responses is controlled. This method is related to
the ABC method described earlier but is used to study specific
antecedents. To record these units, observers note the antecedent, interaction, and consequence. One example is parent or
teacher commands: the antecedent is a request, the child's behavior is recorded (for example, comply), and the consequence
is recorded (praise). Compliance is typically represented as a
percentage. The difference between this class of behaviors and
others is that parents and teachers create the specific opportunities for children's responses (Baer & Fowler, 1984).

Observing More Than One Child

Besides observing interactions between children, there are at
least two other occasions when it is necessary to observe more
than one child in a group or classroom. First, the professional
may want to compare the behavior of the referred child with
other nonreferred or "normal" children. Second, and very different, more than one child may be referred for similar behavior
problems. Momentary time sampling and interval sampling are
good methods for recording several different children.

Micronorms. The term *micronorms* refers to accepted norms for
a particular teacher, class, and activity. Another descriptive

term is the *referred pupil/comparison pupil method.* These judgments
are an important point of basic referral and intervention decisions, either explicitly or implicitly. It is important to consider
whether the behavior of an individual child differs significantly
from other children in a specified way. The "comparison pupil
method" and scan-checking (see below) are used to create micronorms. Walker and Hops (1976) credit Gerald Patterson and
his colleagues as being the first to use samples of randomly selected peers as partial criteria for evaluating intervention effects
for a target child.

Two important questions guide the process of creating
micronorms. First, how to select appropriate comparison children? The most reasonable approach involves random selection
of adequately performing or average children (not necessarily
exemplary performers) of the same age and sex who are engaged
in the same task.

Second, which observation and sampling strategies to use?
For many applications, the most desirable are interval or
momentary time recording (discussed earlier) and *sequential sampling* (Thomson, Holmberg, & Baer, 1974). In sequential sampling, the observation session is divided into brief intervals. The
observer records the behavior of the first child in the first interval, records the behavior of the second child in the second interval, and so on. After all children have been observed, the
rotation process is repeated.

Advantages and Disadvantages of Micronorms. The logic for the
use of micronorms is clear; we view the technique as fundamental. Observations of the referred child can be compared with
micronorms to decide further assessment plans, potential goals,
and intervention outcomes (Alessi, 1988).

Alessi also presented potential problems with micronorms.
First, micronorms may not predict norms in other classrooms
or settings. Second, the micronorms for a classroom still may
not be suitable for establishing goals, if overall rates of targeted
behaviors are unusually high or low. In this case, other classes
in the school or system may yield more adequate comparisons.
Other problems involve basic sampling, reliability, and validity
issues (Alessi, 1988; Barnett & Macmann, in press). The sample

of time may be inadequate or inappropriate. The selection of comparison children may not be reasonable (an ideal performer will exaggerate differences; or the comparison child may also have a behavior problem). As with other observations, the behaviors need to be well defined. Last, since the referral is dependent in part on teacher perceptions, misperceptions of the target child (and other children) will reduce the validity of the procedure. When used to establish goals or measure changes in behavior, the clinical significance of differences may be difficult to determine (see special issue of *Behavioral Assessment,* 1988, *10*[2]). Ultimately, decisions about discrepant performances will be based at least in part on the judgments of teachers (or social validity).

In sum, the use of micronorms is an important part of the process. However, it is also vulnerable to sources of error found in observations in general.

PLA-CHECK (*Planned Activity Check*) is a variation of time sampling (Risley, 1972). A group of children is observed at the end of a specified interval, and the number of children engaged in the behavior of interest is counted. The number is divided by the total number of children in the group to arrive at the percentage of children engaged in the activity. Alessi (1988; Alessi & Kaye, 1983) described a procedure referred to as *scan checking* adapted from PLA-CHECK procedures. At a brief interval (one or two minutes), the observer scans the classroom and records the number of children who are behaving appropriately (reported as a percentage).

For large areas such as playgrounds or cafeterias, a *zone system* of sampling may be used along with time sampling (Sulzer-Azaroff & Mayer, 1991). The space is mapped and divided into zones, and the observer sequentially observes and records the behaviors of individuals within a zone. The observer makes several observations in one zone, then moves to the next.

Multidimensional Observation Codes

Interest in one isolated target behavior is unusual for several reasons. The likelihood of a target behavior occurring may be a function of setting events, behaviors of others, or may occur along with other behaviors (termed a *response class*). Also, children are often referred for more than one behavior. Furthermore, intervention design requires that intended and unintended outcomes be evaluated. For all these reasons, a broad range of behaviors should be considered. Some of the major multidimensional codes are *Ecological Assessment of Child Problem Behavior* (Wahler, House, & Stambaugh, 1976) and *Ecobehavioral System for Complex Assessment of Preschool Environments (ESCAPE)* (see Chapter 10).

Bramlett (1990) developed the Preschool Observation Code for use in preschool classrooms across intervention phases (baseline and intervention monitoring). The code categories were developed from an analysis of real-time recordings of referred Head Start children over a five-year span ($N = 55$), a comprehensive review of interventions found in the literature, and empirically based constellations of behaviors such as conduct disorders and social isolation. The code format (shown in Exhibit 4.3) is based on a state-event model developed by Saudargas (1980). The code requires about five hours of training.

Sequential Analysis

The sequential recording of behaviors adds a level of analysis to systematic observations. The primary questions are how behaviors are sequenced in time, and how behaviors are meaningfully related in time. At a basic level, examples of sequential analysis may be found whenever interactions are studied.

Sequential analysis involves comparing conditional probabilities of events. We use the example of a young child crying in school. A simple probability is that she will cry on fifteen days out of a thirty-day span (probability equals .50). A conditional probability may be calculated based on the days that the father was at home (or any other event). If the father was present for twenty-five days, the conditional probability relative to crying and father's presence is 15/25 or .60. Of course, the statistical and clinical significance of the relationships need to be determined. Other examples include the study of how behaviors vary by different antecedent or consequent events. Child compliance with parental commands may vary by different antecedents

Exhibit 4.3. Categories of the Preschool Observation Code.

State Behaviors

Play engagement [for example, "putting a puzzle together"]
Preacademic engagement [in group instruction]
Nonpurposeful play [playing with puzzle pieces without putting them together]
Unoccupied or transitional behaviors [wandering around room]
Disruptive behaviors [throwing objects]
Self-stimulating behaviors [rocking]
Other behavior (to be used for observations not included in code)
Social interaction with peer [talking to a peer]
Teacher monitoring/interacting [teacher is close to the child and is looking at child or child's activities]

Event Behaviors

Activity changes [changing from puzzle to join another child in play]
Negative verbal interactions [name calling]
Positive motor behaviors [giving a toy to a peer]
Negative motor interactions [pushing]
Disruptive behaviors (same as above)
Child approaches teacher [child asks for teacher's help]
Teacher commands — alpha (clear and direct commands)
Teacher commands — beta (vague commands)
Child compliance [the child performs the task required by the command within approximately five seconds]
Teacher approval [praise or a pat on the back]
Teacher disapproval ["You're in trouble now!"]

From Bramlett, R. K. (1990). "Categories of the Preschool Observation Code."

(types of commands) or different consequences (types of praise). Likewise, the probabilities of successfully entering a play group may vary as a function of different play engagement skills (gaining eye contact, making requests to share, and so on).

Sequential analysis can be much more complex and technical. Relationships between events can be studied both as immediately occurring probabilities and as a function of intervening events. *Lag* sequential analysis (see Bakeman & Gottman, 1986; Sackett, 1978) is a probabilistic approach to the analysis of relationships between events over time. "Lags are defined as the number of event (or time unit) steps between sequential events" (Sackett, 1978, p. 39). Lag 1 refers to probabilities that a target event will occur immediately after a given event. Lag 2 means that the probabilities are calculated after one intervening event. The current applications are mostly research oriented (describing or building models of social interactions), but the practical benefits may be great. Introductory reviews are provided by Bakeman and Gottman (1986), and La Greca and Stark (1986).

Applications of Self-Observation

Earlier, we described self-observation as one of three basic strategies that stem from the question "Who is to observe?" From a practical perspective, self-observation is significant because it is useful for behaviors that are inaccessible to direct observation. Self-observation is necessary for private or covert events such as emotions or thoughts. It may also be used for overt behaviors for which observations may be otherwise costly or inefficient. It has been viewed as a keystone for behavioral change.

In general, children are probably not accurate at self-monitoring (Nelson, Hay, Devany, & Koslow-Green, 1980). However, many conditions and innovations can be used to facilitate self-recording and improve its accuracy. Self-monitoring can be combined with other strategies including caregiver monitoring of behavior and reward systems. Agreement or accuracy checks can be used to improve performance through the surveillance of behavior. For example, a teacher or parent can use a signal system to help the child monitor behaviors. The occurrence of behaviors can be unobtrusively signaled to the child, and the child can maintain tallies on a chart or color in small circles. Kanfer and Gaelick (1986) also note that complete accuracy is not necessary to derive some benefits for assessment and intervention plans.

Self-monitoring may be a critical strategy for various aspects of caregivers' behaviors. Specific behaviors (such as giving approval or using specific types of commands) may be amenable to self-monitoring throughout the assessment-intervention process. Self-monitoring also includes indirect methods such as self-ratings.

Self-Observation as a Keystone Behavior. Keystone behaviors are those for which successful interventions are likely to produce beneficial effects and side effects. Koegel and Koegel wrote that "many researchers and theorists consider the absence of self-monitoring skills to be a pivotal deficit in normal development" (1988, p. 53). Self-monitoring is fundamental to self-control or self-regulation (Bandura, 1978).

Self-Monitoring as a Multistage Process. First, the child must be able to discriminate the occurrence of the state or behavior. Specific training may be needed. Second, the results of self-observations need to be recorded. Third, self-evaluation occurs based on the data produced. Self-evaluations may have the quality of reward versus punishment. While there are some differences of opinion about the various stages, the stages of response discrimination and recording are basic (Mace & Kratochwill, 1988).

The most important aspects of implementing a self-monitoring system are clearly defined target behaviors, training, and uncomplicated recording systems. Self-, social, or other reinforcement may be helpful. Watson and Tharp (1989) have extensive examples of procedures that are useful for adults. We describe interventions that use self-monitoring with young children in later chapters.

The following stages are adapted from Koegel and Koegel (1988, pp. 54–55), based on their work with speech disorders of autistic children, and from the review by Mace and Kratochwill (1988, p. 505).

1. *Preparation for self-monitoring.* Inappropriate behaviors and target responses are defined. Decisions are made about the treatment and generalization settings. Functional rewards (social or tangible) are selected. Time periods sufficiently brief to ensure success are also decided upon.

2. *Training in self-monitoring.* The child is taught to discriminate between correct and inappropriate behaviors. This may be accomplished through modeling and prompting. Clear definitions of the target behaviors are necessary. Pictures representing the target behaviors may be used. Following the training, the child is taught to self-observe, evaluate, and record the

behavior. The child is trained to an individually established criterion. At this point, the child is prompted to perform self-monitoring under natural stimulus conditions, still as a part of training.

3. *Evaluating and rewarding self-monitoring that occurs in the natural environment.* It is necessary to evaluate whether the self-monitoring activities occur in the intended environment. Strategies typically involve participant observation by parents or teachers. If it is not occurring, prompts or rewards may be used.

4. *Fading the formal self-monitoring activities.* Fading may be accomplished in several ways: (a) increasing the number of points necessary for a reward; (b) lengthening the time period of appropriate behavior required for a reward; (c) expanding the amount of "work" required for a reward; or (d) when appropriate, "simply telling the child that because he or she is doing so well the self-monitoring is no longer necessary" (Koegel & Koegel, 1988, p. 55)

Reactivity of Self-Monitoring. Although we have discussed it as an observational method, self-monitoring may result in behavioral changes as well; this is called *reactivity*. The changes in behavior may be consistent with treatment goals. Thus, self-monitoring may be considered as either a supplementary or primary intervention (Mace & Kratochwill, 1988). Self-reinforcement frequently has important social qualities that may be critical in determining the efficacy of self-monitoring in altering behavior. The social consequences of self-recording may be important determinants of intervention outcomes.

When studied as an intervention, the results of self-monitoring have been variable. However, many factors may influence the reactivity of self-monitoring: the type of behavior (pleasant or unpleasant thoughts, verbal or nonverbal behavior); the type of recording strategy and its obtrusiveness; the time period for self-monitoring and recording; other competing tasks and responsibilities; the monitoring of behavior by an independent observer; the instructions and training given to the client; and motivational factors. Behaviors with a negative valence have a potential for unintended negative outcomes. Thus, it may be important to reframe some target behaviors (depression, anger) so that positive behaviors are monitored (pleasant exchanges or activities).

Curriculum-Based Assessment

One of the most useful approaches for making educational decisions involves the systematic and ongoing assessment of children within the context of a well-constructed curriculum. As we saw earlier, developmental measures have frequently been criticized. Curriculum-based assessment circumvents many problems because developmental sequences are tied to ongoing measurement related to instructional efforts and skill progression rather than a "profile" of skills at any one time. It is important to note that curriculum-based assessment is not a panacea, however, and that many questions about the decision process remain unknown (Wolery, 1991).

Characteristics of Curriculum-Based Assessments

To enable decisions about intervention, a curriculum must have (a) a wide range of functional, developmentally sequenced tasks; (b) ongoing measurement of progress; and (c) a variety of teaching and learning strategies. Curriculum-based assessment enables ongoing observations of the child's performance in preacademic, social, and other developmental areas. The observations are used to delineate the classroom environmental conditions necessary for competent performance (LeBlanc, Etzel, & Domash, 1978). Analysis of the child's level of skill development provides information about the appropriate level for instruction and allows for the continuous evaluation of the child's progress. A range of research-based teaching strategies that match instruction to skill development and the needs of individual children are essential to ensure progress. Children who remain at a particular level of a skill sequence, or who are unable to complete a task, may require a change in instructional strategies to progress to the next step.

Through ongoing assessment of the classroom environment and the curriculum, information about the conditions necessary for learning can be obtained. By assessing current performance, altering instruction strategies, and adapting materials for a child, teachers can develop goals and educational techniques that may help the child develop competencies within a specific target area. The information gained from a curriculum-based assessment includes (a) current level of performance or functioning; (b) rate of learning new skills; (c) strategies necessary to learn new skills; (d) length of time the new skill is retained; (e) generalization of previously taught skills to a new task; (f) observed behaviors that deter learning; (g) environmental conditions needed to learn skills (individual, group, peer instruction); (h) motivational techniques used to acquire skills; and (i) skill acquisition in relationship to peers.

Currently, there are numerous preschool curricula. Several are discussed in Chapter Ten.

Task Analysis

Task analysis "involves breaking a complex skill or series of behaviors into smaller, teachable units" (Cooper, Heron, & Heward, 1987, p. 342). To date, it has been widely used with people who have severe developmental disabilities, but its potential for broader clinical applications is promising. Task analysis requires attention to behaviors and settings. "Not only are the behaviors relatively specific, but so are the situations in which they are to occur" (Hawkins, 1986, p. 339).

The first step in a task analysis is to identify how a task is competently performed. The component steps that lead to the overall performance are identified; these are usually sequential steps, but concurrent and alternative performances may be important as well. Hawkins (1986, p. 361) gives an example of a concurrent response where the suggestion of a joint activity, such as play, is "accompanied by a smile or other positive facial expression." Alternative behaviors, such as training in different ways to approach peers in play, may be important for many interactions.

Several practical methods can be used to help construct and validate a task analysis sequence.

1. Observations of competent performers may be made.
2. Experts can be consulted regarding the skills that need to be learned.
3. The task may be self-performed by the person developing the task analysis and the steps may be logically constructed.
4. Sequences may be based on steps observed through skill acquisition.
5. A task analysis can be sequenced by task difficulty and levels of assistance.

Technical Adequacy of Observations

The technical qualities of observational strategies have generated an enormous amount of discussion and research. There are controversies as to whether traditional categories of reliability and validity should be extended or adapted to encompass behavioral assessment, or whether new frameworks are needed (see Suen & Ary, 1989; and Nelson & Hayes, 1986, for very different reviews). Regardless, it is important to consider the overall quality of measurement procedures and to evaluate their impact on decision outcomes.

Reporting Agreement Between Observers

The basic strategy for determining agreement involves comparisons between observers who are coding the same sample of behavior. The quality of data obtained from observations may reflect on the skills or training of the observers, characteristics of the behavior to be observed (difficulties include bursts of behavior, episodic behavior, covert behavior), the clarity of definitions for problem behaviors or units of analysis, different occasions for observations, and different settings. If interobserver agreement is low, these facets represent possible points of analysis. We review several basic methods for determining agreement.

Total agreement refers to an overall summary of agreement concerning the number of behavior occurrences within an established time interval. This index does not measure agreement on specific instances of behavior, and there may be substantial disagreement on occurrences of behavior even when total agreement percentages are relatively high (Page & Iwata, 1986). Even so, it may be useful when other agreement indices are not applicable. To calculate total agreement, divide the smaller estimate by the larger. For example, a teacher may report seven aggressive acts during the day while the teacher aide may report five. The total agreement may be expressed as 71 percent. Similarly, duration may be expressed by dividing the smaller estimate of duration for a behavior (for example, crying) by the larger estimate and multiplying by 100 to arrive at the percent agreement.

Interval agreement involves analyzing specific occurrences of target behaviors within time intervals. The units of analysis are discrete opportunities in which the observers agree or disagree that the target behavior occurred.

Interval agreement takes into account both occurrences and nonoccurrences to arrive at a measure of *overall* agreement. It is calculated by adding the numbers of agreements and disagreements, and dividing that sum into the number of agreements (Hopkins & Hermann, 1976). However, one significant problem is that results vary widely by the rates of behavior. To circumvent that problem, Page and Iwata (1986) suggested reporting three agreement indices for a data set. Through the same basic equation, occurrence agreement, nonoccurrence agreement, and interval agreement may be reported.

Kappa also has been widely used to present agreement indices (Barnett & Macmann, in press); however, it is not free from other problems (see Zwick, 1988). Another practical strategy is simply to co-plot the data for the second observer.

Agreement estimates are necessary to examine the effects of observers, the adequacy of target behavior definitions, and observational systems. Estimates of agreement also are important over different occasions of measurement, and across settings. Measurement occasions include different phases or conditions of the case study such as baseline, intervention, and follow-up.

Interobserver agreement indices also are used to determine whether the intervention is being carried out as planned. General procedures from research provide the foundations for practical considerations related to technical adequacy. In research applications, agreement indices are reported usually for about 20 to 25 percent of the observation sessions. While desirable standards or criteria for reliability indices related to decisions are usually set from .80 to .90, they generally have not been linked to individual decision outcomes. When observations are used for educational decisions, it may be critical to provide basic evidence related to traditional standards of reliability and validity.

Agreement and Accuracy

Agreement stresses the consistency between raters; accuracy shifts the emphasis more stringently to the relationship of observations with objective indices of actual performance. The assessment of observer agreement provides an *estimate* of accuracy (Foster & Cone, 1986). To determine accuracy, observations are compared to a criterion measure. An exact index of the behaviors is necessary. These may be provided by scripts, video, or audio recordings. Specific approaches to estimating agreement also are used for assessing accuracy. Although accuracy is desired, most investigators settle for agreement (Kazdin, 1982).

   Many factors influence the quality of observations (Repp, Nieminen, Olinger, & Brusca, 1988). One is *observer drift,* which means unintentionally adopting idiosyncratic definitions of target behaviors and changing the measurement operations. Another is *expectation bias,* meaning that observers may "see" improvements (or lack of gains) that do not exist. Also, the location for preschool observers may be critical. For example, observers who remain in a fixed position are likely to miss important interactions during freeplay. For all these reasons, training and frequent agreement checks are critical.

Validity of Behavioral Assessment

Surprisingly little has been written about the validity of behavioral assessment. Some argue that the traditional notions of reliability and validity do not readily apply to behavioral assessment (Hayes, Nelson, & Jarrett, 1986); others believe that the traditional concepts have value (Barrios & Hartmann, 1986) or should be extended to decision outcomes (Barnett & Macmann, in press). The challenge for practitioners is to select reliable and valid measures for individual cases and for decision making. We define validity in this case as the appropriateness of the behavior for change. There is no direct correspondence between the accurate description of problem behaviors and their intervention implications. The issues surrounding validity are examined in the next chapter, where the emphasis shifts from measuring behavior to selecting target behavior.

The Interpretation of Behavioral Observations

The final step in conducting behavioral observations is to analyze and interpret the data. The most basic way is to graph the results (Parsonson & Baer, 1978; 1986). We continue this discussion at the end of the next chapter, in considering how to evaluate interventions. An extensive but introductory-level discussion of this topic can be found in Cooper, Heron, and Heward (1987).

Summary and Conclusions

The foundations of assessment for intervention design are problem-solving interviews, observations, and curriculum-based measures. The context for these three strategies is critical. Consultation offers a coherent model based on problem-solving strategies. The focus is on providing needed services to parents and teachers in natural settings.

Observations are fundamental to the analysis of behavior. Other assessment methods are used to simplify, structure, or give meaning to observations. However, many decisions are necessary: what, where, who, when, and how to observe. Each facet of planning and interpreting observations requires professional judgment.

5

Designing
Effective Interventions

INTERVENTION DESIGN SHOULD BE GUIDED BY FACTORS THAT ARE likely to facilitate change: (a) parent and teacher collaboration and involvement, (b) an understanding of problem situations, (c) the analysis of intervention research, and (d) step-by-step or *sequential* (rather than diagnostic) decision-making strategies. The targets of assessment and analysis may be different from those revealed by developmental theories or traditional measures because the goal is altering developmental patterns or reducing risk status, rather than understanding normal development or "defining" deviancy. The differences in emphases, and especially their practical ramifications, are significant. Assessments take substantial time and resources, and assessment practices that lack treatment utility should not be allowed to detract from assessment efforts necessary for interventions.

The Reliability and Validity
of Target Behavior Selection

In the last chapter, we discussed the technical adequacy of behavioral assessment. This section shifts the emphasis to selecting appropriate targets of intervention. The difference is important. There may be high agreement between observers on the measured behaviors, and the behaviors may be related to other important criteria, but still the behaviors selected may not be the most useful as targets for change. Overall, many factors influence target behavior selection, and the quality of the assessment must be established for the individual case. Deciding what target behavior to measure is critical.

Reliability of Target Behavior Selection

Research studies have demonstrated the potential for considerable differences when selecting behaviors for change. For example, Wilson and Evans (1983) sent descriptions of childhood disorders to a sample of members of the Association for Advancement of Behavior Therapy. The profiles described children experiencing fearful and anxious behavior; conduct-disordered and disobedient behavior; and withdrawn, shy, introverted behavior. The psychologists were asked (a) to judge whether treatment appeared necessary, (b) to indicate the child's major difficulty, (c) to identify treatment goals, and (d) to indicate and rank order intervention targets. Agreement on the decision to intervene was high; agreement on specific target behaviors was generally quite low (38.6 percent across all conditions).

Although the study was not based on actual problem behaviors, it does serve to warn professionals of potential disagreement in selecting target behaviors. Perhaps the strongest strategy to help deal with potential differences is ongoing, collaborative problem solving with caregivers where priorities for intervention are carefully considered. Professional judgment in assessment and intervention design may be improved through an analysis of sequential decisions (Bandura, 1969). Diagnostic questions become focused on the most reasonable steps in the assessment-intervention process. The outcomes are subsequently evaluated.

Validity of Target Behavior Selection

The *effects* of selecting different target behaviors fall under the topic of validity. There is not necessarily a direct correspondence between the accurate description of a particular behavior and its implications for intervention. Target behavior selection is guided by the likely probability of changing a current or future problem situation, and not necessarily by the salience of specific behaviors (Kanfer, 1985). Challenges include understanding complex interactions, covariations of responses, and sequences of events, and selecting appropriate treatments for target behaviors. When selecting targets and methods for change, we must take care to design durable interventions that generalize to significant settings.

Content Validity. "Content" pertains to adequate sampling of behavior. Content validity has been termed the cornerstone of behavioral assessment (Linehan, 1980; Strosahl & Linehan, 1986). Content validity requires the following: (a) the "specification of the behaviors of interest," (b) the settings where the behaviors are likely to be of interest, (c) the tasks, expectations, and instructions for the situation, and (d) "self-generated" stimuli that may influence the performance (Strosahl & Linehan, 1986, p. 34). One example is assessing noncompliant child behaviors (Barkley, 1987; Forehand & McMahon, 1981). Examining content validity for an assessment technique for noncompliance may include (a) behaviors — whining, having tantrums, ignoring parental commands; (b) settings and situations where the behavior is evident, such as home, shopping, or school; (c) qualities of commands or requests that are reasonable, developmentally appropriate, clearly stated, with appropriate consequences (praise, positive attention, effective reprimand, discipline); and (d) management of potentially interfering factors such as parental anger, depression, or helplessness.

Criterion-Related Validity. This refers to the correlation between a measure and another criterion of performance; the intervention implications of this type of validity have been examined by Kazdin (1985). Traditionally, criterion-related validity has been applied both to current (concurrent validity) and future status (predictive validity). Concurrent validity includes relationships between the target behavior and other measures of the problem, other behaviors related to possible syndromes, and the impact of the behavior on the child's daily functioning. Predictive validity addresses effectiveness of interventions with alternative target behaviors over long time periods.

The social skills of young children provide an example of criterion-related validity. Concurrent validity is a consideration in measuring behaviors related to successfully joining peer play and maintaining bouts of play. Social competence may be related to other aspects of the problems, including aggression or social withdrawal, and corresponding syndromes of behaviors. Changes in behaviors for improving social skills should be related to meaningful changes in everyday functioning with peers across a variety of tasks and situations. Behaviors related to discrete social skills (such as greetings) may not improve overall success in play.

Perhaps the strongest evidence of predictive validity for social skills comes from developmental research. Many converging lines of research point to the significance of social development in the early years and its impact on overall development. However, deciding on specific strategies to improve social skills requires considerable planning. Some variables related to acceptance (such as physical attractiveness) may be immutable (Strain, 1985b). For many reasons discussed throughout this text, change efforts include peers.

Construct Validity. Many constructs (conduct disorders, social skills) now appear in the behavioral literature, and construct validity has increasing relevance to target behavior assessment. It is important to select multiple measures of a problem area—an issue of construct validity (Hayes & Nelson, 1986). When the assessment is focused on the individual case, the *personal constructs* used by the caregivers and psychologist also are important. Personal constructs (Kelly, 1955) are those that individuals use to "perceive, think, interpret, and experience the world" (Mischel, 1981, p. 486). This underscores the importance of understanding values and beliefs of caregivers, and of consultants.

Social Validity. This is concerned with defining socially significant problems for behavioral change, and establishing and obtaining goals through procedures acceptable to the immediate social community (Kazdin, 1977; Wolf, 1978). The effectiveness of any resulting change should be evaluated in multiple ways by those who interact directly with the child. In other words, the results should have practical significance.

Two general methods stem from this approach. First, social validity involves social comparisons. For example, peer group or individual performance of the target behavior may help differentiate adept from inadequate performance and may suggest behaviors for change. This is essentially a normative approach to target behavior selection (see *template matching* in this chapter).

Second, social validity involves subjective evaluations by others who are in a position to judge the adequacy of the behavior. Parents, teachers, and community members all serve in this capacity. We resume related discussions in the sections on acceptability and naturalistic interventions later in this chapter.

In sum, although concepts of technical adequacy apply in a general way, the topic is not well developed. However, implicitly or explicitly, reliability and validity considerations are a part of every intervention design. No assessment strategy guarantees selecting reliable and valid target behaviors and intervention goals. We believe that the technical questions of reliability and validity are best addressed through ecobehavioral analysis, collaborative problem solving, and functional assessments. Ultimately, validity is assessed by evaluating intervention outcomes.

Planning Interventions

The stages of intervention are (a) defining and clarifying problem or target behavior, (b) designing an intervention, (c) executing the intervention, and (d) modifying or terminating the intervention based on intervention outcomes. Intervention plans are based on at least five considerations, all of which require professional judgment:

1. Applications of change theory and the use of various assessment techniques in the process of problem solving.
2. Child, caregiver, setting, and service delivery characteristics.

3. Analysis of possible and likely interventions.
4. Acceptability of interventions.
5. Relative costs and estimated potential benefits of interventions.

Many children have more than one difficulty; alternative target behaviors have to be ranked or behaviors meaningfully grouped together, and the sequence and loci of intervention efforts must be decided.

Guidelines for Selecting Target Behaviors

Guidelines are based on pragmatic, conceptual, and empirical factors. Furthermore, the selection is accomplished "progressively and with continuing refinement" (Kanfer, 1985, p. 15). Many decisions are necessary.

Evaluate the Basics: Health, Impairment, and System Functioning.
A preliminary question is whether a behavioral intervention is necessary. Children should be screened for medical problems that may be contributing directly or indirectly to the behavior. For example, a child with hearing loss or middle ear infection may be described as inattentive or noncompliant. Sleep patterns, diet, and any medication that might influence behavior should be considered.

Also, children may be referred for behavior problems when it is the classroom or the family that is in chaos. In the schools, teacher consultation for classroom management, curriculum design or modification, and teacher and administrative support for change efforts may take precedence over consultation for individual child misbehavior. Likewise, parents may refer children for misbehaviors when their own lives are out of control through separation, divorce, or illness. We have had children referred when both parents were holding down two jobs and were rarely at home with the child. Basic rebuilding of family and parent-child relationships, or helping to create some stability for at least one parent or alternative caregiver, may be necessary to evaluate the effects of family functioning on child behavior, or to support child-related interventions.

Determine Physically Dangerous Behaviors. Behaviors that threaten lives, either the child's or others', have the highest priority. With children, one of the initial goals may be to ensure a safe environment while behaviors are being monitored and interventions planned. Aspects may involve abusive and neglectful parental relationships, or elements of home and community safety. For example, in a consultation with parents concerning an aggressive four-year-old boy, initial assessment targets involved the parental monitoring of play behaviors, baths, and stair behaviors (to eliminate pushing and shoving on concrete steps) to protect a toddler sister. Health-related behaviors, safety, and injury prevention may take immediate priority over other concerns. Key factors include parental situations, motivation, skills, and stressors — all of which may effect monitoring and responsiveness to child care needs. Thus, risk assessment is an important initial step.

Evaluate Empirically Based Constellations of Behaviors. Empirically based constellations of behaviors or syndromes refer to "multiple characteristics that co-occur and encompass different behaviors, affect, cognitions and psychophysiological responses" (Kazdin, 1985, p. 36). Some (for example, Powers, 1984) believe that appraising the degree to which empirically based syndromes fit an individual child is an important point of assessment. Certain classes of behaviors (such as conduct disorders and social withdrawal) have been linked to later difficulties in adjustment, and these factors also contribute to prioritization of target behaviors.

The basic procedure involves making comparisons of the similarities between a child's profile and the *prototypic* or distinctive features of empirically based syndromes. Practical benefits include making comparisons between the understanding of the construct as it may apply to a child and the general, researched dimensions of the construct. Child and setting characteristics, treatment components and alternatives, the magnitude of expected changes, and the possible utility of observation systems and measures all can be logically compared to the referred child. The use of an empirically based constellation of behaviors may lead to uncovering behaviors, factors, or circumstances that would have been missed otherwise. Many excellent sources for interventions are organized by syndromes (see Bornstein & Kazdin, 1985; Kratochwill & Morris, 1991; Mash & Barkley, 1989), and collectively they represent best practices for specific referral problems.

However, the possibilities for high error rates have not been researched. Other potential vulnerabilities include pressures to diagnose, the politics associated with using alternative diagnostic categories, and stigma and unintended or deleterious outcomes introduced when syndromes are used as labels.

Evaluate the Social and Economic Impact of Behaviors. Behaviors that have potentially damaging social or economic consequences for caregivers also receive high priority. For example, selecting targets for severely disruptive child behavior may include evaluating the impact on the caregiver's economic realities. Initial consultations may be directed to day-care settings and, later, home and community settings. In other circumstances, parents may be discouraging visits from friends and family because of child behaviors that are embarrassing, disruptive, or harmful. These parents may be losing needed support systems.

Consider Values, Goals, and Beliefs. Belief systems are direct and indirect sources of the learning experiences that are provided to children (Sigel, 1985). They also play a significant role in plans for changing behaviors. Parents and professionals may have different priorities for changes. Ecobehavioral assessment practices may help in elucidating these priorities, and considering caregiver priorities in intervention design. Services that more closely match caregiver needs may be associated with beneficial outcomes for families and children.

Some beliefs also may undermine interventions. For example, we have worked with mothers of noncompliant children whose spouses were in jail for violent acts. If mothers do not believe that such behaviors are learned, but instead result from "bad genes," they will invest little in interventions related to improving parenting skills. Questions about beliefs should be included in ecobehavioral interviews even though beliefs that guide actions may be difficult to communicate or may be out of awareness.

Plan for Expanding Positive Behaviors. Whenever possible, target behaviors should specify desirable goals, rather than inappropriate behaviors. Increasing the amount of time spent behaving appropriately will decrease the time spent behaving inappropriately. Selecting target behaviors thus leads to evaluating resources and plans for action (Hawkins, 1986; Mash & Terdal, 1988). Furthermore, because of the time-consuming process involved in sequential decision making, attention should be given to "enabling" behaviors that are likely to have powerful overall effects on adjustment, or "access" behaviors that allow entry into beneficial environments.

Improve Coping as an Intervention Goal. In many situations, such as those involving children with very severe developmental disabilities or degenerative disorders, goals related to improving caregivers' coping skills and examining their sources of satisfaction are appropriate. An important focus may become involving care providers in implementing and revising change programs over the developmental period through adulthood.

Plan for Sequences of Behavior Change. Some target behaviors may be prerequisites for other changes, primarily because they may influence later, more significant, or pivotal behaviors (Kanfer, 1985). Behaviors that are viewed as aspects of a normal developmental progression, and that may result in cumulative deficits if not mastered, are given high priority (Mash & Terdal, 1988). Sequences of behaviors are established through developmental studies and through comparisons of skilled versus nonskilled performances on specific tasks (task analysis and template matching).

For example, before learning preacademic tasks, some children need to be taught *preattending skills:* looking at materials, listening to instructions, and sitting quietly during instruction. Reading to young children is a naturalistic method to teach and improve preattending skills.

Consider Keystone Behaviors. A strategy for target behavior selection is the evaluation of keystone behaviors, where response classes based on research with specific disorders are considered for interventions. (Response classes are discussed further in Chapter Six.) Evans and Meyer defined keystone behavior in the following way: "The keystone behavior is the one on which all the others appear to depend, rather like a pivotal or prerequisite skill" (1985, p. 31). For example, compliance may be a likely keystone behavior for conduct-disordered children.

A related keystone is *rule-governed* behavior. Rules are guides for conduct in specific circumstances based on caregiver commands or setting expectations. One of the initial targets for assessment and intervention is classroom and family rules: how they are introduced and taught, and what the consequences are for appropriate and inappropriate behaviors.

Selecting an appropriate keystone behavior may have beneficial side effects. For example, Firestone (1976) found reductions in verbal aggression and teacher attention, and increases in cooperative play, following a brief intervention for aggressive behaviors. Keystone behaviors should also lead to more cost-effective and efficient interventions.

Evaluate Social Competence. Children's play and social behaviors often are critical assessment targets with broad implications for development. Guralnick wrote, "Establishing successful relationships with one's peers is one of the most important accomplishments of early childhood" (1987, p. 93). Potential targets for assessment include facility with functional social routines (such as taking turns), strategies for gaining access to play, communication skills, and toy play skills. Promising research has examined the effectiveness of peer-mediated strategies (Hecimovic, Fox, Shores, & Strain, 1985; Hendrickson, Strain, Tremblay, & Shores, 1982), teacher-mediated strategies (Fox, Shores, Lindeman, & Strain, 1986), and sibling-mediated strategies (James & Egel, 1986) to extend play and social behaviors, although more research is needed, particularly with respect to generalization effects.

Plan for the Next Educational Environment. A child's likely success in transition settings should be considered. Vincent and colleagues wrote: "Traditional special educational programming may be incompatible with child success in least restrictive programs" (1980, p. 326). They argued that at least some instructional time should be dedicated to "survival skills" necessary for independent functioning in complex educational environments.

Related to social validity and functional assessments, strategies to establish needed skills include temporary placements to determine skill deficits, consultations with receiving teachers, and observations in the next environments. Template matching, discussed next, is a research-based procedure to help with transitions. More broadly, Brown, Nietupski, and Hamre-Nietupski (1976) proposed *the criterion of ultimate functioning* to stress the need for functional assessments that might improve environmental adaptation for severely handicapped persons.

Template Matching. Template matching is a promising target behavior selection strategy with origins in person-environment research (Bem, 1982). Essentially, template matching includes several different experimental procedures to assess discrepancies between client performance and the performance of successful individuals in transition or target settings. The discrepancies are used to (a) predict the likelihood of adaptation in specific settings, and (b) identify target areas for intervention to facilitate transitions to less restrictive settings.

The general strategies developed by Cone (Cone & Hoier, 1986) are straightforward and can be represented by four steps: (1) "the behavioral requirements of situations are conceptualized in terms of behaviors (template items) important to the social context of the particular client child"; (2) "behaviors most characteristic of exemplary performers . . . in that context are identified"; (3) the behaviors are "collected into templates against which the client is compared"; (4) "discrepancies between the client's repertoire and the template indicate targets for intervention" (p. 15). For example, a child's behavior in the current setting (such as special preschool classroom) and adaptive behavior in the transition setting (mainstream kindergarten classroom) are compared. "Index children" in the receiving classroom (those who are successful) are identified to create a template, which is a profile of child and teacher-child behaviors necessary for successful adaptation in the new setting. Discrepancies between the target child's characteristics and the template reveal targets for intervention.

Applications include assessing social skills and the skills needed for successful transitions between settings. Under the rubric of transenvironmental programming (Anderson-Inman, 1981), Walker and associates have used a different approach to the construction of templates (Walker, Severson, & Haring, 1986; Walker & Rankin, 1983). Rather than observe the performance of successful students per se, they developed profiles of caregiver tolerance that are intended to reflect behavioral standards and expectations in specific settings. Teacher skill and tolerance are important factors in considering transitions.

In sum, planning for educational transitions is a critical aspect of assessment and intervention design. Template matching may help professionals identify probable transition settings and select target behaviors to help with transitions. Template matching has also been applied to selecting target behavior related to social skills. Barnett and Macmann (in press) review the technical adequacy of template matching.

Summary of Target Behavior Decisions. Target behaviors are selected based on pragmatic, conceptual, and empirical factors. Hawkins (1986), among others, recommends the conceptual use of a "behavioral assessment funnel" in which the first step involves broad screening, followed by a narrowing focus, and ultimately, the specification of target behaviors. Exhibit 5.1 summarizes issues in target behavior selection. Exhibit 5.2 reproduces the classic framework developed by Kanfer and Grimm (1977).

Intervention Decisions

Interventions may include (a) changes in parent, teacher, peer, sibling, and child behaviors; (b) changes in physical environments; (c) instruction to teach new skills or expand existing skills; and (d) techniques for increased self-regulation. Generally, interventions are selected based on a combination of strategies, including the analysis of situations and potential target behaviors

Exhibit 5.1. Decisions Concerning the Selection of Target Behaviors.

---

1. The question of whether to develop new behavioral repertoires or to reduce troublesome behaviors.
2. The relative focus on the child's versus caregiver's behaviors.
3. The reliable and valid development of skill hierarchies and intervention sequences.
4. The analysis of complex relationships between behaviors (for example, language, social skills, aggressive behaviors).
5. The decisions about changing the level of analysis from discrete behaviors to more global classes of behaviors (such as combining hitting, name calling, and breaking objects into a category of "destructive tantrums").
6. The prioritization of target behaviors.
7. The criterion for effective performance.
8. The determination of *access* behaviors that enable entry into environments likely to enhance development.

---

through problem solving with caregivers, observation, and evaluating the research base for interventions.

Assess the Research Base. There are several broad reasons for this step. First, parents, teachers, and administrators generally expect intervention decisions to be guided by available and pertinent research. These expectations have significant legal, ethical, and professional ramifications discussed in Chapter Twelve.

Second, research may be used as a general guide for both assessment and intervention design. As an example, parental behaviors, in addition to child characteristics, should be a focus of assessment and intervention plans for conduct-disordered children (see McMahon, 1987; Patterson & Bank, 1986).

Third, preschool consultants should be aware of valid and, ideally, replicated intervention strategies that have been successfully applied to specific behavior problems. The process involves making logical generalizations from research to individual cases. This is not a "cookbook" recommendation; functional analyses are necessary to assist with making generalizations, as follows.

Functional analysis is a research-based approach to intervention design. The general strategy is to examine and, if necessary, alter environmental variables to determine their *function*

Exhibit 5.2. Selecting Target Behaviors.

I.   Behavioral Deficits
  A.   Inadequate base of knowledge for guiding behavior
  B.   Failure to engage in acceptable social behaviors due to skills deficits
  C.   Inability to supplement or counter immediate environmental influences and regulate one's behavior through self-directing responses
  D.   Deficiencies in self-reinforcement for performance
  E.   Deficits in monitoring one's own behavior
  F.   Inability to alter responses in conflict situations
  G.   Limited behavior repertoire due to restricted range of reinforcers
  H.   Deficits in cognitive and/or motor behaviors necessary to meet the demands of daily living

II. Behavioral Excesses
  A.   Conditioned inappropriate anxiety to objects or events
  B.   Excessive self-observational activity

III. Problems in Environmental Stimulus Control
  A.   Affective response to stimulus objects or events leading to subjective distress or unacceptable behavior
  B.   Failure to offer support or opportunities for behaviors appropriate in a different milieu
  C.   Failure to meet environmental demands or responsibilities arising from inefficient organization of time

IV. Inappropriate Self-Generated Stimulus Control
  A.   Self-descriptions serving as cues for behaviors leading to negative outcomes
  B.   Verbal/symbolic activity serving to cue inappropriate behavior
  C.   Faulty labeling of internal cues

V.   Inappropriate Contingency Arrangement
  A.   Failure of the environment to support appropriate behavior
  B.   Environmental maintenance of undesirable behavior
  C.   Excessive use of positive reinforcement for desirable behaviors
  D.   Delivery of reinforcement independent of responding

Source: Adapted from F. H. Kanfer and L. Grimm (1977). Behavioral analysis: Selecting target behaviors in the interview. *Behavior Modification, 1,* pp. 7–28, copyright ©1977 by Sage Publications. Reprinted by permission of Sage Publications, Inc.

in modifying or maintaining behaviors (O'Neill, et al., 1990; Skinner, 1953). The ABC analysis presented earlier is one technique designed for this purpose, but due to limitations in events that may be observed through naturalistic observations, environmental events may need to be systematically manipulated. Many of the examples throughout the chapters on basic, family, and school-based interventions represent examples of functional analysis. The result is a data-based method to evaluate possible causes of behavior and ways to test intervention hypotheses.

Last, numerous gaps exist in the intervention research base for certain behaviors, child characteristics, or applicability of interventions to different settings. In such circumstances, accountability procedures are especially important. Strategies for accountability are based on single-case experimental designs (Barlow, Hayes, & Nelson, 1984; Bloom & Fischer, 1982).

Assess the Availability of Resources. A careful analysis of resources for reaching treatment goals is necessary. Interventions require an appropriate environmental context, the availability of caregivers, and a range of specialized personnel. Teachers may require planning time and support services. The roles of babysitters and extended family members may be significant. It is important to differentiate between currently existing resources, those that are accessible, and those that may be creatively identified.

Assess the Acceptability of Intervention Alternatives. Acceptability refers to broad-based judgments by consumers (participants and caregivers) concerning "whether treatment is appropriate for the problem, whether treatment is fair, reasonable, and intrusive, and whether treatment meets with conventional notions about what treatment should be" (Kazdin, 1980, p. 259; see also Wolf, 1978). The general premise is that for many problem behaviors, a range of alternative interventions is likely to be effective. Those viewed as more acceptable are more likely to be "sought, . . . initiated, and adhered to" (Kazdin, p. 260). Wolf wrote: "If the participants don't like the treatment then they may avoid it, or run away, or complain loudly" (p. 206). Unless participants view the intervention as acceptable, important technological advances will not be used. Also, by considering a range of intervention alternatives, professionals help reduce the possibility of intervention biases.

Acceptability research is rapidly expanding (Reimers, Wacker, & Koeppl, 1987); consumer groups such as parents (Calvert & McMahon, 1987; Frentz & Kelley, 1986), teachers (Witt, Martens, & Elliott, 1984), and children are focal points of various studies. One of the major issues is how acceptability ratings may be altered through planned sequences of interventions. Witt and Elliott (1985) hypothesized that acceptability, use, integrity, and effectiveness of the intervention are sequentially and reciprocally related.

Fawcett, Mathews, and Fletcher (1980, pp. 508–511) argued that interventions that are contextually appropriate are more likely to be adopted. Based on their analysis, desirable interventions are (a) "effective," (b) "inexpensive," (c) "decentralized" and controlled by local groups, (d) "flexible" enough to permit input by participants, (e) "sustainable" with local resources, (f) "simple" or comprehensible, and (g) "compatible" or harmonious with existing perceived needs, values, and customs of the setting.

Assess for Motivation. Acquiring significant behavior change for children may require substantial behavior change on the part of the caregivers. In the context of behavioral intervention, motivation refers to "the probability of an individual emitting the behaviors necessary for successful intervention" (Haynes, 1986, pp. 400–401). While there are no panaceas, active involvement by caregivers in assessment is likely to increase participation in intervention decisions (Brinckerhoff & Vincent, 1986).

Reducing rather than increasing caregivers' demands may be an important goal in some situations. Caregivers may spend a considerable amount of time monitoring and responding to behavior of problem children. Preschool consultants need to assess the impact of interventions on caregiver-child interactions, and the caregiver's other roles and responsibilities. When possible, successful interventions should lighten burdens for conscientious, effective, but harassed caregivers. Practical examples include reducing teacher monitoring and number of prompts necessary to manage a child's classroom behavior, and reducing the level of assistance that a child requires in self-care skills such as dressing or feeding.

Estimate Probable Success and Cost Effectiveness. Intervention strategies must be realistically appraised with respect to their likelihood of success in changing selected target behaviors. Probable success rates are determined in part through a review of interventions found in the literature. More complex interventions, or those involving multiple change agents, are more vulnerable to failure. The relative efficiency and cost effectiveness of alternative interventions are additional considerations.

Intervention or *treatment strength* "refers to the ability of a given treatment to change behavior in the desired direction" (Gresham, 1991, p. 28). *Resistance to intervention* is defined as "the lack of change in target behaviors as a function of intervention" (p. 25). An analogy from physics has been used to help explain resistance to intervention. Learned behaviors may be thought of as "possessing momentum" (Nevin, Mandell, & Atak, 1983, p. 49). According to Newton's law, momentum is the product of the mass and velocity of a moving body. Momentum is an indication of the effort needed to move, stop, or change its direction. Behavioral momentum, in the context of intervention design, refers to the resistance of behavior to change. When applied to children's behaviors, the rate of behaviors during baseline can be thought of as velocity, the strength of response or persistence as mass, and the intervention as an external force. The premise is that a behavior with greater strength and rate will be more resistant to intervention. Resistance must be analyzed by behavioral factors — severity, chronicity, generalization, and teacher tolerance of the behavior — and intervention factors — strength of treatment, acceptability, treatment integrity, and treatment effectiveness.

Analysis of resistance has many practical implications. Interventions must have sufficient strength to change the behav

ior. This means that interventions must be carefully planned
and procedures specified, the length and intensity of the intervention must be determined, and change agents with appropriate
expertise must be identified. Behaviors that are resistant to
change require a functional analysis and replanning of target
behaviors, interventions, and appropriate services and support
for caregivers.

In addition, Gresham (1991) has argued that behavior
disorders may be conceptualized in terms of resistance to intervention. The implications are important. First, the framework
shifts professional decision making away from dichotomous classifications (disturbed versus not disturbed) and psychometric
approaches where the number of symptoms or behavioral profiles
are considered, to functional assessments and intervention decisions. Second, and more basic, no classification decision is
made unless the child's behaviors remain unaltered by well-
planned and -executed interventions. The classification logically
leads to stronger interventions. Classifications of resistance also
have applicability to severe learning problems.

The concept of intervention strength may lead to possible misinterpretation, especially related to aversives (giving
louder commands for noncompliance, for instance). Mace and
colleagues (1988) gave a creative yet simple example that merits
replication with noncompliant children. They used high-proba-
bility commands—those likely to be complied with, based on
the child's history ("Come here and give me a hug")—to increase
behavioral momentum of responding that would carry over to
low-probability commands ("Pick up your toys").

Self-Mediated Change. Earlier we described self-monitoring as
a keystone behavior, but, surprisingly, research on self-directed
change strategies has been inconclusive (see Billings & Wasik,
1985; Bornstein, 1985). In large part, this is due to experimental design considerations in determining the extent of self versus
"other" directedness. In other words, because children are guided
through the intervention, self-directed change is actually based
on the efforts of caregivers.

However, despite the controversies, several methods may
be used to encourage and facilitate self-regulation and indepen-

dent problem solving. These include the basics of modeling, prompting, and reinforcing behaviors, and creating sufficient opportunities for practice. As one example, Stokes, Fowler, and Baer (1978) successfully taught preschoolers to judge the quality of their work and to appropriately elicit teacher praise. Overall, external means are important in developing self-regulation.

An example of a "self-mediated" intervention technique is that of "correspondence training." A number of studies have demonstrated the effectiveness of reinforcing children's verbalizations as a way to control behavior. The method, along with other self-mediated change strategies, is reviewed in later chapters.

Based on a series of investigations now spanning three decades, Mischel has proposed *delay of gratification* both as a significant psychological process fundamental to self-control, and as a basic personal competence. Delay of gratification refers to "the ability to purposefully defer immediate gratification for the sake of delayed, contingent but more desired future outcomes" (Mischel, 1984, p. 353). Cognitive strategies that children use, as well as different situations, facilitate the delay of gratification. While effect sizes are modest, measures of delay of gratification during the preschool years predicted parent-rated aspects of social competence when children were in high school.

Agree on Roles and Responsibilities. After intervention alternatives are evaluated and an intervention plan is selected, the responsibilities of the consultants and caregivers must be agreed upon. Gutkin and Curtis (1990) commented that this is an often overlooked but critical step. We elaborate on this topic in the next section on treatment integrity.

Assess Treatment Integrity. Treatment integrity refers to whether an intervention was conducted as intended. Treatment integrity is of major significance and, if not evaluated, casts doubt over intervention efforts. "Real treatments are often complex, are sometimes delivered by poorly trained or unmotivated people, and can be totally disrupted by events in the real world" (Sechrest, et al., 1979, pp. 15–16). Interventions often are altered intentionally or unintentionally, or are not carried out as planned. Threats to treatment integrity include (a) variables of individ-

uals or settings that affect the implementation of the intervention, (b) the complexity and demands of the intervention, and
(c) the length of time the intervention is carried out.

While changes frequently are required to ensure that the
child receives an appropriate intervention, the needed changes
should be identified, planned, and mutually agreed upon. A
common error is changing to a more restrictive or intrusive intervention because the outcomes appeared ineffective when instead
the original plan lacked treatment integrity. The intervention
may not have failed; rather, it may have been inadequately
implemented.

To help control for potential threats to treatment integrity,
several strategies are available. First, using ecological and consultation-based approaches when designing interventions enables
the professional to identify likely change agents, and allows the
individual who will be responsible for implementation to be
aware of the conditions necessary for success. Second, through
training, modeling, role playing, and guided practice, that individual can become competent in the intervention techniques
before they are actually implemented. The most sound and practical strategy is to detail the intervention through the use of written scripts and to role play the complete intervention. Through
agreement (or consensus), the consultant and caregiver can examine necessary skills for the intervention and the need for intervention changes. The intervention can be evaluated and revised as necessary.

Third, using a standardized protocol and simplifying
procedures as much as possible also can help with threats to treatment integrity. In developing the protocol, interventions are re-
cast as specific steps. The caregiver contributes to the intervention design, the sequences of steps, and to the wording of the
steps. Observers also can help by collecting data on the intervention procedures administered in the natural environment.
In addition, other teachers or family members that come in contact with the child may need to be informed about the intervention program so that they support its goals. Sulzar-Azaroff
and Mayer (1991) refer to preparing the physical and social environment to support intervention programs. Thus, caregivers

may use the final form of the intervention steps as a familiar script.

There are many ways to use treatment integrity protocols for implementing and monitoring interventions. After consultation and training in the intervention technique, the caregivers may be given enough copies of the treatment integrity protocol to use until the next scheduled consultation. While the consultant carries out the intervention, caregivers follow the script, to help learn the intervention steps and to become familiar with the regimen. The consultant and caregiver may co-intervene for the first few days of the intervention. Teams may be formed within classrooms to help with monitoring. The caregiver may bring in the completed protocols as part of the ongoing consultation. It is critical that it be viewed as a helpful process, similar to feedback received in learning any new task.

Significantly, poor treatment integrity may indicate that the intervention is unreasonable for a situation and that reconsideration of the steps or redesign of the intervention are necessary. From the framework of naturalistic intervention design, spontaneous changes also may result in improvements. A treatment integrity protocol will enable changes to be noted and evaluated on subsequent trials. Factors related to treatment integrity and evaluation strategies are summarized in Exhibit 5.3.

In summary, implementing and maintaining the planned intervention are significant challenges. Potential difficulties with adherence to intervention plans underscore the need to identify a range of intervention alternatives and change agents, and to find flexible ways to enable caregivers to help modify plans based on realities of situations.

Assess Unintended Outcomes or Side Effects. Interventions may have positive, mixed, or negative outcomes. In addition to the specified target behaviors, other features of the social environment may be altered unintentionally, for better or worse. It is important to evaluate potential negative outcomes. While there are no standard procedures for measuring unplanned outcomes, general procedures involve extending measurement or probes

Exhibit 5.3. Treatment Integrity.

Factors Related to Treatment Integrity and Evaluation
1. Complexity
2. Time requirements
3. Materials and resources needed
4. Number of treatment agents
5. Perceived effectiveness of treatment
6. Actual effectiveness of treatment
7. Motivation of treatment agents
Technical Issues
1. Specification of treatment components
2. Deviations from interventions and behavior change
3. Assessment of treatment integrity
    A. Occurrence/nonoccurrence of intervention components
    B. Percentages of treatment components implemented
    C. Graph of results along with target behaviors

Source: Gresham, F. M. (1989). Assessment of treatment integrity in school consultation/prereferral intervention. *School Psychology Review, 18,* 37–50.

into longer time periods, measuring multiple behaviors, and assessing the behaviors of others in the social environments.

Make Data-Based Changes When Necessary. Interventions require data-based modifications. Time-series methods based on single-case research designs are appropriate for this function because the core procedure involves repeated measures for the same situation over time. Time-series methods may be used to monitor trends in behavior and the effects of interventions. A practitioner-oriented overview of single-case designs and guidelines for data-based decision making are included in the final section of this chapter.

Plan for Generalization. Many target behaviors for young children referred for intervention services require widespread rather than narrowly focused gains. Also, artificial means of control often are linked to difficulties with long-term success of interventions (Kanfer, 1985). Yet, many of the interventions necessarily begin with a limited set of objectives, or are limited by setting or circumstance. Questions about comprehensiveness and durability of change are necessary. Strategies for generalization frequently need to be a part of assessment-intervention plans from the outset; when they are not, outcomes are unknown or possibly limited. Generalization is a long-neglected problem with behavioral interventions. In this section we review principles of generalization programming drawing on the work of Stokes and Osnes (1986, 1988, 1989), which updates the classic paper by Stokes and Baer (1977). Edited books by Haring (1988) and by Horner, Dunlap, and Koegel (1988) examined the topic in depth for severely handicapped learners.

Stokes and Osnes describe generalization: "Generalization . . . refers to the outcome of behavior change and therapy programs, resulting in effects extraneous to the original targeted changes. This occurs in the absence of comprehensive programming across stimuli, responses, and time. In therapeutic activities, these effects are sought across clients, stimulus conditions and settings, and behaviors" (1989, p. 338).

Maintenance of behaviors is determined by the durability of intervention outcomes over time. It is not enough to intervene and hope for effects that generalize and that are maintained. For professionals the issue is how to identify and plan for functional variables in the natural environment that will enhance generalization programming.

Stokes and Osnes (1986, 1988, 1989) discuss three principles and twelve tactics that promote generalization.

A.   *Take advantage of natural communities of reinforcement.* Preschool and family environments have considerable potential for establishing the generality of skill development. Thus, target behavior selection is guided by the degree to which changes in behavior are likely to achieve "entry into the natural reinforcement community of the child" (Baer & Wolf, 1970). This principle focuses the analysis of generalization to settings (Stokes & Osnes, 1989, use the term *exploit*). The principle requires an understanding of the arrangement of antecedents, responses, and consequences that influence behavior in natural communities of reinforcement.

1. *Contact natural consequences.* Stokes and Osnes (1989) stressed that *relevant* behaviors be taught. The rationale is that useful and adaptive behaviors are more likely to be reinforced by natural communities of reinforcement. "Perhaps the most fundamental guideline of behavior programming, as well as generalization programming, is to teach behaviors that are likely to come into contact with powerful reinforcing consequences that do not need to be programmed by a therapist or behavior change agent" (p. 341). In sum, teaching relevant behaviors is an important tactic.

2. *Recruit natural consequences.* Training may focus on both the frequency and skill of behavior, but also individuals in the environment may need to be recruited or trained to "notice and pay off" the appropriate behavior (1989, p. 342).

3. *Modify maladaptive consequences.* Maladaptive consequences may be maintaining inappropriate behaviors; if these are eliminated, appropriate behaviors may be more easily developed and maintained. Thus, environments may be supporting maladaptive behaviors and may need to be modified. An example is misplaced positive social consequences for inappropriate behavior.

4. *Reinforce occurrences of generalization.* Any occurrence of generalization should be noticed, valued, and followed by consequences that may reinforce the behavior. Plan for the conditions to facilitate generalization, but also "take advantage of randomness and good fortune" (p. 343).

B. *Train diversely.* Instead of tightly controlled training conditions, changing to less rigid programming with greater variation in training and antecedent stimuli, responses, and consequences may have a greater impact on generalization.

5. *Use sufficient stimulus exemplars.* A stimulus exemplar is defined as a training condition. The tactic involves using multiple trainers and settings.

6. *Use sufficient response exemplars.* These exemplars are

different child behaviors used in training. Frequently behaviors that are the focus of training function as a part of a response class. It may be necessary to train for subsets of behaviors, rather than specific behaviors, in order for generalization to occur. Examples include teaching a variety of appropriate greeting and play entry skills.

7. *Make antecedents less discriminable.* Also referred to as "loose training" (Stokes & Baer, 1977), this suggestion involves varying the conditions of training. An example is incidental learning based on interactions that the child initiates naturally (Hart & Risley, 1980).

8. *Make consequences less discriminable.* Strategies for increasing the likelihood for generalization include the use of intermittent reinforcement schedules, increasing the delay for presenting the consequences, and making the therapist's presence less predictable.

C. *Incorporate functional mediators.* Mediators are stimuli that facilitate generalization. To increase the likelihood of success, they need to be easy to produce or must be present under relevant conditions. Stokes and Osnes (1989) give the following examples.

9. *Incorporate common salient physical stimuli* (or objects). A strategy to help with generalizing behaviors includes the presence of the same or similar stimuli in both the training and generalization setting. Posting pictures of rules for activity centers in preschool classrooms is an example.

10. *Incorporate common salient social stimuli.* This tactic involves using specific people or gestures to facilitate generalization through appropriate behaviors that become associated with their presence. Peer training in social skills serves as an important example. Another is the use of brief preplanned signals between caregiver and child as a prompt for behavior (Poth & Barnett, 1983).

11. *Incorporate self-mediated physical stimuli.* This strategy

involves the use of a stimulus that is maintained and carried by the child. Self-recording techniques may be used in this way.

12. *Incorporate self-mediated verbal and covert stimuli.* These strategies generally relate to verbalizations, language, and thought. Correspondence training (discussed in later chapters) is an important example.

In sum, planning for maintenance and generalization is a requirement of intervention design. Another related skill is *adaptation.* Adaptation changes the focus from using a skill in different settings and over time, to being able to modify the skill "to meet the requirements of changing demands or conditions" (Wolery, Bailey, & Sugai, 1988, p. 61).

The Use of Aversive or Punishment Procedures. Many procedures that can be used for intervening with children's behavior problems are aversive. Self-injury, self-stimulation or stereotypic behavior, acting out, or psychotic behaviors have been associated with decisions to use aversives (see Matson & DiLorenzo, 1984; Repp & Singh, 1990). Well-established interventions such as time out and overcorrection also may be classified as aversive interventions. Because of the many controversies, decisions about using aversives involve evaluating risks to the child and others, the potential of positive procedures to work efficiently and effectively, and protections for the child. Established safeguards should be employed when these procedures are used, and these are reviewed in later chapters.

Naturalistic Interventions

In this chapter, we emphasized establishing a range of possible interventions as a step in problem solving. Decision making is then guided by factors such as acceptability, analysis of resources, and other elements of planning. As a general guide based on ecobehavioral principles, special consideration should be given to the most natural intervention that is likely to be effective.

Naturalistic interventions are a form of environmental intervention. The interventions are revealed by the natural teaching styles of successful caregivers. Beyond a research foundation (Hart, 1985), there are several basic reasons for examining naturalistic interventions.

First, interventions vary greatly in the demands made on participants. The acceptability and overall outcomes of an intervention depend on many factors. For parents and teachers, the more closely an intervention fits the caregiver's current situation, skills, and plans, the more effective it is likely to be.

Second, interventions are frequently accomplished in specific training environments, which may be considerably different from nontraining environments. To facilitate generalization to other settings, new activities and caregiver behaviors will need to be introduced. In designing interventions with generalization as an objective, Stokes and Osnes (1989) wrote: "Generalization programming seems to be well served by providing the least artificial, least cumbersome, and most natural positive consequences in programming interventions. Such programming most closely matches naturally occurring consequences and their entrapment potential" (p. 341). "Entrapment" refers to the process in which relatively simple behaviors lead to general behavioral change because they are "trapped" by reinforcement that occurs in existing environments (Baer & Wolf, 1970). Assumptions are that techniques in natural settings will parallel those used in training settings, and that trainers and caregivers will work collaboratively to plan and evaluate interventions. A prototypic example is naturalistic language training (Hart, 1985).

Third, naturalistic intervention design also stresses existing competencies of caregivers, and thus may serve to enhance their feelings of efficacy. Children who are hard to teach or parent may have devastating effects on caregivers' self-confidence.

Plans for naturalistic interventions are based on the analysis of caregivers' actual roles, routines, skills, and interests. Assessment plans can be designed to identify (a) a range of treatment options based on research and functional analyses; (b) naturally occurring parent or teacher intervention strategies that are likely to be successful as implemented, or with changes, guidance, and feedback; or (c) interventions that may be adapted to evident styles of parenting or teaching.

For example, interviews and observations may reveal that caregivers use techniques that are consistent with other successful interventions. However, they may not be aware of the importance of their behaviors. Therefore, a role of the consultant may be to evaluate emerging skills of caregivers that can be further enhanced through consultation, practice, and feedback. Planning can be built around these naturally occurring approximations of successful strategies. Naturalistic intervention design includes modifying or extending caregiver interventions, or identifying interventions that may be easily incorporated into the routines of caregivers.

To sum, interventions are selected based on a combination of strategies: the analysis of situations, collaborative problem solving, and the consideration of the research and naturalistic basis. The naturalistic basis is determined by evident skills, emerging skills, and accessible skills of caregivers. Of interest to the consultant are successful naturalistic strategies, partially successful strategies, and skills that may be built upon, and the interventions that may readily fit caregivers' roles, skills, and situations.

Evaluating Interventions

Since the focus of this text is on individual interventions, strategies that stem from single-case research designs are fundamental. While research itself is not the present topic, many have argued for the use of single-case research methods to evaluate practice (Barlow, Hayes, & Nelson, 1984; Bloom & Fischer, 1982; Kratochwill, 1977, 1978). Evaluation is basic to the scientist-practitioner model and to the design of interventions for young children.

Single-case designs generally have at least three important facets: (1) measures of stability, level, and trend of behavior; (2) an introduction of the intervention while maintaining the measurement procedures; and (3) the evaluation of a well-specified intervention over substantial time periods. The outcomes of observations are graphically represented. This visual presentation is used to help overcome the natural limitations of interpreting complex assessment information (although some argue for statistical approaches).

Interventions require data-based modifications. Time-series methods may be used to monitor trends in behavior and the effects of interventions. Lastly, they can be applied broadly to philosophically different interventions and may be used to track behaviors when decisions are made not to intervene.

Professional Practices and Single-Case Designs

Two basic reasons for using single-case designs are to evaluate the effectiveness of interventions and to compare the effects of alternative treatments. Many of the research designs are quite useful for professional-practice decisions. We have elected to not go into detail on this topic because basic information on designs is widely available. Also, we recommend that complementary training in single-case research designs be covered in a separate course. Our goal here is to place accountability methods in the context of professional practices with preschool children.

Conditions and Design Notations. Conditions refer to stable procedures for different phases of the assessment-intervention process. The data in each condition are used to (a) provide information about current performance, (b) predict future performance, and (c) test predictions from previous phases or evaluate interventions (Kazdin, 1982). Thus throughout an intervention, specified conditions must remain consistent if comparisons are to be made over time.

Baseline is the term used to describe level, variability, and trend of behavior *before* the intervention. Another important and realistic view is that baseline data reflect the intervention that is in effect in the environment before a new intervention begins. Level refers to frequency or prevalence of behavior; variability refers to differences in level among observation sessions. For example, a child may have three tantrums on Wednesday and eight on Thursday. Trends are noted across observation sessions and may reflect improving, stable, or deteriorating situations, or observations may be too variable to be characterized by trends. In graphing baseline and intervention phases, the horizontal axis represents time (days or sessions) and the vertical axis represents a quality of behavior (frequency, prevalence, and so on). In some cases a baseline may be *reconstructed* using archival records such as attendance or discipline notes to parents (Bloom & Fischer, 1982). *Retrospective* baselines result from histories given by caregivers. Reports of specific acts such as firesetting or bedwetting may serve as retrospective baselines. Because of errors of memory and verbal reports, a conservative recommendation is that retrospective baselines should be used only with behaviors having zero or 100 percent rates of occurrence (Gelfand & Hartmann, 1984).

The baseline condition is called Phase A; B, C, and so on refer to different intervention phases. Combined treatments are noted through letters depicting discrete components (for example, BC may stand for tokens plus time out). The use of a prime (B', B", B"') indicates that slight deviations were used. Such systematic changes are basic for parametric designs that evaluate such factors as duration and frequency of treatment. Examples include varying the length of time out, or the time interval used for a DRO (Differential Reinforcement of Other behavior). If an intervention was ineffective, it serves as a baseline for the next intervention. However, when baseline phases are alternated with intervention phases, the second and subsequent baselines are altered by the effects of interventions and so are not exactly comparable to the preintervention baseline.

A-B Design. An A-B design represents a baseline followed by an intervention condition. This is not a strong design for a research study, but it is sufficient when the primary goal is to ascertain improved adaptation or skill development, not to demonstrate validity for an intervention. There are many threats to internal validity for A-B designs because of potential unknown factors that may bring about change in behavior. Alternatively, the A-B design is viewed by some as a "cornerstone of accountability" (Barlow, Hayes, & Nelson, 1984, p. 182).

The B design may be used for accountability. The B

notation indicates that a treatment was monitored throughout the intervention but a baseline condition was not established. This might be done when intervening in crisis situations or consulting with a teacher or parent when an intervention is already in place. In fact, it may be highly unusual that a child is experiencing difficulty and nothing is being done. The B design may help evaluate naturalistic interventions, and while not acceptable from a research standpoint, it is still much more desirable than not evaluating an intervention. Conclusions can be made about behavior but not about intervention effectiveness, because the natural course of the behavior is unknown. In other words, the child's behavior may have improved regardless of the intervention.

A-B-A-B or Withdrawal Designs. A-B-A-B designs are a part of a family that includes A-B and B designs. The reason for using the A-B-A-B design is that it provides two chances to observe treatment effects and thus to strengthen conclusions (see Figure 5.1). More complicated designs employing additional phase changes have been used to compare treatments or components of treatments. A related, strong practitioner design is represented by B-A-B (Bloom & Fischer, 1982).

We realize that some concerns about the withdrawal phase may be voiced, and so we summarize some of the attractive features of the design that fit the realities of professional practices. When the intervention is withdrawn and the behavior does not drop to baseline levels, there is evidence that the intervention effects may be durable. In this case, it is important not to provide unnecessary treatments. Also, the second baseline does not have to be long. A possible misconception is that the intervention is withdrawn to "produce deterioration"; rather it is withdrawn to permit evaluation of treatment effects. Sometimes, a good rationale for caregivers is to "take a break" from the intervention and to "see where things are going." Also, since interventions cannot continue indefinitely, it is important to plan for withdrawals. Lastly, withdrawals may occur naturally due to illness or other circumstances. While they are not as convincing as planned withdrawals, these breaks still may help with the evaluation of interventions.

Figure 5.1. A-B-A-B Design.

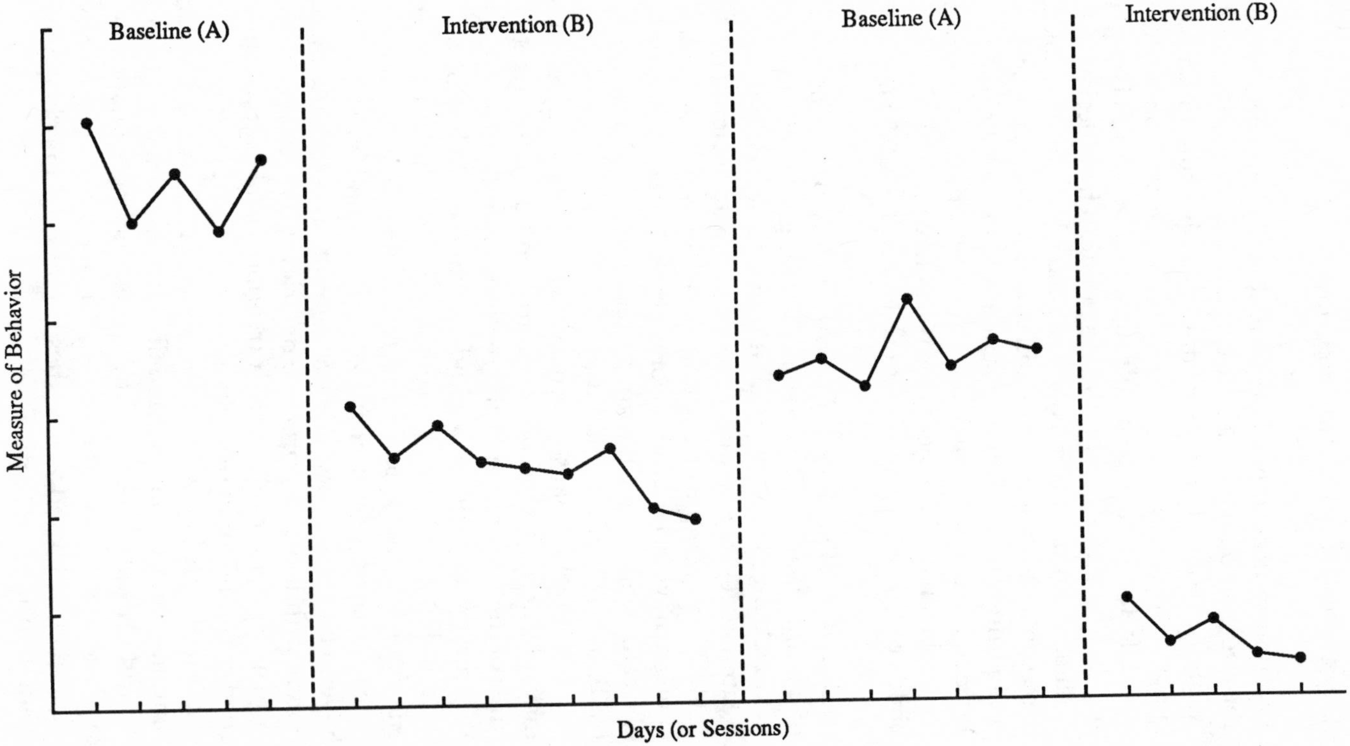

Changing-Criterion Designs. One logical way to view changing-criterion designs is that they are A-B designs on a repeated basis (Barlow, Hayes, & Nelson, 1984). They are useful when it is reasonable to specify a desired pattern of behaviors, and to change the objectives in a stepwise, gradual, or progressive fashion. Changing-criterion designs may be used for goal setting to accelerate or decelerate behaviors and to shape desired levels of performance. Shifts in criteria serve as replications of intervention effects (see Figure 5.2). The design may be useful without a baseline condition.

Sainato, Strain, Lefebvre, and Rapp (1987) used a variation of a changing-criterion design applied to levels of teacher commands and the rate and quality of group responses of preschool children. Also, changing-criterion designs may be very useful for caregivers or children who feel initially overwhelmed by the magnitude of behavioral change needed. For example, the design may be useful for self-monitoring programs for parents to reduce shouting or excessive reprimands, or to set goals for children who are socially withdrawn.

Multiple Baseline Designs. One significant practitioner feature of multiple baseline designs is that they often unfold naturally. They may be applied to interventions across (a) settings (or instructional time periods), (b) behaviors, or (c) children. Also, they are useful when interventions cannot be withdrawn. Because concurrent measures are taken, the design also can be used to study generalization (across settings, behaviors, or children).

The logic is easy for caregivers to understand. A basic assumption is that the target behaviors are independent but will respond to the same treatment. Thus, multiple baseline designs involve simple replications (A-B) of the same intervention across settings, behavior, or different children. Two baselines are useful for practice; for research purposes, three or more are recommended.

An example of a multiple baseline design across settings is depicted in Figure 5.3. Such a design could be used to identify an effective treatment for a behavior in one setting (a resource room), to study the effectiveness of the intervention in

Figure 5.2. Changing-Criterion Design.

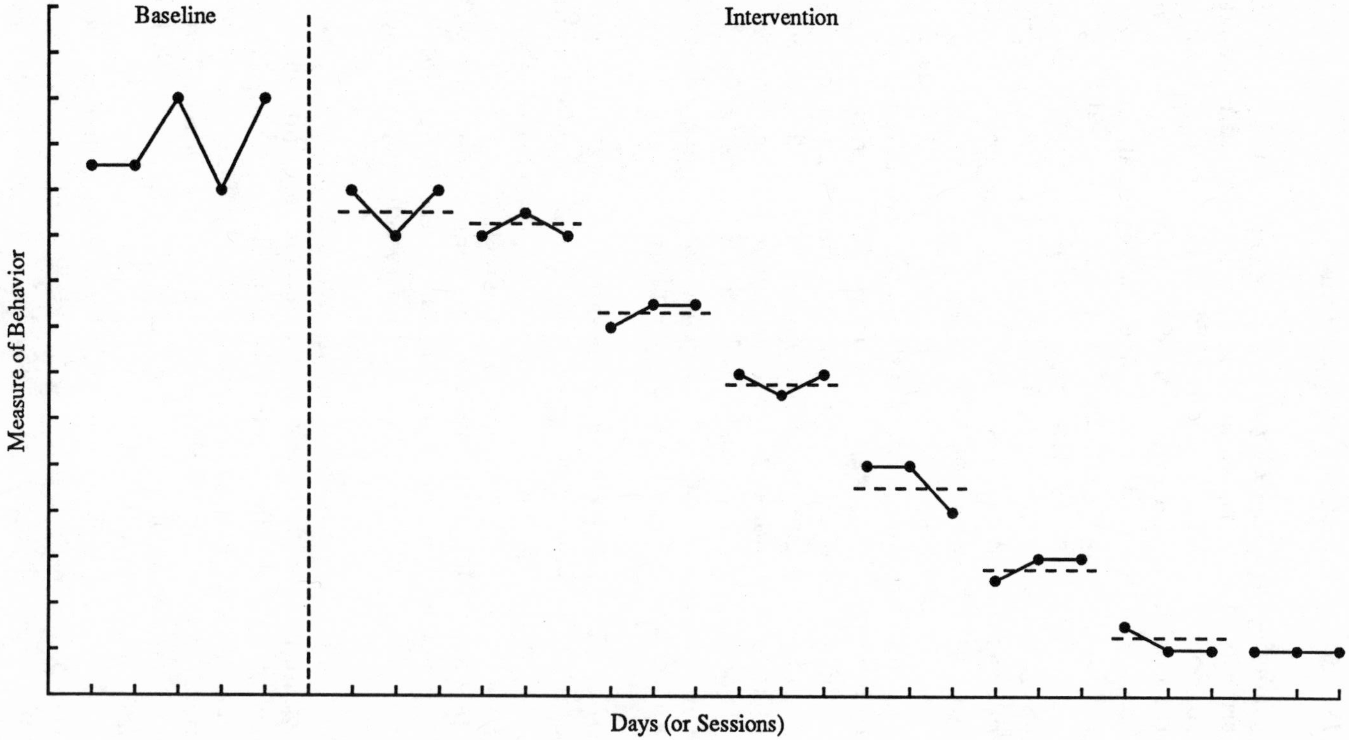

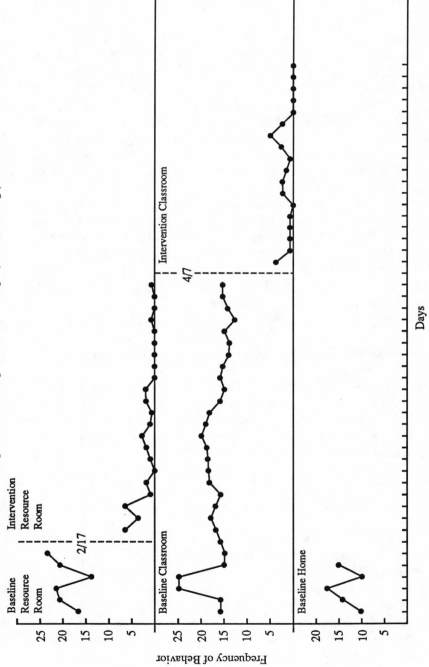

Figure 5.3. Multiple Baseline Design (Across Settings).

Source: Poth, R. L., & Barnett, D. W. (1983). Reduction of a behavioral tic with a preschooler using relaxation and self-control techniques across settings. *School Psychology Review, 17,* 322–330.

another setting (the classroom), and to carry over the intervention to a third setting (the home environment). Poth and Barnett (1983) used this design to identify an effective treatment for the ticlike behavior described in Chapter Seven.

Examples of multiple baseline designs across behaviors may include separate baselines for whining, tantruming, and aggressive acts. Russo and Koegel (1977) used this design to evaluate the integration of an autistic child by modifying, in turn, social behaviors, self-stimulation, and appropriate responses to verbal commands (see Chapter Ten).

Multiple baselines also may be conducted across subjects. Frequently, several children in a class have similar types of problem behaviors (such as social withdrawal). After a baseline period, an intervention may be implemented with one child, followed by other children who have the same problem behaviors. The Classroom Manager intervention (Sainato, Maheady, & Shook, 1986) is an example of a multiple baseline across children described as socially withdrawn (see Chapter Eleven).

The *multiple probe design* is an important variation of multiple baseline designs (Horner & Baer, 1978). The major difference is that continuous measurement is not a requirement. Instead, brief probes or data points are used to monitor baseline conditions and treatment effects. The practicalities are well suited for evaluating instruction and for situations where frequent measures are not feasible or may result in changes in behavior. An important assumption for the use of a multiple probe design is that the child's behavior is stable and not likely to change without intervention. One application includes evaluating instruction for complex skill sequences.

Alternating-Treatment Designs. The alternating-treatment design has many important features for evaluating professional practice. Most significantly, it is useful for evaluating different interventions. Since it involves the rapid, usually semirandom alteration of two or more treatments, this design may be used to quickly compare the effectiveness of alternative interventions. The question of relative effectiveness of interventions is ubiquitous in practice but is frequently associated with differences of opinion or judgment rather than data. The logic is that different levels of behavior will be associated with different conditions or interventions. Other designs used to compare interventions may be longer and more cumbersome (such as A-B-C-B-C).

Conditions may include treatment components, dimensions of treatment, time of day, settings, or behavior change agents. The rapid alteration can be based on natural units by comparing interventions across similar morning versus afternoon conditions such as freeplay, snack time, or bus behavior. Each time the child is scheduled for an intervention condition, it is alternated.

Another feature of the alternating-treatment design is that it can be used with or without a baseline condition. A modified baseline can be incorporated into the intervention by comparing an intervention condition to the data from an alternating nonintervention condition. (While useful, this baseline condition is not the same as a preintervention baseline or natural baseline.) The design also may be used with highly variable behavior. After comparing interventions, the alternating-treatment design ends with the more effective treatment (see Figure 5.4).

In this design, as with others, there are limits and potential problem areas (Barlow, Hayes, & Nelson, 1984). There may be confounding or interference between the conditions or interventions. Also, the conditions may be too brief to examine intervention outcomes. The design may need to be counterbalanced over many variables, such as teacher or time of day. For this reason, we recommend natural conditions as units of analysis.

Sherburne, Utley, McConnell, and Gannon (1988) used an alternating-treatment design, along with a withdrawal phase, to evaluate two interventions aimed at reducing violent and aggressive play. One condition included a contingent statement (a brief reminder and warning) and time out. The children were allowed to participate in violent theme play (involving guns, death, sounds of exploding bombs) only on a small rug identified for such use. Time out was used for occurrences of hitting, biting, and so on. A second condition, without the rug present, employed verbal prompts, inappropriate play was interrupted, and a suggestion was made to engage in alternative

Figure 5.4. Alternating-Treatment Design.

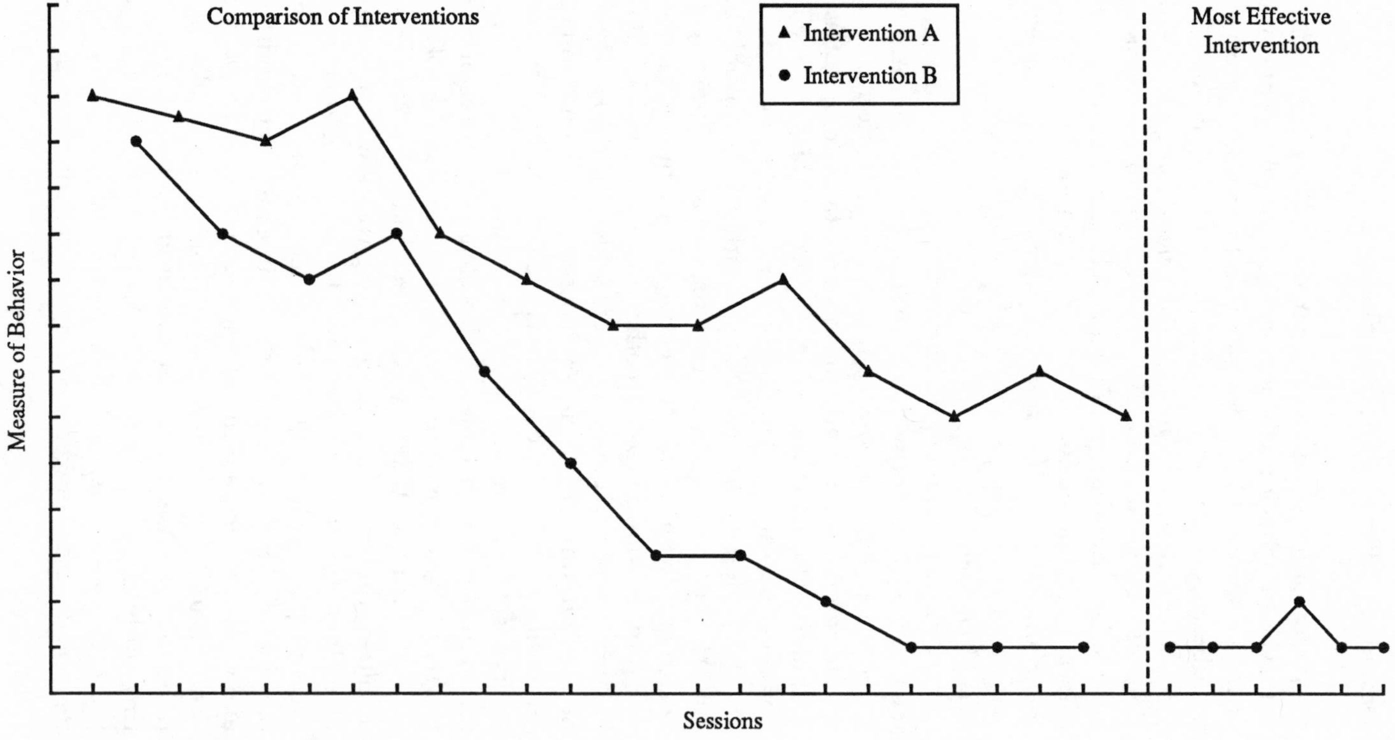

behavior. The two intervention conditions were counterbalanced across two freeplay periods. While both procedures were somewhat successful when compared to the baseline condition, the first was more effective.

Interpretations of Data

There are standard ways of visually evaluating the effectiveness of interventions. Strategies for visual analysis are summarized in Exhibit 5.4. The most basic for professional practices involve changes in behavior level and trend (increasing, decreasing, or stable).

Trend lines are easy to compute and useful for assisting with interpretation (Bailey, 1984; Kazdin, 1984). Examples of trend lines for two different phases are presented in Figure 5.5. While developed to analyze semilog charts (discussed below), the procedure can be used with ordinary graph paper (Kazdin, 1984). Based on procedures established by White (1974) and Koenig (1972), the steps for drawing a trend line for individual phases are (a) divide the data points in half by the median number of days or sessions, (b) divide each half into halves, (c) find the median value or rate of performance, (d) connect the two intersections, and (e) if necessary, adjust the line by keeping it

Exhibit 5.4. Visual Analysis of Time-Series Data.

1.	Stability of baseline
2.	Variability of behavior within phases
3.	Variability of behavior between phases
4.	Overlap of scores of adjacent phases
5.	Number of data points in each phase
6.	Changes in trend within phases
7.	Changes in trend between adjacent phases
8.	Changes in level between phases
9.	Analysis of data across similar phases
10.	Evaluation of the overall pattern of the data

Source: Adapted from Parsonson, B. S., & Baer, D. M. (1978). The analysis and presentation of graphic data. In T. R. Kratochwill (Ed.), *Single subject research: Strategies for evaluating change* (pp. 101–165). Orlando, FL: Academic Press. Reprinted with permission.

Figure 5.5. Drawing Trend Lines.

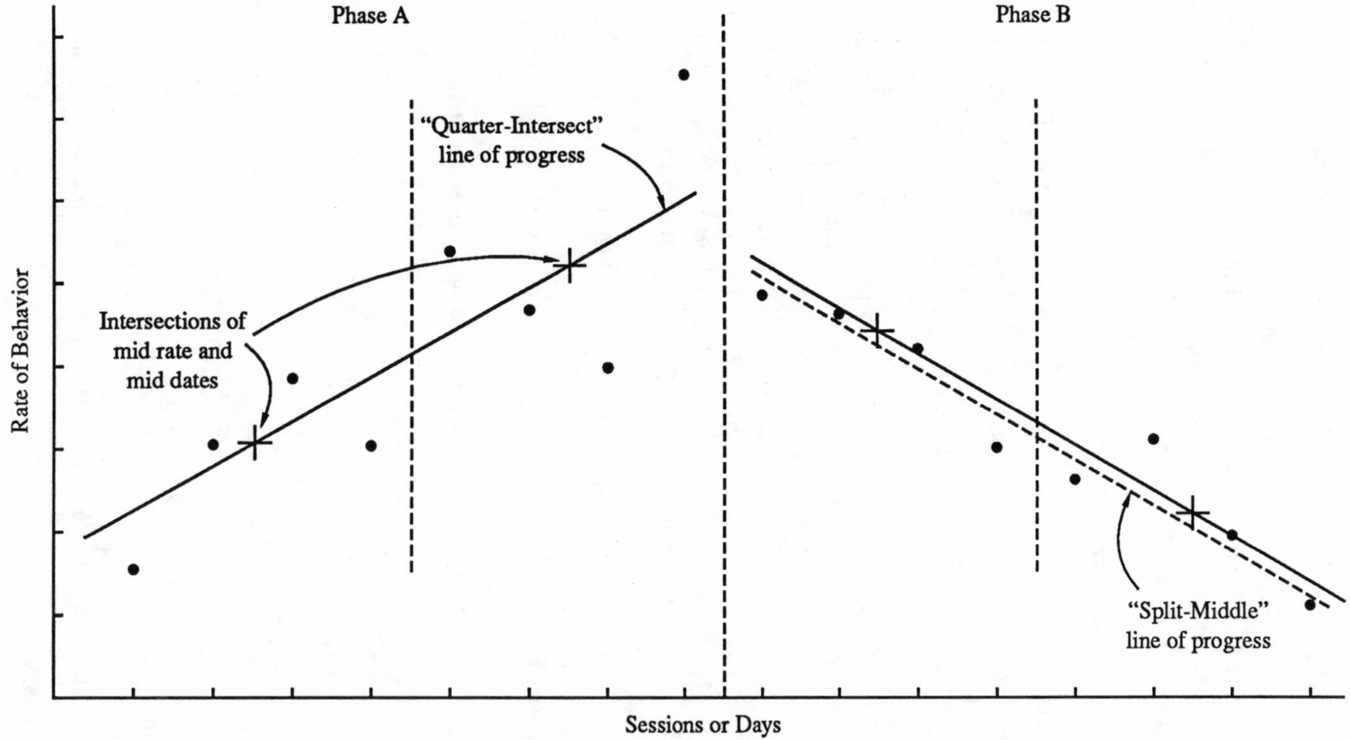

parallel to the intersect line so that half the data fall above and half below the *split-middle* line of progress. Separate trend lines are drawn for each phase.

While description is beyond the scope of the chapter, in some cases there are advantages to plotting children's behavior on a *semilogarithmic* chart. Most charts in the behavioral literature are based on equal intervals. However, when an equal-interval graph is used, certain comparisons may be misleading. One example is changes in behavior rates. A child with fifteen aggressive acts on one day and ten aggressive on another, will represent the same distance on a graph as thirty aggressive acts on one day and twenty-five on another. However, the *rate* of change is much greater in the first case. As discussed by White and Haring (1980) and Wolery, Bailey, and Sugai (1988), the use of a "semilog" chart may more accurately portray changes in rates of behavior and thus may affect intervention decisions. Rather than equal scale intervals, the vertical scale on semilog charts is based on logarithmic units to preserve equal relative changes that occur in behavior. Proportionate changes in rates are represented by the same distance on the chart. In contrast, on standard graph paper, equal absolute changes are represented by the same distance on the chart (Bailey, 1984).

There are numerous challenges embedded in the analysis of intervention outcomes. Decision reliability includes the study of outcomes associated with methodological differences in data analysis (see Barnett & Macmann, in press). While statistical methods also may be used to analyze data, they are not typically useful in practice. Problems are related mostly to the insufficient number of data points that result from applied work. Visual data analysis also has resulted in controversy (Furlong & Wampold, 1982; Greenwood & Matyas, 1990; Grigg, Snell, & Loyd, 1989). The major problems pertain to judgmental differences, and differences that stem from alternative ways data may be graphed.

Decision validity of interventions pertains to the significance of behavioral change and to the planned maintenance and generalization of change. The essentials are tied to the measurement of important personal and social intervention outcomes over substantial time periods. The challenges of these goals are part of the reason for our stress on ecobehavioral analysis and problem solving in natural environments. In sum, visual analysis is the most reasonable approach available, but like any assessment method, it may contain both systematic and random errors of measurement.

Data-Based Decision Making

"'Decision rules' are procedures which guide the evaluation of information to determine if changes in methods and/or content are necessary" (Liberty, 1988, p. 55). Wolery, Bailey, and Sugai (1988), building on the work of White and Haring (1980), and Haring, Liberty, and White (1980), provide guidelines for altering instructional strategies using data-based decisions.

If the guidelines discussed below are to be used, four requirements must be met. First, the goal for intervention and a date by which it is to be attained must be specified. "A well-specified goal is stated as a full behavioral objective, including the acts to be performed, the conditions, and the standards or levels of accomplishment" (Sulzer-Azaroff & Mayer, 1991, p. 290). Second, intervention effectiveness is determined by analyzing trend lines or "lines of progress" and "minimum 'celeration lines" drawn from the present level of performance to the point at which the goal is reached. The line describes the rate of change or progress needed for the child to reach a desired goal. Third, as the data are graphed, intervention effectiveness is monitored frequently by comparing the data to the minimum 'celeration line. Fourth, treatment integrity of the intervention must be ensured.

Once these initial requirements are met, data-based decision guidelines can be used to determine whether intervention modifications are needed. While many questions related to data-based decision making remain, the guidelines described by Wolery, Bailey, and Sugai (1988, pp. 133–137) can help practitioners monitor trends in behaviors and the need for instructional or procedural changes.

1. If correct responses are increasing and errors are decreasing or stable, no modifications are necessary and the intervention should be continued. The minimum 'celeration line is used to check progress toward goals.

2. If only some (for example, 20 percent to 50 percent) of the tasks are performed consistently, the intervention is having limited success or progress is stalled. The intervention should be sliced back to skills the child is able to perform, while teaching one or two new steps in the sequence at a time. High error rates along with some successes also may reveal the need to try a different instructional procedure.

3. If correct responses are near zero, the intervention is having no success. The task is too difficult. The decision should be to step back and teach earlier, prerequisite skills.

4. If correct responses are highly variable or correct responses decrease significantly, compliance may be the problem. The assumption is that the child can complete a task but does not. Compliance training may be needed.

5. If correct responses are stalled at a fairly high level (say, 80–90 percent correct), but rate is not improving, different contingencies or incentives and additional practice time may be required. The child may be bored, and it may be necessary to move to a new phase of learning to build fluency.

6. If a child has met the specified criteria for accuracy and fluency (or rate), it is time to introduce a new skill. The learned skill may serve as a foundation for subsequent skills, and continued practice may be necessary.

The use of formal decision rules to improve practice for children with severe instructional and behavioral problems is gaining substantial attention. For further reading, we recommend Evans and Meyer (1985) and the edited book by Haring (1988).

Naturalistic Decision Making

The methods described here are very similar to those in single-case designs, except that additional procedures have been adapted to facilitate the analysis of professional judgments in ongoing phases. The decision model is based on general principles, related steps, and techniques: (1) ecobehavioral analysis, to evaluate functioning of child systems and barriers to system functioning; (2) decision reliability for targets of change efforts based on collaborative problem solving and analyses of research; (3) naturalistic intervention design, based on existing skills of caregivers; (4) ongoing measurement of behavior and treatment integrity; and (5) decision validity, based on the analysis of intervention effectiveness.

A hypothetical series of decisions is displayed in Figure 5.6. The first row depicts ongoing ecological assessment, placing the child within a family, school, and community context. Evans and Nelson wrote: "Any model which proposes that behaviors interact with each other (and the environment) in a reciprocal or dynamic fashion implicates some type of systems mapping as an appropriate assessment goal" (1986, p. 615). The eco-map (as adapted from Hartman, 1978) uses symbols to depict relevant people and relationships. It is reconfigured as necessary in each phase change. The eco-map in the figure portrays conflicted relationships between the child (4) and the teacher (T), between the teacher and a representative from an outside agency (OA) that is recommending mainstreaming, and between the agency and the school psychologist [SP]. It represents the psychologist's understanding of the situation.

The second row shows multiple target behaviors. Changes in behaviors are evaluated through graphic analysis. Two behaviors are recorded in Phase I. New or postponed target behaviors are depicted in Phases II and IV. Phase III data includes both the trends for behaviors subject to intervention and the one that is being monitored.

The third row, based on "Think Aloud" procedures, summarizes the guiding factors used to develop the plans: target

Figure 5.6. A Prototype for Practitioner Time-Series Methods.

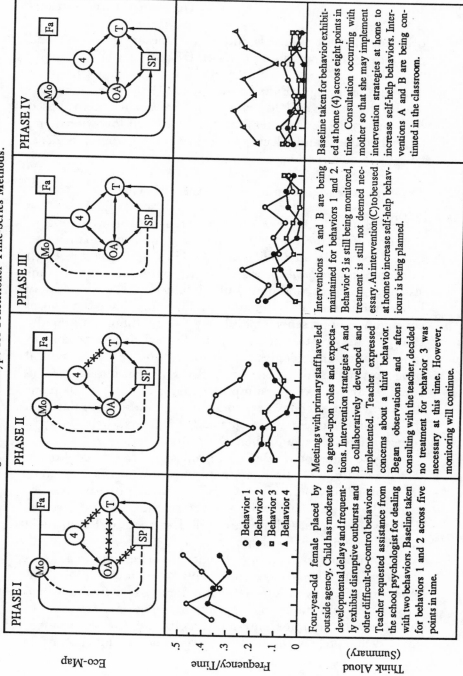

	PHASE I	PHASE II	PHASE III	PHASE IV
Eco-Map				
Frequency/Time (Summary)	Behavior 1 Behavior 2 Behavior 3 Behavior 4			
Think Aloud (Summary)	Four-year-old female placed by outside agency. Child has moderate developmental delays and frequently exhibits disruptive outbursts and other difficult-to-control behaviors. Teacher requested assistance from the school psychologist for dealing with two behaviors. Baseline taken for behaviors 1 and 2 across five points in time.	Meetings with primary staff have led to agreed-upon roles and expectations. Intervention strategies A and B collaboratively developed and implemented. Teacher expressed concerns about a third behavior. Began observations and after consulting with the teacher, decided no treatment for behavior 3 was necessary at this time. However, monitoring will continue.	Interventions A and B are being maintained for behaviors 1 and 2. Behavior 3 is still being monitored, treatment is still not deemed necessary. An intervention (C) to be used at home to increase self-help behaviours is being planned.	Baseline taken for behavior exhibited at home (4) across eight points in time. Consultation occurring with mother so that she may implement intervention strategies at home to increase self-help behaviors. Interventions A and B are being continued in the classroom.

behavior selection (Phase I), intervention design (Phase II), and evaluation and replanning (Phases III and IV).

For each step, specific decision models can be used for intervention design. Evans and Meyer (1985) provide an extensive discussion and flow charts representing a systems-based decision model for teachers that may be used for prioritizing target behaviors and selecting interventions for persons with severe behavior handicaps.

Professional Practices and Time-Series Methods

Time-series methods are considered fundamental to evaluating interventions, but there are difficulties and complexities in their use.

First, *phases* are traditionally used in single-subject research to denote *consistent conditions*. However, conditions are only consistent to a degree, and in real-life circumstances, even this may be a tenuous assertion. In many situations involving behavioral consultation in preschools, it is likely that conditions are rapidly changing in ways that are only partially revealed to the consultant. Changes in ecologies can profoundly influence behavioral programs. Thus, the term *phase* reflects the consultant's understanding and working assumptions that are expressed as plans and professional behaviors. Phase changes also are related to the persistence of change agents and caregivers, their ability to cope with realities, and their creativity.

A second potential point of concern is the concept of internal validity, a requirement that is basic to outcome research. Internal validity pertains to evidence that the treatment—not external or extraneous factors—was responsible for the outcome. Threats to internal validity are well described by Kratochwill (1978); we will briefly review several.

Multiple treatment interference is a potential threat to internal validity if two or more interventions are introduced. Combinations of interventions make it difficult to determine which effects are attributable to a specific intervention. However, in practice, various intervention strategies are often combined, either deliberately or through parent and teacher embellishments (an issue of treatment integrity). While experimental design strategies that compare treatments may fit professional-practice circumstances, ideally they need to be planned before starting the interventions. Most important, time-series methods can be used to evaluate an overall plan. Attributing success to individual facets of the plan may not be possible in many circumstances, but the evaluation of the overall plan is essential.

Another pertinent threat to internal validity involves reactive interventions (Kratochwill, 1978). These are similar to regression effects, where the professional intervenes in reaction to changes in the data. For example, if intervening in a crisis situation (B design), there is an increased probability that the situation will improve as a result of naturally occurring processes rather than (or in addition to) the planned intervention. Practical considerations should prevail, and overrule the need to provide evidence for internal validity. Still, general time-series methods are appropriate for accountability in such circumstances.

Third, in many situations, the requirements of data collection are imposing. For example, it may not be feasible to obtain baseline data. In such cases, time-series methods can still be used to keep track of the trend of the behavior, and to adjust or replan interventions based on the data obtained. Also, the requirement for continuous data collection may be eased with carefully planned time sampling, probes, and structured participant observations.

Fourth, in most (perhaps all) situations, it is necessary to assess outcomes in multiple ways, including behaviors that were not specifically treated and behaviors in alternative settings. This can be done by using a multibehavioral code and tracking caregivers' behavior, satisfaction with the intervention, and difficulties involved with maintaining behaviors. Outcomes may focus on *reducing* the necessity of such caregiver behaviors as extensive monitoring.

In summary, time-series methods are a robust means of determining changes that occur in behavior. To accommodate real-world exigencies, professionals can use "core elements" to evaluate the overall effectiveness of interventions (Hayes, 1981).

Most important, single-case designs imply that behavior is continuously assessed, along with the effects of well-defined and -executed interventions.

Summary and Conclusions

This chapter focused on conceptual and research-based strategies for selecting target behaviors and intervention methods. The selection process goes beyond the technical aspects of assessing behavior; it requires judgments that may range from straightforward to complex. At the focal point are general planning guidelines for practitioners. Specific attention also is required for the maintenance and generalization of behavior. Evaluating interventions for both intended and unintended results is critically important. Many strategies associated with single-case research designs are well suited to professional practice.

Intervention design is guided by the results of assessment. Since these results may be fallible, so may intervention design. We stressed the basics: ecobehavioral principles and collaborative problem-solving methods. While not fail-safe, these methods make it easier to analyze problem situations and to evaluate decision reliability (the convergence of decisions across reasonable approaches to assessment) and decision validity (which emphasizes the personal and social outcomes of decisions).

PART TWO

BASIC INTERVENTIONS

6

Developing New Behaviors and Modifying Existing Behaviors

ONE OF THE MOST SIGNIFICANT FOUNDATIONS FOR PROFESSIONAL practice is the analysis of research-based interventions. In Chapters Six and Seven we review interventions that have research support and that have been used in a wide range of settings. In later chapters, we present examples of intervention applications that have been specifically oriented to home and school.

Naturalistic Learning Experiences[1]

Perhaps the most important foundation of early intervention, and the most difficult to rectify when not present, is a responsive, guiding, caring, and nurturing adult. Safe physical environments that are conducive to development are also necessary. Ecobehavioral assessment and naturalistic intervention design are two important ways to evaluate and plan for these factors. A naturalistic decision model is based on consultation with caregivers and focuses on children's adaptation to home, school, and community environments.

The learning and mediational environments of families (see Laosa & Sigel, 1982) and classrooms (see Rogers-Warren, 1982) may be a point of broad-based intervention. *Mediation* refers to the way adults (or peers) select, focus, organize, and

[1]John D. Hall contributed to writing this section.

145

give meaning to experiences for children. Adult–child and child–child interactions that occur naturally in a variety of situations and environments provide a rich oppportunity for facilitating children's cognitive, language, and social development. For parents, interacting with a child in an educative manner during daily events — dressing, meals, television viewing, reading, play, shopping, or household tasks — holds many opportunities for teaching basic concepts, problem solving, and related language skills within the context of an important relationship. For teachers, classroom and instructional design includes the development of play and learning areas that help promote curiosity, task engagement, and appropriate peer interaction. Opportunities for direct and incidental teaching occur during planned instruction and on serendipitous occasions.

The power of even brief encounters may be greatly underestimated by parents and teachers. Cognitive, language, and preacademic stimulation occurs through play and reading to children. Modeling necessary skills and encouraging social maturity and coping occurs within real-life contexts of problem solving and resolving conflicts. Learning takes place in an interpersonal context characterized by the caregiver's responsivity and warmth. Adult–child interactions should avoid unnecessary restriction and harsh physical and mental punishment.

Play experiences are particularly important. Hobbs wrote, "A child should know joy" (1966, p. 1113). Play behaviors can be explored through interviews and observations. Interventions may include (a) structuring or monitoring play experiences that incorporate cognitive, language, affective, social, and motor learning; (b) facilitating or modifying adult–child and child–peer interactions; and (c) enabling appropriate periods of solitary play. The literature on children's play is voluminous. In subsequent discussions, we elaborate on specific interventions that involve play.

In sum, the most significant elements of intervention design depend on responsive and capable adults and on safe environments that support a wide range of learning objectives that include peers, interesting materials, and functional activities. Initial intervention efforts should be directed toward assisting adults who are available to children and who are capable of fulfilling these roles. Many children are being raised in precarious environments. For this reason, throughout this text we have stressed naturalistic principles in intervention design, because they are intended to fit exigencies and they enhance acceptability and generalizability. We resume these discussions within specific contexts of family and school in later chapters.

Professionals involved in the design of early intervention efforts should consider basic procedures, rather than more complicated ones, at least initially. We present four fundamental intervention strategies that are potentially powerful but can easily be overlooked or misused.

Four Naturally Occurring Strategies

These four strategies are ubiquitous. They are used by effective caregivers to teach, eliminate, shape, and maintain many types of behaviors. However, each may be easily misapplied or abused, and thus also may contribute to maladaptive behavior. Therefore, these strategies deserve systematic attention in interviews and observations, as a starting place for intervention design.

Differential or Systematic Attention. Differential attention consists of approval. It is defined as social reinforcement given to a child contingent on the display of desired behavior. Hall and Hall (1980a) described it as "noticing when someone is doing something desired and then giving him attention by commenting, looking at, touching or expressing approval" (p. 8). The effectiveness of differential attention has been well established in varied research studies, and it is one of the best examples of a systematically replicated intervention. On the other hand, Hall and Hall wrote: "Unfortunately, many persons squander their attention and approval in an unsystematic or haphazard way — worse yet, some give nearly all their attention to unwanted behavior" (1980a, p. 4). *Misplaced* differential attention can serve to reinforce inappropriate behaviors.

Systematic attention is effective only when attention is reinforcing. If attention is not reinforcing, or is having a weak effect, then it first must be paired with an effective reinforcer. Basic steps for providing systematic attention and approval are described here (adapted from Hall and Hall except as noted).

1. Define the behavior to be changed. Systematic attention and approval are designed to increase behaviors to be strengthened. Paine and colleagues described an "if-then" good praise rule: "*If* the student is doing something you want to encourage — something you want the student to do again or do more often in the future (and if you are sure that that is what the student is doing) — then (and only then) you should praise the student for it" (1983, p. 46).

2. Set a goal for the target behavior.

3. Use basic observation procedures in measuring the behaviors to be changed.

4. Select appropriate types of attention and approval. Use a variety of different reinforcing verbalizations immediately following the desired response. Use *specific* and descriptive praise ("I like the way you helped Sally put the blocks away"). Note that praise may be easily misused or overused, or used perfunctorily. It should be convincing: genuine, warm, and sincere.

5. Think about whether to use public or private praise or both, when praise should be given, and how often. A basic principle of systematic attention is that it should occur while the targeted behavior is occurring or immediately after. Also, praise should not be used in a way that disrupts ongoing activities.

6. Systematic attention or approval also may be used in conjunction with back-up reinforcement, other interventions, and treatment packages. The most notable are compliance training and classroom management procedures discussed in later chapters. Another example is the use of positive attention in shaping programs if the child lacks the prerequisite skills or behaviors (discussed in a later section).

Planned Ignoring. Withdrawal of attention in a systematic fashion is referred to as "planned ignoring" (Hall & Hall, 1980b). It may be viewed as a form of time out in which "usual attention, physical contact, and any verbal interactions are removed for a short duration contingent upon the occurrence of the unwanted behavior" (Sulzer-Azaroff & Mayer, 1991, p. 457).

Planned ignoring will not be effective for modifying inappropriate behaviors if positive attention of the caregiver is not serving as a reinforcer. In other words, the child must be responsive to positive attention for ignoring to work as an intervention. Even if the caregiver is appropriately ignoring the misbehavior, the attention of others (peers, adults) may sustain the behavior. Also, ignoring is an aversive procedure. Thus, children may become upset and undesirable behaviors may increase when the procedures are first used.

Hall and Hall (1980b) suggest the following steps for planned ignoring:

1. First inform the child of the inappropriate behavior and of the plans to ignore the behavior. Make the statement only once.

2. Develop specific procedures that fit the behavior, child, and setting. As an example, for a child who whines or tantrums, the adult will focus attention away from the child, show a passive expression, remain silent, and withdraw from the immediate setting within five seconds. At first the undesirable behavior may increase but over time it will likely decrease.

3. Use the procedure consistently. This is essential. Inappropriate behaviors may easily be reinforced inadvertently. Consider difficult circumstances and settings before deciding to use planned ignoring.

4. Combine the intervention with social attention for appropriate behavior. One suggestion is to have the caregiver list behaviors that will receive contingent positive attention and approval.

The term *extinction* is closely related and easily confused. It means no longer reinforcing a behavior that was previously reinforced. All sources of reinforcement that are maintaining the behavior need to be removed for the length of time extinction is in effect. Several characteristics of extinction are well established by extensive research. Its effect in reducing behavior is gradual rather than immediate. At first, the target behaviors are likely to increase in rate and intensity. As the target response decreases, the behavior may be "extinguished," only to reappear at the beginning of a new session. This is termed *spontaneous recovery*. The predicted consequence is important for teachers and parents. Although extinction has been used successfully for a wide range of problem behaviors such as crying, whining, and tantruming, in fact, both planned ignoring and extinction may be difficult for many caregivers to apply.

Modeling. We make reference to modeling throughout the chapters on interventions. Indeed, "most human behavior is learned by observation through modeling" (Bandura, 1986, p. 47). Through observing the behavior of others, children learn rules for behavior that later serve as guides for action. In addition, values, attitudes, patterns of cognition, cognitive competencies, and the consequences of behaviors also are learned by observing others.

In addition to teaching new behaviors, observational learning may have the effect of strengthening, weakening, or facilitating learned behavior. Basic to these processes is observing the consequences of behavioral acts for others. For example, it is safe to say that many children in a preschool classroom have in their repertoires behaviors that are inappropriate to the school or other settings (hitting, spitting, swearing, and so on). When one child behaves inappropriately and receives negative consequences, all the other children may become more "restrained" in similar behaviors. However, if the consequences for inappropriate behaviors are not effective, more children may exhibit the behavior. As another example, if children with high status in the classroom often share and other children observe that, sharing is likely to increase. Another possible outcome is that modeling may enhance the value of the object (or setting) that was the focal point of the modeled behavior. Bandura concluded that the effects of modeling depend on the information that is actually conveyed: "The direction and strength of the impact of such information on personal restraint largely depends on three factors: on observers' judgments of their ability to execute the modeled behavior, on their perception of the modeled actions as producing rewarding or punishing consequences, and on their inferences that similar or unlike consequences would result if they themselves were to engage in analogous activities" (1986, p. 49).

Emotions are "coeffects" of learning and performing (Bandura, 1986). Emotions are an inextricable part of social interactions, and emotional reactions to events are pervasively modeled. Gottman argued that "emotional development organizes social development" (1986, p. 85). Because of these properties, modeling may be useful for dealing with fears and phobias.

Observational learning involves four major processes (Bandura, 1986).

Attentional processes focus analysis on what is observed. Features of the modeled activities and the cognitive processes of the observer both determine what events will be observed, how they are perceived and interpreted, and how they affect subsequent behaviors.

Retentional processes incorporate the ways brief experiences are encoded or remembered. "Retention involves an active process of transforming and restructuring information about events" (Bandura, 1985, p. 90).

Production processes involve the ability to carry out acts based on a cognitive or symbolic organization of the response and a plan for the activity. Actual performance is compared to the conceptual plan. Points of analysis include the physiological or developmental limitations of the person and any factors related to prior learning.

Motivational processes have to do with whether a new behavior is learned and whether a learned behavior is performed. The reinforcement may be external, based on environmental contingencies and on the consequences of behavior. Reinforcement also may be self-generated or vicarious.

All four processes are important for understanding the effects of observational learning. Furthermore, positive changes in behavior can occur through any combination of the four: (1) by improvements in selective observation (attentional processes); (2) by improvements in memory encoding; (3) by enhancement of the child's ability to perform based on sensory, motor, and cognitive processes; and (4) by improvements in the anticipation of the consequences of acts. It may be important to assess what relevant people (child, caregivers, and consultant) *believe* about the likelihood of change.

The practical applications of modeling are unlimited. Interventions that involve observational learning may be applied to individual children, groups of children, parents, and teachers. Furthermore, opportunities for learning through modeling may be planned or unplanned (Striefel, 1981). One of the major points of assessment is the evaluation of the models that are available to children. Striefel includes detailed practical guidelines for using modeling; two important considerations include selecting models and encouraging imitation of the modeled behavior. Wolery, Bailey, and Sugai (1988) discuss vicarious reinforcement of others' behavior as a basic indirect strategy for behavioral change. Children who are behaving in the desired manner are reinforced while the target child observes. Specific examples of interventions using modeling are given in this and in subsequent chapters.

Reprimands. Reprimands are perhaps the most common overt strategy for behavior control. They can be used in combination with many other interventions. However, when used ineffectively, they can intensify maladaptive behaviors. Most important, reprimands should be used in the context of positive attention. Specific training for caregivers in the use of reprimands is often needed.

Van Houten (1980) identified the following guidelines for the use of reprimands.

1. Specify the inappropriate behavior, state why the behavior is inappropriate, and provide an example of an appropriate behavior.

2. Use a firm tone.
3. Use appropriate nonverbal expressions of disapproval.
4. Deliver the reprimand within close proximity.
5. Avoid ignoring inappropriate behavior.
6. Use a more intrusive intervention with a dangerous behavior.
7. Use social reinforcement for appropriate behaviors.
8. If necessary, follow reprimands with other acceptable behavioral strategies.
9. Maintain emotional control.

Developing Language Skills

Many referrals in preschool populations have to do with language problems (Snyder-McLean & McLean, 1987). Language skills are linked to cognitive and social competencies, and they are often the target of formal interventions. Numerous sources extensively discuss various language interventions. We have elected to present naturalistic strategies consistent with the purpose of the book.

Naturalistic Language Training Techniques

Naturalistic strategies focus attention on the roles and skills that caregivers need in order to help children acquire, generalize, and maintain new behaviors. The rationale is straightforward; caregivers, primarily mothers, are natural language teachers for infants and young children, and language learning is a critical part of the preschool curriculum. The most important initial aspect is adaptive caregiver–child communication. "Contingent verbal responsiveness . . . is perhaps the greatest single influence on early cognitive development" (MacPhee, Ramey, & Yeates, 1984, p. 349). In later years, pragmatic language is critical for developing social competence in peer interactions.

Learning "events" include experiences intentionally provided and those that result from incidental opportunities. Caregivers may underestimate the power of brief shared experiences; teaching can be a part of ongoing daily routines. Based on a review by Hart (1985, p. 67), the following characteristics of environments contribute to language development:

1. *Stimulation:* the richness and variety of objects and experiences provided.
2. *Adult–child ratio:* the one-to-one nature of early interactions.
3. *Topic:* child selection of the topic for interaction.
4. *Routines:* the standardized framework of early interactions.
5. *Models:* the language the child hears.
6. *Imitation:* repetition of models by child or adult.
7. *Prompts:* method of evoking language from the child.
8. *Function:* the consequences of language use for the child.

Warren and Kaiser (1986) summarized common premises of naturalistic language interventions: (a) language and communications skills are taught in natural environments, (b) a conversational context is used for acquisition and skill development, (c) dispersed trials are used, (d) learning follows the child's "attentional lead," and (e) functional reinforcers are revealed by the child's "requests and attention" (p. 291). Halle, Alpert, and Anderson (1984) and Warren and Gazdag (1990) review applications for more severely impaired young children.

Pragmatic Language. The emphasis of pragmatic language is on the real-life context of language performance. "Establishing the *function* of the communicative act is as necessary to language development as the acquisition of conventional form (syntax) and content (semantics)" (MacDonald, 1985, p. 95). Social competence is an important context for pragmatic language performance (Prutting, 1982). Parent, teacher, and peer roles and social contexts are critical for improving or facilitating language development. The analysis of pragmatics has two main thrusts (Alpert & Rogers-Warren, 1985, pp. 133–134). The first involves determining how prelinguistic and linguistic behaviors function in communication — as requests, protests, answers, vocatives, declaratives and so on. The second is evaluating social skills that tend to promote effective communication; for example, taking turns, maintaining the topic of conversation, relating new information to old, avoiding saying what the listener already is likely to be aware of, and using the apparent interest level of the listener as a cue for modifying one's verbal behavior.

In the next sections, we discuss three basic naturalistic strategies to facilitate language acquisition: mand-model, the use of brief time delays, and incidental teaching. All are based on naturally occurring strategies used by caregivers, and all have considerable experimental support (Hart, 1985).

Mand-Model. A mand is a request, question, demand, or instruction to respond (Skinner, 1957). The mand-model strategy is a systematization of a type of natural interaction between mothers and young children (typically at twelve to fifteen months) described by Bruner (1978) and Snow (1977). At the most basic level, the mother directs the child's attention, as by saying, "Look." After the child attends, the mother asks a wh—question such as "What's that?" After the child vocalizes, the mother provides a model or a label. Developmentally, labels first are object words or proper nouns (Bruner, 1978). In natural settings where language is readily acquired by children, the interaction is repeated often. While the mother's behavior may remain relatively unchanged, Bruner reported changes in child initiations of the behavior and the frequency of responses to the mother's initiations.

Rogers-Warren and Warren (1980, p. 367) outline the sequence of steps for the mand-model strategy as follows:

1. Teachers direct children's attention by providing a variety of attractive materials children want to play with.

2. When a child approaches material (such that joint teacher-child attention is focused on that material as topic), the teacher asks, "Tell me what this is" or "Tell me what you want." (Open-ended questions that require responses beyond "yes" or "no" are used.)

3. If the child does not respond or gives a minimal response, the teacher provides a model for the child to imitate. The teacher may also prompt within this step, for example, by elaborating the request to "Give me a whole sentence," and then providing a model if the child does not respond appropriately.

4. The teacher praises the child for responding appropriately to the mand, or for imitating, and gives the child the material.

As noted by Wolery, Bailey, and Sugai (1988) and Hart (1985), the mand-model technique has many potential applications across settings because of the brevity of the caregiver–child interactions. It also may have positive effects on general language behavior. Furthermore, the technique may be used naturally and systematically.

Use of a Brief Time Delay. Another normal process is that parents expect and wait for more mature forms of behavior (Hart, 1985). The use of a brief delay (five to fifteen seconds) has been found to help with the development of language (Halle, Baer, & Spradlin, 1981). Delay is an adaptation of incidental teaching (Warren & Kaiser, 1986). The delay serves as a nonverbal cue or stimulus to respond. Hart wrote, "For language acquisition to progress, it is essential that nonsocial stimuli such as materials and activities evoke verbal behavior: that a child want to talk not just to people, but about *things*. The more things in the environment that the child is interested in talking about, the greater is the pressure to acquire language as a means of communicating perceived properties, actions, and relationships" (1985, p. 85).

Halle, Baer, and Spradlin (1981) give an example: the caregiver holds a glass of juice, faces the child, and waits for the child's vocal initiation. Steps in using delay and examples of applications are summarized in Exhibit 6.1. Delay also may be used to fade from the mand-model strategy (Hart, 1985).

The use of naturalistic time delay (Wolery, Bailey, & Sugai, 1988) is related to time delay used in errorless learning (Chapter Ten). Like the mand-model technique, it is used widely in various school and home settings because it capitalizes on brief adult–child interactions and is readily learned.

Incidental Teaching. Incidental teaching takes advantage of naturally arising interactions between adults and children in un-

Exhibit 6.1. Time Delay to Increase Language Use.

1. Use with natural and functional opportunities that occur on a daily basis (freeplay, snack time, lunch)
2. Conditions
   a. The caregiver does not vocalize.
   b. The caregiver is close to the child (i.e., three feet).
   c. The caregiver's head is oriented toward the child.
   d. The child is attending to the adult.
   e. Visual (not verbal) prompts may be used.
   f. The caregiver assumes a questioning or expectant look.
   g. The caregiver may kneel to be at eye level with the child.
   h. Use a five-second delay guideline.
   i. The child's verbalizations should be contextually appropriate.
3. Examples
   a. Gross motor play: put hands on object to be moved (for example, large ball or scooter). Before the caregiver moves the object, use the delay procedure.
   b. Or, stop the moving object, and use delay (wait for request).
   c. Juice in hand, use delay (anticipated response: "I want juice").
   d. Use delay with child in need of help (as with zipper or shoelace).
   e. Use delay before receiving reinforcement (anticipated response: "I want a star").
   f. Use delay for bathroom requests.

Source: Adapted from Halle, J. W., Baer, D. M., and Spradlin, J. E. (1981). Teacher's generalized use of delay as a stimulus control procedure to increase language use in handicapped children. *Journal of Applied Behavior Analysis, 14,* pp. 389–409. Copyright ©1981 by the Society for the Experimental Analysis of Behavior. Reprinted with permission.

structured situations. Through brief interactions, adults transmit new information or enable the children to practice communication skills. Experimentally, the procedure was used to increase compound sentences in spontaneous speech (Hart & Risley, 1975, 1980, 1982), but it may have many other benefits in language as well as personal and social development. The adult focuses attention on what the child says and encourages elaboration. It is described as "loose" training that follows the child's attention; the topic is chosen by the child. Incidental teaching is one of the best examples of a language intervention that combines conversational and behavioral elements. It was developed for children with mild language problems whose language use was sufficient to provide adequate learning opportunities (Hart & Risley, 1975).

Incidental language intervention requires a caregiver to respond to the child's initial request (verbal or nonverbal) or comment with (a) attention or social praise and reinforcement; (b) a request or encouragement for more information (verbally); and (c) a statement related to the request and/or comment that may expand the child's knowledge with respect to the initial request.

Several examples follow (Barnett, Silverstein, & Miller, 1988):

Example 1

Jill: Points to doll.

Caregiver: "She's a pretty doll. What is her name?"

Jill: "Baby."

Caregiver: "Well, Baby has on a bright red dress today."

Example 2

Jill: "Help."

Caregiver: "What do you need help with, Jill?"

Jill: "Help with coat."

Caregiver: "You need help putting on your coat."

Example 3

Jill: Reaching for cup at mealtime.

Caregiver: "What do you want, Jill?"

Jill: "Cup."

Caregiver: "Good, Jill. You asked for your cup with juice."

Incidental learning strategies are expanded in Hart and Risley (1982). Exhibit 6.2 details the steps. Warren and Kaiser (1986) provide a comprehensive review of incidental teaching.

Exhibit 6.2. Incidental Teaching.

Step 1: The setting has materials and activities that are attractive and appropriate.

Step 2: The adult's attention and approval are important to the child.

Step 3: The adult waits for the child to initiate conversation.

Step 4: When the child speaks, the adult looks into the child's eyes, smiles, and focuses on the child's topic.

Step 5: If unsure of the child's topic, the adult clarifies.

Step 6: The adult asks a question that elaborates the child's language.

Step 7: The adult prompts as necessary.

Step 8: The adult models a correct response as necessary, and requests that the child practice the modeled response.

Step 9: The adult confirms that the child's response is correct, models the elaborated language, and gives the appropriate adult response (such as assistance or information).

Source: Hart, B., & Risley, T. (1982). *How to use incidental teaching for elaborating language,* pp. 6–8. Austin, TX: Pro-ed. Reprinted with permission from Pro-ed.

They underscore not only its potential in educational and family settings, but also the need for systematic research. Other potential applications include social skills interventions and problem solving.

Summary of Early Language Intervention

We have stressed language intervention by primary caregivers rather than specialists. This is not intended to minimize the role of professionals or the contributions of specialized disciplines, but rather to emphasize the importance of language for personal and social development, the pragmatic and functional nature of early language acquisition, naturalistic learning strategies, and an ecobehavioral emphasis for assessment and intervention design. While not necessarily causal, if language problems persist into school age, they are likely to be associated with a broad range of academic and social problems. Furthermore, the strategies involving the roles of parents and teachers are directly related to issues concerning skill generalization — a topic for which research is lacking.

Incidental learning experiences are important because they have the potential for flexible adaptation to a wide range of settings and change agents. Incidental teaching should be successful because it incorporates both behavioral principles such as shaping, prompting, and contingent reinforcement (discussed in subsequent sections) and factors gleaned from basic developmental research. Recent research trends suggest the importance of integrating language interventions into the child's usual routines and interactions (Snyder-McLean & McLean, 1987).

Other Basic Intervention Strategies

Early problems with achievement predict later academic and social difficulties. Pronounced forms of antisocial behavior and disturbed peer relationships preclude normal sources of affection and socialization, and also predict later maladjustment. We began the chapter with everyday or naturalistic techniques that serve as a starting place for intervention design. The four techniques that have been introduced — differential attention, ignoring, modeling, and incidental teaching — are powerful, but may not be sufficient by themselves to deal with the complexity of learning or behavior problems. Other strategies to develop new behaviors and modify or eliminate existing ones may be needed. Here we expand discussion of interventions for children that are hard to teach, parent, or befriend.

Reinforcement

A reinforcer is a contingent event that follows a response and increases the "future probability of responses in the same *class*" (Skinner, 1953, p. 87). The concept of response class is important because interrelated behaviors are typically the unit of analysis, not isolated responses. For example, aversive behaviors of children such as whining, tantruming, and crying often are treated as a response class because of their functional interrelatedness (see Chapter Five on keystone behaviors).

Reinforcement may be either positive or negative. In both

cases, however, behavior is strengthened. The reinforcement increases the probability of behaviors belonging to a response class.

Positive reinforcers "add something" to the situation (Skinner, 1953). Positive reinforcement is most widely applied and is a cornerstone of intervention design with young children. One of the best examples, positive attention, was introduced earlier in the chapter. We will return to positive reinforcement in a later section on differential reinforcement.

Negative reinforcement increases the probability of a response class of behaviors through "removing something . . . from the situation" (Skinner, 1953, p. 73). After the child makes the desired response, the caregiver takes away the aversive stimulus. Thus, the use of negative reinforcement requires "a prior worsening of the environment" (Cooper, Heron, & Heward, 1987, p. 261). The potentially undesirable outcomes of negative reinforcement may be reduced by combining it with positive procedures. Negative reinforcement may be a factor in learning disruptive behaviors, such as tantrums, to avoid difficult or unpleasant tasks.

Punishment is different from negative reinforcement. Furthermore, technically it is *not* the opposite of reward (Skinner, 1953). Punishment involves *introducing* (rather than removing) a negative reinforcer or aversive consequence (commonly referred to as Type I) or removing a positive reinforcer (commonly referred to as Type II) (Skinner, 1953). When contingently applied to a response, punishment decreases the rate of the response. Punishment also applies to the contingent *withholding* of positive reinforcement such as in the intervention known as time out. These definitions do not always fit lay interpretations of the term *punishment*.

Current views of punishment and the use of aversives vary widely, and punishment typically is considered a controversial last resort. Wolery and Gast (1990) make the point that aversives may be placed on a continuum, and much of the debate has centered on extremes. What is needed is to establish the conditions for use of specific and effective interventions, whether aversive or nonaversive, mild or extreme. The focus is on a decision model that systematically is used to protect clients' rights; to ensure appropriate planning, implementation, and review; and overall, to establish the reasonableness of professional actions (Wolery & Gast, 1990). At the same time, there is a need to develop alternatives to punishment.

While punishment is common in parental discipline, numerous ethical and legal concerns apply when it is used by professionals. One of the first steps for the professional is often to examine the aversiveness of techniques that caregivers already use for discipline and control. (We resume the discussion of aversives in the next chapter and stress procedural safeguards, guidelines, and resources for aversive interventions in the final chapter.)

Types of Reinforcement. When social attention is not sufficient, it is necessary to consider other types of reinforcement. *Primary* or *unconditioned* reinforcers have biological importance; the most widely used example is food. *Secondary,* learned, or *conditioned* reinforcers become reinforcing only after they become paired with primary reinforcers (or other secondary reinforcers).

Several groups of reinforcers have been used with young children. *Tangible* reinforcers are objects, such as toys or stickers. *Activity* reinforcers are events or privileges that may be used to increase behaviors. These may be superior to edibles and toys for many children (Hall & Hall, 1980c). Novel events may also be highly rewarding, for example, an activity or "surprise box" containing slips of paper with various activity reinforcers (draw a picture, get a drink, and so on). If the contingency is met, the child pulls out a slip and completes the brief activity (Sulzer-Azaroff & Mayer, 1991). *Social reinforcers* include physical contact such as hugs, attention, proximity such as standing or sitting near someone, or verbal statements such as recognition or approval (Hall & Hall, 1980c). *Feedback* from self-recordings or charts showing improvements in behaviors may also be reinforcing for many children. *Tokens* or coupons serve as *generalized reinforcers;* these tangibles can be exchanged for other back-up reinforcers later. Group reinforcement and tokens are discussed in the next chapter. Examples of reinforcers for preschool-aged children appear in Exhibit 6.3.

Exhibit 6.3. Examples of Reinforcers for Preschool Children.

Material Reinforcers
    Snacks of favorite foods, toys, balloons, pennies for bank

Social Reinforcers
    Verbal: "Yes," "Great," "That's right," "I like the way you . . . "
    Physical: hugs, smiles, eye contact, tickles, handshake, piggyback ride

Activity Reinforcers
    Trip to park, zoo, or any special outing; playing with friends; listen-
    ing to stories or songs, singing songs; feeding pet; playing a game;
    talking into a tape recorder; blowing bubbles; helping mother,
    father, or teacher

Source: Adapted from Hall, R. V., & Hall, M. C. (1980c). *How to select reinforcers,* pp. 25–26. Austin, TX: Pro-ed. Reprinted with permission from Pro-ed.

Selecting Reinforcers. A reinforcer is defined by its effect on the behavior of an individual child. Thus, change agents must decide what to try as a reinforcer. Basic strategies involve asking the child, teacher, and parent, and observing the child for data on such factors as play preferences. As a general guideline, the selection of reinforcers should start with those that are "most natural or indigenous to a situation" (Sulzer-Azaroff & Mayer, 1991, p. 179). If artificial reinforcers are selected, natural reinforcers ultimately should be introduced. Several strategies are discussed that are based on observations.

    The *Premack Principle* (Premack, 1959), or Grandma's Law, is a powerful strategy in which access to high-frequency behaviors (playing with favorite toy) is made contingent on low-frequency behaviors (completing a preacademic task). Further analysis of the Premack Principle has led to a contrasting general principle. The *response deprivation hypothesis* (Timberlake & Allison, 1974) states: "If access to one of a pair of events is restricted below free operant levels (baseline), an organism will work to regain access to that activity" (Redmon & Farris, 1987, p. 327). In other words, a low-probability behavior can function as a reinforcer for a high-probability behavior if there are restrictions placed on responses as assessed at baseline levels (Konarski, Johnson, Crowell, & Whitman, 1981). The practical implications are enormous: "Almost any behavior in which the individual engages is a potentially effective reinforcer, provided access to that response can be restricted" (Sulzer-Azaroff & Mayer, 1991, p. 160). Konarski, Johnson, Crowell, and Whitman (1980) used the response deprivation hypothesis with first-grade children and demonstrated that math could serve as a reinforcer for coloring as long as the response deprivation conditions were in effect.

Another strategy involves *reinforcer sampling* (Ayllon & Azrin, 1968; Kazdin, 1977), in which the child is given a brief exposure to the potential reinforcer. If a child does not have experience with an object, it may have only minimal appeal (Sulzer-Azaroff & Mayer, 1991). The child can be given several samples of reinforcers and the child's preference can be observed directly. Modeling of another child using the reinforcer also may be helpful (Ayllon & Azrin, 1968). Once the child begins to enjoy the activity or event, it may become a reinforcer.

Given the array of decisions, one can see that the task of selecting reinforcers may be quite complex. Outside the use of direct observation, it may also be subjective. However, the use of direct observation will restrict the classes of potential reinforcers to those that are currently available. Typically, the process is not carried out systematically. Furthermore, reinforcement preferences may vary by day and by sessions. Satiation may also be a problem for some reinforcers.

In sum, the ongoing assessment of child-preferred reinforcers or activities is strongly linked to intervention outcomes and typically is carried out through interviews of caregivers and observation. However, it is a topic that will likely benefit from the development of structured procedures.

Mason, McGee, Farmer-Dougan, and Risley (1989) studied what they termed a "practical reinforcer assessment package" where children select their own reinforcers on an ongoing basis. The basic strategy followed earlier work by Pace and colleagues (1985) where reinforcement preferences were assessed by sampling from stimulus items selected for accessibility and ease of presentation. The items also represented different sensory qualities (mirror, juice, hug, clap, swing). To determine potential reinforcers, approach behavior and compliance to instructions were observed. This package capitalizes on variety and novelty.

In the study by Mason and colleagues (1989, p. 173), the reinforcer assessment package involved the following categories along with two stimuli, each from one of eight groups:

1. Olfactory: potpourri, coffee beans
2. Gustatory: juice, animal crackers or cookies
3. Visual: flashing light, mirror
4. Tactile: vibrating wind-up toy, fan
5. Thermal: ice, heating pad
6. Vestibular: rocking, spinning
7. Auditory: touch-tone telephone beep, music
8. Social: clapping, hugs

Reinforcement was individualized. About half the child-preferred reinforcers identified in the comprehensive assessment were used in teaching. The range of reinforcements across children and conditions was two to five. The researchers described the comprehensive procedure used at the beginning and end of the study, and the daily mini-session assessment.

Comprehensive procedures. Each item was alternated randomly among stimuli for ten trials. If a child failed to approach (that is, reach for or correctly label) an item within five seconds of its display, the experimenter prompted the child by providing a model of the response (the experimenter picked up and manipulated the item), and then re-presented the trial after a five-second delay. Preferred items were those that children approached on 80 percent of the initial trials.

Daily procedures: The presession mini-assessment consisted of one presentation of each of the items designated as preferred in the initial comprehensive assessment. The experimenter simultaneously displayed two preferred stimuli. The order and position of items varied across presentations, and two stimuli from the same sensory category were never presented as pairs. The child was told once to "pick one." The experimenter continued to display the two items until a selection or active rejection was made. (Adapted from Mason, McGee, Farmer-Dougan, & Risley, 1989, pp. 173–174.)

The results of the study with three preschool children having behaviors described as autistic showed positive effects (on maladaptive behaviors, correct responses on a teaching task, out-of-seat behavior) and positive side effects. One side effect was the broadening of reinforcement interests over the period of the study. Whereas the process of obtaining reinforcer information from teachers was about five minutes, the average experimental procedure based on children's selection of reinforcers ranged from thirty seconds to one minute.

Schedules of Reinforcement. Reinforcement may be given on a continuous basis, where every occurrence of the targeted behavior is reinforced, or it may be administered intermittently. During the initial stages of interventions, continuous reinforcement is used primarily to strengthen behavior. Intermittent reinforcement is used later to maintain behaviors. The term *thinning the schedule* refers to the process of changing from continuous to intermittent reinforcement. Lovaas described the thinning procedure: "How 'thin' you can make the reward schedule depends on many variables, and differs between children and tasks. Thin the schedule and look for *schedule strain;* if his behavior falls apart or begins to fluctuate widely, 'thicken' the schedule, that is, reward him more often. Once you have recovered his behavior, start thinning again" (1981, p. 13).

Advantages of intermittent reinforcement include resistance to extinction for desired behavior, maintenance of relatively high rates of responding, control for satiation, and cost effectiveness. "Intermittent reinforcement is usually necessary for the progression to naturally occurring reinforcement" (Cooper, Heron, & Heward, 1987, p. 277).

The effects of intermittent schedules of reinforcement have been extensively studied in laboratory experiments. The four basic schedules of intermittent reinforcement and characteristics are summarized in Exhibit 6.4. Schedules of reinforcement can be much more complex than this. Cooper, Heron, and Heward (1987) and Sulzer-Azaroff and Mayer (1991) have expanded discussions of schedules of reinforcement.

Herrnstein's Law of Effect. For many interventions, one of the most important and often challenging tasks is to assess for com-

Exhibit 6.4. Schedules of Intermittent Reinforcement.

Ratio Schedules: Reinforcement is contingent on a specified number of responses.

Fixed Ratio (FR): A set number of responses is performed before reinforcement. After the FR schedule has been in effect, there may be a postreinforcement pause or cessation in performance if the interval is relatively large, followed by typically high rates of responding. During extinction, performance may be characterized by bursts of responding followed by increasingly longer periods of nonresponding until it reaches its prereinforcement level.

Variable Ratio (VR): The number of responses required to earn a reinforcement for each trial is variable. The average number of responses across trials is used to describe the ratio. Steady rates, high rates of responding, and greater resistance to extinction are characteristic of VR schedules.

Interval Schedules: Reinforcement is based on the passage of time.

Fixed Interval (FI): The subject is reinforced following the performance of the targeted response after a set period of time. A scalloped performance effect is characteristic of FI schedules whereby the subject responds at a low (or zero) rate following reinforcement, and performs at an increasing rate before the end of the interval. Under extinction, similarly, performance is interspersed with periods of nonresponding. Generally, under extinction, performance is less persistent compared to performance under other schedules.

Variable Interval (VI): The subject is reinforced for performing the desired behavior following a time period that varies around an average interval. Like VR schedules, VI schedules typically generate stable levels of responding, with rates of responses depending on the size of the intervals, and they are resistant to extinction.

---

peting contingencies of reinforcement. Herrnstein's Law of Effect is a mathematical statement that expresses the rate of a target response as a function of *reinforcement context*. Examined in research for over three decades, this is a naturalistic view of reinforcement because it takes into account other concurrent reinforcers present in environments.

The practical importance of Herrnstein's formulation is that "a given rate of contingent reinforcement may produce a high or low response rate depending on the context of reinforcement in which it occurs" (McDowell, 1982, p. 773). Regarding treatment implications, problem behavior may be reduced by extinction, by increasing reinforcement for appropriate response alternatives, or by "increasing the rate of free or noncontingent reinforcement" (p. 777). To increase desirable behavior, the reinforcement rate can be increased for the target behavior, the reinforcement rate for a concurrent inappropriate response can be decreased, or free or noncontingent reinforcement can be decreased. Tryon (1983) pointed out the benefits of selecting modification strategies to reduce reinforcement rates.

More formally, the equation asserts that behavior increases (hyperbolically) as a function of contingent reinforcement of the target response, but also as a function of extraneous concurrent reinforcement. Extraneous reinforcement may include reinforcement for a response other than the target behavior, noncontingent reinforcement, or spontaneous reinforcement (McDowell, 1982).

The equation is expressed as

$$R = k\left(\frac{r}{r + \imath}\right)$$

where R is the rate of target response, k (a constant) is the maximum possible rate of response, r is the rate of reinforcement contingent on the target response, and $\imath$ is the rate of reinforcement for all other behaviors (Herrnstein, 1970). Martens, Halperin, Rummel, and Kilpatrick (1990) successfully demonstrated Herrnstein's Law of Effect for teacher contingent attention and the on-task behavior of a six-year-old boy. Teacher attention for off-task behavior influenced the rate of target responding by changing the relative amount of contingent attention for the target response.

Stimulus Control

Stimulus control — meaning that behaviors are performed in response to specific cues or stimulus conditions — is fundamental to the environmental analysis of behavior (Skinner, 1953). "Stimulus control is always operative in behavior modification programs" (Kazdin, 1984, p. 43). An event that functions as a signal that behavior will be reinforced is termed a *discriminative stimulus*. "A discriminative stimulus sets the *occasion* for the behavior: it increases the probability that a previously reinforced behavior will occur . . . [and] eventually becomes a reinforcer itself" (Kazdin, 1984, p. 38). Thus, these antecedent events help control behavior. The control of the antecedent events over behavior is termed *stimulus control.* The importance of stimulus control is that responsibility for learning rests with the person arranging the "conceptual environment" (Etzel, LeBlanc, Schilmoeller, & Stella, 1981).

There are many examples of simple and effective stimulus control procedures for young children. Modeling and a brief time delay, discussed earlier as ways to promote language development, are two examples. Other examples include improving parental commands for compliance (Chapter Nine) and the use of classroom rules and prompts (Chapter Ten). Stimulus control is used to teach concept formation and in differential reinforcement (Chapter Seven) and "errorless learning" (Chapter Ten). The effects of stimulus control may be used to explain why behavior of children may vary considerably in different settings. Stimulus control may be applied to intervention programs based on self-control procedures (Kazdin, 1984).

Stimulus *generalization* occurs when a response transfers or generalizes from one stimulus condition to other similar conditions. Generalization was discussed in Chapter Five.

In the next four sections, other applications of stimulus control are discussed. Stimulus control procedures also need to be *faded.* Examples of fading procedures are given in the following discussion of the use of prompts.

The Use of Prompts

"Prompts are events that help initiate a response" (Kazdin, 1984, p. 40). Three common prompts are verbal directions, modeling, and physical guidance. Gestures are commonly used as prompts or combined with verbal prompts. Pictures also may be used as prompts to depict rules, goals, steps in completing tasks, or models for performance.

Prompts may be ordered on a continuum of intrusiveness. Physical guidance is the most intrusive. However, without physical prompts, some children will be unable to perform the behavior. *Partial* physical prompts require that caregivers touch the children but not control their movements. *Full* physical prompts involve moving children through the desired behaviors. Modeling may be considered intrusive because the correct response is demonstrated.

Wolery, Bailey, and Sugai (1988, pp. 226–227) suggest the following guidelines for prompts:

1. Select the least intrusive, effective prompt.
2. Combine prompts if necessary.
3. Select natural prompts and those related to the behavior.
4. Provide prompts only after students are attending.
5. Provide prompts in a supportive, instructive manner before the student responds.
6. Fade prompts as soon as possible.
7. Plan fading procedures before using prompts.

Ultimately, the prompts are "faded," gradually diminished until the responses occur without them. There are several methods to accomplish fading. Cooper, Heron, and Heward (1987) described "least to most" (see Exhibit 6.5) as an appropriate fading procedure for most applications involving skill development.

Detailed overview of the steps for the different procedures, and review research on specific applications are provided by Sulzer-Azaroff and Mayer (1991) and Wolery, Bailey, and Sugai (1988). Time delay is another method to fade prompts. Other fading strategies include the following (Wolery, Bailey, & Sugai, 1988):

Most-to-least prompting procedure. In contrast to the least-to-most procedure, most-to-least prompts involve progressively less intrusive prompts or decreasing levels of assistance as children demonstrate performance at specified criteria.

Antecedent prompt and test procedure. This involves presenting children with "prompted trials" and then giving them practice with the prompts removed.

Exhibit 6.5. Fading Prompts: Least-to-Most Procedure.

1.	The child is given the opportunity to perform the response with the least amount of assistance on each trial.
2.	Greater degrees of assistance are provided as successive opportunities are required.
3.	The procedure requires a delay (perhaps five seconds) between presentation of the stimulus and the opportunity to respond.
4.	If the response does not occur within the specified time, a response prompt of least assistance is provided.
5.	If after the specified delay, the correct response is still not given, another prompt and additional assistance (such as a gesture) follow.
6.	Partial or full physical guidance can be provided if the child has not responded to lesser assistance.

Source: Adapted by permission of Merrill, an imprint of Macmillan Publishing Company, from *Applied Behavior Analysis* by John O. Cooper, Timothy E. Heron, and William L. Heward. Copyright ©1987 by Merrill Publishing.

Antecedent prompt and fade. Prompts are given on initial trials, but are faded (rather than removed) systematically by reducing the intensity or frequency of the prompt.

Graduated guidance. This procedure involves beginning each trial with sufficient assistance (or prompt) so that the child is able to perform the desired behavior, but withdrawing the prompt immediately when he or she does so. Prompts are provided as needed. *Shadowing* means that the caregiver's hands follow the child's movements in carrying out the behavior, but do not touch the child. It enables immediate prompting as necessary.

Shaping and Chaining

In *shaping,* a complex behavior is achieved by teaching and reinforcing steps or *successive approximations* to the final behavior (see Exhibit 6.6). The final behavior is achieved gradually. Panyan wrote: "Shaping fosters the gradual development of a new behavior by repeatedly reinforcing minor improvements or steps toward that behavior. Instead of waiting for a new behavior to occur in its final form, we reinforce every resemblance of that new behavior" (1980, p. 1).

Exhibit 6.6. Components of a Shaping Program.

---

1. Define both initial and goal behavior in specific terms, including the condition under which the behavior is to occur.
2. Identify a behavior that the individual currently performs relatively often and that roughly approximates the desired target behavior.
3. Reinforce the current behavior, even though it may only remotely resemble the target behavior.
4. Withhold reinforcers for behaviors that are not clear steps toward the target behavior.
5. Reinforce closer approximations to the target behavior and discontinue reinforcement for previously reinforced behaviors that are less similar to the goal behavior.
6. Increase the requirement for reinforcement when closer approximations begin to occur with some regularity.
7. Consistently reinforce any new approximations.
8. Continue to withhold reinforcers for behaviors that are not in the direction of the goal behavior.
9. Increase the requirement for reinforcement until the goal behavior is fully developed.
10. Reinforce every instance of the goal behavior until it occurs consistently.

Source: Adapted from Panyan, M. (1980). *How to use shaping,* pp. 3–4. Austin, TX: Pro-ed.

Behaviors can be shaped in five ways (Panyan, 1980). First, the time that a child is engaged in an activity can be *lengthened.* An example is allowing a child engaged in appropriate solitary play to continue; shaping is used to increase existing behavior. Second, the time that it takes for a child to engage in a behavior following a stimulus or cue (for example, reply to a request) can be *shortened.* Third, the *frequency* of a behavior can be increased. An example is increasing the rate of spontaneous language in play situations by a child with limited social interactions. Fourth, the *form* of the original response may be changed. Typical examples involve shaping sounds into recognizable language or teaching social skills. Fifth, shaping can be used to modify the *intensity* of a response. An example is shaping the force a child uses in coloring or drawing, or the loudness of a social greeting. Other techniques such as modeling and physical guidance may be combined with shaping.

A *"chaining procedure* is the reinforcement of a specified sequence of relatively simpler behaviors already in the repertoire of the individual to form a more complex behavior" (Sulzer-Azaroff & Mayer, 1991, p. 338). Whereas in shaping the steps are useful only because they lead to the desired response, in chaining the desired goal is typically the sequence of the separate behaviors (Kazdin, 1984). The responses are usually within the child's repertoire. The stimulus conditions and responses are components of the chain. The stimulus linking the components together serves two functions: a reinforcer and a discriminative stimulus for the next response.

There are three major varieties of chaining (Cooper, Heron, & Heward, 1987). *Forward chaining* involves teaching the behaviors identified in a task analysis in temporal order. The first step is reinforced when the initial behavior in the task analysis is achieved. After that, each successive step is reinforced contingent on adequate performance of prior steps to a specified criterion. The steps for *backward chaining* are included in Exhibit 6.7. Lovaas (1981) suggested that backward chaining is useful for skills such as undressing; since undressing is easier to learn than dressing, it may be taught first. Also, backward chaining builds on the reinforcement provided by the completion of the entire chain (Sulzer-Azaroff & Mayer, 1991). *Total task presentation* also begins with a task analysis. The difference is that the child receives training in each step for every session.

Exhibit 6.7. Steps in Backward Chaining.

---

1. All the behaviors identified in the task analysis, except for the final behavior in the chain, are completed by the trainer.
2. When the subject performs the final behavior at the predetermined level, reinforcement is delivered.
3. Thereafter, reinforcement is delivered when both the last and the next-to-last behaviors in the sequence are performed to criterion.
4. Subsequently, reinforcement is delivered when the last three behaviors are performed to criterion.
5. The sequence proceeds backward through the chain until all the steps in the task analysis have been introduced.

Source: Adapted with permission of Merrill, an imprint of Macmillan Publishing Company, from *Applied Behavior Analysis* by John O. Cooper, Timothy E. Heron, and William L. Heward. Copyright ©1987 by Merrill Publishing Company.

Assistance is given as needed for each step, and steps for the entire chain are trained until the child is able to perform to a preset criterion. Skills that may benefit from chaining include dressing, feeding, and chores. Which procedure to use is an empirical question that depends on specific situations.

Preattending Skills

For many children, *preattending* skills may be an important focal point of assessment and intervention. Preattending is a preliminary step in learning; it involves looking at the materials, listening to instructions, and sitting quietly during instruction. With adept learners, preattending behaviors occur with minimal adult prompting.

Attention to tasks can be improved by first teaching specific preattending behaviors through shaping. For example, in teaching a child the preattending behavior of sitting quietly, the adult first verbally models the behavior ("Watch how I can sit quietly in my chair." For some children, other prompts may be added: " . . . without talking to others or getting up."). The teacher then physically models the behavior by sitting next to the child for a brief period (approximately five seconds). Next, the adult verbally prompts the child to exhibit the behavior ("Now show me how you can sit quietly."). Upon successful completion of the behavior, the child may receive a reinforcer such as praise. After each session the time criterion for the reinforcer can gradually be increased. If the child is not imitating the model, different strategies need to be used.

The components for teaching preattending skills are summarized as follows:

1. *Modeling.* The teacher verbally models the behavior for the child. For example, teaching the child to look at a page of a book, the teacher would say, "Watch how I look at the page of this book without looking anywhere else."

2. *Physical prompting.* The teacher physically models the behavior for the child. Continuing the example, the teacher

would look at the book for approximately five seconds while the child watched.

3. *Verbal prompting.* The teacher then prompts the child to engage in the looking behavior ("Show me how you can look at the page of this book just like I did without looking anywhere else."). The interval should be kept brief, five seconds or less.

4. *Reinforcement.* Sometimes children's attention to tasks can be improved simply by providing reinforcement for attending. When the child successfully completes the looking behavior, the teacher should praise the child for looking. Other reinforcers may be added as needed.

5. *Following sessions.* During following sessions, model and prompt as necessary while gradually increasing the time interval for looking (six seconds, eight seconds, ten seconds). Also, shift reinforcement from preattending responses to correct task completions.

Opportunities to Respond

A potentially significant focal point of assessment and intervention plans involves the analysis of ecological and behavioral interactions. One of the most powerful interventions involves giving children more frequent chances for learning and for practice. Greenwood, Delquadri, and Hall provide the following definition of opportunity to respond: "The interaction between: (a) teacher formulated instructional antecedent stimuli (the materials presented, prompts, questions asked, signals to respond, etc.), and (b) their success in establishing the academic responding desired or implied by the materials" (1984, p. 64).

The term includes such factors as practice, time on-task, at-task behavior, and specific child responses, but attention is directed to the *antecedents* of instruction. Greenwood, Delquadri, and Hall give examples of antecedents: "Scheduling and . . . implementation of instructional time on a systematic basis for specific academic subjects; providing level-appropriate materials that facilitate directly the desired academic responses; organization of the classroom physical structure so that it is conducive to academic responding; and teacher interaction patterns with students as individuals or as groups, that support academic responding at high levels" (1984, p. 64). Another important distinction is that children are actively rather than passively responding.

Overall, research has demonstrated a strong relationship between the "quality and frequency of academic interactions" and academic gains (Greenwood, Delquadri, & Hall, 1984, p. 86). The major focus is on identifying instructional methods and materials that promote frequent, diverse, and systematically planned preacademic behavior. Applications are discussed in Chapter Ten.

Summary and Conclusions

This chapter introduced basic interventions for learning new behaviors and modifying or eliminating existing ones. Naturalistic strategies — differential attention, ignoring, modeling, and reprimands — are fundamental techniques for acquiring or modifying behaviors and for learning rules that guide subsequent behaviors. An expanded discussion of language skills emphasized the role of caregivers and the importance of language to other developmental tasks.

In addition, other basic principles and strategies for behavior change were presented, including reinforcement and stimulus control. The use of prompts, shaping, and chaining procedures are foundations for many interventions discussed in later chapters. Important strategies for many preschool referrals that build on these interventions are preattending skills and opportunities to respond.

7

Managing
Severe Problem Behaviors

PROBLEM BEHAVIORS MAY BE VIEWED AS EITHER EXCESSES OR DEF-
icits in desirable behavior; frequently both are present. Well-
designed and well-implemented interventions may increase appropriate behaviors while reducing inappropriate behaviors.

Differential Reinforcement

Differential reinforcement simply means that certain responses
or classes of behaviors are reinforced while others are not. Differential reinforcement is used for building skills or for altering
patterns of behaviors. Differential attention (Chapter Six) is an
application of differential reinforcement. Some of the best and
earliest examples of interventions used parent and teacher attention as reinforcers.

This section presents techniques used to reduce maladaptive behaviors. They are referred to as "positive reductive procedures" for decreasing inappropriate behavior (Deitz & Repp,
1983, p. 35). Since the procedures involve changes in reinforcement, a functional analysis is an important prerequisite (Iwata,
Vollmer, & Zarcone, 1990).

Differential Reinforcement of Alternative Behavior (DRA)

In this technique, a more acceptable behavior is substituted for
the maladaptive behavior and occurrences are reinforced. The

alternative behavior should appropriately "occupy the time" during which a child would otherwise be exhibiting the undesirable behavior (Cooper, Heron, & Heward, 1987, p. 392). For example, if a child is "unoccupied" in the classroom, increasing appropriate play would be an alternative behavior. DRA procedures have great possibilities for reducing classroom disruptions (Lentz, 1988). In addition, DRA is a positive procedure, without known negative side effects.

The alternative behavior must be selected with care. LaVigna and Donnellan (1986) proposed the 100 percent rule: the target behavior and alternative response together cover all possibilities for behavior. "By definition, the learner can either engage in the target behavior or in the alternative response with no third option available" (p. 44). Also, the alternative behavior must be in the child's repertoire. If it is not evident in preintervention baseline data, other procedures such as modeling, instruction, and prompts must be included.

Differential Reinforcement of Incompatible Behavior (DRI). DRI is a subclass of DRA. Reinforcement is presented if the child performs a desirable behavior that is the opposite of the targeted behavior. The rationale is that since both behaviors cannot be performed simultaneously, by increasing an acceptable but incompatible behavior, the unacceptable behavior must diminish. As examples, a child cannot be attending and be off-task, or isolated and engaged in peer play at the same time. The behaviors selected as incompatible should be "natural opposites" (Donnellan & LaVigna, 1990). Exhibit 7.1 suggests guidelines common to both DRA and DRI.

Differential Reinforcement of Functional Behavior (DRF). This technique, described by Rolider and Van Houten (1990), is also logically related to DRA. Based on the functional analysis of behavior, a new behavior that serves the same function as the maladaptive behavior is taught. Examples are how to ask for help (such as signal the need to use the toilet), how to receive attention appropriately, or how to appropriately escape stressful or demanding situations instead of having tantrums. Func-

Exhibit 7.1. Guidelines for the Use of DRA and DRI.

---

1. Alternative or incompatible behaviors should be in the child's repertoire of skills, and should be emitted with regularity. Furthermore, the skills should lead to acquiring additional skills, and should be likely to be maintained by the natural environment.

2. The alternative behaviors should be "as physically different from the target behaviors as possible, in addition to being incompatible" (LaVigna & Donnellan, 1986, p. 52). Thus, alternative and target behaviors cannot be performed simultaneously.

3. Guidelines for the selection and administration of reinforcers should be carefully considered. The reinforcement should be contingently, consistently, and immediately administered. The reinforcers need to be stronger than those maintaining the maladaptive behavior, or, if possible, the maladaptive behavior should be subjected to extinction.

4. A continuous schedule of reinforcement should be used initially, and then should be gradually thinned.

5. DRA and DRI can be effectively combined with other techniques (such as DRO, DRL).

---

tional behaviors are taught because they are likely to help children receive reinforcement that is naturally available in the environment or help them learn appropriate ways to deal with difficult tasks. DRF stresses teaching new and adaptive behaviors to replace maladaptive behaviors. It is important to make certain that the new behaviors are more effective than the current behaviors in earning the desired reinforcers: "the new response should access the relevant reinforcer with a shorter delay, greater consistency, and less effort" (Carr, Robinson, & Palumbo, 1990, p. 367).

Communication skills are frequently targeted as functional behaviors for children. Carr and Durand (1985) proposed a "communication hypothesis of child behavior problems" where behavior problems function as "nonverbal communicative acts" to obtain socially mediated reinforcement (p. 124). This may be referred to as *Differential Reinforcement of Communication.*

Differential Reinforcement of Other Behavior (DRO)

In using DRO, the caregiver provides reinforcement for all responses *except* the target behavior. Reinforcement is given when the child does not perform the target behavior for certain time intervals. Carr, Robinson, and Palumbo (1990) reconceptualized DRO by its stimulus properties. They pointed out that DRO provides systematic discriminative stimuli for appropriate behaviors, thereby reducing problem behaviors.

For children with more than one problem behavior, those prioritized for change may be introduced sequentially or, preferably, target behaviors may be defined by response classes where several behaviors are included in the criteria for acceptable performance (if not, undesirable responses may be reinforced). Also, the child must have functional and appropriate behaviors in his or her repertoire. Most typically, DRO has been applied to self-injurious, aggressive, and disruptive behaviors (Poling & Ryan, 1982). Parent-administered programs for thumbsucking and for inappropriate car behavior are described in Chapter Nine.

There are several possible alternatives in designing a DRO program. For example, "whole" DRO involves a specified time period in which the child must not emit the targeted behavior in order to receive reinforcement. In momentary DRO (Barton, Brulle, & Repp, 1986), reinforcement is provided if the child is not performing the behavior at the moment of observation ("spot checking"). Momentary DRO may be helpful in maintaining behavior change; whole-interval DRO is likely to be more effective in modifying behavior.

Generally, the interval is reset if the target behavior occurs. For example, if a child misbehaves three minutes into a five-minute interval, the timer is reset for another five minutes. Another practical variation is to set the interval at a specified length and provide reinforcement only if the behavior was not emitted during the interval. Intervals also may be variable in length, and may be increased based on the child's performance (termed an *escalating schedule*).

DRO has demonstrated effectiveness over many different applications. Like other differential reinforcement procedures, DRO may require substantial vigilance and effort. However, only the target behaviors (in contrast to the alternative behaviors) and the time interval need to be carefully monitored. DRO may be combined with other interventions. For example,

Rolider and Van Houten (1984) found that the use of reprimands increased the effectiveness of DRO. General procedures for DRO are outlined in Exhibit 7.2.

Differential Reinforcement of Low Rates of Behavior (DRL)

DRL is a procedure to *reduce* rather than eliminate behavior. However, it also may be used as a first step in eliminating undesirable behavior when behavior rates are very high. To use DRL, a criterion is specified for the targeted response and the child is reinforced if the rate of behavior is less than the criterion for a specified time period. DRL is appropriate when it may not be desirable to reduce the behavior to a zero level. For example, a child who makes numerous comments during group discussions may be allowed only a set number (established through the use of micronorms or teacher consultation).

Exhibit 7.2. Guidelines for Using DRO.

---

1. Establish an appropriate time interval for reinforcement. One guideline is to set the initial time interval less than the mean interresponse time (IRT) found during baseline observations (Deitz & Repp, 1983); another is to use half the baseline IRT (LaVigna & Donnellan, 1986).
2. Reinforce the child at the end of the interval if the target behavior, or other inappropriate behavior, was not performed during the interval.
3. Establish procedures to increase the length of the DRO interval by small increments after behavior is effectively controlled. Three recommended ways to increase the interval include: (a) increase by a constant amount of time, (b) increase by a proportionate amount of time (such as 10 percent), and (c) base the interval length on the child's performance (for example, the mean IRT interval from the preceding session can be used to set the new DRO interval) (Poling & Ryan, 1982; see LaVigna & Donnellan, 1986, for other recommendations). It may be helpful to inform the child about the change in interval length.
4. Since DRO is not a constructive procedure, it should be combined with DRA or DRI (Sulzer-Azaroff & Mayer, 1991) or other strategies for positive programming to increase adaptive and appropriate behaviors.
5. DRO can be effectively combined with other reductive procedures (e.g., time out or reprimands).

Except where noted, the procedures described have been adapted from Cooper, Heron, and Heward (1987).

DRL may be specified by the number of responses allowed within a time period or by how much time passes between responses. Once the behavior is under control, the criterion for the number of responses can be changed to lower the average rate of responding. New criteria for performance may be introduced after the behavior has reached a "steady state" (LaVigna & Donnellan, 1986). *Differential reinforcement of diminishing rates* (DRD; Sulzer-Azaroff & Mayer, 1991) means that reinforcement is contingent on a reduction in response rate.

As with all differential reinforcement procedures, there are several alternative strategies (Deitz, 1977). In *full-session DRL,* reinforcement is administered if responses during the session are equal to or below a specified criterion. Full-session DRL involves the fewest demands on practitioners. The practitioner simply has to count the number of targeted behaviors exhibited during the session and reinforce or withhold reinforcement (Deitz, 1977).

Interval DRL requires dividing the session into equal intervals of time. Reinforcement is administered at the end of each interval if the child's responses were equal to or below the set criterion. Longer intervals can be reinforced later, thereby reducing the rate of behavior. In *spaced-responding DRL,* a response is reinforced that is separated by another response by a preset minimum amount of time (interresponse time, or IRT). After behavioral control has been obtained, the length of the IRT is increased. General procedures are presented in Exhibit 7.3.

While these procedures are effective across many applications, some cautions are in order. Appropriate alternative behaviors must be within the child's performance capabilities. Also, DRO and DRL focus on negative and not constructive behavior, although other procedures such as DRA or modeling may be added. Self-monitoring or other feedback systems may be combined with differential reinforcement procedures.

Aversive Procedures and Punishment

Aversive procedures and punishment were introduced in Chapter Five. Their use has prompted many considerations of legal

Exhibit 7.3. Guidelines for Using DRL.

---

1. Baseline data are used to set the initial DRL criterion. When using full-session DRL, the initial criterion should be set equal to or slightly lower than the average response level found in the last three baseline sessions. Similar considerations are used when selecting the initial response criterion for interval DRL or the initial interresponse time (IRT) for spaced-responding DRL.

2. The DRL criterion is gradually and systematically changed. Prior sessions are used to make decisions about new criteria.

    a. For full-session DRL, the criterion is decreased gradually with each new criterion equal to or slightly lower than the average number of responses that occurred while the previous criterion was in effect.

    b. For interval DRL, the length of the interval can be increased if the criterion is one response per interval. If the criterion is more than one response per interval, that number can be reduced while the interval remains constant. If the criterion is not met, the interval is reset.

    c. With spaced-responding DRL, the IRT is increased gradually with each new IRT equal to or slightly greater than the average IRT that occurred while the previous IRT was in effect.

3. A decision rule should be established for changing the DRL criterion in each of the three programs. For full-session DRL, the criterion may be changed when the criterion is not exceeded and reinforcement is received in three consecutive sessions. For interval and spaced-responding DRL, the criterion may be changed when reinforcement is received 90 percent of the occasions in three consecutive sessions.

Note: The procedures are adapted from those described by Deitz (1977), Deitz and Repp (1983), and D. E. D. Deitz (personal communication, August 29, 1991).

and ethical issues that are discussed in Chapter Twelve and comprehensively reviewed in LaVigna and Donnellan (1986) and Repp and Singh (1990). In many ways, punishment should also be viewed as a strategy that is naturalistically used, or misused, by caregivers (Axelrod, 1990) and thus merits analysis in many situations. The punishment administered to children may be reinforcing to caregivers.

In this section, we discuss interventions traditionally considered aversive: the use of time out, response cost, and overcorrection. Other aversive strategies were presented earlier, such as the use of planned ignoring, extinction, and reprimands.

DRO and DRL also may be considered aversive procedures because reinforcement is reduced contingent on inappropriate behavior. Also, both focus on undesirable behaviors and "negative scanning" for occurrences (Sulzer-Azaroff & Mayer, 1991).

Except in unusual circumstances, interventions that involve harsh and restrictive punishment should be considered only after positive procedures have been adequately tried and failed, and only if legal, ethical, and procedural safeguards have been followed. Some think that punishment never should be used (Donnellan & LaVigna, 1990); others argue that for certain behaviors involving risk, harm, or disastrous consequences of intervention failure, interventions involving punishment may be considered from the outset (Axelrod, 1990). Thus, the use of punishment or aversives merits the following considerations: the likelihood of risk or harm to the child or others, the results of functional analysis, and the likelihood of intervention effectiveness. If punishment is used, appropriate alternative behaviors should be reinforced.

Time Out (from Positive Reinforcement)

Time out is considered to be a punishment procedure; it involves a child being denied access to the opportunity to earn positive reinforcement for brief periods of time, contingent on a targeted maladaptive behavior. Nelson and Rutherford (1983) noted that time out "involves a combination of extinction, punishment, positive reinforcement, and negative reinforcement" because it includes multiple contingencies for different possible behaviors (p. 56). Planned ignoring can be considered a form of time out when attention is the major reinforcer.

To be effective, the "time-in" environment must be reinforcing. Thus, the first step in using time out is to assess the *time-in* environment — a step basic to ecobehavioral analysis in general. Schrader and Gaylord-Ross described environmental enrichment in the following way: "Enrichment refers to the provision of a wide range of activities and materials that create a stimulating and reinforcing environment. . . . An enriched environment . . . provides availability of and reinforcement for

interacting with materials and activities, opportunity and reinforcement for the use of language and other forms of communication, a high interest curriculum, novelty in available stimuli,
frequent reinforcement for adaptive behaviors, opportunities
for structured and incidental social interaction, an adequate
amount of personal space, choices within a predictable schedule, and the opportunity for community participation" (1990,
pp. 408–409).

Time out can be easily overused and misused. Reasons
for this are (a) an insufficiently reinforcing time-in environment,
(b) caregiver reinforcement for placing children in time out, (c)
inappropriate use of time out (for mild problems, or for problems that are out of control), and (d) unenforceable time outs
(Nelson & Rutherford, 1983). Time out is subject to significant
criticism when used to exclude or seclude children.

Safeguards for the use of aversive or punishment procedures are discussed in the final chapter. Training procedures
for time out have been researched. Flanagan, Adams, and Forehand (1979) suggested that modeling (such as through the use
of videotape) may be the best procedure to help parents competently perform time out. The effectiveness of the training
should be assessed by observing the parents' use of the technique.
Teachers also will benefit by systematically planning time-out
procedures.

Considerations for planning time out are identified in Exhibit 7.4. Time out can be conducted in many ways, perhaps
best represented on a "continuum of aversive procedures" (Nelson
& Rutherford, 1983, p. 61). Some evidence suggests that one
brief warning may decrease the number of time-out occasions
(Roberts, 1982). Time-out durations for most preschool applications should be relatively brief, but are also dependent on the
child's history with the procedures. Short durations of time out
(two minutes) may be useful if they have not been preceded by
longer intervals (Harris, 1985), but still this would be a function of the attractiveness of time in. A reason for concern about
long or frequent time outs is that they reduce learning time.
Back-up procedures or contingencies are also a necessary part
of plans for time out.

Exhibit 7.4. Considerations in Planning and Using Time Out.

---

1. Enriching time in.
2. Type and location of time out (removing reinforcing conditions or removing child from reinforcing conditions).
3. Selecting the duration of time out.
4. Using a warning first.
5. Selecting and using verbal explanations along with time out. If used they should be brief, and perhaps used only the first time.
6. Presence or absence of a signal to indicate the beginning and end of time out, or that time-out period is in effect.
7. Using verbal instructions (versus physical administration).
8. Scheduling time out (such as time out for each occurrence of misbehavior or the use of warnings).
9. Selecting criteria and procedures to release children from time out.
10. Selecting back-up contingencies.
11. Presence or location of adult during time out.
12. Training staff and monitoring implementation.
13. Collecting and analyzing data (if behavior is improving, the use of time out should be decreasing).

Adapted from Harris (1985), Matson and DiLorenzo (1984), and Wolery, Bailey, and Sugai (1988).

Frequently, time-out interventions include a step whereby the interval is extended if the child behaves inappropriately. This is called contingent delay. For example, if the child is crying, whining, or yelling, at the end of the time-out interval, time out is extended until a brief contingency is met for appropriate behavior (say fifteen seconds). The rationale is that if the child is released from time out while misbehaving, the misbehavior may inadvertently be reinforced. However, the efficiency and effectiveness of the contingent delay procedure have been questioned (Mace, Page, Ivancic, & O'Brien, 1986). Potential problems with the contingent delay include unnecessarily longer time outs, time out for relatively minor offenses, and practical factors related to a more complicated intervention. Mace and colleagues compared time out with and without the contingent delay and found both to be effective across three subjects.

In the original protocol for time out by Roberts, Hatzenbuehler, and Bean (1981), spanking was used as a consequence for noncompliance with the procedure. More recent studies suggest that room time out may be useful for this purpose (Roberts, 1988).

An example of time out. Firestone (1976) evaluated the use of time out with a four-and-a-half-year-old boy in a nursery school. The child had a substantial history of aggressive behaviors and was expelled from a nursery school at age three. In addition to verbal and physical aggressive behavior, other behaviors were observed in order to determine the side effects of the intervention: (a) cooperation (such as compliant, shares), (b) interactions with teachers (such as asks questions, helps with chores), (c) isolation (such as plays alone), and (d) activity level.

For every physically aggressive act, the child was placed in a chair in the corner of the classroom for two minutes. The rationale was shared with the child the first time.

Physical and verbal aggressiveness decreased significantly. In addition, the intervention demonstrated beneficial side effects. Isolate behavior decreased, cooperative play increased. Interactions with teachers were reduced, but were variable. Activity level increased slightly over the baseline condition (however, level was variable and the data did not suggest a trend). The most notable findings were the reductions in physical aggressiveness and increased positive interactions with peers.

Other, more drastic forms of time out, such as isolation or seclusion, are not discussed here as they typically are not recommended for preschool practices. However, these forms of time out are often practiced by parents (sending children to their room). Many other forms of time out have been used in home and educational settings. Parental strategies and the use of time out in treatment packages are discussed in Chapter Nine, and the use of a time-out "ribbon" is discussed in Chapter Eleven.

Contingent Observation

For problem behaviors, a strategy easily adapted to many play routines is contingent observation. Contingent observation involves both incidental teaching and "mild" time out from active participation in an activity (Porterfield, Herbert-Jackson, & Risley, 1976). The steps for the original application are detailed in Exhibit 7.5.

Exhibit 7.5. Contingent Observation.

1. Describe the inappropriate behaviors to the child. ("Don't take toys from other children.")
2. Describe what would have been appropriate in the situation. ("Ask for the toys you want.")
3. Move the child to the periphery of the activity, have the child sit on the floor without the play materials, and tell the child to observe the appropriate play of other children. ("Sit here and watch how the other children ask for the toys they want.")
4. When the child has been watching quietly for a brief period (unspecified, but less than one minute), the child is asked if he is ready to rejoin the play activity and use the appropriate behavior.
5. The child indicates that he is ready to rejoin the group by nodding or verbalizing.
6. If the child gives no response or a negative response, he is asked to sit until ready. ("Sit here and watch the children until you think that you can ask for the toy you want.")
7. The child sits for another brief period (thirty seconds to one minute), and step 4 is repeated.
8. When the child returns to the group, positive attention is given for appropriate behavior. ("Good, you asked for the toy you wanted.")
9. If crying or disruptions continue for a few minutes, and other play or activities of others are disrupted, or if child refuses to sit quietly, he is taken to a "quiet place" (time out) removed from the "sit and watch location."

Source: Porterfield, J. K., Herbert-Jackson, E., & Risley, T. R. (1976). Contingent observation: An effective and acceptable procedure for reducing disruptive behavior of young children in a group setting. *Journal of Applied Behavior Analysis, 9,* 55–64. Copyright © 1976 by the Society for the Experimental Analysis of Behavior. Reprinted with permission.

Response Cost

Response cost is used to decrease inappropriate behaviors. It is defined as the removal or loss of a positive reinforcer held by the child (or one that would normally be available) if a target behavior is performed, with the result of a decrease in occurrences of the behavior. Alternatively, it sometimes involves a fine or penalty for every occurrence of the targeted behavior. Most often, response cost has been applied to earned points, tokens, chips, stars, check marks, money, or similar reinforcers, but can also apply to privileges.

Advantages are that it may result in effective decreases in inappropriate behavior and is convenient in group or classroom settings. In comparison to time out, the child is not removed from ongoing activities. Also, it may be effectively used with token economies. Response cost also is likely to be acceptable to many caregivers.

One potential drawback is that children may become heavily fined and thus so in debt that they may lose interest or be unable to participate in the program. Furthermore, because it is an aversive procedure, unwanted side effects such as aggressive behaviors, avoidance, or emotional outbursts may occur. Response cost should be combined with other positive procedures, because it alone does not teach adaptive behaviors. Cooper, Heron, and Heward (1987) suggest combining response cost with differential reinforcement procedures. Ineffective response cost may undermine a treatment program.

There are different ways of implementing response cost procedures. First, response cost can be used along with a system of reinforcement; the child earns points or tokens for appropriate responses and loses points for inappropriate behaviors. Second, participants may be fined, and reinforcing events such as free play are taken away. In a third strategy, referred to as a "bonus response cost" (Sulzer-Azaroff & Mayer, 1991, p. 442), additional reinforcers that are not typically available to the child are made accessible. An example would be additional time in the gym or play with an attractive toy. The bonus time, but not the usually scheduled time, would be lost in specified amounts for inappropriate behavior. The advantages are the potential use of back-up reinforcers, and less critical legal and ethical concerns since positive experiences available to all children are not removed (Cooper, Heron, & Heward, 1987). Fourth, group contingencies may be involved. These are discussed in a later section.

Guidelines for the use of response cost have been suggested by several writers; they are summarized as follows.

1.   Carefully evaluate the natural reinforcers that are available, or the "bonus" reinforcers that can be made available. Consider the use of token economies.

2. Build in positive attention for appropriate behaviors. Response cost can cause behavioral change agents to focus unduly on inappropriate behavior (Walker, 1983).

3. Depending on the response cost system, children may need to have experience with the reinforcers, and need to be able to earn or build up a sufficient amount to establish a "reserve." However, if the reserve becomes too large, the fine may be of insufficient concern.

4. Clearly define the behaviors or rules and carefully determine the amounts of the fine. The target behaviors should be significant inappropriate behaviors and not minor transgressions. The amount of fines or penalties may need to be determined empirically (Sulzer-Azaroff & Mayer, 1991).

5. The effective use of positive reinforcement is critical. Children need to have clear descriptions of both how to earn positive reinforcement and the behaviors that result in response cost. Role play with the system may be helpful, and prior training in prerequisite skills (such as how to enter play groups to prevent playground fighting) may be necessary (Walker, 1983).

6. The fine should be substantial enough to affect behavior, but not so large as to result in bankruptcy. If response cost results in high rates of loss, the child may give up. Increasing the amount of fine will decrease behavior only to a point, after which large fines are not likely to decrease behavior significantly (Pazulinec, Meyerrose, & Sajwaj, 1983). The child should not be allowed to accumulate fines. "If a child's point total is at zero and an instance of behavior requiring . . . [response cost] occurs, a brief time out or other similar consequence should be applied until additional points have been earned or a new rating period begins" (Walker, 1983, p. 53).

7. Administer the fine as soon as possible following each targeted inappropriate behavior. The fine should not be administered in a harsh, punitive, or personalized way (Walker, 1983).

8. Make certain there are sufficient "reserves" of reinforcement. Baseline data should be used to help determine the amount of reinforcement that may be set aside for possible losses.

9. Plan for collecting response cost fines and plan back-up interventions for children who refuse to give up tokens. Home–school contingencies may be added.

10. Keep records of each inappropriate behavior and resulting response cost.

11. Evaluate the program for unplanned outcomes. Response cost may be overused. The "economics" of response cost need to be considered carefully, to prevent situations where children fall into debt or amass large amounts of the tokens or rewards. In both cases, the procedure is likely to be ineffective (Kazdin, 1977).

Response cost, in one form or another, is used often by parents or teachers — sometimes ineffectively, such as removing toys or other positive experiences in ways that do not decrease misbehavior but limit positive experiences and learning. To use response cost with young children, special attention is necessary because prerequisite skills and prior history with such systems are necessary and may have to be taught (Pazulinec, Meyerrose, & Sajwaj, 1983). Several applications are reviewed in later chapters.

Overcorrection

Overcorrection involves two procedures that may be used separately or in combination: (a) *restitution,* where the child is required to restore the environment to an improved condition, contingent on the performance of a target behavior, and (b) *positive practice,* where appropriate behaviors are practiced in situations that have been associated with misbehavior, contingent on performance of the targeted maladaptive behavior. Conceptually, overcorrection may be viewed as punishment — a mild time out from reinforcement, during which the child is required to perform a positive task (or work) logically tied to the misbehavior (Matson & DiLorenzo, 1984). It is also viewed as a complex treatment package, and can be effectively combined with other interventions such as DRO. In contrast, simple correction means that the child only "corrects" the result of the behavior. *Negative practice* requires the child to engage in the undesired behaviors repetitively for a specified time period under supervision and contingent on the targeted maladaptive behavior.

The intervention originated with toilet training for retarded adults (Azrin & Foxx, 1974). Restitution and positive practice overcorrection have helped with severe problems such as stereotypic behavior (self-stimulation), self-injury, aggression, and disruptive behaviors for severely disabled individuals (autistic, mentally retarded). However, the procedures can also be applied to a wide range of maladaptive behaviors of normal children. "Overcorrection appears particularly suited for eliminating many common minor destructive acts . . . such as throwing food on the floor and leaving toys and clothes strewn all over the house" (Spiegler, 1983, p. 156). Recommendations for overcorrection procedures can follow an analysis of naturally occurring caregiver responses to misbehaviors and incorporating ways to teach socially appropriate behaviors and provide natural consequences for specific maladaptive behaviors.

Overcorrection may have a number of components that vary within specific treatment programs. Important conditions are that (a) the additional task must be similar or related to the original task or behavior; (b) the overcorrection should occur immediately after the misbehavior if the child is calm; (c) the duration of the overcorrection should be longer than the original problem situation; (d) the child must be engaged actively in the positive practice overcorrection task; and (e) appropriate alternative behaviors should be reinforced when not applying overcorrection. Verbal cues and physical prompts are often used.

An example of overcorrection. Shapiro (1979) applied restitution and positive practice overcorrection to reduce paper shredding and book tearing by a five-year-old girl described as nonverbal and moderately retarded. Restitution (two minutes) consisted of instructions to pick up all torn paper and then clean the area (place toys in the toy box). Physical prompting was given when necessary. Positive practice (five minutes) consisted of looking through books with the experimenter without tearing them. The behaviors were successfully eliminated, and the results were sustained through eighteen months after the program ended.

Steps and the corresponding interventions related to over-correction are outlined in Table 7.1.

Overall, overcorrection is potentially acceptable to parents, teachers, and other change agents for a variety of target behaviors. However, it is important to follow established procedures whenever possible. Also, since overcorrection is viewed as a punishment or an aversive technique, special precautions are

Table 7.1. Overcorrection: Steps and Interventions.

Steps	Intervention
Restitution	
1. Request to stop responding ("No")	Reprimand
2. Notation of behavior to be corrected	Feedback
3. Interruption of ongoing activity	Time out and response prevention
4. Removal from others	Social isolation
5. Requirement to do work	Verbal instructions
6. Manual assisting (as necessary)	Physical restraints
7. Proceed to only verbal prompting	Graduated guidance
8. Performance required repetitiously	Aversive contingencies
Positive Practice	
9. Required to perform appropriate behavior	Presentation of alternative incompatible behaviors
10. Performance required repetitiously	Aversive contingencies
Conclusion	
11. Return to activity interrupted	Negative reinforcement of appropriate behavior and decreased probability of reinforcement of avoidance behaviors

Source: Matson, J. L., & DiLorenzo, T.M. (1984). *Punishment and its alternatives: A new perspective for behavior modification,* p. 52. New York, NY: Springer-Verlag. Reprinted with permission.

necessary. The caregivers should be prepared to handle a child who becomes upset or refuses to perform the required behaviors. Overcorrection can be abused by angry or unskilled caregivers.

Thus, it may require close supervision and may be very difficult to use correctly and consistently by some caregivers or in certain situations. Medical consent may be required, in addition to the safeguards outlined in Chapter Twelve. However, durations for overcorrection applications may be quite brief (thirty seconds to three minutes) but still be effective (Wolery, Bailey, & Sugai, 1988). An important application of overcorrection is dry-bed training described in Chapter Eight; an example of overcorrection for fire-setting behavior is described in Chapter Nine.

Self-Mediated Intervention Techniques

Self-Regulation

Self-regulation is considered to be a keystone behavior, and pivotal in behavior change efforts. Self-regulatory processes involve self-observation or monitoring, judgmental processes concerning one's performance, and self-reactions. Kanfer and Karoly (1982) suggest that self-regulation or management "signifies the *gradual* assumption of control by the individual over cueing, directing, rewarding, and correcting his or her own behavior" (p. 576). Methods of external control (by parents, teachers, peers) are used to teach self-management skills. Self-control techniques are best viewed by differences in emphasis rather than as completely different procedures. Furthermore, in practice, interventions often benefit from combinations of procedures.

There are many reasons to further the development of self-regulation. For young children, the following reasons are salient. First, much behavior is missed by parents, teachers, and other potential observers. Second, observers, behavioral change agents, or settings may become "cues" for the target behavior, so that the child performs the behavior depending on the setting or presence of another person. Self-regulation is an inherent mechanism for generalization. Third, practical benefits of successful interventions include giving caregivers additional time for other responsibilities. Successful interventions reduce the vigilance required in monitoring children's behavior that results in fatigue and loss of motivation. Fourth, the goal of intervention is often that of self-control, defined as a set of generalizable skills such as coping responses or rules of conduct in identifiable problem situations.

Self-monitoring may have treatment effects, termed *reactivity*. Thus, self-monitoring may be an important intervention in itself. With young children, we have used self-monitoring with such behaviors as thumb sucking and tantrums, and have included it as a component in other interventions to the greatest extent possible. Other techniques of self-control for young children involve stimulus control, self-instruction and self-statements, self-reinforcement and self-punishment, and alternative response training (Kazdin, 1984).

Teaching Self-Regulation

The general strategies for teaching self-regulation are outlined here; specific home and school applications are discussed in later chapters.

1. The child must be able to observe his or her own behavior. The component strategies of self-monitoring were reviewed in Chapter Four.
2. Appropriate rule learning is essential. Rules involve behaviors that are appropriate for various tasks and situations, and awareness of the consequences of behaviors.
3. The child must have the appropriate skills to perform the behaviors. Furthermore, it may be important to identify beliefs related to capabilities necessary in performing the task, defined as self-efficacy (Bandura, 1978). Self-instruction training involves teaching self-statements related to problem solving. Meichenbaum and Goodman (1971) developed the core procedure: (a) the adult models the behavior while talking aloud, (b) the child performs the behavior while

the adult instructs out loud, (c) the child performs the behavior and talks aloud to him or herself, (d) the child performs the behavior while whispering, and (e) the child performs the behavior while covertly verbalizing. Modeled verbalizations usually consist of (a) questions about the task, (b) answers to the questions, (c) self-guiding instructions, and (d) self-reinforcement (Bryant & Budd, 1982). However, there have been failures in replicating the procedure (Billings & Wasik, 1985).

4. The child is taught to evaluate his or her own behavior and compare it to standards for the behavior.
5. The child is taught to self-record and self-reward.
6. Self-regulation may be used in combination with other interventions, such as DRO, and other reinforcers. Public goal setting may be an important aspect.

An Example of a Self-Regulation Intervention. Poth and Barnett (1983) combined self-regulation with other intervention components to help with a three-year-old boy's ticlike behavior. The child had an extensive history of abuse and neglect. Parent and teacher consultation, plus his educational and psychological history, revealed multiple concerns including delayed fine and gross motor development, attention span, speech, and social skills. Of special concern were ticlike behaviors described as "shuddering episodes" in which the child's upper body and arms became tensed and rigid and he displayed palsylike movements in his hands for two to three seconds. The teacher felt that the behavior interfered with the child's classroom performance, particularly in activities requiring fine motor skills, and drew negative attention from his peers. His adoptive parents noted situational variation in the behavior, but still hypothesized a physical cause even though the child had undergone prior neurological evaluations. They thought that while the behavior might be "outgrown," it could also produce negative social ramifications.

The intervention plan was implemented first in the resource room and then in the classroom. In the first phase, self-observation and -regulation techniques were used, following the general steps discussed in Chapter Four. The child was taught to discriminate tensed from relaxed positions and behaviors, and was reinforced for engaging and completing activities where the shuddering behaviors were not exhibited. The procedural steps were

1. "Charlie, this is relaxed." (Slowly rotate head, shake arms loosely, bend at the waist, hands near the floor. Slowly return to upright position. Extend arms forward in a slow and relaxed manner). Repeat, "This is relaxed."

2. "Charlie, show me relaxed; let's relax together." (Repeat relaxing the body as described in step 1, talking softly through each movement).

3. "Charlie, this is *not* relaxed." (Demonstrate rigid arms, legs, tensing the body, then repeat, "This is not relaxed.")

4. "Charlie, show me *not* relaxed. Let's do *not* relaxed together." (Repeat tensing the body as described in step 3.)

5. Repeat step 2, then step 4, and step 2.

After the relaxation practice, it was explained to the child that if he remained relaxed during the planned activity, he would receive a star for his special card. In the classroom phase, he received stars or stickers on a special card for completing classroom activities while staying relaxed. A silent signal was used as a reminder to be relaxed. Like many interventions, specific techniques were combined. The intervention also used elements of DRO by reinforcing periods of time when the ticlike behavior was not evident. The results were described in Chapter Five, in the example of a multiple baseline across settings.

Correspondence Training

The rationale for correspondence training is quite simple — it involves developing the relationship between children's verbal accounts of behavior and their actual behavior, between saying and doing. It can be viewed as training in "promise keeping" (Baer, Osnes, & Stokes, 1983).

Language is a logical target for self-regulation efforts, for several reasons (Stokes & Osnes, 1986): (a) relatively speaking, it may be a well-developed skill with a pattern that leads to some control over behavior; (b) it can be used readily across different environments; and (c) it may be used conveniently and requires little effort. A potential advantage is that it may facilitate behavioral programs across inconvenient situations and inaccessible settings (Baer, Osnes, & Stokes, 1983). Although the focus of correspondence training is on verbalizations used to mediate behaviors, the procedures have also been used with young, language-delayed children (Osnes, Guevremont, & Stokes, 1986).

The concepts and steps of correspondence training are outlined in Exhibit 7.6. Succinctly stated, "reinforcement is made contingent on both promising to engage in a target response and then actually doing so, or on truthfully reporting past actions" (Baer, Williams, Osnes, & Stokes, 1985, p. 479).

Baer, Osnes, and Stokes (1983) demonstrated that it was possible to train correspondence between verbal and nonverbal behaviors across settings. They studied the effects of the procedure with a four-year-old boy described as having normal intelligence and no major behavior problems. Three behaviors were selected for training: picking up his pajamas after dressing, picking up his clothes after a bath, and choosing fruit for dessert. At agreed-upon times, his mother observed both occurrences and nonoccurrences of the targeted behaviors. She brought the data sheets to the center each day while transporting her child.

The correspondence procedure was examined across two conditions. The first condition was delayed reinforcement. Late in the afternoon at school, the child was questioned in private about specific home behaviors. During the questioning periods the child "was asked what he intended to do at home and a correct promise was praised, with prompts provided when necessary" (Baer, Osnes, & Stokes, 1983, p. 383). Prompts were required for only several sessions, in order to elicit complete sen-

Exhibit 7.6. An Example of Correspondence Training.

Language-delayed or socially withdrawn children

1. Before play period: "What are you going to do in play today?"
2. "I'm going to talk to the kids a lot."
3. Use prompts if step 2 is not spontaneous.
4. After response, "OK, you can go play." Play setting has at least four children.
5. After play period, child was taken aside and given general feedback about play behavior.
6. If criterion was met for "talking a lot," child is given praise and affection, and picks a slip of paper from a "Happy Sack."
   a. The criterion was established by peer comparisons. Criterion for children was individually selected based on baseline information. Level changes were introduced by changing the criterion in planned increments.
   b. Happy Sack: a bag containing ten slips of paper that have attention or activity consequences (piggy-back ride, getting a toss in the air, getting to blow bubbles). All consequences require less than three minutes to dispense.
7. The child returns to play.
8. If criterion not met: "You said you were going to talk a lot today in play but you didn't, so you can't pick from the Happy Sack. Go back to play."
9. Parent components through home–school communications can be added.

Source: Adapted from Osnes, P. G., Guevremont, D. C., & Stokes, T. F. (1986). If I say I'll talk more, then I will: Correspondence training to increase peer-directed talk by socially withdrawn children. *Behavior Modification, 10,* 287–299. Reprinted by permission of Sage Publications, Inc.

tences ("I'm going to choose fruit for dessert"), and were subsequently withdrawn. During this condition, reinforcement was given only if the correct promise had been made the preceding day. Even if the behavior was not performed, the correct promise was reinforced. The consequences were described as follows: "a grab bag containing slips of paper, each with one of the following written on it: 1 Big Hug; 2 Big Hugs; 2 Tosses in the Air; 3 Tosses in the Air; 3 Swings; 4 Swings; 5 Swings; 2 Tickles; 3 Tickles; 4 Tickles; Piggy Back Ride; Pick a Toy. If [the child] drew Pick a Toy, he was allowed to choose from a selection of inexpensive trinkets" (Baer, Osnes, & Stokes, 1983, p. 382).

In the second condition, the teacher gave social praise and tangible reinforcements for actual correspondence between the promise and behavior: "Yesterday you said you would . . . , and you did! That's very good! You get to draw from the surprise bag today." Or "Yesterday you said you would . . . , but you didn't. That means that you can't pick a surprise today."

The results showed the second condition — reinforcement of correspondence — immediately altered existing behaviors. The delay of reinforcement was successful without the correspondence training only when it followed the successful application of correspondence training to two prior targeted behaviors. Thus it was first necessary to establish a history of correspondence. The delay of reinforcement procedure may help with maintenance of behaviors. The authors concluded that the procedure may have utility for more complex home behaviors such as disruptiveness.

Correspondence training may be used for generalization and maintenance of responses. It may help with generalization to facilitate entry into natural communities of reinforcement by increasing the likelihood of reinforcement and positive attention from adults and peers (Stokes & Osnes, 1986). Through correspondence training, children achieve a successful history between verbalizations and actions: what they say they will do, and how they actually behave (Stokes & Osnes, 1986).

Despite the demonstrated effectiveness of correspondence training, some facets of the intervention still merit considerable study. A recent component analysis with normal preschoolers found that reinforcement of compliance ("Today you must do a letter or number worksheet when you get up from your nap in order to get your prize") was just as effective as reinforcement of correspondence (Weninger & Baer, 1990). Thus, the child's verbalization of the target behavior in correspondence training may not play an independent or important role. The results suggest the importance of prompts, and reinforcement of appropriate behavior or rule-governed behavior. Despite the ambiguities, for some children learning rules governed by language and reinforcing its use may be quite beneficial.

Group Contingencies and Tokens

Group and Peer Interventions

There are significant but interrelated reasons for considering the roles of other children in interventions for target children. Interventions for those who have various skill deficits or interfering behaviors related to social competence must take place in a social context. In fact, social behaviors constitute one of the most significant goals of early intervention or prevention programs. Strayhorn and Strain (1986, adapted from p. 288) conclude that three broad-band competencies are essential, all of which require a social context for learning:

1. The ability to be kind, cooperative, and appropriately compliant, as opposed to having a prevailing habit of being hostile and defiant.
2. The ability to show interest in people and things, to be appropriately outgoing, to socialize actively, as opposed to being withdrawn, fearful, and shy.
3. The ability to use language well, to have command of a wide range of vocabulary and syntax such that ideas may be both comprehended and expressed with facility.

In addition, there are practical reasons for including groups of children and peers as change agents. They provide powerful sources of reinforcement for learning and maintaining behaviors. Peers can model, reinforce, extinguish, and monitor broad classes of social behaviors. Peers may have more opportunities to observe specific social behaviors than adults. Similarly, the use of peers may greatly expand the situations where behaviors may be targeted for change. Peer-related interventions encompass situations or behaviors where it would be impractical or impossible to intervene, and they may be both powerful and time efficient for teachers. Examples related to classroom ecologies are expanded in later chapters.

Alternatively, adult-mediated strategies for producing and

sustaining changes in social behavior may result in limited outcomes. In fact, adult behavior may increase the frequency of brief appropriate social behaviors to the detriment of *sustained* social interactions with peers.

While many studies focus on specific skills and relatively brief play bouts, a desired result for children is to increase the likelihood of friendships. Friendships involve mutually established stable and skillful play interactions, and positive affective ties. While children with disabilities do "make friends" (Field, 1984), many of the interventions for improving social competence may not directly lead to friendship patterns. However, there still may be benefits for children in learning effective social skills and increasing positive interactions even when friendships are not the outcome.

Despite the potential benefits, there is relatively little research related to how group behavior of preschool children may be used to either reduce target behaviors or increase developmental skills. The use of group contingencies also raises special ethical and legal questions, which are reviewed in Chapter Twelve. Foremost is the possibility of unplanned negative effects for individual children. As with many interventions, much more research is needed in peer interventions.

Group-Oriented Programs. There are different ways of implementing group-based programs. A classification system described by Litow and Pumroy (1975) is presented in Exhibit 7.7. Using this classification system, Gresham and Gresham (1982) compared outcomes for a classroom of educable mentally retarded children (ages six to ten) with respect to disruptive behaviors. Overall, the results suggested some possible advantages of interdependent and dependent systems.

General guidelines for using group-based programs include the following (Cooper, Heron, & Heward, 1987; Hayes, 1976; Kazdin, 1984; Litow & Pumroy, 1975).

1. Set measurable objectives for behavior change. Objectives may include those linked to individual performance (such as aggressive acts or talking out) or those used for the entire

Exhibit 7.7. Classification of Group-Oriented Contingencies.

Independent Group-Oriented Contingency Systems
"The same response contingencies are simultaneously in effect for all group members, but are applied to performances on an individual basis" (p. 342). *Example:* Children who achieve the set level of performance are reinforced while others are not. Under this system, children are not reinforced for trying to help or encourage others.

Dependent Group-Oriented Contingency Systems
"The same response contingencies are simultaneously in effect for all group members, but are applied only to the performances of one or more selected group members. It is the performance of the selected group members that results in consequences for the whole group" (p. 342). *Example:* A child or subgroup must achieve a goal to earn free-time activities for the class. Failure to achieve the set level of performance would mean that no children are rewarded.

Interdependent Group-Oriented Contingency Systems
"The same response contingencies are simultaneously in effect for all group members, but are applied to a level of group performance" (p. 343). *Example:* Group reinforcers are made contingent upon each child meeting a set performance criterion. If the criterion is not met, no class member is rewarded. Group performance may be evaluated in several ways: (a) by establishing a criterion for the group; (b) by averaging all performances, low performances, or high performances; (c) by randomly selecting a performance; and (d) by selecting the highest or lowest performance.

Source: Adapted from Litow, L., & Pumroy, D. K. (1975). A review of classroom group-oriented contingencies. *Journal of Applied Behavior Analysis, 8,* pp. 341–347. Copyright ©1975 by the Society for the Experimental Analysis of Behavior. Reprinted with permission.

group. Appropriate target behaviors include those that are under peer control and those where it may be difficult to pinpoint individual behaviors, as with classroom noise levels.

2. Plan a group-based program designed to meet goals. Establish methods for feedback about performance. Teacher motivation is an important variable.

3. Set achievable criteria for performance. Baseline measures can be used to set initial criteria. Target children or group members must be able to meet criterion levels.

4. Establish measures for unwanted side effects. Monitor the behavior and performance of the target child and the group. For dependent group-oriented contingency systems, targeted children may experience extreme pressure from peers. Another problem is that a target child or subgroup may control the classroom by never achieving the criterion, thereby creating a situation where no class members receive reinforcement.

5. Select powerful reinforcers. One helpful strategy is the use of a reinforcement menu. An important safeguard was discussed earlier in the section on response cost. Group contingencies can result in bonus reinforcement beyond that which would normally be available to the children, to reduce the possibility of aversive consequences if the criterion is not met by the group.

6. As necessary, combine individual programs with group-based programs. Many individual behavioral programs, for example DRO, can be combined effectively. When a child meets a set criterion for individual objectives, such as reinforcement for appropriate behavior, the entire class can receive a reward.

7. Record keeping may be facilitated in ways that engage children. Teachers may design railroad tracks on tagboard, with "towns" representing intermediate goals at planned intervals. The space between the railroad ties can be used to indicate steps, and children can participate in "moving" the class to goals. If a child is successful in six out of ten DRO intervals, the class may move six "steps" to a group reward.

In sum, group-based programs have many potential advantages, and they may be combined with individual intervention programs. However, they also require special safeguards, as we discuss in Chapter Twelve.

Peer-Mediated Interventions. Rather than sharing the consequences of behavior, as described above, peers (or siblings) may be directly involved as behavior change agents. Peer-mediated intervention strategies have been widely researched. (Sibling-mediated interventions are discussed in Chapter Eight.)

A basic design includes a peer confederate (or group) who is close in age to the target child and who receives specific training in participating in an intervention. Many variables have been studied, such as the functioning level of the confederate child and various target behaviors. The adult role typically involves training, monitoring the intervention, and prompting behaviors, but not directly intervening. For older children, peer tutoring has been widely researched. For younger children, most research efforts have been directed toward improving the social behavior of withdrawn children and integrating children with disabilities into group or classroom settings.

Odom and Strain (1984) outlined three different peer-mediated interventions. First, *proximity* interventions entail placing socially competent children with target children and instructing them to "(1) play with the target children, (2) get the children to play with them, or (3) teach the target children to play" (p. 545). The distinguishing feature is that the socially competent children are not specifically trained for their intervention role and behavior change is dependent on "a natural transmission of social skills" (p. 545).

The second type of peer-mediated strategy is referred to as *prompt and reinforce,* where peers are trained to prompt and reinforce the social behavior of target children. "[A] prompt is an instruction (e.g., 'Come play') to engage in some social activity, and reinforcement is an event that comes after the interaction (e.g., 'I like to play with you') and maintains or increases the frequency of the desired type of behavior" (p. 546).

The third type of procedure is termed a *peer-initiation intervention.* Peers are instructed to make social initiations, including "asking a child to play, giving a toy to a child, providing physical assistance, or suggesting a play idea" (p. 547).

In each case, research suggests at least some success with the strategies, but, overall, proximity alone seems to be less effective than the other approaches. However, direct comparisons between the various methods are limited.

We describe general guidelines for implementing peer initiation strategies (Kerr & Nelson, 1983; Odom & Strain, 1984; Strain & Odom, 1986).

Carefully select peer confederates. Frameworks for decisions include school attendance and naturally frequent and appropriate peer interactions. Critical decision points also include likely compliance with training instructions, and skill in imitating modeled behavior included in the intervention components. Furthermore, the confederate should be able to maintain on-task behaviors related to the intervention; Kerr and Nelson suggest ten minutes. Also, specific play competence may be helpful depending on the game or activity.

Plan to reduce the effects of fatigue. Many variables may contribute to declining rates of social interaction over time, including characteristics of the peer confederate and the target child (such as difficulty in maintaining positive social interactions). A variety of reinforcements have been used to maintain the behavior of the peer confederates. Teacher prompts may be a significant part of the intervention. Also, several confederates may be trained and alternated in play. Overall, the effects on peer confederates have not been found to be negative, and sometimes the effects have been positive (Strain, Hoyson, & Jamieson, 1985; Strain & Odom, 1986).

Monitor the intervention closely. It is especially important to see that the intervention is carried out as planned. There may be positive or negative side effects for the confederate that need to be monitored and evaluated. Kerr and Nelson also suggest the possible use of *cue cards* to help the peer trainer conduct the intervention. For example, each cue card can depict a preferred toy or activity of the target child.

Carefully select specific peer initiations. Strain and Odom suggest "teachable" units based on naturalistic research. Recommendations include play organizers ("Let's play __ "), sharing, assistance, and affection.

Systematically train peer initiations. Training involves teaching the peer confederates specific social initiations. The training suggested by Strain and Odom (1986, p. 546) incorporates the following features: (a) discussion of the importance of the intervention or a review, (b) a description of the target social behavior that is the focus of the daily lesson, (c) modeling and role playing of the behavior, including the role of a nonresponsive child, (d) practice, and (e) verbal feedback. Exhibit 7.8 depicts a sample script.

Exhibit 7.8. Sample Script for Peer-Initiated Training.

Session 1: Introduction to System — Share Initiation — Persistence

Teacher: "Today you are going to learn how to be a good teacher. Sometimes your friends in your class do not know how to play with other children. You are going to learn how to teach them to play. What are you going to do?"

Child response: "Teach them to play."

Teacher: "One way you can get your friend to play with you is to share. How do you get your friend to play with you?"

Child response: "Share."

Teacher: "Right! You share. When you share you look at your friend and say, 'Here,' and put a toy in his hand. What do you do?" (Repeat this exercise until the child can repeat these three steps.)

Child response: "Look at friend and say, 'Here,' and put the toy in his hand."

Adult model with role player: "Now, watch me. I am going to share with ___ . Tell me if I do it right." (Demonstrate sharing.) "Did I share with ___ ? What did I do?"

Child response: "Yea! ___ looked at ___ , said, 'here ___ ' and put a toy in his hand."

Adult: "Right. I looked at ___ and said, 'here ___ ' and put a toy in his hand. Now watch me. See if I share with ___ ." (Move to the next activity in the classroom. This time provide a negative example of sharing by leaving out the "put in hand" component. Put the toy beside the role player). "Did I share?" (Correct if necessary and repeat this example if child got it wrong.) "Why not?"

Child response: "No. You did not put the toy in ___ 's hand."

Adult: "That's right. I did not put the toy in ___ 's hand. When I have to look at ___ and say, 'here ___ ' and put the toy in his hand." (Give the child two more positive and two more negative examples of sharing. When they answer incorrectly about sharing, repeat the example. Vary the negative examples by leaving out different components: looking, saying 'here,' putting in hand.)

Child practice with adults: "Now ___ , I want you to get ___ to share with you. What do you do when you share?"

Child response: "Look at ___ and say, 'here ___ ' and put a toy in his hand."

Adult: "Now, go get ___ to play with you." (For these practice examples, the role-playing adult should be responsive to the child's sharing.) (To the other confederates:) "Did ___ share with ___ ? What did she/he do?"

Child response: "Yes/No. Looked at ___ and said, 'here ___ ' and put a toy in his hand."

Adult: (Move to the next activity.) "Now, ___ I want you to share with ___ "

Exhibit 7.8. Sample Script for Peer-Initiated Training, Cont'd.

Introduce Persistence

Teacher: "Sometimes when I play with ___ , he/she does not want to play back. I have to keep on trying. What do I have to do?"

Child response: "Keep on trying."

Teacher: "Right, I have to keep on trying. Watch me. I am going to share with ___ . Now I want you to see if I keep on trying." (Role player will be initially unresponsive.) (Teacher should be persistent until child finally responds.) "Did I get ___ to play with me?" *Child:* "Yes." "Did he want to play?" *Child:* "No." "What did I do?" *Child:* "Keep on trying." "Right. I kept on trying. Watch. See if I can get ___ to play with me this time." (Again, the role player should be unresponsive at first. Repeat above questions and correct if necessary. Repeat the example until the child responds correctly.)

From "Peer Social Initiations: Effective Intervention for Social Skills Development of Exceptional Children" by P. S. Strain and S. L. Odom, *Exceptional Children, 52,* 1986, p. 547. Copyright 1986 by The Council for Exceptional Children. Reprinted with permission.

Make necessary changes in the physical environment to enable and facilitate interactions. Ecological factors include the availability of play materials and activities and the planning of play areas so that children will be encouraged to interact, play cooperatively, and share. Strain and Odom (1986) suggest that dolls, house materials, blocks, wagons, and kiddie cars help facilitate social interactions. Furthermore, some children may benefit from instruction in toy play. Sociodramatic activities also help promote social interactions.

Conduct frequent intervention sessions. Strain and Odom suggest daily sessions. Strategies to encourage persistence also may need to be programmed, especially for the first few days of the intervention (Kerr & Nelson, 1983). The daily event sequences for peer-initiated interventions are outlined in Exhibit 7.9.

Plan for generalization and maintenance. One important factor is the availability of "socially responsive peers" (Odom & Strain, 1984, p. 554). In addition, entire groups may receive social skills training to promote generalization of treatment effects. The behaviors and activities required in various settings,

Exhibit 7.9. Daily Intervention Sessions for Peer Initiations.

1. Bring the entire group to the intervention setting. The group should include a subject and at least one confederate.

2. Introduce the activities and support or model specific ways in which the children can use play materials.

3. Tell all children to go to the play activity, except the confederate.

4. Take the confederate aside and remind her what she will be doing in the intervention activity. Tell her to go and get the subject to play with her.

5. Observe the confederate closely. If she does not make the appropriate initiation in fifteen seconds, give her a verbal prompt to initiate. The first prompt should be implicit ("Remember, Lisa, you need to get ___ to play with you"). If the confederate does not come up with a good idea for an initiation, give her an explicit verbal prompt that tells the confederate exactly what to do ("Lisa, tell ___ to pour some tea in your cup").

6. Continue to prompt the confederate every fifteen to twenty seconds if she does not initiate to the subject. (As the intervention continues across a one-month period, the teacher should gradually reduce his or her prompts.)

7. If a contingency system is not being used, give verbal reinforcement to the confederate for being a good teacher and the subject for being a good player. Send the children to the next structured play activity or a free play activity.

8. Teacher support to the confederate must be withdrawn systematically: (a) When the confederate is initiating to the subject within fifteen seconds on 75 percent of all possible occasions, the length of time before giving a verbal prompt may be increased to thirty seconds. (b) After three days, the interval may be increased to forty-five seconds. (c) If confederate initiations do not decline, the interval may be lengthened to two minutes and finally to three minutes. (d) Two prompts to the confederate per session is an acceptable criterion for teacher prompt support. (e) Each time the interval is lengthened, the initiations and responding must remain stable for a three-day period. (f) If noticeable reductions occur, the teacher should move back to the previous prompting interval length.

the planned roles of adults, and the timing and sequence of the intervention components, are other important variables.

Long-term treatment effects have not received much attention from researchers. One important caveat before deciding on a peer-mediated intervention is the warning by Odom and Strain (1984, p. 554) that the "maintenance problem must be solved" before peer-mediated interventions can demonstrate clinical significance. For this reason, interventions may need to be carried out in each setting where the targeted behavior is observed. Peer interventions should be considered experimental (see Chapter Twelve). However, the same issues may also be applied to many other interventions, particularly social-skill interventions.

Token Economies

Token economies combine many procedures that have been proved effective. In a token economy, children earn tokens based on a set criterion for performance. The tokens are exchanged for back-up reinforcers at a later time.

Token economies were widely applied in the 1970s and many reviews are available. However, research on token economies has waned since that time. This has been attributed by some (for example, McLaughlin & Williams, 1988) to the demonstrated effectiveness of tokens, resulting in less need for research. An alternative explanation is the availability of other acceptable procedures that accomplish the same goals but require less effort, especially in monitoring and recording. In other words, token systems may not be necessary for instituting change. Examples of effective and less intrusive procedures include the use of performance feedback systems for classrooms (Van Houten, 1984) or daily report cards (Kelley, 1990).

However, token economies are versatile and may be adapted to many situations. One important advantage with young as well as older children is that tokens help bridge the delay between the response and reinforcement. Another benefit is that they may be backed up by a variety of reinforcers and thus may help avoid satiation, or help with children who have reinforcement preferences that are difficult to predict.

The following procedures and guidelines have been used to set up token economies. Kazdin (1982) specifically treats problem areas associated with token economies and possible strategies for dealing with the problems.

1. Define the targeted behaviors and rules. Definitions of the responses to be reinforced (or punished; see the discussion of response cost) need to be specified. Preacademic skills and social behaviors may be addressed by token systems.

2. Select a token that is safe, that may not be easily counterfeited, that is durable and standardized. The token itself may be attractive but not overly valued. The token should be easily administered. Examples of tokens were given in the earlier section on selecting reinforcers.

3. Select reinforcers to serve as backups for the tokens to be exchanged. Activity reinforcers have been widely used. Do not rely on a single reinforcer for an individual. Children may help select back-up reinforcers. Token delivery should be paired with praise or approval.

4. Specify the contingencies, exchange system, and the exchange ratio (or token value) whereby the number of tokens will be "cashed in" for the back-up reinforcers. At first, it may be important to reinforce a minimal performance "to allow for exposure to some sources of reinforcement" (Kazdin, 1977, p. 50). Although different terminology is sometimes used, *response priming* (Ayllon & Azrin, 1968; Kazdin, 1977) is a specific method of prompting: an individual is required to perform the first few components of a response chain (sequence of behaviors) that leads to the desired response. *Reinforcer sampling* is a special case of response priming in which the primed responses result in reinforcement (similar to a "free sample").

5. Plan and establish a way to dispense tokens. Important elements of economic theory are discussed by Kazdin (1977). Guard against satiation by controlling the contingencies for the reinforcement.

6. Plan to implement the token economy. Training staff is an essential part of effective token economies. Assign individual responsibilities for specific occasions. Treatment integrity is a significant consideration.

7. Develop a record-keeping system to monitor the children's performance. Other records can include exchange preferences and reliability in carrying out the procedures. They also serve to reinforce those carrying out the intervention.

8. Plan a way to fade the token economy. Basically, to fade the use of tokens, their use should become reduced over time and should be replaced by natural procedures. Kazdin (1977) discussed a number of procedures for fading, some summarized in an earlier section. One critical approach is to select target behaviors that are adaptive and that are likely to continue to be reinforced after the intervention (Ayllon & Azrin, 1968). While Kazdin (1982) discussed the possibility of having children earn their way off the token program for increasing responsiveness to the system, this may also be used to fade tokens (Kazdin & Mascitelli, 1980). Another practical strategy is to build in a delay between earning and exchanging tokens. Issues related to generalization and maintenance are pertinent. Fading should have the desired outcome of increasing self-regulated behavior.

In sum, the literature surrounding the use of token economies is extensive. It has been applied across many populations and settings (including home, school, and community), and with many behavior change agents. Tokens may be effectively employed with group contingencies. Some of the potential criticisms are (a) whether the target behaviors selected are the most suitable or impactful, and relatedly (b) whether the target behaviors help with adaptation to specific institutional settings or to broader treatment goals (Kazdin, 1977). A further criticism that arose in the 1970s centered on the potential deleterious effects of extrinsic reinforcement. However, these negative effects have not been documented in the research literature on the use of tokens. Perhaps the most important criticism is the relative effectiveness and efficiency vis-à-vis other intervention alternatives. Many other potential concerns, such as the full evaluation of treatment effects, can be applied to most other forms of intervention. Staff and administrative demands may be considerable.

On the other hand, the defining characteristic of the token economy is simply "the delivery of tangible conditioned reinforcers contingent upon specific behaviors" (Kazdin, 1977, p. 283). Thus, even in its simple form, token use may be versatile and effective. Specific family and school-based applications are discussed in later chapters.

Summary and Conclusions

We began the discussion of basic interventions by describing naturalistic strategies. Naturalistic intervention design represents a fundamental approach to address issues of acceptability, maintenance, and generalization.

Interventions commonly used for problem behaviors also were presented. Problem behaviors may involve either excesses or deficits in desired performance. Differential reinforcement represents a family of procedures to increase positive or adaptive behaviors while reducing maladaptive behaviors. Other basic interventions that have been widely used or have potential applicability for young children include time out, response cost, and overcorrection. Building on earlier discussions related to self-observation as a keystone behavior, basic strategies for teaching and enhancing self-regulation in young children were reviewed. We closed the chapter with discussions of group- and peer-mediated strategies, and the use of tokens.

The next chapters describe specific examples of how these and other interventions have been applied in home and school.

PART THREE

FAMILY AND HOME
INTERVENTIONS

8

Changing Roles
Within Family Systems

PARENTS ASSUME MANY ROLES IN DESIGNING AND CARRYING OUT
interventions for young children, whether the intervention is
at school or at home. For school-based interventions, parents
participate as problem solvers and decision makers. When the
locus of the intervention is at home, these roles are expanded;
parents become observers and teachers or change agents. Many
interventions successfully combine home and school elements.

Family needs and parent–child relationships need to be
studied idiographically. In addition, social networks and work-
related responsibilities, apart from child responsibilities, often
are critical considerations when working with parents. For these
reasons, we have emphasized strategies to enhance parent–child
relationships and naturalistic interventions based on parental
and family realities and goals.

An important caveat is necessary. There is a considerable literature that discusses professional roles related to family
assessment and intervention, role boundaries, and professional
qualifications that is outside the scope of this book. We present
general legal and ethical guidelines in Chapter Twelve. Many
other sources discuss professional-role issues. Despite potential
difficulties, preschool professionals frequently consult with family
members, and this chapter is generally written from the perspective of the parent-consultation model described earlier.

A second omission involves the intricacies of home-based instruction for early developmental skills. The topic has many complexities and insufficient research for summarization, especially for the age ranges of children and purposes that are the focus of this book.

Family Systems Issues

The overall significance of family systems for assessment and intervention design can be stated succinctly: "The child is an inseparable part of a small social system of an ecological unit made up of the child, his family, his school, his neighborhood, and community" (Hobbs, 1966, p. 1108).

We begin with one assumption—that the relationship between child and caregiver is the primary factor in establishing a *general* model for early intervention. However, many factors may interfere with that relationship. Family realities affect intervention decisions, and may have direct and indirect effects associated with children's risk status and adjustment or learning difficulties. For these reasons, our focus is on family *systems* rather than solely parent–child relationships. Although there are many other frameworks for early intervention, we place the child and the realities of families at the focal point of our analysis.

Family Realities

The assessment of family realities is an important first step in intervention design with young children. Family realities that may affect child behavior and child-rearing practices include social, economic, and personal stress, illness, and disruptive life events. The daily care of a child who places unusual demands on parents also contributes to stress.

Family situations often fall short of various ideals. However, it is likely that many alternative strategies for rearing children and different social arrangements will lead to the development of children's competence. Children also vary greatly with respect to their vulnerabilities (Rutter, 1987).

Families, like other environments, present both "risks and opportunities" (Garbarino & Whittaker, 1982, p. 3). While risk status for young children may be increased in response to family stressors, early stressors have the potential for both beneficial and harmful consequences. "There may be *sensitization* to the effects of later stressors," thus compounding risk factors, "but also there are *steeling* effects involved in overcoming stress and adversity" (Rutter, 1981, p. 347). The effects of stressors may be buffered by at least one caregiver who provides a relationship characterized by warm, reciprocal, and supportive interactions; a continuity of experiences; and the active promotion of competence (Werner, 1986).

Last, it is important to recognize that there is not one "global" environmental effect for children, even those being raised in the same family. Aspects of the environment uniquely influence individual development, and may operate at different times.

Mental health professionals frequently work with families in crisis, and, unfortunately, parents that most need help may be quite hard to reach. At the same time, demographics suggest increased numbers of single-parent families, use of day care by mothers joining the work force, and considerable divergence from traditional practices in the structure of families. Therefore, because of their potential effects on parent–child relationships and early experiences, parental stress and coping may be important targets in assessment and intervention design.

Relatedly, risk status for young children is associated with the quality of the learning and mediational contexts provided by families where opportunities likely to encourage growth and competence are provided. Qualities of the family system and interactions transform day-by-day events into learning experiences. Methods of control, punishment, and underlying parental belief systems influence learning and behavior outcomes.

Parents as Teachers and Change Agents

The assessment of the parental role requires careful consideration. Parental contributions to problem solving, decision making, and observation were discussed in Chapters Three, Four, and Five. The dimensions of parental "teaching" and family environment have been researched by Caldwell and Bradley (1979). Their widely used research instrument (HOME) is organized by (a) emotional and verbal responsivity of the caregivers, (b) avoidance of restriction and punishment, (c) organization of the physical and temporal environment, (d) availability of play materials, (e) degree of maternal involvement, and (f) opportunities for variety in daily stimulation.

Shearer and Shearer (1972, 1976) developed a model project based on the parental teaching role. The program included curriculum-based assessment, behavioral principles, parental input into curriculum planning and implementation, and a "home teacher" who demonstrated tasks and observed and gave feedback to the parent teaching the child. In addition, parents were taught the basics of recording behavior.

Griest and associates (1982) found that a *parent enhancement* program, including discussion and training in individual adult and family functioning, improved treatment outcomes, especially generalization. The program encompassed parental perceptions and expectations about child behavior, parental mood and adjustment, marital relationship, and extrafamilial interactions and relationships. The multifaceted training included direct instruction, discussion, modeling, role playing, and homework.

Thus, although much attention has been focused on the parental role, many factors mediate the effectiveness of parent–child interventions. While it often leads to successful outcomes, parental involvement in early intervention is not a panacea, nor are the effects of parent-based treatments well known. Sometimes parents will not be able to fulfill responsibilities because of a range of complicating factors, such as illness or economic stressors.

The role of parents in dealing with learning and behavior problems of children has received considerable attention and applications are expanding rapidly. Important dimensions include problem behavior, amount of parent versus professional involvement, the locus of involvement (home versus office or center), and cost effectiveness. Throughout the chapter we describe a variety of interventions where parents assume the role of change agent.

Maternal (or Caregiver) Responsiveness

Maternal responsiveness is a key behavior that underscores early competence in many developmental skills. There are many facets to the analysis of responsiveness, including social, environmental, and person variables, as well as specific skills, competencies, and behaviors. In addition, parental factors such as depression, or child factors related to temperament or other variables may at least partially determine qualities of interactions related to responsiveness. Martin (1989) outlined the following *person and relationship variables* underlying maternal responsiveness.

1. Interpersonal sensitivity: to be aware "of the interpersonal dimension of experience" and attuned "to characteristics of and variations in the interpersonal field" (p. 7).
2. Empathic awareness: to experience "another person's emotional reality as his or her own" (p. 8). Affective and cognitive components may be included.
3. Predictability: to provide "a stable, safe context for self-expression." Without predictable behaviors, the child may "experience the relationship as unsafe, unstable, and unresponsive." Excessive predictability may "result in relationships that are flat and arid" (p. 8).
4. Nonintrusiveness: to not intervene when the situation does not require intervention. An example of intrusive behavior is overprotectiveness.
5. Emotional availability: to be "affectively involved in a relationship and available for authentic exchange of feelings" (p. 8).
6. Engagement or involvement: to freely exchange values and ideas while considering the "needs and wishes" of the other person (p. 9).
7. Contingent reactivity: to respond to the behaviors of the child in appropriate ways regarding "content, timing, and intensity" (p. 9).

8. Interpersonal relations: to embrace "both personal and inter-personal components of mutually responsive mother–child relationships" (p. 11).
9. Interpersonal system: to consider responsiveness as a "do-main" consisting of multiple variables "imbedded within an interpersonal system" (p. 12).

In summary, a first step in intervention design for early learning and behavior problems is to consider the relationship between parent and child. The outcomes of this step may affect the range and quality of personal, social, and educational ex-periences provided in the home, or, if necessary, may help ad-dress parental needs to accomplish this goal. Despite the difficul-ties, the focus of early intervention decisions often may be directed to improving the realities of family circumstances, since other factors in the caregiver's experience may be precluding the adequate expression of the parental role. However, there are many times when it may not be possible to alter family cir-cumstances. In these cases, goals are associated with coping with realities. In the next sections, several factors related to plan-ning family interventions are examined.

Parental Beliefs, Self-Efficacy, and Empowerment

Parental beliefs directly and indirectly influence experiences that are provided to children and child-rearing practices. Further-more, they are likely to play a significant role in the decision process, including goals, efforts, and persistence related to change, and the acceptability of various intervention alternatives. How-ever, beliefs are difficult to assess. Individuals may be unaware, unwilling, or unable to communicate beliefs that affect behav-iors. Willingness to reveal belief systems to professionals is likely to be a function of rapport. Home observations and interviews reveal parental beliefs only to a degree. They are difficult to ob-serve directly in limited interactions because they are subtle and cumulative, because they are related to the basic organization of the home and family, and because of their links to factors outside the parent–child relationship (McGillicuddy-De Lisi, 1985).

Bandura (1977, 1981, 1986) has proposed *self-efficacy* as a broadly integrative, developmental construct central to the study of behavioral change. Self-efficacy reflects personal beliefs about competency, and thus it has the potential for influencing caregivers (and consultants) in making decisions about interventions, and in carrying them out. Self-efficacy influences the choice of activities, persistence in difficult tasks, thoughts, and emotional reactions.

Although parents may receive technical assistance in the course of an intervention, it should be provided in a way that is likely to encourage independent problem solving and relationship building through naturalistic means. Interventions can have the unintended effects of *reducing* self-sufficiency and confidence.

Dunst and his associates (Dunst & Trivette, 1987; Dunst, Trivette, & Deal, 1988) argue that professionals should strive for relationships with families that enable and empower the family, so that parents may meet their own needs with increased self-sufficiency. Major factors are the selection of intervention goals and strategies that promote competence, expand opportunities, and facilitate the client's personal attributions for success. To accomplish these goals, assessment outcomes should identify (a) family needs and priorities; (b) family strengths, resources, and "functioning style"; (c) "the family's personal network" for support and resources; and (d) "helping behaviors that promote the family's acquisition of competencies and skills necessary to mobilize and secure resources" (Dunst & Trivette, 1987, p. 444). Characteristics of the model proposed by Dunst and Trivette are summarized in Exhibit 8.1.

Home and School Interventions

Collaboration between home and school is a central theme of early intervention efforts. Collaboration may be expressed in many ways. First, parents may have a significant role in developing and conducting preschool programs. In fact, one of the most important legacies of Head Start is the focus on meaningful parental participation in programmatic decision making. Second, parent volunteers may be used for specific classroom

Exhibit 8.1. A Model of Enabling and Empowerment.

Empowerment deals with the effects of giving and receiving help.

1.   Help is positive and proactive.
2.   Help is offered.
3.   The locus of decision is with help-seeker.
4.   Aid and assistance fit the client's own culture.
5.   Aid and assistance are congruent with the help-seeker's appraisal of the problem or need.
6.   Costs of seeking and accepting help do not outweigh the benefits.
7.   Help can be reciprocated or "repaid."
8.   Help bolsters self-esteem; parents may experience immediate success in solving problem.
9.   Use of natural support networks is emphasized.
10. Cooperation and joint responsibility are characteristic of the helping process.
11. Acquisition of effective behavior that reduces need for help is emphasized.
12. It is important not only that problems have been resolved, but that the person was an active, responsible agent.

Source: Adapted from Dunst, C. J., & Trivette, C. M. (1987). Enabling and empowering families: Conceptual and intervention issues. *School Psychology Review, 16,* 451–453.

interventions. In Chapter Ten, we discuss a classic "switching task" intervention that was maintained by parents. Third, a critical area of professional practice involves conducting center-based interventions for parents, based on collaboratively identified needs. For example, preschools may offer programs on parenting skills, or intensive structured programs for specific aspects of parenting. Fourth, certain problem areas may benefit from collaboratively developed home–school plans for assessment and successful intervention. Examples are discussed in detail in Chapter Eleven.

In this section, we discuss strategies for developing home–school interventions and present examples. The basic procedures involve establishing ongoing parent–teacher communications and mutually agreeing on target behaviors, contingencies, and reinforcement strategies. The behavior of concern — and the reinforcement — may occur at school or at home, or both.

The potential benefits are many (Atkeson & Forehand, 1979; Budd et al., 1981; Stokes & Baer, 1977; Kelley, 1990;

Kelley & Carper, 1988): (a) such programs help promote parent involvement and reduce "blaming," (b) they can be time and cost efficient, (c) they may be nonintrusive in the classroom, (d) for some children the range of rewards in the home may be greater than in the school (although the opposite may be true), (e) there may be general beneficial outcomes for parent–child relationships in addition to those targeted, (f) the delay of reinforcement may enhance generalization efforts, and (g) home-based reinforcement may deal effectively with ethical concerns related to school-based behavior modification programs. While home–school interventions may be applied to a wide range of target behaviors, they will not be effective in all situations, especially with severely dysfunctional families.

The following steps are suggested (Atkeson & Forehand, 1979; Kelley, 1990; Kelley & Carper, 1988).

1. *Use parental and teacher consultation strategies to evaluate realistic and acceptable roles.* For initially unwilling or resistive parents (or teachers), the individual roles may be minimal but still meaningful. In comparison with parent training programs or other classroom interventions, the involvement by a caregiver may be drastically reduced.

2. *Define target behaviors and decide on ongoing measurement strategies.* The general strategies discussed in earlier chapters apply. Frequently we use parent and teacher consultation to design simple participant-observation strategies involving frequency counts (such as number of fights). In addition, direct observations or probes may be useful when specific activities are targeted (such as behavior in group freeplay).

An important decision is whether to apply the measurement procedure (and intervention) for the whole day, for a portion of the day, or for a specific activity. These decisions need to be made individually.

3. *Decide on a home–school communication system.* The most likely strategy involves a home–school *note.* The system should be tied to the target behavior and intervention, and behaviors and conditions should be described in ways that are appropriate

for daily use (weekends require separate plans). The note should be easy to use. An important decision involves whether the note will include very specific information or a global description of the behavior (Kelley & Carper, 1988). Related factors include the complexity of the target behavior and the degree of possible involvement and acceptability by parents and teachers. Messages can be delivered either daily or weekly, or only contingently (when the child meets specified criteria).

For children with behavior problems, we have frequently used DRO, or modifications of DRO, for home–school programs. In these cases, the child may take home the record of intervals showing the occasions that reinforcement was earned in school and the occasions that will be reinforced by the parent. Many developmentally appropriate and attractive means may be used for home–school communications that are engaging to children. For example, a railroad ticket format: each section of the ticket is punched or marked when a task or planned activity is completed successfully.

Parents are frequently the recipients of bad news. Thus, home–school notes that address accomplishments rather than misbehavior are effective. Phone contacts also may be useful with some parents. Lahey and associates (1977) reported the effective use of daily "report cards" for disruptive kindergarten behaviors.

Young children may be able to self-record behaviors, with assistance and structure. A prearranged private or silent signal can be given to the child when the targeted behavior is observed, and the child can be taught to mark a paper. The tallies, such as small circles colored in on a paper, can be recorded by the teacher or parent, and can serve as the basis for social and or tangible rewards. Strategies for self-observation and regulation may be considered adjunctive procedures initially, but may have important long-term benefits.

4. *Develop plans and scripts for teachers and parents concerning ways to carry out the daily communication.* It is necessary to plan the specifics of how to introduce, monitor, and send the home–school communication, and the way parents receive it and pro-

vide consequences. One of the possible dangers involves the natural variability of behaviors in the treatment phases of interventions, and subsequent parental and teacher reactions. This variability, and the possibility of "bad days," needs to be discussed. Plans may range from simple, brief, nonpunitive discussions about the behavior to the use of tokens, where each reinforced activity contributes to a weekly goal. Potential disruptions in family life and dysfunctional parent–child relationships need careful consideration. Parent and teacher training in the intervention is critically important in determining successful outcomes and should not be neglected.

Scripts for parents and teachers can help deal with the problem of treatment integrity. A script is essentially a model to follow when carrying out aspects of the intervention. Natural language and setting events, derived through parent and teacher consultation, should be used. Scripts are developed from the parents' or teacher's viewpoint, and encompass the intention and the strategies of the intervention. Scripts are developed collaboratively with parents and teachers, are tried out in role play and in actual interventions, and are revised as necessary. Behavioral contracts may be used to specify the roles and contingencies.

5. *Evaluate the intervention periodically and plan for ultimately fading it.* Given the many procedural variations that have an impact on the overall effectiveness, evaluation is essential. The home–school report is one important measure; it may be supplemented by direct observation probes conducted in the home or school. In other words, key elements of assessment and intervention design apply. Kelley (1990) has developed a comprehensive checklist of variables related to the overall effectiveness of school–home notes.

Interventions to Expand Learning Opportunities

One of the major parental roles is expanding learning opportunities in the home and community. Events such as shopping, dining, and sibling interactions hold potential for developing social, cognitive, and language skills.

Shopping with Children

Clark and colleagues wrote: "While shopping offers many opportunities for constructive and educational family interactions, parents rarely seem to use them!" (1977, p. 606). At the opposite extreme are coercive demands, punishment, and frequently embarrassment for family members. "Indeed, many family shopping trips occasion a high level of inappropriate child behavior and an equally high rate of apparently ineffective parental coercion" (p. 606). Studies that focus on shopping behavior of parents and young children are described in this section.

Barnard, Christophersen, and Wolf (1977) assessed the effectiveness of two traditional interventions on shopping behaviors: token reinforcement and response cost. Three mothers, who had received prior training in behavior management, and their three boys (ages five to six) participated in the study. The study was conducted in a supermarket; the shopping visits ranged from eight to twenty-two minutes. Mothers were encouraged to shop in their usual manner except that children were not permitted to ride in the carts.

Parent *proximity* (being "within reach" of the child) was measured. This behavior was viewed as a prerequisite for effective parent–child verbal interactions and instructions in the supermarket setting. *Product disturbance,* defined as the child picking up, moving, pushing, or disturbing merchandise without permission, was also measured. For two children, mothers' complaints were recorded after each store visit. Mothers also rated satisfaction with their child's behavior. Last, verbal interactions were obtained via a cassette tape recorder for one mother–child pair (coded as positive, negative, or neutral verbalizations).

An outline of the intervention is presented in Exhibit 8.2. Follow-up observations (from eight to twenty-two weeks) were also conducted.

The results indicated the treatment package was effective for all three children. Follow-up measures demonstrated that the behaviors were maintained at very high levels for two children; outcomes for the third child were variable. The evalua-

Exhibit 8.2. A Parent Intervention for Shopping Behavior.

Proximity

1. Before the store visit, the experimenter described the appropriate behaviors (staying within reach of the mother) and modeled them in the home.

2. The child was given an opportunity to practice engaging in the appropriate behavior and received praise and verbal feedback about his performance.

3. Mothers were instructed to award one point at periodic intervals (two or three times per store aisle) when the child was in reach and to subtract two points each time they judged the child to be out of reach.

4. Mothers were also instructed to give descriptive verbal feedback to the child about his behavior. *Examples:* "That's a point; you're here with me." "That's too far ahead. I'll have to take off two."

Product Disturbance

1. Appropriate behaviors were discussed in the home.

2. The same procedures for proximity were maintained.

3. Identical procedures were used for product disturbances.

Combined Procedures

1. Children periodically received one point for being within reach of the mother, and an additional point for not disturbing products.

2. Two points were deducted for each instance of nonproximity or product disturbance.

3. Mothers carried pencils and point cards.

4. At the end of the store visit, the number of points earned and lost was announced to the child.

5. The balance was added to the child's daily home balance and was exchangeable for goods and privileges as defined by his specific home point system.

Source: Adapted from Barnard, J. D., Christophersen, E. R., & Wolf, M. M. (1977). Teaching children appropriate shopping behavior through parent training in the supermarket setting. *Journal of Applied Behavior Analysis, 10,* 45–59. Copyright ©1977 by the Society for the Experimental Analysis of Behavior. Reprinted with permission.

tion of caregiver satisfaction found reduced complaints about shopping behaviors. Verbal interactions recorded for one child demonstrated that positive talk increased during the treatment, and was maintained at a level higher than baseline. Negative comments dropped to a low level during treatment, and to zero during followup. The results also suggest the importance of training for skills in the setting in which they occur. The researchers conclude that parents may be able to use these procedures "without prior home training" (Barnard, Christopherson, & Wolf, 1977, p. 59).

Clark and colleagues developed an extensive intervention package to help with family shopping problems, reported in three interrelated studies. The objectives were to "develop and maintain children's courteous behavior and enhance family interactions on shopping trips" (1977, p. 607). The program components were described in the following way:

> 1. The management component consisted of a response-cost system. Children were allotted a 50-cent allowance at the outset of the shopping trip. Each time a child violated a guideline (made a distracting comment or engaged in a distracting behavior), a nickel was withheld from the child's shopping allowance.
> 2. The enhancement component consisted of parental instructions "to prompt and encourage interesting conversation about shopping and other topics to involve the children" in the family activity. [p. 607]

The first study evaluated the contribution of the components. The children, ages seven to ten, were from group homes for neglected children. The "parents," in this initial study, were actually surrogates involved in training as a "teaching parent." Observations were conducted in stores located in a shopping center. The methods are described in Exhibit 8.3.

In the initial study, money withheld under the response-cost procedure could be spent during the next shopping trip, if

Exhibit 8.3. A Family Shopping Advice Package.

Guidelines for Good Shopping

1. The following guidelines were used during the baseline condition; and during the two intervention conditions.
2. On the way to the shopping center, the parent described the guidelines:
   a. "Stay close enough to reach out our arms and touch hands—this means we will be close enough to talk to one another."
   b. "Do not touch things for sale in the store or things like cash registers, candy machines, or mannequins."
   c. "I have a lot of errands to do, so please do not distract me by saying, 'I want to go to the candy store,' or 'Buy me one of those,' or by tattling on the other children."
   d. "Please do not roughhouse, run, yell, fight, or hang on the other children in the store because this will slow up our shopping and bother other people in the store."
   e. Each child was asked to repeat an abbreviated version of the rules.
   f. The children were told that they would have 50 cents of their allowance to spend during "their" ten-minute shopping at the end of the trip.
   g. Any time a child did not follow a guideline, the parent would hold back 5 cents of that child's allowance. If the child failed to follow the guidelines again, then the parents would hold back another 5 cents.

Management plus Enhancement Condition

1. The same conditions were in effect.
2. In addition, the parent was instructed to talk to the children about the shopping they were doing in the store, such as interesting merchandise they saw, quality, prices, and so on. ("Where could a ___ be found?")
3. After shopping was finished, parents told children how much money each could spend, and the children were allowed to shop.

Source: Adapted from Clark, H. B., et al. (1977). A parent advice package for family shopping trips: Development and evaluation. *Journal of Applied Behavior Analysis, 10,* 608–609. Copyright © 1977 by the Society for the Experimental Analysis of Behavior. Reprinted with permission.

the child qualified as a "good shopper." However, this step was later eliminated from the treatment package because of the additional complexity (personal communication, H. B. Clark, March 29, 1991).

Comprehensive measures were taken of children's distracting behaviors and comments, children's social and educational comments, parents' teaching comments, and parents' coercive comments. In addition, parental consequences for behaviors were measured (such as parental description of why 5 cents was being withheld). The comments were tape recorded. The results were stated succinctly by the authors: "The management component significantly reduced distracting behavior and distracting comments but *also reduced social and educational comments* [emphasis added]. However, adding the enhancement component increased social and educational comments to well above baseline levels" (p. 610).

A second study replicated the package with natural families and with younger children (ages ranged from four to nine). The parents in the second study were paid $4 for their participation plus a bonus for meeting scheduled appointments. In addition, a four-part "advice package" was developed to describe the components. The first part described how to use the procedures. The second part included three quizzes on the components and scripts of shopping trips based on the "advice package." The third part included a form for the following: "space for a shopping list, a tally for keeping track of the nickels withheld . . . , and five self-feedback Yes/No questions for the mother to answer at specific intervals" (p. 613). The last part included a simplified version to help parents explain the new procedures for shopping trips to their children. Four days of practice were used to teach the mothers to use the procedures.

The effectiveness of the advice package was demonstrated and social validity evaluations were positive. Mothers reported that the advice package resulted in "more pleasurable and frequent shopping trips" (p. 617). They reported that the shopping trip was a better learning experience for the children. Three mothers reported spending *less* than usual for their children when using the procedures. Ratings on parental effort were mixed, although the mothers who thought that the procedure required more effort still thought that it was worthwhile. A third study replicated a slightly modified shopping advice package without professional intervention.

Together, the three studies convincingly demonstrated the potential use of behavioral techniques in the community to help make family outings more enjoyable and more of a learning experience. The authors discussed a *graduated practice procedure* as an important feature of the program. Initially, families shopped for only half their usual time, to help ensure that the children would be able to follow the guidelines and be reinforced. Otherwise, because of the response-cost procedure, children could lose all their spending money despite improved behavior. Also, the briefer shopping trips at the beginning were likely to reduce the strain associated with the parents' newly learned behaviors. A booklet written for use by parents is available (Greene, Clark, & Risley, 1977).

Dinnertime Conversations and Dining Out

Correspondence training was used to enhance dinnertime conversation for preschool children, making it "more mutually interesting" (Jewett & Clark, 1979, p. 590). The locus of the intervention was in the preschool. The authors described the rationale in the following way: "If the teacher could obtain reasonably accurate information on the children's dinnertime conversation, she/he could reinforce their corresponding verbal behavior on a delayed basis in the preschool group setting" (p. 590).

While most of the studies reported throughout this book are based on clinical or at-risk samples, the subjects in this study were volunteers. The study has potential for clinical applications, however. Also, the locus of the intervention could be clinic- rather than school-based.

The subjects were four children ages four and five described as middle class, having intelligible speech, and with at least one sibling over the age of four. Families were paid a nominal amount for participation. The evening meal was tape recorded and was returned each morning to the school.

Outcome measures of conversations were (a) children's statements of appreciation, (b) conversational questions, and (c) comments "to prompt or to coach the target child" (p. 591). Conversational comments included initiating a topic, continuing a topic, or restating a comment.

Exhibit 8.4. Correspondence Training
for Dinnertime Conversations.

The prelunch practice

1. The amount of practice varied according to teacher judgment (from one to ten minutes).
2. On the first day for a new topic category, the teacher modeled examples of comments for that topic.
3. The comments were then taught, using prompting, modeling, practice, and social reinforcement.
4. The criterion was met when the child was able to verbalize the comments independently or within 30 seconds of a modeled comment.
5. The child had to verbalize the appropriate set of comments for the next meal.
6. Practice was directed to the child's difficulties.
7. Correct sentence structure and variation of comments were also prompted.

The simulated family meal held by the preschool teacher

1. Lunches were eaten family style, and were used to role play. The teacher assumed the role of various family members in responding to the child.
2. Social reinforcement was given within the context of the role.
3. Prompts were used freely during the first day of each training condition.

Predinner practice

1. Predinner practice, held in the afternoon, was the same as prelunch practice, except the focus changed to the evening meal.

The feedback sessions

1. At 10:30 A.M. a feedback session was held to check correspondence between what the children reported and what comments were actually made at dinner the previous evening.
2. A prompt was given and the child was asked to repeat the comments.
    a. "Did you say all of the right things at dinner?" (This established "eligibility.")
    b. "Who did you ask questions to and what did you ask them?"
    c. Further prompts and modeling of the correct responses were allowed for "eligible" children.
    d. If the teacher had to assist the child, a brief delay was used. ("Now you're saying it right, but I had to help you. I'll come back in a minute to see if you can remember all by yourself.")
    e. Assistance was given to those children who had not met the criterion.
    f. The prompts were continued until the child met the criterion without assistance and earned the reward.

Exhibit 8.4. Correspondence Training for Dinnertime Conversations, Cont'd.

---

3.   The criterion was one comment to *each* specified family member in each planned category.

2.   A social and snack reinforcement was provided contingent upon the correspondence between verbal report and the use of the comments during the family dinner.

5.   Lunch feedback, in the afternoon, was identical, except that it focused on the simulated family meal.

Source: Adapted from Jewett, J., & Clark, H. B. (1979). Teaching preschoolers to use appropriate dinnertime conversation: An analysis of generalization from school to home. *Behavior Therapy, 10,* 589–605. Copyright ©1979 by the Association for Advancement of Behavior Therapy. Reprinted by permission of the publisher and author.

The correspondence training procedure followed that of Risley and Hart (1968). The central features of the study were (a) the taped dinnertime conversations between family members, (b) the simulated family meal held by the preschool teacher, (c) the training sessions, and (d) the feedback sessions. These components are outlined in Exhibit 8.4.

Conversational comments within the categories being studied did not occur under the baseline condition. The experimental conditions convincingly demonstrated the effectiveness of the intervention across all subjects. Furthermore, the results were maintained after the preschool facet of the program was withdrawn and during a two-week followup. The authors wrote: "Conversational participation was apparently being maintained by natural consequences, such as parental attention, increased interaction with family members, and interesting new topics of discussion" (p. 601).

The experimenters also evaluated parental satisfaction and social validity. A questionnaire was used to evaluate the program in terms of improvements or disruptions in mealtime. "Three sets of parents reported that their child's conversational skills made mealtime much more pleasant" (pp. 597–598). The fourth set of parents did not report enhanced enjoyment, "but all four sets of parents reported that it was more pleasant for their children" (p. 598). All families indicated that the procedure was either less disruptive or no different in comparison to the nonintervention condition. Furthermore, all families reported that more time was spent in interesting conversation.

Social validation was studied by having five judges (parents of preschoolers not involved in the study) rate a set of dinnertime tapes for two families selected from baseline and experimental conditions. The social validity tests supported improved conditions, or no change, but no negative results.

The experimenters also addressed the issue of feasibility. Little parent or teacher time was required, and new behavioral repertoires were established quickly. The preschool procedures required a maximum of two twenty-minute periods, and were quickly faded. A resource that evolved from this research is available for parents and practitioners (Clark, McManmon, Smith-Tuten, & Smith, 1985).

Parent advice packages have been developed for mealtime and dining out (Bauman, Reiss, Rogers, & Bailey, 1983). Steps are identified in Exhibit 8.5. An innovative study by Green, Hardison, and Greene (1984) examined the use of special placemats to stimulate family conversation during restaurant meals.

Exhibit 8.5. Parent Advice Package for Dining Out.

---

1. Specify appropriate behavior for children in restaurants.
2. Find a table or booth away from the crowd.
3. Seat children on the inside next to the wall.
4. Separate the children.
5. Provide the children with a premeal snack, such as crackers.
6. Order food the children enjoy.
7. Provide interesting toys to occupy their time.
8. Move dinner utensils from the children's reach.
9. Remove the toys when the food arrives.
10. Periodically praise the children for appropriate behavior.

Source: Adapted from Bauman, K. E., Reiss, M.L., Rogers, R. W., & Bailey, J. S. (1983). Dining out with children: Effectiveness of a parent advice package on pre-meal inappropriate behavior. *Journal of Applied Behavior Analysis, 16,* 55–68. Copyright ©1983 by the Society for the Experimental Analysis of Behavior. Reprinted with permission.

Sibling Interventions

Without a doubt, sibling interactions can be a significant so-
cializing force for many children. "[A] potential, virtually un-
used resource for training handicapped children to engage in
social interaction is the handicapped child's nonhandicapped sibling" (James & Egel, 1986, p. 173). Also, many parents request
specific help for problem behaviors between siblings.

Powell and Ogle (1985) reviewed in detail the topic of siblings and exceptionalities within a family context, and wrote:
"If the sibling and the child with a handicap do not socially interact with each other, the loss of the benefits of such interaction will be more detrimental for the handicapped child than
a nonhandicapped child" (p. 107). Conversely, improved interactions enable expanded interactions with normal children.

The study by James and Egel (1986) evaluated direct
prompting as a way of increasing reciprocal interactions between
siblings. The authors also were interested in generalizations to
peer play and interactions across settings. The children targeted
for the interventions were two girls and one boy (all age four)
in a noncategorical special education program. They were selected because of limited interactions with siblings or peers. Two
of the children had cerebral palsy; one was nonambulatory and
required a wheelchair. The third child was diagnosed as mentally retarded and had a number of maladaptive behaviors such
as body rocking. All were described as having IQs in the 30s.
The nonhandicapped siblings ranged from ages six to eight. Based
on parental report, the older siblings "occasionally" initiated play,
but the young handicapped child "rarely initiated or responded
to interactions" (p. 174). In addition, two friends of the nonhandicapped older siblings participated in the study, both age
seven. The third child lived in a rural location, and no peer was
available to participate in the study.

The intervention setting for two children (for play, training, and generalization) was in the usual play area in the home,
containing household furnishings including a television set. The
generalization setting for the third participant was an outside
porch. The experimenters also conducted a "toy preference as-

sessment" to choose reinforcing toys. The duration of toy play was recorded during brief structured observations.

The training for the siblings is outlined in Exhibit 8.6. The training was conducted in the home play area. The training sessions ranged from twelve to fifteen minutes, and were held an average of five days a week, with no more than two per day, four to six hours apart.

Exhibit 8.6. Increasing Interactions Between Handicapped and Nonhandicapped Siblings.

Modeling

1. The experimenter demonstrated the initiation of interactions, prompts, and the reinforcement of initiations and responses, with the handicapped child in play with the most preferred toy.
2. As an example, the trainer would say, "Let's play cars" and would push the car to the handicapped child.
3. If the target child responded, the trainer gave social praise. ("I like playing with you.")
4. If the handicapped child did not respond, the trainer used physical guidance to push the car.
5. At least four interactions were modeled, and explanations were given to the nonhandicapped sibling.

Practice with Feedback

1. The trainer asked the nonhandicapped sibling to use the modeled strategies to get the targeted child to play.
2. The trainer gave instructional cues and feedback to the sibling for five minutes while observing the interactions.
3. If no positive social behaviors were observed (for a ten-second interval), the trainer prompted the sibling to initiate an interaction.
4. A variety of prompts, varying in obtrusiveness, were used: from "Make sure he is watching you" to "Put his hands on the car." Social reinforcement was given.
5. If the sibling did not respond within ten seconds of the cue (or if it was incorrect), the verbal cue was repeated, the response was prompted, and reinforcement was provided.

Source: Adapted from James, S. D., & Egel, A. L. (1986). A direct prompting strategy for increasing reciprocal interactions between handicapped and nonhandicapped siblings. *Journal of Applied Behavior Analysis, 19,* 173–186. Copyright ©1986 by the Society for the Experimental Analysis of Behavior. Reprinted with permission.

Additional procedures were added to increase the targeted child's initiations if the rate of initiations was low. Based on incidental teaching and delay (see Chapter Six), the sibling held a desired toy and waited for the targeted child "to initiate," using verbal requests, signs, or gestures (p. 177). Mothers prompted interactions when observations showed that interactions were occurring in less than half of the intervals for two targeted children and their siblings.

The results indicated low levels of interactions during baseline. For each target child/sibling dyad, substantial increases in reciprocal interactions were found during the intervention. Follow-up data obtained six months after the study indicated that the level of reciprocal interactions had increased. Evidence for generalization to the groups with a friend of the nonhandicapped child was also found, although the probes for assessing generalization were limited to two children in the same setting used for training.

Social validity of the intervention was assessed. Parents gave generally favorable ratings to items concerning increases in positive interactions and the responsiveness of the targeted child. There was some agreement that the targeted child was more likely to initiate interactions. The siblings did not appear to express negative statements concerning interactions.

Schreibman, O'Neill, and Koegel (1983) trained sibling pairs to teach specific tasks to autistic brothers or sisters. In one of the three cases, an eight-year-old girl was trained to teach her autistic five-year-old brother. The tasks included (a) concepts of before/after and first/last; (b) coin identification; (c) classification of picture cards (for example, animals, clothes); (d) pronoun concepts of "I have" and "you have"; (e) one-to-one correspondence; (f) spelling skills; (g) capital letters; and (h) responses to short-term memory questions ("Who went to the store?").

The training and teaching sessions took place in the home. Two generalization probes were conducted at a research site resembling a living room. The sibling was taught reinforcement techniques, shaping, chaining, and discrete trial strategies through a videotaped presentation, after which the older sibling and the trainer discussed the various techniques. The trainer also provided examples of how the techniques could be used in situations other than those described on the tape and how they could be applied to everyday problem behaviors and situations.

During the next phase, the sibling worked on one of the specified target behaviors with her younger autistic brother for thirty minutes while the trainer observed. The trainer interrupted periodically to provide corrective and positive feedback to the sibling. When the sibling had difficulty performing specific techniques, the trainer modeled the procedure and asked the sibling to try it again. After each training session, a new task was selected and the sibling worked another fifteen minutes without interruption from the trainer. Probes were taken during this period to determine the extent of skill generalization. A total of eight training sessions were conducted.

The results of the study indicated that the sibling used the strategies 73 percent of the time during baseline and increased her performance to 100 percent with training. The autistic child's responses increased from 15 percent at baseline to 45 percent during training. Setting generalization probes indicated maintenance of performance for both children.

Other studies report the successful training of siblings in teaching one skill to a handicapped sibling (Bennett, 1973; Cash & Evans, 1975; Colletti & Harris, 1977; Miller & Cantwell, 1976). For example, Bennett taught a four-year-old girl to teach her hearing-impaired three-year-old sister to use plurals. The hearing impaired child had intelligible speech but had never used the plural endings of -s ("forks") and -z ("bags"). The child could hear vowel sounds at a distance of twelve feet but consonants only at three feet. During training, the children were three feet apart and face to face. Training consisted of imitating and requesting responses from the hearing-impaired sibling (such as showing picture cards and saying, "What's this?"). Tokens (cashed in for candy) and praise were used. Training required seven sessions lasting between twenty and thirty-five minutes. The intervention was successful in increasing the hearing-impaired child's use of the plural -s; use of the -z ending, a control measure that was not taught, remained unaffected.

James and Egel (1986) caution that "the long-term effects of sibling training programs on the siblings have not been assessed empirically" (p. 185). They point out the need to directly assess outcomes for the siblings in future research. As discussed by Powell and Ogle (1985), numerous factors may affect the success of such interventions. Exhibits 8.7 and 8.8 summarize potential advantages of sibling interventions and issues in implementation. Exhibit 8.9 lists some activities that may promote sibling interactions at the preschool age level.

General guidelines for a sibling teaching program include (a) clarifying treatment expectations, (b) seeking voluntary participation, (c) planning to ensure successes, and (d) rewarding both children for participation. A two-year age advantage for the sibling teacher is recommended. Sibling rivalry may undermine such efforts, and strategies to reduce jealousy and competition may be necessary (Powell & Ogle, 1985).

Exhibit 8.7. Advantages of Sibling Training.

1. *Teaching new skills.* Normal siblings often have intensive contact with their handicapped siblings and teach them many skills. However, such teaching is often intermittent and based on the interests of the normal sibling. Training siblings in what to teach and how to teach can result in beneficial outcomes for targeted children.

2. *Consistency.* The inclusion of siblings in training programs can result in the consistent application of procedures and strategies taught. With all the immediate family responding in the same manner to behaviors exhibited by the targeted child, maintenance and generalization may occur more easily.

3. *Parenting.* Often it is easier for parents to reward the sibling for implementing the intervention than to implement the intervention themselves.

4. *Enthusiasm.* Siblings generally have fewer preconditioned biases toward handicapped persons. They may be more enthusiastic, committed, and successful in implementing interventions than others.

5. *Increased positive interactions.* Siblings may feel enormous responsibility for caring for the handicapped sibling or may feel neglected by parents for the amount of time spent with the handicapped child. If the time and content of interactions between a sibling and the handicapped child are structured, benefits may accrue for both.

Source: Miller & Cantwell, 1976, p. 449; Weinrott, 1974.

Exhibit 8.8. Issues in Sibling Training.

---

1. *Training sessions.* Training sessions should be well planned and divided into short segments. Incidental teaching, direct prompting, modeling, role playing, and rehearsal strategies can be effective in sibling training. Length of sessions should depend on the age and behavior of the siblings.

2. *Rules.* When parents and siblings participate in intervention training, it is necessary to establish rules. Some may be interpreted as telling of "family secrets." For example, if family members observe another member not carrying out the intervention as planned, such behavior may be subject to discussion with the professional. Miller and Cantwell presented a case in which a sibling reported that the father had spanked the target child rather than following the intervention procedure, resulting in the father's increased anger toward the sibling.

3. *Following through.* It will be necessary to have the parents monitor the sibling to make certain that the intervention is being carried out as planned. Frequent therapist–family member contact will facilitate treatment adherence.

4. *Presence of target child.* If parents and siblings are being trained, it may be most beneficial if the target child is present for only a portion of each session. Providing someone to watch the target child may be necessary.

5. *Participation by family members.* Participation by other family members during sessions may need to be assured to help with a domineering parent or shy child.

Source: Adapted from Miller, N. B., & Cantwell, D. P. Siblings as therapists: A behavioral approach. *American Journal of Psychiatry, 133,* 447–450, 1976. Copyright ©1976, the American Psychiatric Association. Reprinted by permission.

Problem Behaviors

Fears and Phobias

Early investigations of fears are an important part of the history of psychology, but fears and phobias in young children account for only about 5 percent of all referrals for intervention (Ollendick & Francis, 1988). They are discussed here because interventions in this area generally require parents to seek assistance from professionals (Morris & Kratochwill, 1983). However, few single-case studies exist, and most involve children described as having a single fear or phobia.

Exhibit 8.9. Activities for Sibling Interaction.

Catching balls
Kicking balls
Rolling balls back and forth
Block play
Playing with Tinker Toys
Beanbag activities
Acting out stories, television shows, movies
Tee-ball
Bowling pins (indoors)
Balloon play
Playing tea party
Playing house
Playing doctor or dentist
Playing dress-up
Blowing bubbles
Playing spaceship
Playing store
Dolls
Cars and trucks
Playing school
Wagons
Dancing
Singing songs
Marching band
Playing cowboys and Indians
Playing policeman, fireman, mailman, and so forth
Marbles
Toy telephones
Fixing simple snacks
Pretending to be animals
Using puppets

Source: Powell, T. H., & Ogle, P. A. (1985). *Brothers and sisters: A special part of exceptional families,* p. 113. Baltimore, MD: Brookes, P. O. Box 10624, Baltimore, MD 21285-0624, 301-337-9580. Reprinted with permission.

Fears may be described as intense emotional reactions with behavioral, cognitive, and physiological manifestations of anxiety. Fears may be expressed in reactions related to any or all three of these systems (see Evans, 1986, for an analysis of the "triple response mode"). Fears generally help children learn to adapt to stressful and environmental realities because they promote learning caution and seeking protection. But fears also can be disruptive, and can be linked to anxiety and panic.

In young children fears of the dark, ghosts, monsters, animals, bugs, separation from parents, and particular persons, objects, or events are common. However, when these fears persist over a long period (two years or more), a distinction between fears and phobias may be made. Marks (1969) identified criteria for distinguishing phobias from common fears: (a) the fear is unreasonable for the situation; (b) the fear persists even when given explanation and reason; (c) the fear cannot be controlled voluntarily; and (d) the fear results in the nonadaptive avoidance of the object, event, or situation. Furthermore, a phobia may be present when the fear does not change with age, as many fears are age-specific (Miller, Barrett, & Hampe, 1974). Three broad categories of *DSM-III-R* (American Psychiatric Association, 1987) relate generally to fears and phobias: separation anxiety disorder, avoidant disorder of childhood or adolescence, and overanxious disorder; several other diagnostic and empirical approaches to classification exist (Morris, Kratochwill, & Aldridge, 1988).

Jersild and Holmes (1935) anticipated many current interventions by stressing that effective techniques "help the child to become more competent and skillful and . . . encourage him to undertake active dealings with the thing that he fears" (p. 102).

Emotive imagery involves presenting emotionally arousing situations to the child. Rosentiel and Scott (1977) outlined four considerations: (1) images presented should be age-appropriate; (2) images should be based on the child's current fantasies; (3) nonverbal cues should be used to gain access to the child's perception of the intervention; and (4) the child's descriptions of the images should be used in treatment.

Jackson and King (1981) demonstrated the effectiveness of emotive imagery with a five-year-old boy who was fearful of the dark, noises, and shadows. He particularly liked the comic character Batman (he wore a cape and mask in the home, watched the television program, and had several "Batman" toys). A fear hierarchy was created, and the child was instructed to pretend that "he and Batman had joined forces and that he was appointed as a special agent" (p. 326). The child was told to imagine Batman at his side, close his eyes, and gradually imagine the fearful events. Four sessions of emotive imagery were required to eliminate the fears, and gains were maintained through eighteen months. The procedure was adapted from Lazarus and Abramovitz (1962).

In vivo desensitization is one of the variations of systematic desensitization. It involves developing a hierarchy based on the real, feared situation. Items on the hierarchy are gradually exposed to the child. The treatment principle is referred to as *reciprocal inhibition:* "If a response inhibitory to anxiety can be made to occur in the presence of anxiety-evoking stimuli, it will weaken the connection between these stimuli and the anxiety responses" (Wolpe, 1962, p. 562). The technique has been found to be successful in the treatment of school phobia (Garvey & Hegrenes, 1966), water fears (Pomerantz, Peterson, Marholin, & Stern, 1977; Ultee, Griffioen, & Schellekens, 1982), fears of medical treatment (Freeman, Roy, & Hemmick, 1976), and fears of high places (Croghan & Musante, 1975).

Live and symbolic modeling have been used to decrease fears in young children. Bandura, Grusec, and Menlove (1967) investigated children's fears of dogs using live modeling procedures. Forty-eight preschool children were assigned to one of four groups: (a) "modeling-positive context," in which children observed a fearless model interact with a large dog in a party atmosphere; (b) "modeling-neutral context," where children observed the model approach the dog while the children were seated at a table; (c) "exposure-positive context," in which the dog was present at a party but no modeling occurred with the dog; and (d) "positive-context," in which the children were at a party but the dog was not present. Eight ten-minute sessions were conducted over four days. Children in the first two groups, where a modeling context was provided, were significantly less afraid of the dog than children in the exposure or positive context groups at post-test and one-month followup. Modeling also has been found to be useful with fears related to surgery (Melamed & Siegel, 1975), dental treatment (Klorman, Hilpert, Michael, LaGana, & Sveen, 1980; Melamed, Hawes, Heiby, & Glick, 1975; White & Davis, 1974), and social withdrawal (O'Conner, 1969, 1972; Rao, Moely, & Lockman, 1987).

In other studies, multicomponent *verbal self-instruction* training has been used successfully to reduce fears in children (Graziano & Mooney, 1980, 1982; Graziano, Mooney, Huber, & Ignasiak, 1979). Kanfer, Karoly, and Newman (1975) divided kindergarten children into three groups. All children were described as fearful of the dark. Each group was given statements to repeat and practice. The first group, characterized as the *competence group,* practiced active, positive control by repeating "I am a brave boy [girl]. I can take care of myself in the dark" (p. 253). The second group rehearsed statements intended to reduce the fearful stimuli, such as "The dark is a fun place to be. There are many good things in the dark" (p. 253). The third group rehearsed neutral statements ("Mary had a little lamb"). Each group was also given brief elaborations on the themes. For example, the competence group was told the following:

> When you are in the dark you know that you can turn on the light when you feel like it. In your room, when it's dark, you know exactly where everything is — your bed, your dressers, your toys. When you are in the dark, if you felt like talking to someone you could always talk to your parents and they could hear you. Even though you are in the dark, when the door is closed you know that nobody can come in that you would not know [Kanfer, Karoly, & Newman, 1975, p. 253].

Results indicated that children in the first two groups were able to reduce their fear of the dark, but members of the "competence" group benefitted most. Giebenhain and O'Dell (1984) reported the results of a parent treatment package that uses desensitization, reinforcement, and verbal self-control techniques.

Operant-based interventions also have been used with some success in the treatment of many children's fears (Morris, Kratochwill, & Aldridge, 1988). Leitenberg and Callahan (1973) assigned fourteen kindergarten children to either a treatment or control group. During eight sessions, children in the treatment group were told to enter a darkened room and remain in the area until they became fearful. Children were told that they would receive a prize if they could remain in the room longer than their previous longest time. At post-testing, children in the treatment group were able to remain in the darkened room significantly longer than children in the control group. Similar techniques have been found to be successful in eliminating emotionally disturbed and developmentally disabled children's fears of dogs and riding on school buses (Obler & Terwilliger, 1970).

Often, fears are maintained because caregivers give attention to children when they are fearful. *Extinction* of the reinforcement may be necessary to eliminate the fears. In a study by Waye (1979), a five-year-old girl's fear that her thumbs (and later, other body parts) were shrinking was eliminated through the use of extinction and other treatment components. The parents were instructed to ignore all comments related to the child's hands and to praise and reinforce her when she engaged in appropriate play. Combinations of extinction and in vivo desensitization have been found to be useful in eliminating children's fear of noises (Stableford, 1979) and fears of specific foods (Boer & Sipprelle, 1970).

In sum, many methods have been advocated to intervene with children's fears and phobias. Given an absence of research-based decision rules, the most likely procedures for many children may involve in vivo desensitization and contingency management. Setting social standards may be an important aspect of interventions based on self-statements or information learned through modeling (see Rosenfarb & Hayes, 1984). Thyer and Sowers-Hoag (1988) discuss the diagnostic category of separation anxiety, for which surprisingly little research exists.

Thumb Sucking

Habits that persist and that cause undue negative social or parental attention merit intervention consideration. Thumb sucking may have these attributes, and also may interfere with responding during freeplay and structured learning situations. It may also result in dental problems (Christensen & Sanders, 1987).

Many interventions have been recommended to parents to help with children's thumb sucking; most have been insufficiently evaluated. Christensen and Sanders (1987) compared the effects of habit reversal and differential reinforcement of other behavior (DRO) for treating this behavior with thirty parents and their children (ages four to nine). Key issues were intervention effectiveness, generality and maintenance of change, undesirable outcomes or side effects, and acceptability of the intervention by parents.

The authors of the study had the parents select one training setting (such as watching television) and two generalization settings (such as bedtime). Observations included thumb sucking, noncompliance, complaints (whining, screaming), aversive mands, aggression, oppositional behavior (rule breaking), and appropriate interactions and play.

The habit reversal procedure was developed by Azrin and colleagues (Azrin, Nunn, & Frantz-Renshaw, 1980). The first phase included discussion about (a) working together to stop thumb sucking, (b) identifying the stimulus conditions for the behavior and cues for the onset of the behavior, and (c) modeling and feedback for performing the alternative and competing response. The procedure "involved clenching both fists, ensuring that the thumb was enclosed by the fingers, and slowly counting to 20" (Christensen & Sanders, 1987, p. 286). The procedure was repeated three times if thumb sucking occurred in the training setting. Parental counting was faded. The second phase required that the child remain in close proximity to the parent in the training setting for thirty minutes. Parents asked children to take the thumb or finger from the mouth, and prompted the above procedure contingent on thumb sucking, using manual guidance if necessary.

The training session was repeated in the third phase. The child was "reminded to become aware of the earliest sign of thumb sucking and to perform the exercise and counting" (p. 286). Parents reminded children not to thumb suck outside the training sessions as well. Children were requested to perform the exercise (fist clenching and counting) contingent upon thumb sucking or the agreed-upon early cue that signaled the behavior.

Parents were requested to observe as closely as possible and cue the child once if thumb sucking occurred.

The DRO training format was identical. The procedure was implemented in two phases. In phase one, a token system and rules were explained to the child. In the second phase, the parent implemented the training procedure. Children examined the tokens and selected possible rewards. The DRO involved an "escalating schedule" outlined in Exhibit 8.10.

Both interventions lasted for ten days, and both were effective in reducing thumb sucking in comparison to a control group. In addition, both interventions generalized to the other settings. Intervention effects were also noted during three-month follow-up observations. An increase in oppositional behavior was ob-

Exhibit 8.10. A DRO Procedure for Thumb Sucking.

1. Five "rules" were established, and each rule applied for two days or longer if needed.
2. The rules specified that a set number of tokens would be earned contingent upon the absence of thumb-sucking for a specified time interval (e.g., "rule one stated that one token would be earned every 3 minutes where no thumb-sucking occurred" during a 30 minute training session) (pp. 286–287).
3. The child had to be successful for at least 80% of the intervals for consecutive days, or the same rule was applied for the next day.
4. Each "rule" increased the inter-reinforcement interval. For rule 5, the 30 minute session equalled one interval.
5. A "clock face" was used to help explain the contingencies to the child.
6. The parent was required to "discreetly watch the child" (p. 287). If the contingencies were met, that is, no thumb-sucking was observed during the interval, the child was given a token and recorded a mark on a record sheet.
7. If the contingency was not met, the parents told the child that no token was earned and marked a record sheet accordingly.
8. After the 30 minute period, the parent and child counted tokens, and if the criterion was met, the reward was delivered when practical.
9. Children were also able to earn "privileges" at other time during the day. The parents were requested to divide the day into 30 periods, and to observe as much as possible.

Source: Reprinted with permission from the *Journal of Child Psychology and Psychiatry, 28,* A. P. Christensen and M. R. Sanders, Habit reversal and differential reinforcement of other behavior in the treatment of thumb-sucking: An analysis of generalization and side effects. Copyright 1987, Pergamon Press plc.

served during the intervention, but was not evident during followup. Both procedures were judged as acceptable by most parents. Overall, the authors reported that habit reversal may hold some clinical advantages in comparison to DRO: increased collaborative efforts and fewer negative side effects. Other possible treatments include increasing children's engagement in interesting activities to reduce opportunities for self-stimulation (DRI).

We have used self-control procedures in case studies with parent-reported success. The child is taught to discriminate the behavior, and prearranged "silent signals" are used to cue the child to self-record occurrences of thumb sucking. Improvements in daily performance are co-charted with the child, and earn rewards.

Bedwetting

The treatment of bedwetting, or enuresis, has one of the most extensive literatures in behavioral psychology. A review reveals a wide range of treatments, including drug therapy, surgery, various forms of psychotherapy, training in bladder control, the buzzer pad techniques, and a multicomponent procedure termed *dry-bed training* (DBT).

A medical evaluation is advised as standard practice, to rule out urological or neurological pathology or infection. However, a review of the literature suggests two additional considerations. First, organic causes are estimated to be less than 1 percent (Forsythe & Redmond, 1974). Second, behavioral interventions are likely to succeed even when other more radical or drastic treatments have failed. In many studies that demonstrated success with behavioral interventions, from 30 percent to 100 percent of the children had received prior medical treatment, including drugs or surgery.

Neither ignoring enuresis nor radical medical treatment seem to be sound advice with a large proportion of enuretic children ages five and older. Although "spontaneous cures" sometimes occur (Forsythe & Redmond, 1974), the result is not predictable for specific children; wetting is likely to persist through the childhood years for many, and into adulthood for some. Before age five, intervention for enuresis is questionable (Doleys, 1979; Walker, Kenning, & Faust-Campanile, 1989). One factor leading to a possible decision to intervene is a sustained prior history of dry nights followed by wetting.

The multicomponent strategy of dry bed training for functional (versus organic) enuresis builds on many basic interventions introduced earlier and has considerable research support. Many of the component strategies, such as self-monitoring, reinforcement for dry nights, and the supplemental use of a urine alarm, are also successful as independent interventions (Walker, Kenning, & Faust-Campanile, 1989).

As an overview, dry bed training (Azrin & Besalel, 1979) includes training in inhibiting urination and increasing functional bladder capacity, self-correcting of accidents, self-recording of successes and failures, using tangible and social reinforcers, and training specific habits in rapid awakening and urination (described as most important by Azrin & Besalel, 1979). Self-regulation, overcorrection, and reinforcement procedures are the basic procedures.

The treatment package has gone through many years of development. Major changes have occurred, especially recommendations about professional involvement. However, while the program was written for parents, professional assistance is likely to increase chances for success.

The DBT program requires complete parent commitment for the duration of the training. A supportive emotional family climate is important. The three training phases are outlined as follows:

Intensive Training Day. This includes a special shopping trip to buy salty food snacks, favorite drinks, and a sixteen-ounce graduated measuring cup. In the early afternoon, after all procedures have been carefully explained to the child, the child is encouraged to drink as much as possible. This increases opportunities for intensive practice.

Every half hour, training in bladder control is carried out. If the child reports a need to urinate, he or she is encouraged to "hold back" as long as possible. If the need to urinate does not pass, the child is asked to pretend to sleep. An attempt is made to increase the duration of "holding back." Instead of the toilet, the child urinates in the measuring cup kept in the bathroom. The amount of urine is recorded, and the child tries to beat earlier marks.

Also as a part of the training day, parents teach children, even three- and four-year-olds, how to change bed sheets. Disposing of wet sheets and clothing, and getting fresh ones, are rehearsed.

The next major facet of the training day is referred to as "getting up practice." This consists of twenty trials of (a) pretending sleep, (b) concentrating on bladder sensations, and (c) hurriedly arising from bed to urinate. The child pretends to sleep for about a minute. The room is darkened to make practice similar to bedtime. Just before the pretended bedtime, the parents review the procedures with the child and give encouragement. The positive practice is especially important after the first day. The twenty trials are instituted after a child wets (after changing sheets and nightclothes), and before bedtime of the succeeding evening if wet the night before.

The last major feature of the training day is the hourly awakenings after the child is asleep. If the child is asleep at 8:00 P.M. on the training day, the child will be awakened every hour until 1:00 A.M. First, the parents check the sheets. If dry, the child is softly awakened, and is asked to concentrate on bladder sensations. The child makes the choice of either going to the toilet, or waiting until the next hourly awakening. Praise is given, and more drinks are offered (terminated before the last two awakenings). If wetting occurs during the training night, the child has already practiced the procedures during the day: changing the bed and self, and completing the twenty getting-up exercises.

Post–Training Day Program. Three major features from the training day are maintained: attempts at increasing bladder capacity via urinating in the measuring cup, the "getting-up" practice, and the child's responsibility for correcting wetting accidents.

Bedtime review of the program, progress, and encouragement for success and effort continue throughout.

The nightly awakenings are simplified. On the second night, the child is awakened once, at the parent's bedtime instead of on the hourly schedule. If the child is dry, the nightly awakening is moved forward on the next night one half hour, until it is eventually discontinued. If wet, the awakening is kept the same.

The child is shown how to self-record or chart progress. Also, a system of rewards is used. For example, a kitchen drawer near the chart may be filled with treats and small toys, giving the child a choice of rewards for dry nights. Social rewards also may be significant.

Phasing-Out Procedures. The procedure is maintained for two weeks. After that time, nighttime control has probably been acquired. Wetting is likely to recur for some children (about 25 percent). If so, the getting-up practice and responsibility for changing wet bedsheets and clothing are reimplemented.

Other Problems of Elimination

A successful multicomponent toilet training approach has been developed by Azrin and Foxx (1974; Foxx & Azrin, 1973). Daytime wetting may be treated successfully with frequent checks for dry pants, cleanliness training, frequent toileting, positive practice, differential reinforcement for communication, and reinforcement. Also, for functional encopresis (soiling), many of the basics that have been discussed apply, although medical conditions that may contribute to encopresis should be checked first. Crowley and Armstrong (1977) reported details of a successful home-based treatment of encopresis using positive practice, overcorrection, and behavior rehearsal procedures.

Sleep Disturbances

Sleep disturbances, including difficulty getting to sleep and frequent awakenings, are prevalent with young children and may be highly disturbing to both children and other family members. Surprisingly, many young children are medicated for sleep disturbances, but such treatments may be contraindicated. Behavioral interventions that have been used include extinction (for crying or tantrums), positive reinforcement for desired behavior, shaping by gradually making the bedtime earlier, and cuing through bedtime rituals.

Durand and Mindell (1990) modified an intervention suggested by Ferber (1985) for a fourteen-month-old girl who had difficulties going to sleep (tantrums) and who was waking up from one to three times during the night. The intervention, described as graduated extinction, was effective for the sleep problems and had positive outcomes for the parents in terms of marital satisfaction and maternal depression. The steps are outlined here.

1. One of the child's parents entered the room for a brief period (fifteen to thirty seconds) upon the child waking. The parent was instructed to provide reassurance (such as saying "It's okay, go to sleep now" in a neutral voice, p. 40), and to check for problems.

2. The parents were instructed to wait for progressively longer periods of time before entering the child's room on subsequent nights (increased by five-minute increments). The longest period was a delay of twenty minutes.

3. Two weeks later, the same basic intervention was applied to tantrum behaviors. The child required parental presence before going to bed. A parent put the child to bed, and waited for progressively longer time periods before entering her room for a tantrum. They provided brief but neutral reassurance.

Seymour (1987) studied the effects of a comprehensive treatment for sleep difficulties across four families. The program included the following components: (a) explaining night waking to parents in terms of habit formation; (b) describing ways that parents accidently maintain night waking (such as insufficient routines prior to bedtime or rewarding consequences for children's maladaptive behavior); (c) assessing the physical sleeping arrangements; (d) setting routines for before bedtime and for bedtime (meals, baths, etc.); (e) ignoring crying after bedtime or giving minimal attention if needed; and (f) returning children to bed without cuddling or anger. Parents also were instructed to set daytime naps in a similar manner. Reinforcement was given to children when they slept through the night. A treatment program for children with severe disabilities and multiple sleep problems was described by Piazza and Fisher (1991).

Summary and Conclusions

Family systems are of primary importance, for several reasons. First, they help define the quality of social and cognitive learning experiences provided to children and the environments that may contribute to child adaptation and a broad array of behavioral and developmental functioning. Second, family realities are related to intervention decisions. The role of the parent as change agent is dependent on many aspects of parental functioning apart from parent–child relationships.

In this chapter, we examined the role of parent as teacher and change agent within the context of family systems, the basics of home–school interventions, strategies to expand learning opportunities, and interventions for relatively common problem behaviors. The chapter builds on parent–professional collaboration, and assessment strategies, targets for intervention, and basic interventions presented in earlier chapters. The next chapter continues the discussion of family interventions in the context of severe challenges.

9

Interventions for Severe and Risk-Related Problem Behaviors

THIS CHAPTER FOCUSES ON THE MORE SEVERE PROBLEMS OF CHILDREN and situations associated with risk. Many parents are raising children under perilous economic, personal, and social circumstances. These factors directly and indirectly influence the care given to children and intervention decisions on their behalf. In some problem situations, such as abuse or neglect, the parents themselves are targets of intervention efforts.

Problem Behavior in the Home and Community

There are many potential obstacles to successful parent-child relationships. Major barriers include factors related to the adult's world that may create or exacerbate difficult child behaviors or demands.

Insularity

The term *insularity* is used to describe mothers who are "'cut off' from social contact," and who view the limited contacts they do experience as unsolicited, or aversive (Wahler, 1980, p. 208). Wahler and his associates (Panaccione & Wahler, 1986; Wahler & Afton, 1980; Wahler & Dumas, 1986) have examined the hypothesis that extrafamily contacts, especially when they are few or aversive, significantly affect child-rearing practices. In

256

these situations, the demands of parenting may lead to neglect or coercive parent–child interactions.

Insular mothers also are at increased risk of treatment failure. The absence of problem-solving discussion between insular mothers and family members, friends, or professionals has been hypothesized as a keystone behavior that may explain why these parents have problems with parenting skills (Wahler & Hann, 1984).

The findings by Wahler and his associates suggest that points of assessment must include more than child characteristics or those of the parent–child dyad. Interventions need to have positive outcomes for parents in their relationships with their children, and perhaps in their own lives as well. Tremendous conflict may be involved in child-care efforts, depending on child characteristics and parental circumstances. If family needs are not addressed, parent–child interventions are more likely to fail (Dunst, Leet, & Trivette, 1988).

Compliance Training

Noncompliance — ignoring parental requests — is considered to be a keystone behavior that merits intervention in many home and school situations. Generally, noncompliance occurs as part of a constellation of behaviors: whining, tantruming, aggressive behaviors, "talking back," aversive demands ("I want it now!"), and other behaviors related to conduct disorders.

Two important foundations for this section are social cognitive theory (Bandura, 1986) and Patterson's theoretical *coercion model*. The central idea of Patterson's research, which spans several decades, is that antisocial behaviors stem from deficits in parenting skills *and* maladaptive child behaviors: an unskilled parent interacting with a temperamentally difficult child. Patterson's coercion model is defined by three components: (1) learning antisocial behaviors through family interactions, (2) "stress amplifier effects" (such as economic stress or divorce), and (3) possible generalization to the school (Patterson & Bank, 1986).

Ineffective discipline is a key variable. Patterson's research group found that parents of antisocial boys tended to "scold, threaten, and nag as a reaction to both trivial and significant behaviors. Most significant . . . was their failure to back up their threats consistently" (Patterson & Bank, 1986, p. 57). Extreme forms of punishment, or explosive discipline, were also characteristic.

A second major variable is *parental monitoring.* This construct has less adequate convergent validity than the other constructs proposed by Patterson, and needs to be revised for younger children. Examples include increased unsupervised street time and failure to believe that children engage in major antisocial acts outside the home. Patterson and Bank hypothesized that monitoring has a relatively minor role in the early progression of antisocial behavior. However, based on numerous research studies reviewed, we consider this construct highly promising. Many parents have difficulties with monitoring child behaviors or are inappropriately responsive to reports of adaptive or maladaptive behaviors. We also have used this construct to help guide assessment and intervention design for behaviors associated with risk, such as fire setting.

A third variable, termed *coercive child,* refers to a reciprocal process where family members "train" each other to elicit coercive behaviors. For example, a three-part sequence might include an aversive behavior by a parent (an unpleasant request), a coercive reaction by the child (whining), and the termination of the initial parental behavior. Very high levels of noncompliance can be produced quickly through such interactions. "The child learned that he could react aversively to demands made on him, and that if he persisted, probably 'won.' The child also learned that he could use a wide range of coercive means to produce rapid changes in the behavior of other people" (Patterson & Bank, 1986, p. 59).

Patterson and his associates have developed an extensive program based on social learning principles; it has both family and school components (Patterson et al., 1975). The major features of the treatment program are outlined in Exhibit 9.1. The program, intended for children aged three to twelve, has been well researched (see review by McMahon & Wells, 1989). The strategies are to teach parents of antisocial children more effective

Exhibit 9.1. Some Features of Patterson's
Program for Aggressive Children.

---

1. The parents are assigned a text written expressly to provide parents the necessary background for skill training (*Living with Children* or *Families*). The target child is included in interviews and discussion.
2. Parents are trained to pinpoint two problem behaviors and two prosocial behaviors and to track the behavior. Parents monitor two to three target behaviors for a one-hour period for three days. The professional uses frequent phone calls to monitor the data.
3. Parents are trained in the use of a positive reinforcement system that includes praise and tangibles (a simplified token economy). Contingency contracts are used.
4. A time-out procedure is introduced. Response cost also may be used.
5. Through contracting, parents are trained in problem solving and negotiation.
6. Classroom intervention may be necessary, including reduction of disruptive behavior, home–school communication, and help with academic skills.

---

ways for dealing with coercive behaviors and to reinforce socially appropriate behaviors. A key feature is training parents (as well as professionals) to observe behavior. Patterson (1975) noted that without careful observation by parents or teachers, it is likely that they will experience difficulty in changing behavior.

Forehand and McMahon (1981) provided a detailed description of an intervention program for noncompliant children based on considerable research, primarily with children of ages three to eight. The program was originally developed by Constance Hanf at the University of Oregon. It is similar to the program developed by Patterson and earlier work by Wahler and colleagues. An outline of the treatment program is shown in Exhibit 9.2.

The most salient features are two stages used to address parent–child issues. In the first stage, the parent is taught to effectively attend to appropriate child behaviors and to ignore inappropriate behavior. In other words, the parent is taught to be "a more effective reinforcing agent" (Forehand & McMahon, 1981, p. 51). The parent is trained to effectively monitor the child's appropriate behaviors and to stop using ineffective "commands, questions and criticisms" that are linked to noncompliant

Exhibit 9.2. Characteristics of a Compliance
Training Program (10 sessions)

Phase I: Differential Attention

1. Parent is taught to be a more effective reinforcing agent.
2. The parent is trained to increase the frequency and range of social re-
    wards and eliminate verbal behaviors that are associated with deviant
    child behavior.
    a. The parent is taught to attend and to describe the child's ap-
        propriate behavior.
    b. The parent is required to eliminate all commands, questions, and
        criticisms directed to the child during the training sessions.
    c. The parent is trained to use rewards contingent upon compliance
        and other appropriate behaviors (use praise statements in which
        the child's behavior is labeled—"You are a good boy for picking
        up those blocks").
    d. The parent is taught to ignore minor inappropriate behaviors.
    e. In the home, the parent is required to structure brief (ten- to
        fifteen-minute) "child's games" to practice skills learned in the clinic.
        (1). Child chooses the activity.
        (2). Watch with interest what the child is doing.
        (3). Describe enthusiastically what the child is doing.
        (4). Participate in the activity without restructuring (handing
              materials, taking turns).
        (5). Do not ask questions or give commands.
        (6). Do not teach or test.
    f. With the aid of a therapist, the parent identifies lists of child be-
        haviors to increase, discusses the use of attends and rewards, and
        develops a program to increase two child behaviors outside the clinic.

Phase II: Decrease Noncompliant Behavior

1. The parent is trained to use appropriate commands and time out.
2. The parent is trained to give direct, single commands and to allow the
    child five seconds to initiate compliance.
3. If compliance is initiated within five seconds, the parent is taught to re-
    ward or attend to the child within five seconds.
    a. If compliance is not initiated, the parent is trained to use time
        out, as follows:
    b. A warning is given that labels the time out consequence. ("If you
        do not ___ , you will have to sit in the chair in the corner.")
    c. If the warning is ineffective within a five-second interval, the child
        is placed in the chair.
    d. The child must remain in the chair for three minutes and be quiet
        and still for the last fifteen seconds.
    e. The child is then returned to the uncompleted task and given the
        initial command.
4. Compliance is followed by contingent attention from the parent.

Adapted from Forehand, R. L., & McMahon, R.J. (1981). *Helping the
noncompliant child: A clinician's guide to parent training*. New York: Guilford.

behavior (p. 51). Also, parents are trained to use rewards to increase compliance and positive parent–child exchanges, and to ignore minor problem behaviors. A "child's game" is used in the home to practice parent–child play skills learned in the clinic. The second stage consists of specific procedures to increase compliance with parental commands. The parent is trained to use appropriate commands and mild time out.

In other research, adjuncts to the program have been studied. Positive effects are reported for including training in social learning principles and self-control. Zangwill (1984) reported a replication of Hanf's procedure; he also found that the parents in his sample expressed approval of a "bug-in-the-ear" technique that enabled immediate therapist–parent feedback in training sessions.

Effective and Ineffective Commands. Promising points of analysis for many caregivers are the qualities of the commands given to the child. The rationale for evaluating parental commands is straightforward. The evaluation of child misbehavior must include attention to settings, events, parental behavior, and child behavior. The appendix provided by Forehand and McMahon (1981) is excellent reading for professionals working with caregivers of noncompliant children, and provides an extensive discussion of coding parent–child interactions. While we dwell on the analysis by Forehand and McMahon because of their research with conduct-disordered children, note that very different analyses of child compliance exist (for example, see Parpal & Maccoby, 1985).

Forehand and McMahon define an *alpha* command as "an order, suggestion, question, rule, or contingency to which a motoric or verbal response is appropriate and feasible" (1981, p. 191). Often, these are in the form of imperatives such as "come here," "please stop making that noise," or "pick up your toy." They also include under this category *indirect commands* ("See if you can be quiet"), *question commands* ("Why don't we sit here?"), *permission statements and rules* ("There will be no more fighting"), *if/then statements* ("If you don't stop running, you'll hurt yourself"), and *chain commands* ("Stand up, come here, and sit down").

Beta commands include those for which child compliance is difficult or impossible. These include the above form of commands that are interrupted or ended in some way by the parent so that the child is unable to comply in a reasonable time period (say, five seconds), or are carried out by the parent before the child is able to comply. The second type of beta commands are those that result in confusion so that the child is unable to determine what behavior is expected. These include *if/when* statements ("Put it up here if you want to"), and *vague* commands ("Just be good for a while longer"). Other problem areas for commands include frequent and intense commands, a lack of reasonable proximity or closeness to the child, and repetitions of the original command.

Forehand and McMahon note that effective commands are "specific and direct," "given one at a time," and "followed by a wait of five seconds" (p. 76). They also suggest five types of commands that have the effect of *lowering* child compliance (pp. 74–75): (1) chain commands; (2) vague commands; (3) question commands ("would you like to take your bath now?"); (4) "Let's . . . " commands ("Let's pick up your toys") when the parent actually has no wish or intent to be involved in the activity; and (5) commands followed by a rationale or other verbalization (the rationale should come *before* the command).

Roberts and Powers (1988) described the extensive development of the "compliance test," which measures compliance with standardized chorelike instructions from the parent. They developed the rationale for the test based on several ambiguities of the Forehand and McMahon procedure. A low degree of compliance may be related to ineffective commands or noncompliance with effective commands; a high rate of compliance may be due to effective commands or child compliance with ineffective commands. One limitation of the compliance test is that a task to measure children's behavioral inhibition to parental signals needs to be constructed. Roberts and Powers remarked on the potential intervention benefits of compliance test analysis. Children who comply with parental commands in the analogue setting may be treated through teaching more effective command strategies and differential attention. Other noncompliant children may need additional intervention, such as time out.

Defiant Children. Barkley (1987) has made available a treat-ment package building on the earlier work by Hanf and McMa-hon and Forehand. The program has been designed for chil-dren between ages two and eleven, but he states that it may be possible to use the program with children as young as eighteen months, depending on language development. Barkley has also enhanced the usability of the program for clinicians by provid-ing a step-by-step workbook.

In Barkley's program, the following definitions are ap-plied to noncompliance behaviors.

1. The child does not initiate behaviors within ten to fifteen seconds after a request or command from an adult. [Note: Fore-hand and McMahon used a five-second guideline. For training parents in the use of time out, Barkley recommends the five-second rule. We think that the delay interval is an issue of so-cial validity and behavior context, and thus may be an impor-tant point of parent consultation. Circumstances may indicate the need for flexibility in using these guidelines.]

2. The child does not sustain compliance until the stipu-lations in the request have been met.

3. Other well-established rules are not followed in the sit-uation (aggressive behaviors are emitted).

Barkley's changes include (a) a section that explains in more detail for parents the development of misbehavior and non-compliance, (b) strategies for increasing appropriate indepen-dent play, (c) a token ("chip") system for reinforcement for chil-dren who are less responsive to praise or positive attention, (d) sessions to deal with noncompliance in public places, and (e) strategies to prepare parents for possible future misbehaviors.

Since many of the overall features in Barkley's program are similar to those outlined by Forehand and McMahon, only two steps will be summarized here. Overall, Barkley's manual is highly recommended. Step 8 focuses on noncompliant behav-ior in places other than the home (stores, restaurants, church). Parents are taught a strategy referred to as *think aloud—think ahead,* in which the need for future plans for misbehavior is anticipated. The three facets are (a) establishing a plan for misbehavior before entering a public building, (b) sharing the plan with the child(ren), and (c) carrying out the plan as needed. Step 9 deals with planning for *future* problem behaviors. The parents are required to anticipate "new" problem behaviors, and to learn how the basic procedures may be applied. They are expected to be able to "design" a behavior program based on the methods described in the overall program.

Other programs have been extensively developed for parents and young children (ages three to eight) with conduct problems. Webster-Stratton (1981a, 1981b, 1982) has developed a videotape modeling program. Three conditions were compared: (a) self-administered, including ten to twelve sessions of over two hundred videotaped parent-child interactions; (2) group discussion plus videotape modeling; and (3) group discussion only. While all were effective, the most effective program included videotapes and group discussion (Webster-Stratton, Hollingsworth, & Kolpacoff, 1989). Breiner and Beck (1984) reviewed intervention programs for noncompliant behaviors of developmentally delayed (as opposed to conduct-disordered) children.

Parental Self-Regulation

This component is intended to increase the generalization and maintenance of behavioral change. The core concerns are that parents may not continue with effective intervention programs once contact with the professional ends, or they may not automatically apply the intervention program to new or untreated problem behaviors, different settings, or other children with problem behavior. Furthermore, it is likely that different settings (home, stores, community, neighborhood) place different demands on parents and provoke different antecedents or cues that result in effective or ineffective parental responses. Sanders and Glynn commented that "some settings may be 'high risk' occasions for [treatment] program inaccuracy. . . . Parents' ability to alter, control, and rearrange their own parenting environment so that the environment prompts and reinforces the continued application and extension of skills once therapist support is withdrawn may require different strategies from those currently used in training parents" (1981, p. 224).

Sanders and colleagues (Sanders & Christensen, 1985; Sanders & Dadds, 1982; Sanders & Plant, 1989) have investigated an intervention referred to as *planned activity training* to help with problems of generalization to home and community settings. Seven skills were introduced sequentially to the parents, using discussion, modeling, role play, and feedback:

1. How to prepare for situations in advance by organizing and managing time more effectively.
2. How to discuss rules about desired and undesired behavior in a relaxed and noncoercive manner.
3. How to select engaging activities for children in specific home and community settings.
4. How to encourage and extend children's engagement in activities with incidental teaching procedures.
5. How to select and apply practical incentives for motivating children's desired behavior in different child-rearing situations.
6. How to select practical consequences for undesired behavior in the same settings.
7. How to hold discussions with children following an activity, to give feedback on desired and undesired behavior. [Sanders & Christensen, 1985, pp. 108–109]

Sanders and Glynn (1981) demonstrated the effectiveness of teaching five two-parent families self-management skills using a treatment package when intervening with disruptive behavior. The intervention was effective, overall, but it was not possible to determine the effectiveness of the self-management component alone, since multiple components were used.

The steps and components are summarized as follows.

1. After a baseline phase, each family was instructed in the use of behavior modification techniques during a two-hour meeting. The strategies included (a) discussing baseline data

and effects of parental attention; (b) pinpointing problem behaviors in training and generalization settings; (c) checking parental perceptions; (d) explaining consequences for appropriate and inappropriate behaviors; and (e) explaining the intervention program. Examples of ineffective parenting strategies were taken from baseline data. Target behaviors included demands, tantrums, aggression, arguing, and interrupting.

2. The treatment included giving examples of descriptive praise in addition to "other contingent consequences . . . to increase appropriate behavior," and techniques for "behavior correction" (p. 228). The instructions were "(a) gain the child's attention, (b) describe calmly what the child has done wrong, (c) describe and prompt the correct behavior, (d) give a further prompt if required, (e) speak up and praise the correct behavior if it occurs, (f) if the problem continues or worsens, deliver a firm verbal reprimand describing the incorrect behavior and back this reprimand up with a natural consequence (e.g., remove troublesome toy and give a brief explanation)" (p. 228). In addition, if the child was noncompliant following the reprimand, given demanding, tantruming, aggressive, arguing, and interrupting behaviors, a brief time out (three minutes) was used. Detailed instructions for each step were printed on cards. Also, the accuracy of implementation was assessed for five intervention components: giving social attention, prompting, instructing, ignoring, and providing consequences.

3. Feedback sessions were held two times a week for ten-minute periods during home observations. Written feedback included (a) percentage of appropriate child behavior observed, (b) number of praise comments, and (c) percent accuracy of implementation. Three samples of interactions were analyzed with the parents. In addition, part of the session focused on parental verbal behavior and expanding play activities.

4. Parents were introduced to self-management in addition to continuing the above procedures. They were provided with a rationale for self-management, and were trained in goal

setting, self-monitoring, and planning related to parenting skills. The skills were taught sequentially in two phases.

Phase 1: Parents were introduced to goal setting and self-monitoring. Parents recorded on a "self-change card" whether or not they had implemented the home program each day, and if they had applied the procedure in the generalization setting. In addition, the therapist "illustrated" problem solving for one setting.

The steps summarizing specific components for child management were listed on a "self-monitoring card," illustrated in Exhibit 9.3. The cards were used to cue parents for planning skills. After three successful trials using these procedures, the parents were introduced to the second phase.

Phase 2: Parents selected another community setting, devised a management plan, implemented the plan, and evaluated whether the goal had been reached over three occasions. The step was repeated for a third community setting.

5. Self-maintenance training was initiated. Prompts and cues provided by the therapist, home feedback sessions, self-monitoring cards, and checklists were withdrawn. Parents were asked to continue using the behavioral techniques in different settings.

Aspects of self-regulation also are addressed in the treatment programs described by Barkley (1987) and Forehand and McMahon (1981). Extensive discussions of self-regulation for adults are included in Kanfer and Karoly (1982), and the very readable book by Watson and Tharp (1989). The basics were discussed in earlier chapters. Also, there is some evidence that parenting skills generalize to siblings (Humphreys, Forehand, McMahon, & Roberts, 1978).

Parent-Administered Time Out

Time out was discussed in the chapter on basic interventions; here we focus briefly on parent applications. There is much research support for the use of parent-administered time out with

Exhibit 9.3. An Example of a Self-Monitoring Form Used During Self-Management Training.

HANDLING DISRUPTIONS WHILE VISITING

Instructions: Each time you take your child visiting, mark Date and Time, Yes, No, or N.A. (not applicable) for each of the steps below.

Steps to be followed:							
1. Prepare the child for the outing by describing the expected behavior. Describe where you are going and how long it will take.							
2. When you arrive involve the child in an activity and make sure the child has something to do, and you have a snack available.							
3. Speak to, ask questions, and praise the child for desired behavior every so often.							
4. If a disruptive behavior occurs (e.g., grizzling, demanding, tantrums) gain the child's attention immediately.							
5. Describe the problem (i.e., the undesired behavior) and state the correct behavior (e.g., waiting).							
6. If the child obeys, speak up and praise child for doing what he/she is told.							
7. If the problem continues give a direct terminating instruction.							
8. If child does not comply, immediately provide back up consequence (i.e., a logical consequence, or time out).							
Number of steps completed correctly:							

Source: Sanders, M. R., & Glynn, T. (1981). Training parents in behavioral self-management: An analysis of generalization and maintenance. Table. 1. *Journal of Applied Behavior Analysis, 14*, 223–237. Copyright ©1981 by the Society for the Experimental Analysis of Behavior. Reprinted with permission.

oppositional child behavior. A noteworthy feature of the treatment packages described here is that they advocate increasing positive experiences and training in the use of positive approaches to discipline before aversive forms of discipline. The brevity of time periods is also significant (three minutes in the program described by Forehand & McMahon, 1981; three to five minutes in the Patterson program; one to two minutes per year of the child's age, with a limit determined informally by the severity of the misconduct in the program described by Barkley). Many suggest a contingency: the child remains in time out until he is calm and behaving appropriately; but this procedure also has been questioned.

There are numerous studies of time out and various modifications. Exhibit 9.4 outlines a slightly different alternative to time out (Wahler & Fox, 1980). Hamilton and MacQuiddy (1984) present innovative research to support the use of a "signal seat"—a plastic seat with a battery-powered buzzer that alerts the parent when a child leaves time out too soon.

Roberts (1988) has an extensive review of procedures that have been advocated when children do not stay in time out. He compared two different procedures to use when "chair" time outs fail. A "room" time out (sending children to their room), lasted one minute and was followed by a return to the chair time out.

Exhibit 9.4. An Example of Parent-Administered Time Out.

---

1. If the child violated a household rule, or did not comply with a parent's instruction, the child would then be required to go to a designated room (such as bedroom).
2. The child would remain there alone and quiet for five minutes. Quiet was defined as not engaging in behavior loud enough to attract attention.
3. Refusals were followed by a parent closing the door to the room and securing it if necessary.
4. A kitchen timer was used by the parent.

Source: Wahler, R. G., & Fox, J. J. (1980). Solitary toy play and time out: A family treatment package for children with aggressive and oppositional behavior. *Journal of Applied Behavior Analysis, 13,* pp. 23–39. Copyright ©1980 by the Society for the Experimental Analysis of Behavior. Reprinted with permission.

In the second procedure, control-group children were spanked if they escaped from chair time out. Both were effective, but the procedures for room time outs do not use physical violence and are brief. The parent stays by the door while monitoring the child's behavior. Parent consultation for the use of time out should include strategies to handle possible resistance to the procedures.

Walle, Hobbs, and Caldwell (1984) examined different sequences of interventions involving differential attention and time out. They found that differential attention may enhance the subsequent effectiveness of time out.

Parental Use of Tokens

Use of tokens is mentioned often in the preschool literature, and they may be used in many ways. Christophersen, Arnold, Hill, and Quilitch (1972) provided an extensive description of the use of tokens by families and evaluated the use of tokens in two families. The program was effective with both families, but we describe here only one, since the second family had no young children. The first family included a nine-year-old boy described as being truant, noncompliant, and "sassy"; an eight-year-old girl with cerebral palsy enrolled in an EMR class who was also hyperactive and exhibited tantrums; and a five-year-old boy described as "whiny." All three children "bickered," and both boys had difficulty with bedtime.

Target behaviors, including household chores, were explicitly defined for each child and were posted on the bedroom door. For example, the bedtime posting was "the absence of talking, laughing, verbal or physical interaction . . . following 5 minutes in which to settle down" (p. 486). Whining was defined as "a verbal complaint conducted in a sing-song (wavering) manner in a pitch above that of the normal speaking voice" (p. 486). Tokens were earned for chores completed and other nonregular duties, and were lost (response cost) if chores were not completed, if completion did not meet the posted definition, or if behaviors such as whining or bickering occurred. A "point card" was used to keep a record of the points earned and lost. The total intervention time for the first family was ten hours.

The study details an extensive multicomponent parental training program including a film, written materials, discussion, home visits, and phone contacts. Parents were requested not to make any changes in the token "economy" without the therapist. Parental motivation, cooperation, and involvement were critical for success.

Parental Praise

Praising children for appropriate behaviors is frequently offered to parents as advice for misbehaviors. However, in three inter-related studies, Roberts (1985) raised questions about the usefulness of parental praise to induce compliant behaviors, although it has other important functions. For severe noncompliant and disruptive behaviors, treatment packages developed by Patterson, Forehand and McMahon, or Barkley recommended earlier, should be considered. Another demonstration of the contributions and limitations of social attention, and need for broader treatment components, was provided by Budd, Green, and Baer (1976).

An Example of Home–School Intervention

A treatment package illustrative of home–school interventions was developed by Budd and colleagues (1981). The intervention had three facets: (1) teacher monitoring of school performance across the school day, (2) feedback to children on performance, and (3) a note to parents communicating school performance. A description of this DRO-based program is presented in Exhibit 9.5. Comparisons also were made to evaluate the importance of home and school privileges.

Overall, the results demonstrated convincing evidence of the effectiveness of the procedure. However, two children in one group were unresponsive (out of a total of eighteen children), but behaviors improved when school-based reinforcement was added to the intervention. It should be noted that the study was conducted in a special summer program.

Exhibit 9.5. Home School Reinforcement
Package for Severely Disruptive Behavior

---

1. The school day was divided into about twelve periods, four to eight minutes each.
2. The teacher met with each child individually to explain the intervention and when a new behavior was added to the contingencies. The target behaviors were defined for the child, and examples were given of how to earn or not earn stickers.
3. The child was required to verbalize the behaviors necessary to earn a sticker. Verbalizations were prompted as necessary.
4. Each child received a brightly colored sticker after each period in which no targeted behaviors occurred. The stickers were placed on a token card. The performance was monitored by the classroom aide by using a kitchen timer and recording form. The aide communicated the child's performance to the teacher following each period.
5. The teacher provided frequent praise and feedback on performance.
6. Following a preset criterion, stickers earned were exchanged for home privileges through the use of the token card (snacks, activity reinforcers). Privileges were established before the program began, through consultation with the parents.
7. The criterion was increased over time, based on the child's performance.
8. If the criterion was exceeded ("bonus" stickers), the child received "enthusiastic praise" but no additional rewards.
9. The procedure was implemented as a multiple baseline across different disruptive behaviors, which may have contributed to the program's success.
10. Informal but frequent contact was maintained with parents to monitor the program and help with problems.
11. Each day parents recorded the activity earned (or if one was not earned) on the back of the token card. The token card was returned to school the next day.

Adapted from Budd, K. S., Leibowitz, J. M., Riner, L. S., Mindell, C., & Goldfarb, A. L. Home-based treatment of severe disruptive behaviors: A reinforcement package for preschool and kindergarten children. *Behavior Modification, 5,* pp. 282–283. Copyright ©1981 by Sage Publications. Reprinted by permission of Sage Publications, Inc.

Attentional Problems and Activity Level

Syndromes involving child difficulties in sustaining attention, controlling impulses, and changing activities at a high rate, have a long history of parental and professional concern and are currently an area of active research (Barkley, 1989, 1990; Whalen, 1989). This constellation of behaviors is now most often referred to as attention deficit-hyperactive disorder, or ADHD (*DSM-III-R;* American Psychiatric Association, 1987), although further diagnostic changes are inevitable.

While there is no question of the significance of these behaviors for young children and caregivers, and the educational, personal, and social problems that result from severe manifestations of the behaviors, many diagnostic and treatment approaches to this syndrome are controversial. Major problems include (a) the classification soundness of the syndrome (Taylor, 1988; see also Chapter Two), (b) the possibility of and problems associated with multiple etiologies (Whalen, 1989), (c) the question of unintended negative outcomes associated with syndromal classification (Chapter Two), and (d) questions about intervention decisions and utility.

Classification of these children using conventional observations and rating scales is likely to be quite tenuous, given the situational variability of the behaviors and the frailties associated with the recommended measurement devices. The behavior of children described as ADHD varies by the type and amount of structure in settings, in response to different caregivers, and the novelty or demands of settings. Disorganized and chaotic settings can create corresponding behaviors. Whalen commented that "the phenomenon called ADHD has achieved only a fragile consensus" (1989, p. 160). More to the point of this book, "it is possible to design and implement effective educational interventions for children with attentional difficulties, even if one is unaware of whether or not the child is ADHD" (Browning, 1991, p. 1).

For all these reasons, we argue against ADHD diagnosis for preschool children; it may not be useful and may result in unknown or even harmful consequences. Instead, "a descriptive approach may be more helpful in obtaining needed services for the children and in targeting behaviors for interventions without adding the potential stigma of a diagnostic label that may prove inaccurate in the future" (Shelton & Barkley, 1990, pp. 220–221). Because the label ADHD currently affects great numbers of children, core features of the syndrome and professional practices are reviewed in this section. Classroom management strategies are presented in the next chapters.

A major question involves the relationship between ADHD and conduct disorders. A likely proposition is that these behaviors may co-occur for a large number of children (say, 60 percent) but not for all children characterized as ADHD (McGee, Williams, & Silva, 1984). Some children described as ADHD may also be anxious and shy, along with many other problems. A significant theme of the research is the difficulty of causal analyses and separating out other influences such as family characteristics.

While the behaviors underlying ADHD classification are multidimensional, Barkley considers ADHD to be a developmental disability "in the regulation and maintenance of behavior by rules and consequences" that result in other problem behaviors (1990, p. 71). Four interrelated behaviors have been considered prototypic in describing the syndrome: problems with sustained attention, difficulties with impulse control, frequent activity changes, and problems with rule-governed behavior. Barkley (1989) noted that an important facet may be "diminished persistence," especially in uninteresting activities. Restlessness and fidgeting are other characteristics. The best indicators for the disorder are thought to be tasks that require sustained attention and complex problem solving (Whalen, 1989), but many characteristics associated with ADHD overlap with other syndromes and descriptions of problem behavior. All the behaviors associated with ADHD may affect specific daily tasks encountered in home or school, and also social behaviors. Having difficulties with both peers and adults means that children are cut off from normal socialization experiences.

For a *DSM-III-R* diagnosis, eight of the fourteen behaviors listed in Exhibit 9.6 have to be identified at a rate significantly greater than children of the same mental age. The disturbance should appear before age seven and should have persisted for at least six months (American Psychiatric Association, 1987). However, Barkley (1990) argued strongly that a duration of twelve months for preschool children is more defensible. Furthermore, the *DSM-III-R* criteria do not take into account developmental trends and are not appropriate for young children. The use of mental age has been subjected to significant criticism.

Exhibit 9.6. Diagnostic Criteria for ADHD.

1. Often fidgets with hands or feet or squirms in seat.
2. Has difficulty remaining seated when required to do so.
3. Is easily distracted by extraneous stimuli.
4. Has difficulty awaiting turns in games or group situations.
5. Often blurts out answers to questions before they have been completed.
6. Has difficulty following through on instructions from others (not due to oppositional behavior or failure of comprehension).
7. Has difficulty sustaining attention in tasks or play activities.
8. Often shifts from one completed activity to another.
9. Has difficulty playing quietly.
10. Often talks excessively.
11. Often interrupts or intrudes on others; for example, butts into other children's games.
12. Often does not seem to listen to what is being said to him or her.
13. Often loses things necessary for tasks or activities at home or at school (toys, pencils).
14. Often engages in physically dangerous activities without considering possible consequences.

Adapted from the American Psychiatric Association. (1987). *Diagnostic and statistical manual of mental disorders, third edition, revised.* Washington, D.C.: American Psychiatric Association, p. 4.

It may be difficult to untangle problems with sustaining attention and performance from impulse control, and activity level from "restless" behaviors. These are all related characteristics. Browning presents the following analysis: "The extent to which children and adults effectively allot their attention is determined by a variety of factors, including that individual's interest level in the task at hand; his emotional status; and the strategies he possesses for determining such things as what to attend to, and what to ignore. Though an adult may be able through reflection to identify why her own attention is waning (i.e., preoccupation with a personal stressor), it is much more difficult to determine why a child or another adult is inattentive" (1991, p. 1). From a practical standpoint, if sustained attention and performance can be improved, then so will impulse control and associated behaviors.

Children described as attention deficit disordered are hypothesized to have difficulty with *rule-governed* behavior. The earlier discussion on compliance with parental commands illustrates a major application of this general topic. Expressing rules in developmentally appropriate ways and altering the consequences of compliance to instructions may lead to improvements in the behavior, and even the amelioration of the problem for some children (Barkley, 1989, 1990).

There are strong rationales for behavioral interventions for young children and interventions to improve coping behaviors of parents. First, despite successes achieved with stimulant and antidepressant drugs for many children, the responses may be temporary, difficult to predict, and associated with a range of side effects. Second, rule-governed theory — that ADHD behaviors stem from deficiencies in "the regulation of behavior by its consequences" (Barkley, 1989, p. 53) — underlies both drug and behavioral interventions. This suggests that behavioral interventions that focus on alterations in the antecedents and consequences of behavior, and teaching these relationships, may be effective.

Another significant issue for assessment and intervention design is that attention-related behaviors may vary widely by tasks or situations. Thus, the degree that these behaviors are found across tasks and settings is an important consideration. The nature of the tasks is critical (salience, interest level, rate of presentation, instructions to tasks, length, and so on). These factors are related to stimulus control (see Chapter Six).

For preschool children, one important assessment strategy is the analysis of activity changes in freeplay and task engagement in structured activities. Overall, tasks should be structured for successful completion. Two examples of possible interventions related to rule-governed behavior are using timers to help children limit activity changes or stay on task while completing activities, and using cues such as drawings on cards to prompt various responses. However, interventions may have to be sustained over long time periods and across settings to help with severe manifestations of these types of behaviors. Programming for response generalization and maintenance is critical.

Relatively little research has focused specifically on parent-training applications. Barriers to effective parenting stemming from family ecology and parental characteristics influence intervention decisions and outcomes. The strategies that have been used are based on behavioral principles (Anastopoulos & Barkley, 1990; Barkley 1981, 1989) and system theory (Cunningham, 1990). Intervention programs for families of ADHD children are closely related to the work of Forehand and McMahon (1981) outlined in the section on compliance training, and so they will not be reviewed further here. The reasons for considering the programs described earlier for noncompliant children are fairly reasonable (Barkley, 1989). First, the goal of the intervention is to improve parent–child relationships. As examples, objectives focus on positive attending to play, improving parental commands (stimulus control), and teaching rule-governed behaviors. Second, a significant number of children described as ADHD also have conduct-disordered types of behaviors (oppositional or defiant). Third, the programs deal with practical issues of family life.

In sum, combining treatments in sustained programs and across settings may be necessary. Many intervention efforts have used multiple components: parent training, self-control training, social skills intervention, medication, and educational interventions. There is considerable evidence of success for multicomponent treatments across a wide range of academic, social, and community-related behaviors.

Barkley (1989) stated that there has been more research on stimulant medication than any other treatment for childhood psychiatric disorders. He concluded that stimulant medications are highly effective "for the management of ADHD symptoms in most children older than 5 years" (p. 51). However, the benefits may be short-lived (Carlson & Lahey, 1988; Dupaul & Barkley, 1990). Stimulant medication should not be considered sufficient for intervention, but should be viewed as "respite rather than as a solution" (Whalen, 1989, p. 160). Regardless, the drugs should not be recommended for children younger than six (see *Physician's Desk Reference*).

Safety and Health-Related Interventions

In Chapter Five, we identified evaluating the danger of situations and behaviors as a priority in selecting target behaviors.

In this section, we discuss interventions related to helping to ensure a safe home environment. Unintentional injuries are the "leading cause of death of children" (Peterson, 1988, p. 593). Mori and Peterson (1986) wrote: "Preschoolers appear to be the group most vulnerable to injury due to their developmental limitations in dealing with stressful or dangerous situations" (p. 106).

In this section, we discuss interventions that may be valuable for individual work with parents. Many research-based interventions have been developed for use at school; they are reviewed in Chapter Eleven. Barone, Greene, and Lutzker (1986) described a program to reduce home accidents in high-risk families.

Fire Setting

Fires are one of the leading causes of death for preschool children (Peterson, 1988). With regard to intervention decisions, three issues stand out. First, family dysfunction may be an important context for intervention decisions. Other factors, such as parental depression and stress, can contribute to the danger. Peer and family interest in fire-related activities also may be a significant factor. Among the many variables that may have intervention implications, especially important are parental monitoring of behaviors, rule enforcement, effective use of discipline (versus detachment or noninvolvement, and ineffective discipline), and basic safety.

Second, fire setting frequently has been discussed as a behavior evidenced by at least some conduct-disordered children. Thus, the research-based interventions for antisocial and noncompliant children, discussed earlier, have important implications. Differential reinforcement, tokens and response cost, behavioral contracts, supervised negative practice, and overcorrection all may be considered when planning interventions.

Third, intervention programs often have an educational component concerning fire. It is frequently appropriate to deal with children's curiosity and safety in addition to parental and child behaviors related to conduct disorders. Naturalistic supervised opportunities include campfires, candles, and barbecues.

There is limited research-based information on the elements of interventions designed specifically for young fire setters. Studies have methodological and sample limitations, and little follow-up data. Based on our review of the literature and experience with parent referrals for this problem behavior, we offer the following suggestions. (However, the most important recommendation is to refer to specialists. Local fire departments have been very helpful.)

Interventions Dealing with Fire Setting

Discuss with the parents the seriousness of the behavior and overall safety-proofing of the home. Establishing the danger of the behavior is a central concern. Kolko and Kazdin (1989a, 1989b) describe a fire-setting interview for parents, and one developed for use with children. A major point of an interview is to determine factors related to conduct-disordered behavior and parental risk factors, and those related to normal curiosity. The Federal Emergency Management Agency (1988) also has developed semistructured parent and child interviews, a parent questionnaire, and recommended school interviews, to aid in the determination of risk. The handbook is intended for use by fire service personnel but has many excellent suggestions for educational and psychological service providers.

Fire prevention and basic safety instruction form an important component of treatment. Included are a room-by-room inspection for fire sources and combustibles, use of smoke detectors and fire extinguishers, and emergency fire procedures such as an evacuation plan and telephone numbers (see Chapter Eleven for school-based fire safety interventions).

Develop a contract with the parents. Key elements of a contract include (a) childproofing the house or apartment, (b) parental vigilance in monitoring child behavior, (c) enlisting the aid of others who smoke (babysitters or guests) in securing lighters and matches, (d) installing alarms and safety equipment, and (e) participating in a *structured multicomponent parent program* for noncompliant or defiant children, such as the programs by Barkley, Patterson, or Forehand and McMahon. If parents do not agree with the contract, refer them to another agency that has the authority to evoke protective services for the child.

Consult with the parents about parental monitoring. Until the behavior is under control, the parents will have to dedicate complete attention. This may serve as negative reinforcement to get the behavior under control. Problem solve steps to help with parental monitoring. For example, in a case study by Barnett, a young child was turning on burners and "torching" stuffed animals. The mother placed bright "safety" tape in the area in front of the stove. If the child crossed into the "safety zone," the mother used time out. Also, knobs may be removed from stoves. One parent who lived in a situation where matches and lighters were easily available outside the home effectively "frisked" her young child upon returning from play.

Examine with the parents any sources of stress or parental functioning that may be interfering with monitoring the behavior. We have had situations of severe marital conflict where an uncooperative spouse deliberately left lighters and matches in places available to the child. The interviews described in Chapter Three (waking-day and problem solving) may help identify dangerous settings and time periods.

Discuss other possible sources of support for the parent. Older siblings, grandparents, or friends may contribute to monitoring of behavior and intervention plans.

Train for self-control. Young children can be instructed and reinforced for finding matches or lighters and reporting them to an adult. Treated matches that will not burn may be "planted" around the home to train for self-control.

Maintain close contact with the parent. While the programs for noncompliance generally involve weekly meetings, daily contact through telephone calls or brief office visits should be considered, especially for the first two to three days. Based on the contract, there should be no attempts at fire setting because the materials should be unavailable. The program should be immediately effective, or a referral to another agency should be made.

Evaluate the potential utility of a range of interventions for fire setting. In general, it may be important to examine settings, supervision, and parental responses to fire-setting attempts, and to design a multi-element treatment based on family realities and child problem behaviors. In addition to educational strategies, negative practice, as a part of a multistep intervention sequence, is recommended (Federal Emergency Management Agency, 1988). Although reported without supporting data, negative practice involves striking two hundred matches while under close supervision. Restitution (see Chapter Seven) also is recommended.

Carstens (1982) described a "work penalty threat" in the successful treatment of a four-year-old fire setter. The penalty was described as one hour of "hard labor" that did not include regular chores. Examples included "scrubbing off the back porch, washing walls or cleaning the spaces between the kitchen tiles with a toothbrush" (p. 160). Time-out procedures also were taught to the parents to treat aggressive and noncompliant behaviors.

Exhibit 9.7 presents a treatment program using satiation and overcorrection, based on the work by Kolko (1983) and an earlier report by McGrath, Marshall, and Prior (1979). Insufficient research has been carried out to recommend the procedure in terms of general applicability, but it appears powerful.

Assuming normal curiosity and strict parental supervision, *educational programs may be an important intervention or adjunct to one.* Rather than the admonishment "Don't play with matches," which inadequately teaches children about the function and use of matches and lighters, step-by-step programs teach safe fire-related skills in a way that satisfies curiosity. One good program is *A Match Is a Tool* from the Shriners Burns Institute (202 Goodman Street, Cincinnati, OH 45219). Appropriate fear of consequences of fires is also a part of educational programs.

Car Behavior

Car misbehaviors may be quite severe and in need of immediate attention. We also have had parents report that they simply have stopped taking their children places unless absolutely necessary. In either case, car behaviors are an important point of parent consultation. Fortunately, the basics of intervention design may be applied.

Exhibit 9.7. Multicomponent Parent Treatment for Fire Setting.

---

1. The parent directs the child daily to start a fire. Materials (collected by the child) include: matches, two sheets of paper, large metal basin, pail of water, hose, scrub brush, dishwashing liquid.
2. The parent assists the child in setting the fire with paper in the metal basin.
3. Once the fire is started, it is extinguished with the hose.
4. The child is directed to clean the basin with the scrub brush and dishwashing liquid, and then rinse the basin.
5. As the child cleans, the parent verbally repeats the training sequence to the child and discusses fire safety with the child.
6. The parent questions the child to determine the child's understanding of the dangers of fire setting.
7. Daily implementation is conducted for four weeks.
8. After four weeks, the same procedures are conducted every other day.
9. On days when fire setting is not practiced, the parent asks the child if he would like to set a fire. If the child responds "no," no fire is set. If the child responds "yes," the procedure is carried out.
10. Continue to fade the firesetting procedure to one fire per week before terminating.
11. Along with this procedure, a token reinforcement system for appropriate behavior can be instituted. On days when the child does not light fires, he can be rewarded with a piece from a puzzle he has selected. When the puzzle is complete, allow the child to keep the puzzle and select a back-up reinforcer. If the child sets a fire, all the puzzle pieces are lost. Puzzles with increasing numbers of pieces resulted in intermittent reinforcement; social reinforcement was included.

Adapted from Kolko, D. J. (1983). Multicomponent parental treatment of firesetting in a six year boy. *Journal of Behavior Therapy and Experimental Psychiatry, 14,* 349–353. Copyright ©1983 by Pergamon Press.

In a case reported by Niemeyer and Fox (1990), a five-year-old boy diagnosed as having Down's syndrome attacked his mother and sister while riding in the family car. Disruptive behaviors included grabbing and pulling their hair, hitting them, throwing objects at them, and unfastening his seat belt. Often the mother had to stop the car at the roadside to bring his behavior under control.

The sister was trained to collect and record data for the duration of the study. During the first phase of the DRO intervention, seat-belt behavior was targeted. If the child did not remove his seat belt during a three-minute interval, he received a sticker and praise. Upon arrival home he received a small toy and verbal praise if he obtained the required number of stickers to meet a set criterion.

Once the boy had been wearing his seat belt consistently for two days, aggressive behavior was targeted. The procedures were the same: stickers, praise, and back-up reinforcers, contingent upon the absence of aggression. Aggressive behavior was significantly reduced during eight intervention sessions.

The intervention was then faded. Intervals for obtaining stickers were gradually increased. Initially, intervals were increased to five minutes over three sessions and then to ten minutes over two sessions. The final interval consisted of the entire ride (thirty to forty minutes). Upon arrival home he received a small toy and no stickers were presented. Other school-based interventions for bus and car behavior are reported in Chapter Eleven.

Challenges and Difficulties in Working with Families

The family is a foundation of early intervention efforts, especially a responsive and guiding caregiver. There are many challenges to ensuring this foundation. First, professionals working with families need to make certain that barriers to family intervention are not the result of clashes of style, cultures, or values. Very different situations are created when parents are not able to fulfill the normal roles for reasons such as illness, marital conflict or family dysfunction, parental adjustment problems, or psychopathology. In this section we review interventions that may be necessary when parents are not acting in the best interests of their children.

Parental Adjustment Difficulties

Perhaps counterintuively, except in extreme cases *direct* links between family and parental difficulties and children's risk status or vulnerability are not always evident. Some children do seem to be less vulnerable than others (Garmezy, 1985; Weintraub, Winters, & Neale, 1986). Even so, the evidence for *indirect* links is substantial and includes both affective disorders (Panaccione & Wahler, 1986; Webster-Stratton & Hammond, 1988) and conduct disorders (Patterson & Bank, 1986; Wahler & Dumas, 1986). For example, maternal depression may be a significant variable in parental perceptions of their children's behavior (see Friedlander, Weiss, & Traylor, 1986), the experiences that are provided to children, and opportunities for modeling various behaviors. In such cases, the school-based professional is likely to seek outside help for parents through referral to community or private resources for personal, family, or marital therapy.

Child Abuse and Neglect

Child abuse and neglect may be defined as "the degree to which a parent uses aversive or inappropriate control strategies with his or her child and/or fails to provide minimal standards of nurturance" (Azar & Wolfe, 1989, p. 452). The topic of child abuse and neglect is of growing concern, and both institutional and professional responses are necessary. The problem has a journal dedicated to its cause (*Child Abuse and Neglect*). Certainly, much needs to be learned about very different types of abuse (psychological, physical, and sexual) and about responsiveness to interventions.

Child maltreatment is best placed within the framework of dysfunctional family systems (Wolfe, 1987; Wolfe & Bourdeau, 1987). An important context is the parent's lack of control or restraint in conflicted parent–child interactions. Psychological maltreatment may be difficult to detect, but it also may be considered as a "core" component of abuse (Brassard & Hart, 1987). Seven specific acts have been identified to help define situations involving psychological maltreatment: rejection, degradation, terrorization, isolation, corruption, exploitation, and denial of emotional responses (Brassard & Gelardo, 1987).

Wolfe (1987) presented a three-stage model of abuse and neglectful behavior (see Figure 9.1).

There are important limitations to behavioral interventions with abusive or neglective parents. However, these are

Figure 9.1. Transitional Model of Abuse and Neglect.

Destabilizing Factors	Compensatory Factors

STAGE 1

Reduced Tolerance for Stress and Disinhibition of Aggression

Weak preparation for parenting	Supportive spouse
Low control, feedback, predictability	Socioeconomic stability
Stressful life events	Success at work, school
	Social supports and models

STAGE 2

Poor Management of Acute Crises and Provocation

Conditioned emotional arousal	Improvement in child behavior
Sources of anger and aggression	Community programs for parents
Appraisal of harm/loss, threat	Coping resources

STAGE 3

Habitual Patterns of Arousal and Aggression with Family Members

Child's habituation to physical punishment	Parental dissatisfaction with physical punishment
Parent's reinforcement for using strict control techniques	Child responds favorably to noncoercive methods
Child's increase in problem behavior	Community restraints/services

Source: Wolfe, D. A. (1987). *Child abuse: Implications for child development and psychopathology,* p. 50. Copyright ©1987 by Sage Publications, Reprinted by permission of Sage Publications, Inc.

best viewed as limitations of the scientific and professional understanding of the syndrome, and contexts of abuse and neglect,
not an indictment of behavioral interventions in such situations.

First, there may be limitations in behavioral approaches
with parents having severe forms of psychopathology. Second,
involvement with the legal system may lead to questions, conflicts, and dilemmas for parents and professionals. For example, parents must have opportunities to practice new skills, but
they may not have custody of the child because of abuse or they
may be allowed only brief visitations.

Also, reporting data is required for behavioral interventions, but parents may be reluctant to do so because of their
concern that the data may be used to help build a case against
them. Since abuse is usually a private matter, data collection
other than through indirect means is problematic. However,
without strong data, treatment efficacy and recidivism are serious questions. The complexity of intervention design and evaluation is substantially compounded by the fact that abuse is frequently a private event.

Third, behavioral interventions may be insufficient in
scope, given a family's limited personal, social, and economic
resources and sometimes chaotic lives. Fourth, because of crisis situations, systematic solutions may not be sought. Fifth, often
abusive parents do not refer themselves for treatment, and may
not view themselves as having a problem. Sixth, early intervention is necessary. By the time that abuse is reported to child
abuse workers, the situations may be so severe that children have
been significantly harmed (Wolfe, Edwards, Manion, & Koverola, 1988).

In Chapters Three, Four, and Five, we included aspects
of assessment and intervention design that are critical in these
cases: determining danger and risk, general factors related to
family ecology and problem identification, and assessing children's needs and behaviors. Of special importance are harsh verbal and physical discipline, and emotional responses such as
anger that may interfere with more adaptive plans for discipline.
Anger-control interventions may be necessary. Also of great importance are annoying, difficult, or disruptive child behaviors.

Systematical daily reports by parents of significant behaviors and emotional reactions may be critical. Further discussion of assessment issues is given in Wolfe and Bourdeau (1987) and Reid (1985).

Given these considerations, one of the most important aspects of decision making is parental motivation for intervention. Many suggestions have appeared in the literature to deal with this problem, but it may be necessary to develop individual strategies based, at least initially, on forming a treatment alliance (Weitzman, 1985). A promising approach is the use of behavioral contracts (Azar & Wolfe, 1989; Conger & Lahey, 1982; Reid, 1985; also see the earlier discussion of fire setting). A sample contract is depicted in Exhibit 9.8.

The consultant may act as an advocate for the parent in dealings with protective service agencies and the courts as long as objectives in treatment are being met. Reid suggested initially framing the problem by "the daily problems the parent is experiencing with the child" and not by the abuse incident (1985, p. 779). Wahler's (1980) concept of insularity, described earlier, placed emphasis on the needs of the parent. Acceptability of treatment is likely to be critically important.

With regard to specific intervention approaches, a wide variety of techniques can be found. The approach developed by Patterson and his associates, described earlier, has been applied to abusive families (Reid, 1985). Typically, interventions have been focused on the parent, while child-related needs have been comparatively neglected. Interventions that are skill oriented include parent training in behavioral principles, anger control, and stress management (Azar & Wolfe, 1989). Techniques include many of those described in earlier chapters, including rehearsal, feedback, and modeling appropriate parent–child interactions and ways to handle disruptive behaviors. Other points of analysis are the cognitive styles and belief systems of the parents. A safety-oriented approach to abuse and neglect was described by Tertinger, Greene, and Lutzker (1984).

Because abusive and neglectful situations are complex, multicomponent treatments that include parent and child interactions are perhaps the safest alternative (Isaacs, 1982). The

Exhibit 9.8. Sample Contract for Child Abuse Interventions.

SERVICE CONTRACT

Between: _____ and _____

Date: _____

In undertaking to assist our family, [the therapist] agrees to help us explore the effectiveness of our parenting approaches with our son, and to improve in areas that are identified by ourselves and [the therapist]. In this manner, we hope to assist our son in developing more acceptable and desirable behavior at home.

We agree to attend scheduled appointments regularly (approximately once per week for 2 hours), and to follow through on suggestions provided by [the therapist]. We will provide [the therapist] with comments as to the problems and successes we may encounter along the way, to allow for a better "fit" between our style and [the therapist's] suggestions.

The goals of our involvement, as discussed between ourselves and [the therapist], focus on increasing the amount of time we spend with Ben, particularly in terms of active play, developmental stimulation, and positive attention. As well, we hope to improve our methods of discipline with Ben, in order to reduce our use of criticism, harsh punishment, and anger.

(If applicable or agreed to):

We agree to permit [the therapist] to discuss our progress with our caseworker, Ms. ___ , for the purpose of assisting in case planning and fulfilling our agreement with the agency. A written report at the completion of the program will be provided to our caseworker by [the therapist]. *We will have the opportunity to discuss in full the contents of this report with [the therapist] prior to its being sent.*

We understand that any person with whom we may be involved in this program is obligated to report to the child welfare agency any *suspicions of harm or risk* concerning our child that they may have. Such concerns, whether minor or major, will be brought to our attention by [the therapist] in all cases, in an effort to improve on the situation.

All information from our contacts with this treatment program are treated as confidential, with the exception of information required by law or agreed to by our signature.

Signed, for family: Dated:

Signed, for agency:

Source: Wolfe, D. A. (1991). *Preventing physical and emotional abuse of children* (p. 50). New York: Guilford Press.

child's characteristics that elicit abuse, strategies to enhance parent–child bonding, and the parent's extrachild relationships are important considerations. Crozier and Katz (1979) presented evidence of a successful intervention with two families based on social learning theory and multiple treatment components: written material on parenting skills, role playing, and behavior-management strategies, including parental self-control. A "crisis hotline" phone number also was provided.

Also using a social learning approach, Wolfe, Sandler, and Kaufman (1981) taught child-management skills to known abusive mothers. We describe this program in more detail. The age of the children ranged from two to ten, with a mean age of 4.6 years. The sample consisted of poverty parents who were court ordered to participate in the intervention or referred by the child welfare agency. A control group of other abusive mothers received standard services provided by a child welfare agency.

Multiple measures were used in designing the pretest-post-test control group. A core measure was the *Parent-Child Interaction Form* (PCIF), described as an observational system to code the antecedents and consequences of appropriate parental responses. During the observation the parent was requested to interact with the child in different contexts: (a) interacting freely, (b) teaching the child a new task, and (c) commanding the child to complete specific tasks (such as picking up specific toys).

Two interventions were implemented with the treatment group. The first was a group intervention of two-hour parent training sessions two nights per week for eight weeks. Components included teaching parents (a) concepts related to child development and management, including positive reinforcement, time out, shaping, and appropriate use of punishment techniques; (b) problem-solving skills and modeling of appropriate management skills; and (c) relaxation training and methods to control impulsive behaviors.

Second, an individual criterion-based family intervention was completed in the home. Families were visited by clinical psychology graduate students for approximately one hour per week (mean hours in the home = 8.9). The goal of the home visits was to help parents implement the techniques learned in the group intervention. Parents initially were instructed to record any child behavior problem that occurred during the week. Each week parents selected a target behavior for resolution. The parent then was asked to select a positive method for resolving the problem, and the strategy was rehearsed with the graduate student or the child. More difficult skills on the PCIF were not attempted until the parent demonstrated proficiency at basic skill levels.

Results of the parent training program indicated improvements in the use of child-management skills and self-control techniques. Ten weeks later, five subjects were reassessed and the maintenance of effects was observed. After one year, a review of the files of the sixteen families indicated that none of the eight treatment-group families or the six control-group families who received delayed treatment after the initial study had been reported for child abuse. (One of the subjects in the control group who had declined treatment was reported for abuse, and one family moved out of state). However, Azar, Fantuzzo, and Twentyman (1984) questioned the emphasis given to teaching child development and child-management techniques in abuse interventions without more adequate attention to the actual patterns of maltreatment responses. They argued for studies with more careful analysis of the context and interactions that result in abuse.

Most of the research pertains to physical abuse, although Wolfe and Wolfe (1988) provide an excellent discussion of sexual abuse. It is difficult to be a scientist-practitioner in cases of sexual abuse because of the limited research base. The results of assessments such as children's self-reports may be tenuous, and parental ratings may not be valid. The different intervention implications and long-term outcomes of intrafamilial (incest) and extrafamilial (such as by a babysitter) abuse are enormous. The symptoms associated with abuse vary across internalizing behaviors (anxiety, fear), externalizing behaviors (aggression, restlessness), and sexually acting-out behaviors. Furthermore, the symptoms may be delayed in their expression.

As with many problem situations, prevention efforts may be important. Miltenberger and Thiesse-Duffy (1988) evaluated a parent-taught prevention program to help children resist abduction and identify "good" and "bad" touches. They found that behavioral skills training (rehearsal, modeling, praise, and feedback) was a necessary adjunct. However, they warned that the procedures may not help with sexual abuse by family members or persons known to children. At present, many questions also are being raised about prevention efforts. School-based interventions are discussed in Chapter Eleven.

Respite

Respite care is defined as short-term relief (day or night) for families with developmentally disabled members. Respite care is often, by itself, a highly significant intervention for families. It also may have profound direct personal, social, and economic benefits for parents and indirect benefits for children (see Turnbull & Turnbull, 1986). Many interventions place increased demands on parents, but for some parents, "respite may be more important and beneficial than increased involvement" (White, 1985–86, p. 413). Respite-care providers also may be included in intervention plans. There are many alternatives, including in-home, extended-family, and community-based services. Potential benefits are

1. Relief from emotional and economic stress.
2. Accessibility of families to child-care facilities, other appointments, errands for periodic and emergency needs.
3. Enjoyment.
4. Help prevent abuse and neglect.
5. Eliminate need for out-of-home placement for difficult children.

There is little research on the topic. Rimmerman (1989) found that respite services of at least six hours per week provided to mothers of children with developmental disabilities resulted in ratings of less stress and enhancement of coping.

Summary and Conclusions

We discussed atypical problem behaviors in the home and community within the contexts of family systems and parenting behaviors. Noncompliance is a keystone behavior that relates to many interventions discussed in the chapter. Treatment programs for noncompliance focus on improving the quality of parent–child relationships and behavior management in the home and community. Parental planning is a significant component.

Another critical aspect of preschool services involves attention to dangerous behaviors. Special attention was given to fire setting and abuse. For both situations, a contract serves as the basis of services, clearly delineating the parent and consultant roles. Interventions for both typically comprise multiple components that build on many topics considered throughout the book. Improving the relationship between parent and child, parental monitoring of behavior, and effective strategies for misbehavior are primary, but interventions also may need to deal more broadly with parental needs apart from child-related responsibilities.

PART FOUR

SCHOOL-BASED INTERVENTIONS

10

The Classroom
as Ecosystem

THE RANGE OF PRESCHOOL PHILOSOPHIES, THEORIES, AND CURRIC-
ula — and the resulting controversies — is enormous. Preschool
classrooms may be organized along many dimensions depending in large part on the beliefs, values, and training of educators and the goals of the programs. At one extreme, preschool
teachers may be highly permissive, and may focus on encouraging the child's interests or selecting experiences assumed to facilitate normal development. Others may be highly structured and
prescriptive.

Some preschool classrooms are specifically tied to individual theoretical orientations (Montessori, Piaget). Bereiter and
Englemann's curriculum (1966) is an example of the application of behavior principles to preschool education. However, even
when a particular curriculum is adopted by an agency, implementation may differ greatly across classrooms. Moreover, it is
likely that many preschool educators are guided by eclectic or
unspecified personal theories or philosophies.

Given these broad potential differences in philosophy and
practice, we have elected to focus on possible roles of caregivers
and children in intervention design and to emphasize preschool
classrooms as ecosystems. Hobbs wrote: "The group is important to the child. When a group is functioning well, it is extremely

John D. Hall contributed to the writing of this chapter.

difficult for an individual child to behave in a disturbed way" (1966, p. 1112). Well-functioning classrooms help prevent behavior problems (Nordquist & Twardosz, 1990).

Organizational and Systems Interventions

The philosophy, quality, organization, curriculum, and available services directly affect assessment and intervention decisions. There are numerous sources on model curriculum. One framework for early childhood programs is provided by the National Association for the Education of Young Children (NAEYC). Their guidelines for curriculum are reproduced in Exhibit 10.1.

Guidelines for adult–child interactions, home–school relationships, and developmental evaluations are included. The interaction guidelines focus on responding to children's needs, expanding opportunities to communicate, facilitating task completion, and detecting stress in children's behavior. Adult roles in the development of self-esteem and self-control are included, along with adult roles in developing independence. Parental rights in decision making, the teacher as resource to parents, and interagency communication are emphasized in the section on home–program relationships.

A recent study examined thirteen public school preschools based on these guidelines (Mitchell, Seligson, & Marx, 1989). Among the major findings were uneven program quality and frequently great differences between stated philosophies and actual practices found in preschools. Another was the difficulties in transitions between preschools and kindergartens that stem from different curriculum philosophies. Settings frequently lacked art, science, math, and multicultural activities and materials. Areas for sociodramatic play, private spaces, and gross motor play also were absent. Of particular concern was the emphasis in many programs on "worksheet tasks" requiring "closed-ended" responses that were deemed inappropriate and frustrating for young children, and that also may damper creativity, curiosity, and desire to learn.

While the NAEYC guidelines serve as a major framework for preschool design, there are other concerns beyond implemen-

Exhibit 10.1. Guidelines for
Developmentally Appropriate Curriculum.

---

1. Developmentally appropriate curriculum provides for all areas of a child's development: physical, emotional, social, and cognitive, through an integrated approach.
2. Appropriate curriculum planning is based on teachers' observations and recordings of each child's special interest and developmental progress.
3. Curriculum planning emphasizes learning as an interactive process. Teachers prepare the environment for children to learn through active exploration and interaction with adults, other children, and materials.
4. Learning activities and materials should be concrete, real, and relevant to the lives of young children.
5. Programs provide for a wider range of developmental interests and abilities than the chronological age range of the group would suggest. Adults are prepared to meet the needs of children who exhibit unusual interests and skills outside the normal developmental range.
6. Teachers provide a variety of activities and materials; teachers increase the difficulty, complexity, and challenge of an activity as children are involved in it and as children develop understanding and skills.
7. Adults provide opportunities for children to choose from among a variety of activities, materials, and equipment; and time to explore through active involvement. Adults facilitate children's engagement with materials and activities and extend the child's learning by asking questions or making suggestions that stimulate children's thinking.
8. Multicultural and nonsexist experiences, materials, and equipment should be provided for children of all ages.
9. Adults provide a balance of rest and active movement for children throughout the program day.
10. Outdoor experiences should be provided for children of all ages.

Source: National Association for the Education of Young Children. (1986, September). NAEYC position statement on developmentally appropriate practice in early childhood programs serving children from birth through age 8 (pp. 6–11). Washington, D.C.: Author.

tation. The general principles on which they are founded may not be valid for all children and situations. Carta, Schwartz, Atwater, and McConnell wrote: "The philosophy of early education . . . proposes that preschool programs should be child centered, allowing children to make choices about what is to be learned. While this approach may be logical for typical young children, it falls short as a standard of effective programming for young children with disabilities" (1991, p. 2). They emphasized the need for "specialized" teaching and practices for children with special needs, including structured classroom experiences and research-based interventions for instructing and managing behavior.

For the time being, personnel preparation for child-care workers is quite variable, and for many, intervention-related training may be minimal or nonexistent. Also, preschools are in a rapid state of development and difficult to characterize. Therefore, a first step in establishing educational and psychological services for children with learning and behavior problems is organizational assessment and development. The major findings by Mitchell, Seligson, and Marx (1989) do not include considerations related to intervention decision making or special services.

A wide range of intervention alternatives may need to be examined to meet the desired goals for individual children. A likely initial focus of educational consultation is effective teaching and learning strategies that encompass functional developmental skills. Functional skills emphasize the "usefulness of learned responses" (Bricker, 1986, p. 302). The goals of a functional curriculum are to expand opportunities and to facilitate independence and adaptability (Bricker, 1986; LeBlanc, Etzel, & Domash, 1978).

Furthermore, the mental health of young children is enhanced by successful participation in well-functioning social groups established and maintained in preschool classrooms. Social problem-solving skills are modeled, taught, prompted, and reinforced in ongoing interactions through the efforts of peers and teachers.

Classroom Ecologies

From the viewpoint of professional-practice decisions, it is helpful to view each preschool classroom as a natural ecosystem. Any change for individual children may affect other children's and teachers' behaviors in planned and unplanned ways. Thus, preschool classrooms are "interdependent systems" (Carta, Sainato, & Greenwood, 1988). The list of potential variables is vast, and relatively few empirical studies are available to guide practice (Burstein, 1986; Carta, Sainato, & Greenwood, 1988; Rogers-Warren, 1982). A special issue of *Education and Treatment of Children* was dedicated to this topic (McEvoy, 1990).

While it is not possible to separate the physical from the social aspects of the environment, these two major classes of variables serve as the basis for ecobehavioral analysis. First, physical, fixed, or programmatic classroom attributes are assessed. Examples include availability and arrangement of play and work (or curricular) materials, spatial arrangements of classroom, and classroom social memberships (for example, percentage and needs of children with disabilities). Many alternative physical and social arrangements are likely to promote personal and social competence among group members if core design principles are applied. We return to discussions of relatively fixed qualities of classrooms throughout this and the next chapter. Several examples of classroom organization have been developed to help facilitate social interaction and skill acquisition (Bailey, 1989; Bailey & Wolery, 1984; Nordquist, Twardosz, & McEvoy, 1991). Recently, preschool classroom design also has focused on facilitating early literacy through play (Morrow & Rand, 1991; Neuman & Roskos, 1990).

Another broad class of variables that falls under the "fixed" category is *routines*. Several facets of routines are significant for intervention design. Routines provide children with predictable learning situations where cues and models of appropriate verbalizations and behaviors are consistently available. A wide variety of social and preacademic skills may be taught through the use of routines and rules for conduct. With increases in skill development, children are able to perform and learn how to anticipate the necessary behaviors (Rogers-Warren, 1982), and thus are able to perform more independently. Furthermore, routines are important for caregivers. Thus, the behavior of children who are unsuccessfully adapting during classroom routines may be considered targets for assessment and intervention.

The sequence of routines also may be an important variable. Krantz and Risley (1977) found that scheduling a quiet period, such as story time, after an active period resulted in more disruptions than the reverse order. One reason for the importance of the waking-day interview described in Chapter Three is that the preschool consultant can identify routines (or absence of meaningful routines) throughout the day, from awakening to bedtime.

A second class of variables, such as teacher and children's behavior, is interactive or *dynamic*. Teacher behaviors include planning and arranging daily learning activities, creating play areas and assigning play groups, managing activities, and interacting on countless occasions in both obvious (attention, praise, reprimand) and subtle (eye contact, affective tone) ways. The power of contingent attention and praise for teaching and improving behaviors and for classroom management is unquestioned. The form of teacher requests is also an important research topic (Atwater & Morris, 1988; Strain, Lambert, Kerr, Stagg, & Lenkner, 1983). Thus, the environment has significant social and interactive qualities that merit analysis.

Considering the great number of variables that may need to be examined, an ecobehavioral framework has potential value for guiding both classroom design and consultative services to preschool teachers. The two major features of ecobehavioral classroom analysis follow.

1. *Necessity for child environment fit.* The most obvious point of consultation is whether a child can receive instruction within a particular classroom or whether some factors need to be modified to enable the fit. Many variables may lead to success or failure and are potential points of analysis. Examples include methods of instruction and effectiveness of classroom management, group size and composition, teacher tolerance, and support services for teachers.

2. *Necessity for kindergarten survival skills.* One of the important lessons from special programming for older children is that specialized settings may actually decrease chances for success in mainstream or integrated settings. The discrepancies between special and mainstream learning environments may increase problem behavior and decrease skill generalization in transition

settings (Vincent et al., 1980). Special settings, in contrast to mainstream classrooms, are characterized by teacher effort in supervising and monitoring behavior of individual children with special needs and reducing the complexity of tasks for children. Thus, it is of critical importance to directly teach skills needed in anticipated environments. Examples of relevant skills include independent work habits and responding appropriately in group instruction.

Table 10.1 includes the categories and codes of the Ecobehavioral System for Complex Assessment of Preschool Environments (ESCAPE) (Carta, Greenwood, & Atwater, 1985; Carta, Sainato, & Greenwood, 1988). Harms and Clifford (1980) present a rating scale for early educational environments that has seven dimensions (personal care routines for children, language-reasoning skills, adult needs, and so on) with a total of thirty-seven subscales. Another environmental assessment scale is described by Dunst, McWilliam, and Holbert (1986; Project Sunrise, 1989). Earlier, template matching was presented as a strategy to assess both skills and environmental demands.

Curriculum-Based Intervention

Certainly one of the most important aspects of early intervention is inherent in the design and execution of a preschool curriculum. An ecologically based curriculum for young children includes the continuous assessment of skills in ways that are linked to teaching. Curriculum-based assessment also includes the assessment of the classroom ecology (Fuchs & Fuchs, 1986) to enable observations of children's performance in preacademic, social, and other developmental areas. The assessment should yield information to help delineate the conditions necessary for competent performance. There are currently many alternative preschool (or day-care) curricula.

The *Carolina Curriculum for Preschoolers with Special Needs* (CCPSN) (Johnson-Martin, Attermeier, & Hacker, 1990) is an extension of a curriculum for infants. The CCPSN divides developmental domains into teaching sequences that may be used

**Table 10.1. Preschool Observation System
for Measuring Ecobehavioral Interactions.**

	Description	*Code examples*
Ecological categories		
Designated activity	Subject of instruction	Free play, pre-academics, language, fine motor
Activity initiator	Classification of person choosing activity	Teacher, child, no one
Materials	Objects with which the student engages	Manipulative, art materials, large motor equipment
Location	Physical placement of the observed student	On floor, at tables, on equipment, in chairs
Grouping	Size of group in same activity as observed student	Small group, large group, one-to-one
Composition	Mix of handicapped and nonhandicapped students in instructional group	All handicapped, mixed, all nonhandicapped
Teacher behavior categories		
Teacher definition	Primary adult interacting with observed student	Teacher, aide, student teacher, ancillary staff
Teacher behavior	Teacher behavior relative to observed student	Verbal instruction, physical assisting, approval, disapproval
Teacher focus	Direction of teacher's behavior	Target child only, target child and entire group, other than target child
Student behavior categories		
Appropriate behaviors	Specific on-task responses	Fine motor, gross motor, academic work
Inappropriate behaviors	Behaviors which compete with appropriate behaviors	Acting-out, off-task, self-stimulation
Talk	Verbalizations	Talk to teacher, talk to peer

Source: Carta, J. J., Greenwood, C. R., & Atwater, J. B. (1985). *Eco-behavioral system for the complex assessment of preschool environments: ESCAPE.* Kansas City, KS: Juniper Gardens Children's Project, Bureau of Child Research, University of Kansas. Reprinted with permission.

within home, preschool, or day-care settings. The domains include cognition, communication, social adaptation, fine motor, and gross motor skills. Curriculum sequences referred to as "areas" are embedded within the domains. For example, cognition contains attention and memory, concepts, symbolic play, reasoning, and visual perception.

The CCPSN has many important features. Characteristics of the setting are considered: the physical setting (areas for pretend, "messy," quiet, constructive, manipulative, visual-motor, and active play), the structure of the day, strategies to optimize appropriate behavior, and the importance of story time. The authors review a wide range of handicapping conditions and their effects on instruction. Also, they emphasize skill *sequences,* not individual items. Testing and teaching (both individual and group) activities are described for each skill.

Entry into the curriculum is based on an *assessment log,* which serves as a criterion-referenced instrument. Item selection was based on clinical experience, research, and other developmental scales. The assessment log is completed through naturalistic classroom observations that occur over time (one day to several weeks). Both emerging and mastered skills are recorded on a developmental progress chart.

The HICOMP Preschool Curriculum (Willoughby-Herb & Neisworth, 1982) is based on behavioral and developmental principles. Appropriate for children from birth to age five, HICOMP includes over eight hundred objectives organized by communication, self-care, motor, and problem-solving domains. Behavioral strategies for teaching related developmental skills also are included. Another significant feature of HICOMP is that developmental objectives may be individually tracked over successive years. One of the best examples of comprehensive educationally related programming for children with more severe developmental problems may be found in *The Me Book* (Lovaas, 1981).

A different strategy for curriculum development has been introduced by Bergan and co-workers (Bergan, Feld, & Swarner, 1988). They use the term *macroconsultation* to refer to broadly conceived instructional management consultation to help plan learning activities and curriculum and to help with the learning process. The concept fits well within the organizational and systems context of this section by focusing on long-range instructional and program goals. Their instructional approach involves four by-now familiar phases or cycles: assessment, planning learning opportunities, implementation, and evaluation.

One unique aspect of the program is the *Head Start Measures Battery* (HSMB), comprising six scales that assess cognitive and social development. The HSMB was developed through the use of statistical methods to derive instructionally relevant developmental sequences. The assessment technology provides individual and class developmental profiles after fall and spring testing. Among the stated advantages of the assessment system is that a child's developmental level is related to needed and appropriately challenging educational experiences. The children's ability is associated with probabilities of adequately performing the tasks in a developmental sequence. Performance is characterized as mastery, partial mastery, or nonmastery. In addition to a mastery score, a developmental level score is also provided for the six scales.

To evaluate goal attainment, a measure of teaching level is also necessary. Teaching level (TL) refers to skills that are taught to children, and the system provides a TL for each child. Bergan, Feld, and Swarner (1988) pointed out that a close relationship between developmental and teaching levels means that teachers have accurately targeted teaching on the child's ability level. Analysis of teaching levels in relationship to developmental progress may help with instructional planning. Bergan, Feld, and Swarner also discuss broader applications of macroconsultation, involving communication aspects, such as teleconferencing, that may be especially helpful in rural areas.

Curriculum development also may be related to specific content areas (language development, social skills, and so on). Bracken and Myers (1986) provide an attractive program for teaching 250 basic concepts, including the following subdomains: color, comparisons, shapes, direction/position, social and emotional, size, texture and materials, quantity, time and sequence, letter, numbers and counting.

The concept development program also may be used with the *Bracken Basic Concept Scale* (Bracken, 1984). A similar instrument has been developed by Boehm (1986). An extensive intervention related to early language development has been made available by MacDonald and his associates (see MacDonald, 1985, for an overview). McGinnis and Goldstein (1990) have downwardly extended a comprehensive intervention for teaching social skills to young children.

In summary, curriculum-based assessment provides information about a child's educational and developmental levels. It provides information about learning environments and the effects of instructional interventions. A well-developed curriculum (a) includes a wide range of functional, developmentally sequenced tasks, (b) enables ongoing measurement, and (c) facilitates the use of a variety of teaching and learning strategies. Curriculum-based assessment is fundamental to preschool service delivery and facilitates screening and assessment for intervention purposes. The overall curriculum should focus on preacademic, personal, and social outcomes. Specialized or focused curricula have been developed that may be useful for intensive interventions in such areas as language or social skills.

Improving Preacademic Skills

The elements of good instruction apply. These include the appropriateness of objectives and instructional techniques, frequent opportunities to practice skills, feedback related to performance, error correction, progress monitoring, and contingencies for improved performance. Several key strategies are discussed in this section.

Preattending. For many children, preattending skills are an important point of assessment and intervention. Preattending skills include looking at the materials, listening to instructions, and sitting quietly during instruction (see Chapter Six).

Opportunities to Respond. This simply means analyzing the occasions for learning and practice. Giving children frequent chances to practice is fundamentally related to skill acquisition. In many preschool classrooms, such opportunities may be much less than expected. As reported in Carta, Sainato, and Greenwood (1988), transitions and unoccupied time actually may be more prevalent than learning time in preacademic environments. Interventions to improve transitions between activities are reviewed in a subsequent section.

An application of the concept of "opportunities to respond" is provided by Sainato, Strain, and Lyon (1987) in a study of choral responding in a preschool classroom for disabled children (developmentally delayed). They studied the effects of increasing opportunities to respond in relationship to children's rate and quality of responses in group instruction. Appropriate behavior during group instruction is critical because it increases the chances for successful integration of children with disabilities and their preparation to function in less restrictive settings.

The study included the three preschoolers out of a class of ten who were the most disruptive during group instruction. The intervention focused on morning group circle time where receptive and expressive language skills were practiced. Data were collected on the following behaviors: teacher commands (individual and group), type of response (correct, incorrect, no response), and child engagement (defined as on- or off-task). A changing-criterion design was used with the criterion applied to the rate of teacher commands.

The first phase involved twenty days of teacher training, including practice in implementing the following classroom rules: (a) stay in seat, (b) hands to self, (c) look at teacher, (d) be quiet when teacher talks, (e) ignore inappropriate behavior, and (f) praise good behavior. A brief time out was administered if the first efforts to control behavior were insufficient. In addition, the teachers were trained to (a) model desired responses, (b) call on children individually, and (c) give commands to the entire group. Group responses were cued by "Simon Says."

Two different intervention criteria, three and five teacher commands per minute, were used. The procedures are described as follows: "Teachers seated the children in a semicircle and began the morning's circle activities with the calendar, the weather, and children's names. They also called on each child to respond to a command. At a signal from an observer they began the group responding procedure by holding up a stimulus card and modeling the response: Simon says, 'red.' The children in unison responded: 'red' (p. 26). Children were praised for attention and correct responses. If they were compliant and responded during 80 percent of the session, they received a sticker to place on a wall chart.

The results demonstrated the effectiveness of the procedure in several ways. On-task behavior increased after the teacher training began. The group-responding procedure successfully increased the rates of correct responses by the target children. In addition, social validity was assessed by having ten kindergarten teachers rate the children's behavior based on videotapes. The most positive ratings were given for the five-commands-per-minute condition. The kindergarten teachers also commented that, based on the behaviors, all the handicapped children "could be easily mainstreamed into their classroom" (p. 29).

Errorless Learning and Delayed Prompting. In learning new skills, it is important to maximize the amount of early success. Errorless learning stresses the control of antecedent teaching procedures to enable the child to perform with no (or few) errors. There are two basic types of procedures. One involves a system of teacher prompts to help children perform. A second (and more elaborate) procedure uses systematic stimulus modifications where the task is initially made easy and progressively becomes more difficult by fading prompts. Sulzer-Azaroff and Mayer (1991) and Wolery, Bailey, and Sugai (1988) include a discussion of errorless learning strategies. Examples of delayed prompting follow because of its practicality and demonstrated success.

Delayed prompting is a form of errorless learning (Touchette & Howard, 1984) based on stimulus control. The basic procedure involves transferring control from a prompt (or assistance) to the natural stimulus by using a systematic time delay. The intervention has been used with young children who have difficulty acquiring preacademic skills such as letters, numbers, colors, shapes (Bradley-Johnson, Sunderman, & Johnson, 1983) and sight words (Alig-Cybriwsky, Wolery, & Gast, 1990). In the study by Bradley-Johnson, Sunderman, and Johnson (1983),

Exhibit 10.2. Delayed Prompting.

---

1. The child was first taught to wait before responding. The child was reinforced with a penny and praise. The delay interval was gradually increased. When the child was able to wait four seconds on five consecutive trials, the pretraining phase was discontinued.

2. Six 2″ × 2″ cards containing letters or numbers were prepared; three included numbers or letters to be taught, while the other three contained reversals. The selection of stimuli was based on failures during a pretest. The sets consisted of stimuli with similar characters (m, n, u). After mastery of one set, another was introduced.

3. For each trial, the trainer selected a letter (or number), and said, for example, "Point to m and remember to say 'm' before pointing" (p. 330). The trainer waited, and if the child pointed to the correct card and said "m" before the four-second limit she/he was reinforced (as in step 1).

4. If the correct response was not made within the time interval, the trainer prompted the child by pointing to the correct card. If imitation occurred, the child was reinforced.

5. The next trial included the same cards, but their positions were changed. Another card (or stimulus) was randomly selected.

6. When the child failed to repeat the letter or number, a reminder was given. For incorrect responses, the child was told "No" and ignored for fifteen seconds.

7. The criterion for mastery of a letter or number was five consecutive correct anticipatory responses. When this criterion was met, this was followed by a ten-trial criterion test. The mastered stimulus was presented with the other five training stimuli. Training continued on stimuli that had not been mastered. A delayed post-test followed one week of training.

8. Training consisted of two weekly sessions lasting fifteen minutes each. The pennies served as tokens, and were traded for small toys.

Source: Reprinted with permission from *Journal of School Psychology, 21,* S. Bradley-Johnson, P. Sunderman, and C. M. Johnson, Comparison of delayed prompting and fading for teaching preschoolers easily confused letters and numbers. Copyright ©1983, Pergamon Press, plc.

clear benefits were shown over a fading procedure (see Exhibit 10.2). Alig-Cybriwsky, Wolery, and Gast (1990) presented a procedure to use time delay in an instructional group. The description of the procedures is complicated, but salient features are included in Exhibit 10.3. Schuster and Griffin (1990) describe the use of errorless learning with task analysis and chained (multistep) tasks.

Exhibit 10.3. A Group Time-Delay Procedure.

1. A small group of children (four) were selected to participate. Children selected were able to "(a) sit and attend to the trainer and materials with three other children present for 15 minutes; (b) verbally imitate letter and word names; (c) match all words used in the study; (d) wait 3 seconds for a prompt [this was trained . . . if children did not wait]; (e) comply with verbal directions, 'Let's say the letters' . . . ; and (f) select a reinforcer from a provided array" (p. 101).

2. Six unknown target sight words were identified for each child.

3. During the first session, two of six words were selected for each child, and six trials were provided for each word (twelve trials per child).

4. General attentional cues ("Look"), and specific attentional cues ("Let's say the letters") were given. Children's performance was assessed in probe sessions. As each word was presented in a flashcard format, the teacher cued the child, saying, "[Child's name], what word?"

5. A "no delay" procedure was used for the first session of each instructional condition. Subsequent sessions used the three-second delay as follows.

6. If the child did not respond within three seconds, the teacher modeled the correct response ("This word is red") and waited another three seconds for a response.

7. When the child correctly anticipated and waited for the model, the child was praised and received edibles as reinforcement. The edibles were first given on a continuous schedule but were thinned to every third response.

8. If the child responded incorrectly within the first three seconds (prior to the model) the teacher said, "No. The word is ___ ; remember to wait if you don't know."

9. If the child responded incorrectly after the delay and model, the teacher said, "No, the word is ___ ."

10. If another child responded before the target child, the teacher said, "Only say the answer when it's your turn."

11. Review trials at the beginning of instructional sessions were included for previously learned words.

Adapted from Alig-Cybriwsky, C., Wolery, M., & Gast, D. L. (1990). Use of a constant time delay procedure in teaching preschoolers in a group format. *Journal of Early Intervention, 14,* 99–116.

Sociodramatic play. Sociodramatic play is ubiquitous in preschool settings. Still, its power as an intervention may be overlooked. Rosen characterized sociodramatic play in the following way: "Sociodramatic play . . . occurs when several children take on different roles and interact with each other in terms of a situation that they have spontaneously created (e.g., a doctor's office . . .). . . . sociodramatic play, being complex, activates the emotional, social, and intellectual resources of the child" (1974, p. 920).

Evidence suggests that sociodramatic play can be taught, and that potential gains may include cognitive and social problem-solving skills (Rosen, 1974; Saltz, Dixon, & Johnson, 1977; Saltz & Johnson, 1974). Seminal work on this topic was reported by Smilansky (1968). There are important individual, social, cultural, and environmental aspects of play that unfortunately are beyond the scope of our review. Many interventions use aspects of sociodramatic play, and they are discussed at various points in the chapter. An excellent discussion of practical play techniques and materials related to disabled children's developmental needs is provided by Musselwhite (1986).

In the study reported by Saltz and Johnson (1974), children enacted folk tales such as Billy Goats Gruff. Children listened to stories, were assigned roles, and with teacher prompts, narration, and at times, role taking, they dramatized the story. Successive sessions enabled children to play various roles. Children also discussed the story plots. The results showed an increase in spontaneous sociodramatic play and some preliminary evidence for cognitive growth.

Classroom Management

Strategies for classroom management are necessary for providing learning activities and developing well-functioning groups, and many research-based principles exist. The topic is large. Here we discuss several aspects of classroom management that have been of special significance in our consultations with preschool teachers.

Classroom Rules

Rules are used to communicate the expectations for behavior in the classroom. "Only by actively teaching what the rules are and how to follow them can teachers be fair in their classroom management efforts" (Paine et al., 1983, p. 55). Rules also are used as a basis for determining successes and criteria for positive attention when teachers "catch" children being "good." The use of effective rules is common to most studies evaluating classroom management procedures.

The book by Paine and colleagues (1983) contains many strategies for classroom management. Except as noted, the following principles for developing effective rules are abstracted from it (pp. 55–58, 63); we recommend the entire book.

Developing rules. Use as few rules as possible for classroom situations; use developmentally appropriate wording; use positive statements (do's rather than don'ts); post the rules prominently. Rules can include developmentally appropriate outcomes such as task completion (Fowler, 1986).

Establishing rules. Plan rules before the first day of school; decide rules (and behavior) appropriate for each activity; teach rules and their rationales (for expectations, fairness, safety, and discipline) immediately; have children participate, if possible, in developing and discussing rules.

Implementing rules. Use brief mini-teaching sessions to train rules before activities; give "rule-following practice"; use positive attention for rule-following behavior; encourage children to help each other in following rules.

Maintaining rules. Gradually reduce teacher prompts and feedback based on desired behavior for activities (Fowler, 1986). This may be accomplished in many systematic ways. For example, on Mondays, during the first several weeks of school, after vacations or holidays, or when necessary, review rules; periodically (several times a day), catch children following rules and use positive attention; continue to develop peer support for rule following. Essentially, rule behavior may be governed by the task and activity, and ultimately by children with teacher supervision (Fowler, 1986).

Excessive Activity Changes

Early studies by Jacobson, Bushell, and Risley (1969) illustrated several valuable components of preschool interventions. The studies also are noteworthy because they were conducted by parents who functioned as staff members in the Head Start classrooms. The research focused on "excessive switching" from task to task by the children — a frequent concern of preschool teachers.

The major feature of the intervention involved a *switching system*. The system included (a) the definition of activity areas (blocks, manipulative toys, creative area) and (b) a "switching task." The components are described in Exhibit 10.4.

In the first study, the switching task required "matching colored pegs on a pegboard" (p. 44). The results indicated a reduced rate of switching as expected (from 5½ switches to 2 per hour for a group of 30 children). The experimenters also studied different levels of the switching task (such as the number of rows in a matching task). Again, as expected, the rate of switching was related to the demands of the task.

In a second related study, the task was altered: tickets were earned "by placing 10 to 30 individual letters or 3 to 4 individual short words alongside matching letters or words on a sheet of paper" (p. 45). When the switching requirement was not in effect, the rate of switching was approximately 3 per hour. With the requirement, the rate dropped to 1 per hour. However, there were large individual differences among children in rates of switching.

Exhibit 10.4. A Switching Task to Reduce Activity Changes.

---

1. Initially the children were free to enter any area of their choice. Each activity was defined by boundaries (such as a block area).
2. Changing activities required a "switching task":
   a. To stop at a special table
   b. To complete a task (such as matching or preacademic)
3. Upon completion of the task, the child received a "ticket" to select and enter another activity area. The child could stay in the area as long as desired. The child's name was written on the ticket, and the time was indicated to keep track of the frequency of activity changes.
4. Movement to other areas required the completion of another "switching task" and a ticket.

Source: Jacobson, J. M., Bushell, D., & Risley, T. (1969). Switching requirements in a Head Start classroom. *Journal of Applied Behavior Analysis, 2*, 43–47. Copyright ©1969 by the Society for the Experimental Analysis of Behavior. Reprinted with permission.

We comment that the overall rate achieved by the switching task seems rather low. We have had many children referred to us who changed activities several times per minute. Nonetheless, the use of switching tasks offers potential advantages. First, a switching task may help reduce unproductive movement during activity periods. Second, it may help introduce activities that may not be well attended by some children because of other interests (learning letters versus playing with blocks). As Jacobson, Bushell, and Risley suggested, a switching task may reduce the pleading and coaxing sometimes used to complete less interesting learning activities. For some children, the rate of activity change may be an important target behavior, which may be modified through a switching task. One potential negative outcome is that if the switching requirement is too difficult, children may elect to remain in an activity area and use the time unproductively.

Studies by Rowbury, Baer, and Baer (1976) also examined access to more desirable activities through the completion of required preacademic activities. The emphasis of the study has several important facets. First, a "natural classroom reinforcement system" (p. 87) was established. Natural reinforcers included such activities as play and freetime, supported by interesting materials. Second, the focus was on both learning and maintaining preacademic skills for children described as having severe and diverse problems. The children had been referred to a special preschool classroom because of comprehensive behavior problems including short attention span, hyperactivity, disruptive and aggressive behaviors, bizarre or eccentric mannerisms, and language and cognitive deficits. The researchers reported the use of token reinforcement to mediate access to the play area contingent upon completion of preacademic tasks. A second study analyzed the functions of teacher attention and guidance within the token system of management.

In the first study, the classroom was divided into two areas: a work area equipped with preacademic learning materials, and a play area with enjoyable activities. The work area contained fourteen preacademic tasks taken from preschool curricular materials (seven tasks were used at any one time). Dividers were used to separate the areas, but a gap was present to enable movement between areas. Tokens were available in the work area, and timers for each child were present in the play area to control for the length of play time.

An overview of the steps is presented in Exhibit 10.5. The experimenters also manipulated the number of completions required for reinforcement.

The results of the first study indicated that the system was effective in creating and maintaining high levels of work com-

Exhibit 10.5. The Use of Tokens and Teacher Guidance to Mediate Work and Access to Play.

1. In the preacademic work area, the tasks were arranged on either tables or the floor.
2. The "work area" teacher announced that it was time to work.
3. Children were led into the area if necessary.
4. Children were invited to complete a task. ("How about doing a puzzle?")
5. The child was free to select one out of the seven tasks.
6. The teacher remained available to:
   a. help by demonstrating
   b. assist the child through a response
   c. instruct
   d. praise appropriate work behavior
7. If the child met the criterion for the task, the child received praise and a token.
8. The token was given to the teacher in the play area and the child's timer was set for five minutes. A small snack was also offered if the child requested it.
9. The child was able to select a play activity. The activities were varied, but included at least one activity highly preferred by individual children.
10. The "play area" teacher distributed materials and interacted with children.
11. After the time was up, the teacher announced "token time." The child returned to the work area and the sequence was repeated (the teacher gave an invitation to a different task, and so forth).
12. The alternating sequence was in effect for one and a half hours a day.

Adapted from Rowbury, T. G., Baer, A. M., & Baer, D. M. (1976). Interactions between teacher guidance and contingent access to play in developing preacademic skills of deviant preschool children. *Journal of Applied Behavior Analysis, 9,* 85–104. Copyright ©1976 by the Society for the Experimental Analysis of Behavior. Reprinted with permission.

pletion, and that increasing the number of completions necessary for reinforcement brought corresponding increases in completion levels. When access to play was not contingent on work completion, levels of work completion dropped.

The second study, reported in Rowbury, Baer, and Baer (1976), focused on the teacher's role within the token system, including teacher guidance for preacademic tasks. Teacher behaviors included prompting, physical guidance, explaining, and praise. The results indicated that teacher guidance appeared to be a "vital component" in the development of preacademic skills.

"Do I Have to Be Good All Day?"

Another problem frequently encountered in managing classroom behavior is the timing of reinforcement. This issue was examined by Fowler and Baer, who wrote: "Social and economic factors often limit the frequency and immediacy with which behaviors, once established, can be reinforced. Thus, the ability to tolerate inconsistent schedules of reinforcement and delays in reinforcement often becomes critical for maintenance of specific behavior changes, as well as for generally successful functioning in society" (1981, p. 13).

While delayed reinforcement is not typically effective as a means of changing behavior, it may be helpful in *maintaining* behavior. As Fowler and Baer point out, the delay of reinforcement also may assist with efforts to promote generalization.

Seven children participated in the study reported by Fowler and Baer. Two had behavior problems (noncompliance and tantrums); the others were considered "normal." Target behaviors were individually selected: sharing, cooperative play, positive comments about classroom activities, in-seat posture, and conversation with peers. The teachers' use of prompts and praise also were recorded. The study was carried out in the preschool classroom. Training sessions were conducted in an adjacent room. Two procedures were compared: (a) an early feedback and reinforcement condition, which occurred directly after the period the behavior occurred, and (b) a late feedback and reinforcement condition (with intervening class periods).

The training sessions were described as follows. First, a brief session (two to five minutes) was held to rehearse the target behavior and to remind "the child to perform the behaviors the criterion number of times in the classroom" (p. 17). A second session (held either early or late) was used to provide feedback about behaviors and to give reinforcement. Stickers or points were used to obtain an immediately available small toy, or were saved and later exchanged for a larger prize.

The late-reinforcement condition helped promote generalization "for children whose behavior did not generalize spontaneously" (p. 20). The authors of the study suggest that monitoring one activity period and providing reinforcement at the end of the day may help maintain behaviors and increase generalized results. They explain the results through the use of *indiscriminable contingencies,* whereby children are unaware of "the time or setting" during which the appropriate behavior is reinforced (p. 20; see the review of generalization principles in Chapter Five). For example, two children asked, "Do I need to share all day?" Once generalization is established, the timing may be less critical.

Fowler and Baer (1981) concluded that "reinforcement delays should be considered routinely for teaching programs, both for maintaining appropriate social behavior . . . and for maintaining academic performance" (p. 23). The procedure may have economic and practical benefits for teachers.

Recruiting "Natural Communities of Reinforcement"

Children in some settings do not receive sufficient positive attention for their learning successes. Also, the generalization of skills is a major concern for behavior-change programs. Furthermore, one of the primary objectives for young children described as normal, with disabilities, or at risk, is teaching independent work behaviors. In two interrelated studies reported by Stokes, Fowler, and Baer (1978), children were taught to evaluate their work and to appropriately gain the teacher's attention for praise. The studies illustrate possibilities of training children to adapt to classrooms.

Participants in the first study were four normal children. The four children in the second study were described as having comprehensive academic and behavior problems. The studies were conducted in the regular preschool classroom and a remedial summer class.

The studies focused on the effects of teaching the children independent work skills and ways of prompting teacher comments on their work. In a training condition, children were taught the dimensions of good work such as working consistently and quietly. The children also were taught to prompt or cue for evaluative comments from teachers following self-evaluation. The children's skill in *cuing* was the major dependent variable. Cues were defined as the child's statements "inviting favorable comments or positive evaluations of . . . work or general behavior, e.g., 'Look how much I've done' and 'Is this right?'" (p. 287). The children's work involved tracing lines and letters. The cues were taught through "instructions, role-playing, feedback, and praise" (p. 288). The following behaviors were taught: "Do good work, then evaluate the quality of that work, and, when the quality of the work was good, cue the trainer to evaluate that work" (p. 288). Children were reinforced by the trainer for following the instructions in their regular classrooms.

After training in one setting, the targeted work skills were observed in a second (generalization) condition with different teachers. The second study, with several modifications (diverse work, adding hand raising, and so on), replicated the first in a preschool setting. The intervention steps are summarized in Exhibit 10.6.

In sum, the results of the study successfully demonstrated the influence of the child's behaviors on adult behaviors for both normal groups and for those with problem behaviors. The children were taught to evaluate their work, and then to draw their teacher's attention to the work. Stokes, Fowler, and Baer (1978) discussed the importance of the results in terms of children becoming active change agents in their own environments. They suggest that such intervention may be "important to young children who find themselves bereft of attention in classrooms, perhaps because they are labelled deviant, or perhaps because

**Exhibit 10.6. Training Independent
Work Skills and Recruitment of Praise.**

---

1. The children were taught the dimensions of good work.
2. The children were asked:
    a. to practice good lines by staying close to the dashed lines on the writing pages
    b. to erase and correct errors
    c. to work consistently and quietly
3. Feedback and praise were given based on the child's performance.
4. The children were taught to prompt or cue the trainer for positive evaluations of high-quality work:
    a. "Have I worked well?"
    b. "Have I been working carefully?"
    c. "How is this work?"
    d. "Look how careful I've been."

Source: Stokes, T. F., Fowler, S. A., & Baer, D. M. (1978). Training preschool children to recruit natural communities of reinforcement. *Journal of Applied Behavior Analysis, 11,* 285–303. Copyright © 1978 by the Society for the Experimental Analysis of Behavior. Reprinted with permission.

they do not represent a problem to their teachers" (p. 287). The social realities were addressed: children were taught to "ask . . . a few times about the quality of their work, but do not ask too often" (p. 289). Appropriately low rates of behaviors for cuing teachers are desirable. A rate of two to four cues per ten-minute session was the authors' goal, based on the opinions of preschool teachers. To effectively deal with the potential problem of children using the same repetitive cues, diverse cues and prompts were stressed ("Try to say something different each time" [p. 292]). Skills related to judging the proximity of teachers also were necessary.

Transitions Between Activities

Transitions may be difficult for both children and teachers. In this section we present several interventions for improving transitions.

Carden Smith and Fowler (1984) compared a teacher-monitored token system and a peer-monitored token system for reducing disruptive behavior during transitions. The setting was a special class designed for children with behavior problems. Three kindergartners who were the most disruptive during transition periods served as targets.

The token systems were implemented during three transition activities: (1) cleanup (children received one point for helping to clean up the assigned space without disruption); (2) bathroom (children received one point for walking to the restroom, using it within three minutes, and returning to class); and (3) waiting (children received one point for selecting a book, sitting on a mat without disturbing others, and returning the book on teacher request). The procedure is described in Exhibit 10.7.

Results indicated that both teacher monitoring and peer monitoring were effective in reducing disruptions during transition periods. However, peer-monitoring procedures were superior. In addition, the level of participation by the target children during transition activities increased during both monitoring phases.

In a follow-up study involving nine children attending a remedial kindergarten classroom, the initial teacher-monitoring procedure was eliminated. The children identified as monitors were trained in the token system, role played the procedures, and practiced awarding points and providing corrective feedback. The results demonstrated that peer monitoring was effective in reducing disruptive behavior during transitions as well as increasing the target children's participation in the activities.

The progressive use of teacher-monitoring strategies followed by peer monitoring and self-monitoring for the management of transitions was investigated by Fowler (1986). This study replicated the peer-monitoring intervention by Carden Smith and Fowler (1984), and extended the analysis to the use of self-monitoring. Major features of the study are described here.

The transition periods included cleaning up learning centers, using the restroom, and waiting for a large group activity on mats. While on the mats, children were allowed to look at books and eat snacks. Children targeted for the study, described as having behavior and learning problems, were assigned to teams. The behaviors of interest for three target children in-

Exhibit 10.7. Teacher and Peer Monitoring During Transitions.

Teacher Monitoring

1. The teacher described the token system, role played transition behaviors, and questioned the children concerning their understanding of the procedures (three sessions). In addition, the target children (and other children as needed) received brief daily training sessions.

2. Children were assigned daily to different teams. The teams were directed to perform specifically defined transition activities (such as clean up activity area without disruption).

3. The teacher publicly awarded the children for appropriate behavior following each transition.

4. Children who obtained the maximum number of points voted for a back-up reinforcer. Back-up reinforcers included different outdoor activities (kite flying, playing with frisbees, softball).

5. Children obtaining two out of three possible points were given access to the back-up reinforcers but were not involved in the lottery selection (see point 8). Children who obtained one or no points were not involved in the selection of back-up reinforcers and did not participate in the activity. They remained inside and cleaned other classroom areas.

Peer Monitoring

6. The point system and back-up reinforcers were maintained.

7. The children were divided into groups, and team captains for each group were selected. The team captains monitored team performance and awarded points in the same manner as the teacher had.

8. Subsequently, captains were selected from those children who had obtained the maximum number of points on the previous day. A lottery system was used to determine the three team captains for the day.

9. Team captains were reminded daily of their roles (to participate in activities, observe their peers, remind peers of appropriate behaviors, and award points for successful participation).

10. At the end of the transition activity, the team captains awarded points publicly to themselves and their peers. Back-up reinforcers were selected in the same manner as above.

11. The teacher assisted the peer monitoring in awarding points by asking the monitor if team members had met transition responsibilities.

Source: Carden Smith, L. K., & Fowler, S. A. (1984). Positive peer pressure: The effects of peer monitoring on children's disruptive behavior. *Journal of Applied Behavior Analysis, 17,* 213–227. Copyright ©1984 by the Society for the Experimental Analysis of Behavior. Reprinted with permission.

cluded participation or engagement in the transition activities, inappropriate behavior, and teacher and team-captain prompts for rule following. The behavior of the other class members also was monitored. Points were awarded for cleanup, restroom, book time, and snack responsibilities.

Peer monitoring was introduced after three training sessions (each about ten minutes), which were described as follows: "The teacher met with small groups of three or four children, reviewed the class rules with the children, role-played the duties of the team captain and teammates, and practiced point awards" (p. 576). Instamatic photographs of children completing the routines were used for review and for reminders of expected behavior. In addition, the children were given an oral quiz on appropriate transition behaviors. Classroom rules were reviewed daily in brief meetings just before the transition.

Children were assigned to groups, and team captains were appointed. Team captains had the tasks of helping teammates participate in transition activities, and prompting and praising participation. The pictures were posted as reminders for children. "Report cards" with pictures of activities and of each teammate were used for feedback. Team captains also monitored their own behavior, thus building in self-monitoring practice. "The teammates reported the activities in which they had participated appropriately to the team captain. If the team captain agreed with the report, he or she handed the report card to the teammate who made checkmarks next to the appropriate activities in the column under the teammate's picture. If the captain disagreed with a teammate's report, the captain was instructed to not hand over the report card and to say why he or she disagreed. In these cases, the team captain completed the report card" (p. 577).

The teacher supervised the discussions and point awards and intervened if she disagreed with the point awards. The points were used in the following way. Children with four points could vote for and participate in an outdoor activity (such as kite flying). They also were eligible to be the next day's team captain. Children with three points could participate but could not vote on the activity. Children with two points missed five minutes of the activity. Children with one or zero points remained indoors without recess and cleaned the classroom (the reward system was structured so that this contingency was rarely needed).

In the *self-monitoring* condition, team captains passed out report cards and teammates checked activities with regard to appropriate participation. Team captains and the teacher did not change the points.

The results of the study demonstrated increased rates of participation for the three target children as well as reductions in inappropriate behavior in both the peer- and self-monitored conditions. However, the peer-monitoring condition may have been slightly more powerful. While the appropriateness of behavior tended to be overestimated through self-monitoring, the team captain or teacher corrected these inaccuracies in the peer-monitoring condition. In the self-monitoring condition, where corrections were not provided, errors ranged from 10 to 25 percent.

A peer-mediated strategy and an antecedent-prompt procedure for facilitating transition periods were compared by Sainato, Strain, Lefebvre, and Rapp (1987). The peer-mediated strategy involved assigning nonhandicapped children to handicapped peers as "buddies" during the transition period. The antecedent-prompt procedure consisted of instructing handicapped children to ring a bell when the transition period was completed.

Six "normal" children and three children diagnosed as autistic participated in the study. The setting was an integrated preschool classroom housed in an elementary school. Transition periods included (a) group circle to lesson, (b) snack to bathroom, and (c) group circle to language. The rate at which children moved from one activity to the next was recorded, along with other child and teacher behaviors.

During an initial baseline phase, the teachers conducted transitions in the usual way. Stimulus cards representing three different conditions were present but were not explained to the children. Card 1, with a large stoplight showing a green light, represented a nontreatment setting; card 2 represented the bell condition and had a large bell drawn on it; card 3 represented the buddy condition, with a large "smile face" drawn on it. During a second baseline, teachers refrained from helping children through transitions (except for those who were still wandering after four minutes).

During the peer-mediated strategy (a "buddy" system), the teacher showed card 3 and told the children they would help their friends get to the next activity. The teacher then modeled taking a peer's hand and leading the child through the transition with prompts. For the second transition condition, children were shown card 2. Each target (handicapped) child was given a specific direction to go to another area and ring the bell. The peers were instructed to "let their friends go by themselves" (p. 288). During the no-treatment transitions, the teacher showed card 1 and then instructed each child to go to a designated area. The final phase involved the use of the bell across all transition periods.

Although the results indicated that the peer-mediated strategy was effective in reducing off-task behavior during transition periods, the bell procedure (card 2) was superior in increasing the transition rate. In addition, verbal and physical prompts by the teacher were significantly reduced. The results suggest that the bell may have been reinforcing to the children, while the peer-mediated strategy provided no direct reinforcement, but relied on prompts. However, extensive use of a bell may be irritating to teachers (D. M. Sainato, personal communication, June 27, 1991).

A simple and effective intervention designed to improve clean-up routines was described by Wurtele and Drabman (1984). During baseline, kindergarten children took an average of 11.6 minutes for morning clean-up tasks. The children tended to ignore teacher prompts and encouragement during this time. The intervention consisted of the following announcement (p. 405):

> Boys and girls, today we are going to play a game. I am going to set this timer to ring in __ minutes, and I want to see if you can get the room cleaned before the buzzer rings. All the areas must be cleaned and you must be sitting in the circle when the buzzer goes off. Get ready to beat the buzzer (set timer) . . . Go!

For the first four days of the study, the timer was set for eight, six, five, and four minutes; after that, the timer was always set for four minutes. No specific consequences were given for beating or not beating the timer. The average time for cleanup during the intervention was 4.3 minutes. Teacher acceptance was reported to be quite favorable.

Staff arrangements also may have important differential outcomes for transitions. In an often-cited study, LeLaurin and Risley (1972) found that assigning teachers to "zones" or activity areas was more efficient than assigning teachers to small groups of children. The study focused on transitions from lunch to nap time that included stops at the bathroom and a "shoe area."

Integrating Children with Disabilities

Integration generally refers to providing services in the *least restrictive environment* or the most normal setting in which the child can function effectively (Abeson, Burgdorf, Casey, Kunz, & McNeil, 1975). In many respects, the concept originated as a philosophical and moral imperative against institutional settings for the retarded. There are significant social, physical, and academic qualities of "mixing" handicapped and nonhandicapped children. *Social integration* is the foundation of integration efforts; it may also affect many other outcomes, including "(a) improvements in general social and communicative development; (b) more realistic and adaptive social consequences; (c) opportunities for handicapped children to cope with problems directly related to their handicaps; and (d) opportunities for observational and tutorial learning" (Guralnick, 1981, p. 72).

The Division of Early Childhood of the Council for Exceptional Children stresses the importance of integrating children with disabilities with normally developing children (McLean & Odom, 1988). In fact, if integration is not achieved, the division recommends documentation explaining why integration was not achieved, descriptions of attempts at integration, and a timeline for further attempts at integration. The critical factor is the "quality of the educational program" (p. 1), not simply the presence of children without disabilities.

Integration is not a panacea, however, and it is unlikely that integration will occur automatically for many children with disabilities. Beyond broad variables related to classroom ecologies, integration strategies, and interventions to achieve integration, child-specific factors include the severity and type of disabling condition, group composition, and factors related to interpersonal attraction (Strain, 1985a, 1985b). Most important, intervention plans must be developed to encourage and maintain interactions between children with disabilities and peers. Attention must be given not only to the frequency of interaction but also its quality.

Outcomes for parents and other family members also need to be addressed. Bailey and Simeonsson wrote: "Families in mainstream programs observe their child interacting with non-handicapped children and are constantly reminded of their child's abnormalities. Furthermore, they must interact with families of nonhandicapped children and may therefore feel excluded or isolated" (1988, p. 17).

While the challenge of integrating severely disabled children are more obvious, early research did not reveal difficulties with social integration for mildly handicapped children (Guralnick, 1986). However, subsequent research has documented differences in interactions between mildly disabled and preschool children without disabilities (Guralnick & Groom, 1987, 1988).

McDonnell and Hardman (1988) have provided a summary of best-practice guidelines for early childhood services (see Exhibit 10.8). Integrated services play a predominant role. The potential benefits of integration are many, and include social, emotional, communication, and preacademic skills.

Many program alternatives may affect integration efforts. Important factors include the ratio of disabled to nondisabled children, the child-to-teacher ratio, the teacher's background and training, support for families, in addition to other child-related, setting, instructional, and curriculum factors. Basically, children with disabilities may be mainstreamed into regular preschool classrooms, or nondisabled children may be integrated into special education programs (termed *reverse mainstreaming*). A special issue of *Topics in Early Childhood Special Education* (1990) was dedicated to preschool mainstreaming.

Exhibit 10.8. Best-Practice Guidelines for Early Childhood Services.

Integrated	*Adaptable*
Supported placement in generic early childhood service sites. Systematic contact with nonhandicapped peers. Planned integration at all levels.	Flexible procedures within noncategorical models. Support of different family structure. Emphasis on function rather than form of response. Programming changes based on individual, formative evaluation.
Comprehensive	*Peer and family referenced*
Comprehensive assessment, planning, programming, service coordination, and evaluation. Models theoretically and procedurally well defined. Transdisciplinary approach to the delivery of related services. Direct instruction of generalized responding.	Curriculum that is referenced to individual child, family, peers, and community. Parents are full partners in educational planning and decision making. Systematic communication between family and service providers. Planned enhancement of child's skill development within daily family routine.
Normalized	*Outcome-based*
Support for parenting role. Age-appropriate skills and instructional strategies. Concurrent training across skill areas. Distributed practice across settings. Establishment of self-initiated responding. Avoidance of artificial reinforcement and aversive control techniques.	Variety of outcome measures. Preparation for future integrated settings. Curricular emphasis on skills with present and future utility. Transition planning.

Source: McDonnell, A., & Hardman, M. (1988). A synthesis of "best practice" guidelines for early childhood services. *Journal of the Division for Early Childhood, 12,* 328–341. Reprinted with permission.

Some children may not be successfully integrated under one set of circumstances (a failed intervention) but may be under another. The guiding premises are that integrated settings must be considered as ecosystems, family outcomes should be considered, and the overall quality of the program is paramount.

The Effects of Integration on Children without Disabilities

Integration should meet the educational and social needs of *all* children: A question that comes to mind for many parents and educators is the potential effects of integration for children without disabilities. Few methodologically sound studies are available that directly pertain to this question. Many program variables are likely to affect the outcomes for children who participate in integrated programs. Given the many facets of integration, it may be difficult to generalize across early intervention programs.

Esposito (1987) found that eight of nine studies reviewed did not report any deleterious effects of integration, while one study suggested that nonintegrated settings may be more positively related to social development for nondisabled peers. Odom, Hoyson, Jamieson, and Strain (1985) reported beneficial outcomes for nondisabled peers participating in an integrated special education program. Odom and McEvoy (1988) also reviewed parental and teacher attitudes concerning integrated programs.

Interventions to Increase Effective Integration

There are numerous ways to plan for effective integration. Odom and McEvoy (1988) categorize methods in three ways. First, strategies to prepare nondisabled peers may be used prior to integration. There has been little research on this topic.

Second, various classroom or environmental designs are likely to facilitate integration. However, again there is an absence of systematic research and the number of potentially relevant variables is quite large (nature of disability, quality of interactions, nature of the peer group, adult mediation of interactions, program quality, and so on). In a review of research examining mainstreamed versus specialized settings, Buysse and Bailey (in preparation) found that increases in positive peer interactions, levels of play behavior, and positive ratings of social competence by teachers were noted in sixteen out of nineteen studies.

While no beneficial or detrimental effects were found in relation to developmental progress, program designs were variable.

Third, a variety of teacher-mediated and peer-mediated intervention strategies and activities may be used to promote social integration. In Chapter Seven, we introduced interventions to increase appropriate play and social interactions between children. In brief review, researched interventions include teachers' use of prompts and reinforcement of social interactions. Likewise, peers may be trained to prompt, reinforce, or direct social interactions of handicapped peers. Other interventions include teaching and encouraging affection and imitation or modeling. An extensive description of activities to promote social integration are provided by Brown, Ragland, and Bishop (1989) and Odom and others (1988).

One study designed to achieve integration actually had negative outcomes. Children who were exposed to extensive and multifaceted integration training had subsequently fewer social interactions with hearing-impaired peers (Vandell, Anderson, Ehrhardt, & Wilson, 1982).

In the remainder of this section, we review specific examples of interventions related to integrating children with disabilities in preschool settings.

The Use of Tokens. Russo and Koegel (1977) reported a study whereby a five-year-old autistic girl was successfully integrated into a regular kindergarten classroom. Appropriate social behaviors, self-stimulation, and appropriate verbal responses to commands ("What color is this?") were targeted. First, the researchers used pretraining in a small room apart from the classroom to establish the use of tokens. Second, the therapist established the efficacy of the intervention in the classroom. Third, after successful treatment by the therapist, the teachers were trained to carry out the procedures. During the initial week of first grade, retreatment for two of the three target behaviors was necessary. The authors reported followup through the third grade without further problems. The steps used in the intervention are summarized in Exhibit 10.9. Note that the intervention focused mainly on academic integration, not social integration.

Exhibit 10.9. Integrating an Autistic Child into Kindergarten.

1. Three one-hour pretraining sessions were used to establish the reinforcing value of tokens, where tokens were exchanged noncontingently for food.

2. In the treatment-by-therapist phase, each occurrence of social behavior was followed by a token and praise. The therapist sat next to the autistic child. The treatment sessions lasted one hour and were held twice a week. The child saved the tokens in a cellophane bag.

3. After the session, the tokens were cashed in at a small "store" in the back of the classroom. The treatment condition lasted three weeks and was followed by a withdrawal phase. The therapist then reimplemented the condition.

4. The next targeted behavior was self-stimulation. Each occurrence of self-stimulation was consequated by the removal of a token and a "No"! Nonoccurrence of self-stimulation during progressively longer intervals enabled the child to earn tokens and praise. Early in the procedure, physical prompts were also used to control self-stimulation (the therapist placed his hands on the child's hands when she began to self-stimulate).

5. The third targeted behavior was verbal responses to commands. A token was awarded for each question answered requiring a verbal response. Correctness of the response did not matter, and the questions included those directed to the target child or to the class as a whole. Initially, prompts were used, and the child was rewarded for repeating the correct response.

6. The teacher training included the components of general instruction, practice, and feedback in four steps: (a) reading, discussion, and review of behavior principles; (b) discussion of the definitions, contingencies, and use of tokens that pertain to the target child; (c) practice and feedback in identifying occurrences of the targeted behaviors; and (d) practice and feedback in administering social reinforcement.

7. Concurrently with teacher training, the tokens were faded in the classroom. Tokens were used for rewarding intervals of appropriate behaviors (10 minutes). Social reinforcement and "No" for self-stimulation were continued.

8. Following training, the teacher used social reinforcement and tokens to reward appropriate behavior, and response cost for self-stimulation. Initially, the teacher performed under the therapist's direction. The child was placed in the front of the classroom to facilitate the teacher's role.

9. During the time that the program was transferred to the teacher, the therapist was present at least four days each week for two weeks. An aide also assisted by taking charge of the class for parts of the day. Feedback was given to the teacher during breaks in activities.

Adapted from Russo, D. C., & Koegel, R. L. (1977). A method for integrating an autistic child into a normal public-school classroom. *Journal of Applied Behavior Analysis, 10,* 579–590. Copyright ©1977 by the Society for the Experimental Analysis of Behavior. Reprinted with permission.

Affection Activities. In a very different direction, affection activities have been used to help promote social integration. Group affection activities center on facilitating friendship and showing acceptance. They are developed from games, songs, and materials typically found in preschool classrooms.

Based on research and naturalistic design implications, affection activities show a great deal of promise. Interventions designed to promote social interactions between handicapped and nonhandicapped children should be intrinsically reinforcing, should be relevant to the behaviors of all children, and should be easy to use in daily classroom activities (McEvoy, Twardosz, & Bishop, 1990; McEvoy, et al., 1988; Twardosz, Nordquist, Simon, & Bodkin, 1983). Many of the interventions discussed throughout this chapter that are intended to increase social participation of target children do not readily meet these criteria. Research using similar activities has targeted the behavior of children described as socially isolated, autistic, and developmentally disabled.

The affection activities described by McEvoy and colleagues (1988) were based on songs such as "If You're Happy and You Know It" with modifications. Instead of stomping feet, clapping hands, and shouting "hooray," children were asked to "hug your friend," "give your neighbor a high-five," or "pat your friend on the back" (p. 195). Similar modifications were made for "Duck-Duck-Goose," "Farmer in the Dell," and "Ring Around the Rosie." For two of the three targeted children, the intervention demonstrated clear improvements over baseline conditions for peer interaction and for reciprocal peer interaction (reciprocal interactions were counted when social behavior persisted for more than three seconds beyond the original initiation and response). The results were partially successful for a third child. Gains in reciprocal peer interactions were maintained in followup. Generalization to freeplay was delayed for two of the children; another child's reciprocal interactions increased in the generalization phase with the addition of teacher prompts.

In studies reported by Twardosz, Nordquist, Simon, and Bodkin (1983), interventions related to increasing appropriate physical contact (such as shaking hands, clasping arms) and group affection activities were examined, with positive results.

The outcomes associated with affection training may be explained best through the multicomponent nature of affection activities that include a rationale for friendships, in vivo desensitization, modeling, practice, teacher attention, and reinforcer sampling. Related strategies are discussed in the section on social skills and play in the next chapter.

Transitions Between Settings

Planning for transitions between settings requires consideration of many factors. Some strategies have been introduced earlier, including planning for "entry into natural communities of reinforcement" (Baer & Wolf, 1970) and template matching. Meetings between sending and receiving schools or agencies are helpful to clarify expectations and skills that tend to enhance or impede transitions. In this section, we give major emphasis to organizational strategies and to the parental role.

Organizational Strategies. One major organizational strategy to help with transitions is to identify functional skills that are related to adequately performing in the receiving setting. One of the greatest problems is deciding the likelihood of successful transitions to kindergarten. While a broad array of factors typically are considered, such as global developmental level or IQ, a functional and ecobehavioral approach may prove to be more effective in making predictions and planning transitions.

Teacher ratings of "transition" behaviors may be very useful. These include the degree that a child (a) stays on task without undue teacher attention; (b) sits appropriately; (c) focuses attention on the speaker and shifts focus appropriately; (d) follows directions in large groups; (e) responds appropriately in groups; (f) participates appropriately by waiting for a turn, or waiting to be recognized; (g) works and plays without bothering peers; (h) waits appropriately; and (i) modifies behavior upon receiving a verbal directive (Sainato & Lyon, 1989; Strain, 1988). Other likely transition behaviors include the ability to complete directions with two or three steps, to stay task engaged while the teacher is absent, and to follow routines at the end of work periods (Sainato & Lyon, 1989).

An obvious advantage of an ecobehavioral and functional approach is that attention is focused on factors that will enable children to benefit from instruction without requiring excessive teacher monitoring and effort. Alternatively, potential problems are that individual instructional needs are not necessarily addressed solely through improving group adaptation. A promising technique to assess skill related to kindergarten success has been developed by Atwater, Carta, and Schwartz (1989).

Sainato, Strain, Lefebvre, and Rapp (1990) developed a self-evaluation treatment package to help integrate preschoolers with disabilities into regular kindergartens based on self-assessments of appropriate academic behavior. An important feature of the intervention was an "independent seatwork rating scale" comprising nine behaviors (such as "listening to the teacher's directions"). The rating scale was used to assess the match between teacher's ratings and children's self-ratings. Children were photographed modeling appropriate behaviors, and "happy faces" (or "yes" for appropriate work behavior) and "sad faces" (or "no" for inappropriate work behavior) were placed next to the photographs. At the end of "table time," children were instructed to rate session behaviors. They then met with the teacher to compare ratings. Praise was given for appropriate behavior and accurate assessment. A reinforcement component also was included, where children were able to select small toys for accurate self-assessment (seven out of nine behaviors). Later intervention phases enabled comparisons with components of the package removed. The final phase included only children's self-assessments.

We summarize some of their results. Agreement in the initial phase between teacher and child ratings ranged from 60 to 95 percent. In later phases, the ranges were from 91 to 100 percent. The treatment package overall had positive effects on children's behavior and also reduced the need for excessive prompting of appropriate behavior. The results were maintained over systematic reductions in the complexity of the treatment package.

Parental Strategies. Parents can help with transitions in a number of ways. First, they can assist others with understanding their child's educational and developmental needs. Second, they can be made aware of various program alternatives and strategies to help make choices. It is important that the parents visit the alternative sites, to make informed decisions.

Preschool programs are often the first setting where complex educational service-delivery strategies are presented to parents. Some parents will have many years ahead of them in making difficult decisions and in unraveling the complexities of service delivery. They can be given assistance in learning to identify and resolve problems as a part of the transition process. Once the child is enrolled in a new school program, for many children and parents, new issues are likely to arise. Identifying effective problem-solving strategies for parents to deal with program modifications and changes may be a significant part of the process. Special attention also should be given to their understanding of legal rights.

For example, parents can be provided with questioning strategies, with the goal of obtaining information while minimizing defensiveness. They can ask for the teacher's perceptions of problems, focus on behaviors and problems to be solved while not seeking sources to "blame," and can demonstrate concern and willingness to share responsibility. Parents may find ways to facilitate home–school communications. Many of these strategies are reviewed in Barnett, Zins, and Wise (1984).

Summary and Conclusions

The range of early education philosophies and practices is enormous. In this chapter we focused on organizational and systems issues and possible roles of teachers and peers in intervention design. Major emphasis is given to the class as an ecosystem. The first step in many referral situations is to consult with teachers about the overall functioning of the group throughout the day.

With regard to learning and behavior problems, an important point of teacher consultation is the child's progress through a coherent and functional curriculum that includes a wide range of personal, social, and preacademic objectives, and corresponding teaching and classroom-management strategies. Integration of children with special needs was discussed as a part of overall early intervention philosophy and practice that includes preparation for the next environment.

11

Social Skills, Disruptive Behaviors, and Safety-Related Interventions

PERHAPS ONE OF THE MOST IMPORTANT PERSPECTIVES OF PRESCHOOL psychological and educational services is the emphasis on system goals, harmoniousness, and integrity. Regardless of theoretical differences, well-functioning classrooms hold the potential for a broad range of learning opportunities.

Evidence also suggests that for children described as high risk or disabled, important personal, social, and developmental gains may not happen automatically. Many children will benefit from a functional and developmental curriculum that integrates social problem-solving skills. Children referred for behavioral or learning difficulties may require specific plans founded on the intervention design components discussed in earlier chapters, and creative and practical intervention strategies based on an analysis of settings and behavior, problem solving, and research.

Social Skills and Play

One of the most important developmental accomplishments is successful play with peers. Also, social competence is a foundation of integration and early intervention efforts. Successful peer play depends on a range of social skills that frequently are the target of intervention efforts. In this section we describe a series of studies that have investigated behaviors that facilitate entry into play groups and the maintenance of play behaviors. Age, sex, cultural differences, factors associated with poverty, and severity and type of handicapping conditions, all have been shown to have differential effects on play behaviors.

Greenwood, Walker, Todd, and Hops (1981) analyzed social interactions of preschool children in freeplay to provide descriptions and norms for play behaviors. The normative data are important for problem identification and to help establish criteria for determining the social significance of intervention efforts. The study included 461 children from 17 preschools in Oregon. The average time observing children in freeplay was 359.5 minutes. The behaviors measured included the frequency of interactions, initiations (the social responses beginning an interaction), continuing responses (interactive behavior exchanges following the original initiation and the response), and termination (cessation of communication for longer than five seconds).

The results are briefly summarized here. Significant differences existed across classrooms (the means for interaction rates varied from .48 to .96; overall there were .63 interactions per minute). Thus, as might be expected, variables such as location, class size, space, program structure, toys, and child–teacher ratio were significant. These figures are not likely to be comparable to other play areas such as outdoor play. Males had more interactions than females for all age levels, but the differences in interaction rate were not numerically very great (.68 versus .58). The analysis showed similarities in interaction rates for ages four, five, and six. However, significant differences were found between age three and ages five, six, and seven. Children termed "low interactors" had low initiation rates and lower probabilities of responding to peer initiations (for females), and received more initiations from peers than they made to members of the peer group.

The intervention implications of the study are at least twofold, according to the authors. First, it is necessary to "establish reciprocity in social responding" (p. 364). The intervention methods include teaching or modifying children's skills to increase reciprocal interactions. Second, it is necessary to "transfer stimulus control" associated with reciprocity "to the social

bids occurring in the peer group" (p. 364). An example is initiating an appropriate response after receiving attention from
another child. These strategies are examined in detail in the
studies that are discussed next.

In contrast to normative social interactions, Hendrickson,
Strain, Tremblay, and Shores (1982) studied social interactions
of children described as behavioral handicapped. They reported
two studies that attempted to examine the utility of three classes
of play behaviors found in normal children for socially withdrawn children (Tremblay, Strain, Hendrickson, & Shores,
1981; and adapted from Hendrickson, Strain, Tremblay, &
Shores, 1982, p. 325): (1) *play organizers* (such as "Let's play
school" and "Let's play ball"); (2) *shares* (basic exchange of ball,
blocks, cars), and (3) *assists* (such as help child onto a play object). In two phases, a peer confederate was trained in the three
social initiation behaviors. The first phase, an extensive preintervention component, introduced the child to the "helper role,"
taught different ways to initiate the target behaviors, and gave
practice in initiating the behaviors and using play materials.
The second phase was described as follows (p. 331).

1. The experimenter began by telling the confederate she was
    to try and get [*name of child*] to play with her for the next
    five minutes.
2. The experimenter reminded the confederate to use "ask-
    ing," "sharing," and "helping" to get the other child to play.
3. The experimenter then questioned the confederate about
    what she was going to try to get [*name of child*] to play. If
    the child did not know (or answer), the experimenter made
    suggestions.
4. The experimenter also asked the confederate what she should
    do if [*name of child*] did not respond. . . . The experimenter
    would prompt the confederate to initiate if she did not be-
    gin a new initiation within fifteen seconds of the last initia-
    tion or interaction.
5. A reward system (session, daily, and weekly) was also used
    for the confederate.

The three types of initiations by the confederate were highly effective in promoting responses from the socially withdrawn child. The results were replicated with two other socially withdrawn children. A second study replicated the effects with a confederate described as handicapped. However, the children were older (ages six and seven) and the confederate training took substantially longer to accomplish.

Despite the changes in interactive play during the intervention, there was an immediate return to baseline conditions when the intervention was withdrawn. Thus the intervention may not be durable or may require sustained efforts. Through confederate prompts and praise, but not spontaneously, interactions generalized to another play area. For future research, the authors suggested that generalization and maintenance may be improved by (a) using multiple peer confederates for individual target children, (b) teaching approach behaviors to target children, and (c) examining more intensive training efforts by expanding interventions to other parts of the school day. Other factors that may affect such efforts include the relative numbers of socially unresponsive children in various settings, established friendship networks, and prior histories of negative social contacts between target children and peers. In other words, such efforts may require extensive ecobehavioral analysis and modification.

Hecimovic, Fox, Shores, & Strain (1985) built on the Hendrickson intervention. They examined the differential effects of returning the socially withdrawn children on alternating days to either developmentally segregated or developmentally integrated freeplay settings where the peer confederates also were located. The results are complicated and suggest again the need for considerable analysis. Among the results, the training procedures increased the target children's initiations and interactions with confederates. However, the behaviors were not maintained by two of three children when the intervention was briefly withdrawn. While the integrated classroom provided the target children with more "social opportunities in the form of initiations from other children" (p. 385), these bids mostly came from children not involved in the research. The segregated setting produced more adult–target children interactions than the integrated setting. Adult–child interactions may interfere with subsequent play interactions between children. Overall, there was a lack of generalization to both integrated and segregated settings.

Kohler and Fowler (1985) studied the effects of a social-skills training package for three young girls (ages five to seven). Two of the target children were described as domineering, another as passive. As in the above studies, the behaviors of interest were play invitations. They included (a) verbally and physically offering to share play materials, (b) offering assistance ("Can I help you?"), (c) inviting another child to join a play activity, and (d) requesting permission to join an ongoing play activity ("Can I play?") (p. 189). They also studied the use of amenities for two children ("please," "thank you," "I'm sorry"). The authors found that training for play invitations resulted in reciprocated play behaviors for two children. Outcomes associated with amenities were less clear but overall appeared somewhat promising. For one child, the use of amenities appeared to increase as a result of training in play invitations. For a second child, reciprocal peer responses were delayed until after the training phase. In both cases, peer responses to the use of amenities were variable.

For a third child, the intervention was unsuccessful. However, an interdependent group contingency (see Chapter Seven) to increase invitations from peers resulted in an increased rate of reciprocated invitations. This phase consisted of appointing three volunteer children to offer an invitation to the target child in freeplay, and to have a fourth child prompt the peers to make social invitations. Different children were used each day. The target child was instructed to offer between three and six invitations and to avoid negative behaviors. The target child and peer confederates received stickers on days that the specified criterion for invitations was met. The whole class received a reward for meeting the criterion on three successive days. A subsequent phase included only training for the target child's peers. The target child spontaneously increased her use of social amenities to peers during the group contingency phases. After the group contingencies were withdrawn, the acceptance ratio for play invitations was maintained but at a lower level. Follow-up observations suggested modest improvements over baseline in overall rates of reciprocated play invitations.

The results show that it may be important to train target children in behaviors likely to be reciprocated by peers, but that this may be insufficient for some children. It also may be important to train peers in reciprocating the targeted behavior to help with the problem of limited generalization of social behaviors. Kohler and Fowler (1985) pointed out that the following conditions may be necessary for the reciprocation of play invitations: "(a) a decrease in (or absence of) behaviors that compete with invitations . . . ; (b) an appropriate rate of invitations, distributed across members of the peer group; and (c) the availability of a peer, not already engaged in an activity who can respond" (p. 197).

A report by Lefebvre and Strain (1989) focused on group-oriented contingencies to further interactions between autistic and nondisabled preschoolers while also examining the teacher's role in prompting integrated social activities. All children, including those described as handicapped, were included in the peer training activities, and all peers acted as change agents. The study was conducted during daily seven-minute sociodramatic play activities (such as grocery store or camping). Each handicapped child was paired with two peer confederates. To improve maintenance and generalizability, the confederates were rotated every three days.

In the training phase of the intervention, the "morning circle time," lasting ten to fifteen minutes per session, was used to demonstrate strategies for engaging peers in play. The strategies were role played by the teacher and a second caregiver. Each child was given the opportunity to role play, and the strategies were reviewed one minute before the play activity began. The strategies included (p. 332):

"Say your friend's name."
"Face him or her."

"Keep trying."

"Ask for a toy and hold out your hand."

"Listen and help."

"Give a toy to your friend by placing it in his or her hand."

"Ask a friend to wait (after a request by the peer) and
    remember to give (the toy requested)."

The training phase was continued until the nonhandicapped peers met an 80 percent criterion level; this took nine
days.

A token reinforcement system was then implemented during the morning circle time; children were given an opportunity to earn tokens by engaging in appropriate strategies. During the intervention, tokens were exchanged for the "reinforcer
of the day." Each morning when the children arrived, they would
place their names in one of four boxes, indicating the reinforcer
of their choice. Reinforcers included a "popcorn party, popsi-
cle . . . , photographs with friends, listening to records" (p. 333).
The group reinforcer was determined by the box that contained
the most names. Response categories used to determine the effectiveness of the intervention included appropriate and inappropriate initiations and responses, play organizers, teacher prompts
and consequences, and children's responses to teacher prompts.

Three different conditions were compared, to assess the
most effective way to implement the treatment package. First,
the teacher was trained to limit the use of verbal models and
prompts. The teacher continued reinforcing appropriate interactions, strategies, and correction procedures, including prompting the targeted child to engage in peer interactions, expanding the targeted child's verbalizations, and modeling articulation.
Prompts were allowed only after one minute of no interactions
between target children and peers.

The second intervention condition was implemented after peer training and the group contingency were presented. It
was built on a poster displaying the reinforcer of the day, with
empty circles surrounding the reinforcer. The circles contained
the number of appropriate interactions needed by each of the
three groups to obtain reinforcement. Every time the teacher

observed the targeted child and peer confederate engaged in appropriate interaction, a token was placed in the circle and the peer or target child was praised. If all three groups met the established criterion, reinforcement was awarded. During this phase, the teacher was again instructed to refrain from prompts. Thus, all children were able to monitor group progress.

The third, and most effective, condition continued the limited use of prompts, but a change was made in the type of group contingency. Each group could obtain reinforcement noncontingent on the other groups' success. In other words, on any day, one, two, or all three groups could obtain back-up reinforcement. Overall, teacher prompts were significantly reduced for all three groups. The most effective teacher strategy for target children was verbal expansion, which not only increased the targeted child's utterances but also provided models for the peer confederates. *Verbal expansion* was defined as adding to the length of a target child's verbal response or providing a verbal response for a target child's nonverbal response. Generalization of strategies occurred for one of three targeted children and a specific peer confederate during other activities, and one peer confederate used the strategies with a handicapped child not targeted in the study.

Sharing and Prosocial Behaviors

A prosocial behavior that is worthy of facilitating is sharing. This behavior is often regarded as a major component of interactive play. Many preschool children may have difficulties with interpersonal relationships because of problems with sharing behaviors, and numerous reviews and studies are related to this topic. In addition, sharing and other prosocial behaviors are alternative responses for disruptive behaviors. The potential social ramifications are great. In other sections of this chapter and earlier, we have addressed applications of sharing with socially withdrawn and handicapped children. This section specifically reviews sharing interventions.

In a comprehensive study, Barton (1981) compared several different techniques used to teach sharing. The interventions

consisted of instructions, modeling, modeling plus praise, behavioral rehearsal, in-session prompts, and in-session praise.
Only the last three demonstrated substantial changes in sharing behaviors; in-session praise showed the greatest effects. However, the experimental design could not tease out the potential
additive effects of the prior instruction and modeling conditions.
Barton concluded that children must be given (a) opportunities
to practice sharing, (b) feedback concerning the adequacy of
their performance, and (c) praise for practicing sharing. Research has found that the intervention effects may generalize
to untrained peers (Barton & Bevirt, 1981). Barton and Osborne
(1978) documented the effectiveness of teacher-administered
positive practice for increasing classroom sharing with hearing-
impaired preschoolers.

Barton and Ascione (1979) concluded that teaching sharing should include both physical and verbal strategies. Physical sharing was defined as "(a) handing a material to another
child, (b) allowing another child to take his/her material, (c)
using a particular material that another had used during the
same observation interval, or (d) simultaneously using a material with another to work on a common project." Verbal sharing included "(a) requests to share another's materials, (b) compliance with a request to share materials, (c) invitations to share
one's own materials, or (d) acceptance of invitations to share"
(p. 420).

Bryant and Budd (1984) implemented a multicomponent
intervention aimed at improving sharing that replicated and extended the study by Barton and Ascione. The intervention was
mainly conducted by a teacher and six young children. Behaviors
measured were (a) offers to share, (b) requests to share, (c)
responses to offers or requests to share, (d) refusals to share,
(e) taking without asking, (f) "opposing" play, and (g) aggression. The intervention occurred in the classroom, using toys
and materials from a specified area. Overall, five out of six children increased their rate of sharing and decreased negative behaviors. The steps are summarized in Exhibit 11.1.

Correspondence training was used by Rogers-Warren and
Baer (1976) to increase sharing behaviors. This type of intervention is important because of its potential for improving gen-

Exhibit 11.1. An Intervention for Sharing.

---

1. Two children at a time received training in sharing by the teacher. The training occurred during the first ten minutes of freeplay for four consecutive days.

2. Training included a discussion of sharing, modeling, rehearsal, and feedback. At the end of each session, sharing was briefly reviewed, and children were instructed to share with other children in the classroom dramatic play or building area.

   a. *Day 1:* A rationale for sharing and examples of sharing and nonsharing behaviors were given. The teacher modeled sharing behaviors with one child. Examples: "We can share by giving other children things when they ask nicely for them. We can also share by asking for toys that other children have. It is not sharing to hit or push other children, take toys they are playing with, or tell them they cannot play" (p. 50).

   b. *Day 2:* The teacher reviewed sharing behaviors. The second child practiced with the teacher. Last, the two children played together and shared while the teacher used praise and prompts for play offers, requests, and acceptances. Following refusals to share, acceptable examples of sharing were given. Sharing behavior was prompted.

   c. *Days 3 and 4:* Sharing was practiced by the two children. The teacher praised and prompted sharing.

   d. After each training session, sharing was reviewed. For example: "Now that you've had a chance to share and play together, remember it is very important to share with all the children in the classroom, not just each other. Sharing is asking another child for something, giving someone something, and using the same things together" (p. 50).

3. Following training, children received prompts to share and praise for sharing. Nonsharing behaviors were corrected. Contingent observation was used for severe aggressive behaviors.

Adapted from Bryant, L. E., & Budd, K. S. (1984). Teaching behaviorally handicapped preschool children to share. *Journal of Applied Behavior Analysis, 17,* 45–56. Copyright ©1984 by the Society for the Experimental Analysis of Behavior. Reprinted with permission.

eralization, and because of possible cost benefits. However, as Barton (1986) noted, direct training may be important. Rogers-Warren and Baer also included modeling in their intervention. Barton stressed that correspondence training may be more effective for maintenance once sharing behavior is well established.

In sum, multicomponent training of prosocial behaviors appears effective. Barton (1986) further discussed many related aspects of intervention design, such as the potential effects of different activities and materials, number of children, adult presence, different change agents, and other considerations. Both the target behaviors and training methods must fit the individual needs of children and settings.

Social Withdrawal

Many interventions to help increase social interactions of withdrawn children have been described in the literature. Previously described interventions involving play behaviors and other social skills have been applied. In this section, we review additional interventions that may help with withdrawn or isolative behaviors.

Sainato, Maheady, and Shook (1986) described a "classroom manager" intervention in which socially withdrawn children were placed into leadership positions: "They were required to direct their peers in activities that had previously been designated as being highly preferred by the class" (p. 188). The rationale was described as follows: "By placing withdrawn children in 'status' positions and making them the dispensers of preferred activities, their positive peer interactions would be increased and new friendships would be formed" (p. 188).

Three target children described as socially withdrawn were selected to participate, based on a variety of measures: direct observation, teacher rankings, and peer sociometrics. The setting was a regular kindergarten classroom with sixteen children.

Four behavioral measures were used: (a) positive vocal-verbal (verbalizations directed to another child except shouting, crying, whining); (b) positive motor-gestural (such as hugging or sharing toys); (c) negative vocal-verbal (such as crying or whining); and (d) negative motor-gestural (hitting or punching). The behaviors were coded as either "initiated" or "responded" events. The measures were obtained during twenty-minute freeplay periods. Sociometric measures were also obtained, to help evaluate the intervention.

The classroom manager procedure is described in Exhibit 11.2. Each child in the study assumed the role of classroom manager for a ten-day period. The procedure was discontinued after

Exhibit 11.2. The Classroom Manager.

1.	The teacher announced to the class that she had selected a new helper.
2.	She then called the child to the front of the class.
3.	The child was given a large "manager" button to wear for the 2 week period.
4.	The "job" consisted of leading and/or directing preferred activities such as feeding a class pet, collecting milk money, etc.
5.	The classroom manager duties were reviewed each day with the target child and class.
6.	A picture board displaying the major tasks in front of the classroom was used to prompt the child with respect to responsibilities.
7.	Following the 10 day period, the teacher complimented the child on a "great job" and suggested that the class applaud the efforts.

Adapted from Sainato, D. M., Maheady, L., & Shook, G. L. (1986). The effects of a classroom manager role on the social interaction patterns and social status of withdrawn kindergarten students. *Journal of Applied Behavior Analysis, 19,* 187–195. Copyright ©1986 by the Society for the Experimental Analysis of Behavior. Reprinted with permission.

the third child had participated, and follow-up measures were used to assess maintenance effects four weeks later.

The results were analyzed for the number of interactions, the positive versus negative quality of interactions, and initiations by peers or target children. Baseline conditions revealed that social interactions were relatively rare. The intervention demonstrated effectiveness, indicated by significant level changes for positive behaviors of both target children and peers. Level changes dropped slightly following the end of the classroom manager role, but the change was still higher than the baseline condition. The sociometric ratings similarly reflected positive changes.

The results demonstrate the effectiveness of the technique and the possibility of durable changes. While interactions diminished somewhat when the classroom-manager role changed to another child, the results also can be considered reasonable. The experimenters discussed other potential benefits of the intervention: (a) little teacher time was required; (b) children were not removed from ongoing activities; and (c) changes to the usual classroom routines were minimal. Furthermore, similar practices may exist in many preschool classrooms that may be "systematically 'tapped' to derive social benefits for infrequent interactors" (p. 193).

Tarpley and Saudargas (1981) described a teacher-mediated intervention that resulted in rapid increases in peer interactions and expressions of positive affect (laughing or smiling) and decreases in crying for a four-year-old boy. The intervention consisted of the following five teacher behaviors (pp. 410–411).

1. The teacher would "conspicuously" participate with the child's peers as much as possible.
2. After group activities, the class discussed positive aspects and "feelings" associated with group activities and play.
3. Brief comments were made during group play about satisfying aspects of interactions.
4. Private social reinforcement or praise was given to the withdrawn child who joined a peer group.
5. Ignoring was used when the child was not participating or was distanced from other children. Importantly, the child's withdrawal served as a cue for the teacher to increase the first three steps.

Social reinforcement by teachers has been used to increase the social interactions of an isolated preschool child (Allen et al., 1964). The intervention consisted of attention to the isolated child who played with another peer, and minimum attention for isolate behavior or interaction with an adult.

Several investigators have used symbolic modeling to increase socially isolated preschoolers' peer interactions. Rao, Moely, and Lockman (1987), building on earlier work by O'Conner (1969), designed an intervention that required the target children to view a film depicting other preschoolers engaged in social interactions. The film was shown twice. The models in the film initiated interactions while a narrator described socially effective behaviors and positive responses of other children. The behaviors were maintained over a three-week followup. Gottman (1977), however, failed to replicate the modeling procedure reported by O'Conner.

Greenwood, Hops, Todd, and Walker (1982) reported the adaptation of the PEERS ("Procedures for Establishing Effective Relationships Skills") program originally developed for use in primary grades (Hops et al., 1978). The program contains "tutoring" for social interactions and a reporting procedure where children give the names of peers with whom they interact. Significant gains were made when children earned rewards for the class by increasing their time in social interactions. This was accomplished by (a) recording the total time the target child interacted in a fifteen-second period, (b) assigning two peer "special helpers" the role of assisting the child to reach a set criterion, and (c) if the daily criterion was met, providing special games during recess. The first criterion was the baseline average, and thirty seconds were added following each successful day.

Reluctant Speech and Elective Mutism

Children who have some but minimal verbal behavior in social situations outside the home may be described as having *reluctant speech*. Morin, Ladouceur, and Cloutier (1982) used a contingency management procedure with a six-year-old boy described as having reluctant speech within a kindergarten classroom. The child received "school money" for verbal responses to the teacher's questions. The tokens were exchanged for tangible reinforcers selected by the child, such as arts and crafts materials. During the intervention, nonverbal communication by the child was ignored. Verbal responses also received teacher praise, attention, and physical contact. During the final phase, an intermittent variable ratio schedule was used. The child was instructed that the "school money" would be available only on certain days, to increase the delay between earning "school money" and the exchange for tangible rewards. The intervention was immediately successful and was maintained over a one-year followup. Verbal responses decreased during the intermittent schedule, but they were still much higher than found at baseline levels.

Calhoun and Koenig (1973) also investigated the use of classroom interventions for children who talked only infrequently. The children ranged in age from five to eight, and all were enrolled in different classrooms. Four children received treatment; four others served as untreated controls. Classroom rewards, agreed on by the teachers, were contingent on verbal interaction by the targeted student with the teacher. Results indicated that the experimental children significantly increased their rate of verbalization and that gains were maintained at one-year followup.

Elective mutism is a similar but more serious condition. It is defined in *DSM-III-R* as a "persistent refusal to talk in one or more major social situations (including at school)" while having the "ability to comprehend spoken language and to speak" (American Psychiatric Association, 1987, p. 89). The syndrome typically becomes manifest when the child begins preschool or day care; parents of young electively mute children generally report no speech difficulties in the home. The literature related to other aspects of personal, social, and family functioning for electively mute children is mixed. Some children seem to be without other major difficulties, while many other concomitant problems also have been reported for children described as electively mute (Cunningham, Cataldo, Mallion, & Keyes, 1983; Wilkins, 1985).

Treatment of elective mutism has consisted of both psychodynamic and behavioral approaches. However, behavioral interventions generally have been found to be more successful in eliminating the problem. Social and tangible reinforcement have been the most common methods used for encouraging electively mute children to speak in the school setting (Labbe & Williamson, 1984); relatedly, shaping and fading techniques also have been implemented (Kratochwill, 1981). Contingency management procedures are likely to be the most effective for children with reluctant speech; additional procedures (such as stimulus fading and response cost) may be needed for electively mute children (Cunningham, Cataldo, Mallion, & Keyes, 1983; Labbe & Williamson, 1984). Nash, Thorpe, Andrews, and Davis (1979) reported an investigation of unusual aversive procedures with a five-year-old girl considered to be an elective mute. However, the classification of this child was ambiguous, since speech was present in the classroom situation and the child was noncompliant to instructions.

We now describe several representative interventions. Lipton (1980) combined stimulus fading with contingency management in the treatment of a six-year-old electively mute kindergartner. The initial locus of intervention was a room separate from the classroom. Semiweekly sessions lasted thirty minutes. The following activities were used to elicit speech: "structured game playing requiring verbal interaction, working on an exercise book using verbal instructions, and doing picture completion tasks orally" (pp. 147–148). Beads that could be strung on a necklace were used as reinforcers. A 1:1 ratio was initially used for the reinforcers, but this was changed to a variable ratio as speech progressed. A shaping procedure also was used, involving a string held vertically about five inches from the child's mouth. To earn a bead, the child was required to move the string by whispering the desired response. However, the string was needed for only two sessions. The criterion was changed by requiring verbal responses to questions at increasingly louder volumes. The final criterion was conversationally appropriate speech. This second phase was accomplished in three sessions.

The sixth session took place in the library in the presence of the librarian and other children. The teacher instructed other children not to answer questions for the mute child. The seventh and eighth sessions took place in a corner of the classroom but without participation of classmates. The ninth and tenth sessions included another child selected by the mute child. The mother was present for all ten sessions. Conversational speech occurred consistently by session ten. A six-month followup indicated that gains were maintained.

Williamson, Sanders, Sewell, Haney, and White (1977) described a variety of behavioral interventions to treat two cases of elective mutism. We summarize their use of reinforcement, shaping, modeling, and fading to increase verbalizations of a seven-year-old girl. The parents reported that the child had not spoken outside the home since kindergarten, although she spoke frequently at home and even answered the telephone.

Initially, the intervention involved approximations to speaking. Eye contact, blowing, and a voiced "*mmm*" sound were modeled for the child by the therapist; imitative responses were rewarded with a penny. During this phase, the child imitated making eye contact and blowing but did not make the "*mmm*" vocalization.

The mother was then engaged in the intervention. She was given a list of eighty words and instructed to get the child to repeat each word after her. The child received ten cents for every ten correct responses. When this task was successfully completed, the requirements for reinforcement were altered. A question requiring more than a one-word response was substituted for every fifth word on the list, and the experimenter began standing in the far corner of the room. The child did not speak during this trial, so the experimenter moved to the doorway. Again, the child did not respond, so the experimenter stood in the doorway with the door partially closed. The child then responded 100 percent of the time.

Rollerskates were then used as a reinforcer to elicit responses while in the presence of a stranger. The child was told that if she would engage in verbal behavior while the experimenter was in the doorway she could take the skates home for three days. She complied with this request and was rewarded with the skates. She was then told that she could keep the skates if she could read a passage from a book to her class for ten minutes. She complied with the request.

Reinforcement fading was then implemented, with the child first receiving a dollar and then a dollar plus a "card" (token). The cards were used to earn class parties for reading to the class. Results indicated significant increases in verbal compliance and speech initiation, and follow-up gains were maintained at one month.

Cunningham, Cataldo, Mallion, and Keyes (1983) reported the successful treatment of a three-and-a-half-year-old boy. Initially, the child interacted with his family in the preschool setting, in three ten-minute play sessions. In the second phase, employing stimulus fading, the child's teacher was silently present during the family sessions ("in a distant corner"; p. 38). The rest of the intervention was described as follows:

> If [the child] continued speaking [the teacher] gradually moved closer, periodically spoke to other family members, commented on [the child's] activi-

ties, and finally spoke directly to him. Once speech had generalized to [the child's] individual sessions with his teacher, her play sessions with the family were discontinued. One peer was then introduced into family play sessions while another joined [the child] in play sessions with an adult to whom he now spoke. In the final phase, the adult to whom [the child] spoke comfortably joined him for a series of classroom sessions [p. 38].

"Self-modeling" has also been used to treat children considered to be electively mute. Dowrick and Hood (1978) altered videotapes of two electively mute children (ages five and six) to produce the illusion of appropriate behavior in different settings and situations. The tapes were edited by altering school target situations with appropriate responses made by the children in their homes, where they talked freely. Together the two children watched the five-and-a-half-minute tapes three times per week. Results indicated that the "self films" were more effective in producing verbalizations from the children than were films of peers. Follow-up observations at six months revealed that gains had been maintained.

Children with elective mutism traditionally have been viewed as difficult to treat; interventions must be carefully developed. However, there are many reported successes based on behavioral interventions. Labbe and Williamson (1984) suggested a flow chart for decision making that is reproduced in Figure 11.1.

Disruptive Behaviors

Many interventions previously discussed are likely to reduce the overall disruptiveness of behavior. The consultant's initial considerations should include instructional and social environments, basic rules, routines, and classroom-management procedures. In this section, we highlight specific interventions for disruptive and aggressive behaviors.

Figure 11.1. Assessment and Therapeutic Strategies for Elective Mutism.

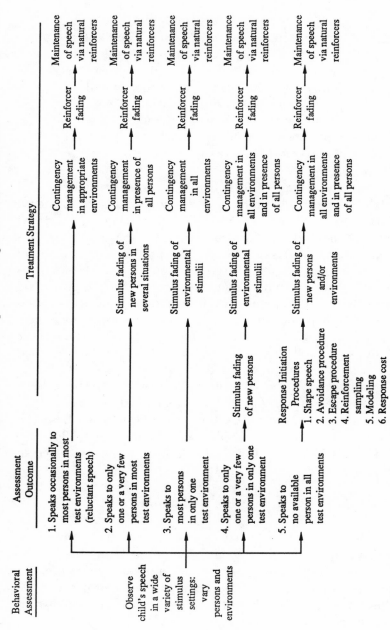

Source: Reprinted with permission from *Clinical Psychology Review*, *4*, E. E. Labbe and D. A. Williamson, Behavioral treatment of elective mutism: A review of the literature. Copyright 1984, Pergamon Press plc.

Basic Interventions for Disruptive Behaviors

Naturalistic strategies should be given primary consideration prior to decisions to use intrusive interventions. Differential reinforcement and time-out procedures, alone and combined with other intervention components, have been used extensively and effectively with disruptive behaviors. These are likely interventions for many lively preschool situations. Contingent observation is a mild form of time out that includes teaching about behavior.

Allen, Turner, and Everett (1970) and Pinkston, Reese, LeBlanc, and Baer (1973) described differential attention and extinction procedures to eliminate aggressive behaviors. In both reports, teachers were instructed to ignore the disruptive behavior of children and attend only to the victims. Teachers were also instructed to attend to the children described as disruptive when they were engaged in appropriate social interaction with their peers. The results of these studies support the use of differential attention and extinction to reduce aggressive behavior and increase positive peer social interaction.

Contingent observation has been used to decrease disruptive behaviors. Tyroler and Lahey (1980) compared the effectiveness of contingent observation and redirection procedures with a two-year-old girl. Disruptive behaviors included aggression, crying, fussing, destroying toys, and creating dangerous situations (throwing objects, standing on a counter). During the redirection phase, when the child engaged in disruptive behavior she was told of the inappropriateness of her behavior and was redirected to a more appropriate activity ("Look at the book"). Contingent observation was implemented, following procedures described in Chapter Seven. Results demonstrated that contingent observation was more effective in decreasing disruptive behaviors than redirection procedures.

The "Good Behavior Clock." Kubany, Weiss, and Sloggett (1971) described the "good behavior clock" procedure for reducing disruptive classroom behavior. It is an example of a modification of time out.

A six-year-old first-grade boy was the target of the intervention. Disruptive behaviors included refusal to sit at his desk, refusal to engage in academic tasks, talking out, and loud outbursts. The teacher also reported that the boy often left the classroom during recess and stayed away until lunchtime.

A false face was placed over a fifteen-minute electric timer. The numbers 1 through 6 were placed on the face at two-minute intervals, and a red star on the clock face indicated the completion of a cycle. When the child was quiet and in his seat, the clock would run. For every two minutes of "running time," the child would receive a treat that was then placed in a "sharing jar" for distribution to himself and his classmates at the end of the school day. Intervals were scheduled so that each child could receive a treat each day if the target child did not engage in any disruptive behavior. When the interval was complete, the child earned a red star, which was placed on his "good behavior chart" posted in the front of the classroom.

When the child engaged in disruptive behavior, he was given a mild prompt for appropriate behavior, and the clock was turned off. The teacher was instructed to ignore him. After fifteen seconds, if quiet and in his seat, he was praised and the clock was turned back on. If he continued to engage in disruptive behavior, the clock remained turned off and he did not earn treats.

At the end of the school day the child dispensed the treats, first to himself and then to his peers. Each day the first child who received a treat was the student at the desk next to the one who had received the last treat the day before. The intervention was successful until the middle of the first intervention phase, when the child's behavior significantly deteriorated. To receive a treat himself, he needed to behave appropriately for only one two-minute interval, as he was receiving the first treat each day. The intervention was altered: the target child was placed in rotation with classmates for the receipt of a treat. This significantly reduced the disruptive behavior. Furthermore, the intervention also generalized to the other behavior of leaving the classroom and not returning. During the intervention phase, he returned promptly from recess on every occasion.

Time-Out Ribbon. In a modified time out from reinforcement procedure, Foxx and Shapiro (1978) used ribbons as a discriminative cue for reinforcement. Five retarded children (ages eight to eighteen) were each given different colored ribbons to wear as ties and were rewarded with edibles and praise approximately every 2.5 minutes for engaging in appropriate behaviors. For any misbehavior, the ribbon was removed for three minutes; during this time the child was not given any edibles or praise, and was denied participation in activities. The teacher named the specific behavior that resulted in the removal of the ribbon. If the child continued to engage in disruptive behavior after the three-minute interval, the interval was extended until the misbehavior had stopped.

The results indicated that the ribbon procedure significantly decreased disruptive behavior in comparison to baseline. However, when the children were not wearing their ribbons (when entering the classroom in the morning or leaving the classroom in the afternoon), disruptive behaviors reappeared. The authors pointed out that the procedure may be effective with less obtrusive objects than ribbons.

Safety and Health-Related Interventions

Accidental injuries are the leading cause of children's deaths, and health and safety programs have a broad base of research support. We describe several interventions that may be adapted for children with risk behaviors or in risk situations.

Pedestrian Safety Skills

Yeaton and Bailey (1978) evaluated an instructional package for street crossing. They noted that although many schools may contain curricular materials for safety, the skills may not transfer to real-life situations. The study was conducted at actual intersections where an adult crossing guard was present, and also at streets without a crossing guard, to assess generalization. The ages of the twelve children ranged from five to nine.

The training procedure involved four phases, outlined in Exhibit 11.3. After the instructional package was presented, the children practiced the safety steps. At one school, the crossing guard signaled each child from the center of the street. At the other, children were allowed to safely initiate the steps with a crossing guard in close proximity but behind the children. After formal instruction, the guard administered a prompt each day to use all the safety steps. Procedures varied slightly between the two schools.

The results showed very positive changes in pedestrian skills, and the level of performance was maintained by the prompts. A one-year followup demonstrated the maintenance of skills at "high levels" or skills that "could be quickly recovered from intermediate levels with only a minimum of remedial training" (p. 327).

Exhibit 11.3. Pedestrian Safety Instructional Package.

---

1. Four phases were used to teach the skills.
2. Eight steps were included in each phase: wait at curb; look all ways; watch vehicle distance; walk (do not stop in street, run, etc.); continue to look; use crosswalk; walk on sidewalk; and cross on corner.
   a. Phase I: "*Tell Them.*" The trainer described correct behaviors for all eight steps.
   b. Phase II: "*Show Them.*" The trainer demonstrated the street-crossing sequence, verbalizing and modeling the steps.
   c. Phase III: "*Ask Them.*" In a varied order, the trainer asked questions about the eight steps and praised correct responses.
   d. Phase IV: "*Let Them.*" The children practiced the steps with the safety guard present. The guard also gave feedback for correct and incorrect responses.
3. Before crossing, the children were asked to verbalize what they would do as they crossed the street.
   a. Correct responses were praised.
   b. Mistakes were corrected, and the child was asked to repeat the correct answer.
   c. Children were asked to observe the crossing of the child ahead of them and verbalize any errors. Praise and corrective feedback were given. The procedure was repeated for the next child.

Adapted from Yeaton, W. H., & Bailey, J. S. (1978). Teaching pedestrian safety skills to young children: An analysis and one year follow-up. *Journal of Applied Behavior Analysis, 11,* 315–329. Copyright © 1978 by the Society for the Experimental Analysis of Behavior. Reprinted with permission.

The procedure was successful and easy to implement. The training time for individual sessions ranged from ten to twenty-five minutes, for eleven sessions. The procedure potentially can be administered by a range of personnel including crossing guards or other adults. However, the authors noted that generalization was more of a problem and that research is necessary to improve generalization.

In a later study, Yeaton and Bailey (1983) evaluated two training packages. The Guard Training Program (GTP), using videotape and role-playing techniques, was designed to train methods for teaching pedestrian safety. The Pedestrian Safety Instructional Package (PSIP; see Exhibit 11.3) was field tested by safety personnel. A total of 108 kindergarten and first-grade children participated in three studies.

Three experiments were conducted to examine the effectiveness of the training packages. First, crossing guards were provided with one training session of the GTP and taught children how to cross streets safely. Skills remained high, as they taught new groups of children to cross streets safely.

In the second experiment, crossing guards were provided with written training instructions and told to read them carefully before implementing them with the children. Results of this phase revealed minimal increases in children's pedestrian safety skills. The crossing guards then participated in the GTP training. Increases in pedestrian safety skills of the children were somewhat higher after this phase, although the guards required prompts to follow procedures when training new groups of children.

In the third experiment, the children were presented with a briefer version of the PSIP. Children were only "shown" and "told" how to cross the street safely. Results indicated minimal gains in crossing streets safely.

Although followup was not conducted, the results of these studies provide evidence of the components necessary for training pedestrian safety skills to children. For children to successfully learn such skills, critical training components include the opportunity to practice newly learned skills and to receive feedback and praise from the adults implementing the training.

Bus and Car Behavior

Disruptive behavior by children while riding in a bus can have extreme negative consequences for all involved. In this section we review an intervention found helpful with bus behavior.

Allen, Turner, and Everett (1970) used consumable reinforcers to improve the bus behavior of a four-year-old boy with multiple problem behaviors. The child had been banned from riding on the Head Start school bus for disruptive behavior. Reported behaviors included refusing to sit in the seat with the seat belt fastened, attempting to open the door while the bus was in motion, playing with the instrument panel of the bus, and throwing himself on the driver while the driver was operating the bus.

The child was placed in a seat and his seat belt was fastened by an aide. Immediately, the aide put a peanut in the child's mouth and praised him for sitting quietly and having his seat belt on. Peanuts and praise were then provided to all the children on the bus for appropriate bus-riding behavior. The reinforcers were dispensed every thirty to ninety seconds to all children throughout the fifteen-minute bus ride.

During the following four days, the interval length for receiving reinforcers was increased. On day 6 of the intervention, peanuts were saved until the bus arrived at the school and the children were off the bus. This phase was implemented for three days. During the final phase, the child rode the bus without an aide present. The bus driver praised the children for appropriate bus behavior and was instructed to ignore any disruptive behavior. When the bus arrived at the school, the teacher and aide rewarded the boy with a small sucker for receiving praise from the driver. Fading procedures were then used to eliminate the consumable reinforcement. Results indicated that the intervention eliminated disruptive bus behavior and gains were maintained throughout the school year.

Seat Belt Usage

Each year over 1,500 children under the age of fourteen suffer fatalities and more than 125,000 are injured in vehicle collisions

(National Safety Council, 1983). Many states have implemented mandatory seat belt and child-restraint laws, although parent compliance is questionable (Roberts & Layfield, 1987).

In a study by Sowers-Hoag, Thyer, and Bailey (1987), sixteen children ranging in age from four to seven who were never observed to be restrained while riding in a car were trained to initiate seat belt usage and ask for assistance when needed. The children were educated about the importance of seat belt usage, and famous persons who used seat belts (airline and jet fighter pilots, race car drivers, and television stars) were discussed. Role playing of scenarios was used to teach children to assert themselves to gain assistance in fastening seat belts before the car was in motion. Behavioral rehearsal was then used, and the children practiced putting on and taking off seat belts. Three cars with different types of seat belts were used for practice, until children were able to buckle and unbuckle the seat belts in less than ten seconds. Training lasted ten minutes or less.

Children who were observed to have their seat belts on when arriving at school were then eligible to participate in a lottery. Of the eligible children, half were selected each day to receive stickers, small toys, or "safety award certificates." Results indicated that seat belt usage significantly increased during intervention as compared to baseline and gains were maintained at followup two to three months later. Relatedly, Roberts and Layfield (1987) found that rewarding children for use of seat belts was more effective than providing information to parents.

Responding to Emergencies

Jones and Kazdin (1980) evaluated the effectiveness of a program designed to teach young children skills necessary in making emergency phone calls. Such skills may be especially important for children who are not well supervised in the home.

The study was implemented based on the interest of the preschool staff. The ages ranged from three years to six. However, some children were excluded because of absences, change of programs, or a lack of skills, as determined by a pretest. The checklist of emergency dialing skills is reproduced in Exhibit 11.4. The training was carried out by the preschool teachers

Exhibit 11.4. Checklist of Dialing Skills.

Dials

1.	Picks up the receiver. (Push dial tone.)	Yes	No
2.	Places receiver on ear.	Yes	No
3.	Dials zero ("0").	Yes	No

"Let's pretend that I am the operator." "Operator."

Reports fire

4.	"There is a fire at my house."	Yes	No

Gives Name

5.	First name	Yes	No
6.	Last name	Yes	No

Gives Address

7.	House number	Yes	No
8.	Street name	Yes	No
9.	City	Yes	No

Tell the child to put the receiver down.
Tell the child to pick up the receiver and put it to his ear.
"Let's make believe the operator is listening."
"Tell the operator what your full name is."

10.	My name is ____(first, last)____ .	Yes	No

"Tell the operator to send the firetruck to your house."

11.	"Send the firetruck to my house."	Yes	No
12.	House number	Yes	No
13.	Street name	Yes	No
14.	City	Yes	No

"Put the receiver down."
"Thank you."

Source: Jones, R. T., & Kazdin, A. E. (1980). Teaching children how and when to make emergency telephone calls. *Behavior Therapy, 11,* p. 511. Copyright 1980 by the Association for Advancement of Behavior Therapy. Reprinted by permission of the publisher and author.

in the classroom. Three conditions were compared: a behavioral program (outlined in Exhibit 11.5), a "teacher-devised method," and a control group of children without training experiences. The behavioral training program resulted in a significant difference in comparison to the other method and the group without training.

In a second study, Jones and Kazdin (1980) extended the

Exhibit 11.5. Behavioral Training of Emergency Dialing Skills.

1. Teachers were supplied with a telephone training device that enabled simulated calls with an operator.
2. The methods included instructions, modeling, prompting, remediation, feedback, review, and reinforcement. Training was conducted sequentially across the following tasks.
    a. *Dialing the operator*
        (1). Picking up the receiver.
        (2). Picking up and replacing the receiver
        (3). Picking up the receiver, dialing "0," listening for the operator, and replacing the receiver
    b. *Reciting name and address*
        (1). Giving full name
        (2). Giving full address
    c. *Providing emergency information*
        (1). Taught singly
        (2). Taught in combination with name and address
3. The tasks were first taught independently, then combined in sequence.
    a. Dialing the operator
    b. Giving name and address
    c. Providing emergency information
    d. Providing emergency information, name and address
    e. Dialing the operator and providing emergency information, name, and address
4. During lessons both the teacher and students played the role of a parent giving instructions to contact emergency agencies (the firetruck, the police, and the ambulance).
5. Emergency situations included such stimuli as yelling "fire" and pretending to be disabled by an accident.
6. Training was conducted in a group, but children practiced individually.
7. Reinforcers were provided for the completion of the component steps and for the sequence.

Source: Jones, R. T., & Kazdin, A. E. (1980). Teaching children how and when to make emergency telephone calls. *Behavior Therapy,* pp. 512–513. Copyright 1980 by the Association for Advancement of Behavior Therapy. Reprinted by permission of the publisher and author.

research to the children's skills necessary to discriminate situations requiring emergency calls. They used a total of thirty pictures to represent three different conditions: "*fire scenes* (e.g., kitchen stove or couch on fire)"; "*injuries* that warranted emergency assistance" (such as cuts or falling down stairs); and "*neutral situations* (child reading a book or lying in bed)" (adapted from p. 515). The pictures were shown daily in random order, and the children were asked who they should call.

The training included the direct teaching of responses:

"When we see fires like this, we call the fire truck. The fire truck brings water and puts the fire out. Now here are some pictures with fires in them." The child was then shown each fire scene individually and asked, "Can you tell me what's on fire?" [p. 516].

Following direct teaching, the children were prompted by showing the different scenes. "What should you do when you see this?" (p. 516). A correct answer was praised and reinforced. Incorrect responses "were followed by . . . 'no,' an explanation . . . , and modeling of the desired response" (p. 516). Modifications were made for two children who experienced difficulty. The results indicated that improvements occurred as a function of training.

It is likely that telephone training occurs in many preschools, and is also conducted by parents in the home. A carefully constructed behavioral training program may have greater benefits than other methods. Children's ability to discriminate situations requiring emergency phone calls improved as a result of a straightforward procedure. Jones and Kazdin (1980) gave several suggestions that would be helpful for practice: using more realistic and naturalistic stimuli (such as videotapes); responding to different operators who ask questions in different ways; and including factors such as busy signals. The procedures may be carried out in about thirty days of fifteen- to twenty-minute sessions.

With similar goals but different methods, Rosenbaum, Creedon, and Drabman (1981) evaluated a treatment package to teach preschool children to discriminate emergency situations, to dial 911, and to appropriately respond to questions relating to the emergency. Six emergency and six nonemergency scenes were presented by videotape. Children's responses included the discrimination task, phone-dialing skills, and providing information that included their name, address, a description of the emergency, the number of injured people, and whether an ambulance was needed. Experience with push-button phones also is necessary.

Self-Protection Training

Poche, Brouwer, and Swearingen (1981) presented a program to teach young children (ages three to five) safe responses to attempted abductions such as kidnapping or molestation. They cite research that suggests that force is less likely to be used than enticement. Thus, training children to resist enticement may be important in reducing such threats. Three preschool children described as having normal intelligence and social skills were included in the study. To aid in generalization, lifelike schoolground settings were used. The components of the intervention are summarized in Exhibit 11.6. The research has been extended to incorporate videotape training (Poche, Yoder, & Miltenberger, 1988).

In a study by Harvey, Forehand, Brown, and Holmes (1988), kindergarten children were provided with a prevention program for sexual abuse. Twenty children participated in the program; twenty others served as controls. At preintervention, postintervention, and followup, each child was asked to view a series of pictures and to identify whether a picture was depicting good (five pictures) or bad touches (five pictures). Each child also was asked five questions (p. 431): "(1) Is it OK to ever break a promise? (2) Do you think that children should always obey grown-ups? (3) If a person forces or tricks you into a bad touch, should you tell? (4) Do you think that sometimes grown-ups trick children into a bad touch? (5) Do you think that children should decide with whom they want to share their bodies?"

A direct test and generalization tests also were administered to children. Each test contained two stories of sexual abuse; one involved an adult, the other a teenager. The child was then asked six questions about whether the abuse was wrong and what the child should do. Stories presented in the direct test were discussed in the treatment program, while the generalization scenarios were not discussed.

The program consisted of three half-hour sessions over three consecutive days, in which sexual abuse was defined, the differences between good, bad, and sexually abusive touches were explained, safety rules to prevent abuse were provided, and

Exhibit 11.6. Teaching Self-Protection to Young Children.

---

1. Normal preschool children were selected, in part based on their inappropriate behavior in an analogue situation where an adult confederate asked the child to leave the preschool.

2. Training occurred in three locations within fifty feet of the school. In addition, performance was measured on sidewalk locations from 150 to 400 feet from the school.

3. "Suspects," or adult confederates used for training, were selected to resemble "local norms" for possible molesters.

4. The following "lures" were employed: "(a) a simple request for the child to go with the molester; (b) a request to leave with the implication that an authority figure (e.g., the child's parents or teachers) approved of the child's leaving; and (c) a request to leave with the promise of an incentive" (p. 171).

5. Definitions of appropriate responses to the lures were developed with parents. Parents "preferred that their child make a brief verbal statement, so as not to offend the good intentions of a benevolent person, but not so long . . . as to permit [an abduction]. They also preferred that their children then quickly move from the vicinity" (p. 171).

6. Two adults were used as trainers. One played the role of a suspect, while the other modeled child responses. In addition, behavioral rehearsal and social reinforcement were used.

    a. The "suspect" used one of three lures described above per day.

    b. The adult trainer modeled appropriate verbal and target behaviors.

    c. The child was asked to rehearse the scene with the suspect and to employ the modeled behaviors.

    d. The child was given positive social reinforcement (and occasionally material or activity reinforcers) if correct.

    e. If the child's responses were incorrect, instruction, modeling, and rehearsal were again used.

    f. When responses to the first lure were learned, responses to the other lures were observed and were trained if incorrect.

Adapted from Poche, C., Brouwer, R., & Swearington, M. (1981). Teaching self-protection to young children. *Journal of Applied Behavior Analysis, 14,* 169–176. Copyright ©1981 by the Society for the Experimental Analysis of Behavior. Reprinted with permission.

the identities of persons who could possibly abuse (strangers, familiar adults, or teenagers) were discussed. The teaching procedures consisted of instruction, modeling, and rehearsal. Stories and a film about sexual abuse also were presented to the children. Results of the study indicated that the children participating in the program demonstrated increased knowledge about abuse, including safety, rules about sexual abuse, and how to handle potential abusive situations, as compared to the control group. The results were maintained at a seven-week followup.

Comprehensive Programs

Mori and Peterson (1986) extended Peterson's earlier efforts (1984a, 1984b) to demonstrate the successful training of safety skills for preschool children based on the "Safe at Home" game, using preschool teachers as trainers. The game is intended to provide preventive services to children who may be at greater risk for injury or trauma from molestation because of more unsupervised time in the home.

The "Safe at Home" game includes three domains, with two modules in each: *emergencies* (cut hand and fire), *encountering strangers* (door and phone), and *food selection and preparation* (nutrition and safe preparation). The game consists of four "safety response rules" for each module; the rules are illustrated and mounted on cards. Several games were used to teach correct responses. Thus, safety rules were presented verbally and visually. Teacher praise was also used, along with social and tangible reinforcement.

The cards were faded gradually, and children were then required to act out and explain the rules without the cards. Rehearsal was used on a repeated basis, and the children also were required to give the rationale for their response. Criteria for discontinuing training were met when "the majority of subjects could act out in proper sequence all four safety responses for each module, while simultaneously reporting its underlying rationale" (p. 110).

Mori and Peterson (1986) warn that the program should be considered only a beginning phase of injury intervention. Furthermore, how well preschool children will actually apply the skills under stress remains untested. Christophersen (1989) also reviewed research-based health interventions for low-income minority groups.

Biting

Biting is a leading cause of injury to children and to adults in day-care centers (Solomons & Elardo, 1989). The victims of bites may face serious consequences, such as infection and scarring. In one study of 1,324 accidents in a university day-care center composed mostly of children (median age thirty-eight months) from white, middle-class two-parent families, 171 accident reports were related to bites received from another child, and 44 were self-induced. Overall, nearly half the day-care children received human bites, the most common circumstance being aggressive acts. However, only four bites actually broke the skin, and most of the bites were described as "not serious."

Among the recommendations by Solomons and Elardo are consideration of play materials, anticipation of conflicts and redirecting children, and vigilance in monitoring play behaviors. Factors such as child–adult ratios and in-service training on the management of aggression also are appropriate considerations. Solomons and Elardo suggested the following steps: using time out, comforting the victim, and examining the bite. If the skin is broken, medical treatment should be sought, the parents should be contacted, and an accident report should be completed.

Matson and Ollendick (1976) reported a series of uncontrolled clinical replications for a brief but aversive "biting" treatment package that may be helpful when severe biting occurs at a low rate. Following baseline, situations were structured (play where the children could not "get their way") to elicit the biting behavior (termed *promptings*). Mild punishment was made contingent for biting, while appropriate behavior was reinforced (praise and hugs). Four fifteen-minute promptings were attempted daily. Bites and attempted bites resulted in having an unpleasant-tasting mouthwash sprayed into the child's mouth. All the safeguards described in the next chapter should be followed. In addition, medical permissions should be obtained. Furthermore, a program like this may benefit from differential reinforcement of alternative or functional behavior (see Chapter Seven). However, intervening with low-rate behaviors presents difficulties, and a prompting strategy to create occasions to practice alternative behaviors may be helpful.

Summary and Conclusions

We reviewed basic interventions for social competence, disruptive behavior, and other problem behaviors, building on earlier chapters. It is important to establish a range of intervention alternatives for problem behaviors to help fit naturalistic styles of teaching, to promote acceptability, and to help guard against intervention biases. A final section outlined interventions related to safety and health-related issues. Systematic instruction for emergencies and risk situations may be a significant part of the preschool curriculum and may help children having special needs.

PART FIVE

INTEGRATING RESEARCH AND PRACTICE FOR QUALITY PROFESSIONAL SERVICES

12

Accountable and
Ethical Practice

THE OVERALL OBJECTIVE OF THIS BOOK IS TO PROVIDE A CONCEPTUAL
and research-based guide for services to preschool children with
behavior and learning problems. We conclude with a discussion of the scientist-practitioner framework. The purpose of the
scientist-practitioner model is the integration of research and
practice to improve the quality of professional services. To meet
these goals, methods for collaborative decision making and accountability are needed.

The Scientist-Practitioner in the Preschool Setting

The foundations of this book are based on a professional model
of practice that is defined by the scientist-practitioner tradition.
The model has several important facets.

    First, the scientist-practitioner is empirically based and
thus is a critical consumer of research. To perform in accor-
dance with the research foundations of practice, the professional
must be aware of findings that affect practice. In our review,
we have analyzed practices and interventions that have considerable research support or show promise of effectiveness. In Chapter Two, we also reviewed practices that have been ineffective
for designing interventions or making educational decisions, such
as those associated with various traditional developmental-
assessment techniques.

371

In fact, most consumers of psychological and educational services may expect that professional recommendations have sound research foundations. An important role of the professional is to help parents sort interventions that have efficacy data or strong evidence of promise from those that do not.

Of course, being a consumer of research is not easy. Several issues stand out. Even interventions that appear likely for a given problem behavior may benefit from an ecobehavioral and functional assessment. Most often it is not possible to take a prescriptive approach to intervention design (such as recommending time out for behavior problems) with much confidence. Also, it is impossible to be fully informed of all pertinent conditions under which a study took place. Little research is carried out under natural conditions. Therefore, generalization is always a question.

Second, the scientist-practitioner should have the necessary skills to evaluate interventions. In other words, scientist-practitioners use the scientific method to evaluate their own professional behaviors through the use of strong accountability methods. Time-series methods associated with single-case experimental designs can be used flexibly to analyze the effects of plans across a wide range of problem behaviors, interventions, and philosophies (Barlow, Hayes, & Nelson, 1984). If established interventions are used, the process is similar to clinical replication, the end result of systematically conducted technique building, where treatment "packages" are tried out with clients similar to the subjects in the original research. Time-series methods can be used to monitor troublesome behaviors even when decisions are made *not* to intervene, and to determine unintentional negative outcomes for children, families, and teachers based on ineffective interventions. The process of *sequential* decision making is used to revise plans as needed.

Third, the practitioner is a researcher. This role is significant for several reasons. One is that professional knowledge often is inadequate to the specific problems that need to be resolved. Problem situations are defined by the fact that solutions are not certain. Frequently, changes need to be made in intervention plans. In fact, it may be best to assume that alterations in plans will be needed. Without adequate data, it is impossible to perform appropriately.

Another reason for the researcher role for practitioners is that research is needed on many aspects of intervention design with preschool populations. At the most basic level, replications are needed to evaluate the effectiveness of various interventions. Many of the practices described in Chapters Three, Four, and Five provide important foundations for reporting studies to the scientific community. Central are (a) descriptions of the child, setting, and behavior; (b) observation procedures related to planned changes in behavior; (c) evidence that a well-defined intervention was carried out as planned; and (d) data showing that the intervention was associated with reliable and valid measures of change (or that it was ineffective).

Idealized Versus Real-World Issues

The realities of practice also merit attention. Presently, the most difficult issues facing practitioners are the tenuous links among theoretical perspectives related to changing children's behavior, research-based interventions, idealized measurement and intervention situations, and the challenges and difficulties of real-world practice. There are many facets to these issues, but perhaps the most fundamental in many situations is the lack of resources, training, and support needed to fully implement and evaluate interventions in an exemplary manner. School district and building-level policies and practices are important in creating effective environments for professionals to provide services (Graden, Zins, & Curtis, 1988).

Psychological and educational services should be based on a coherent theoretical model, on appropriate research, and on a workable practitioner model. Given the absence of rules, formulas, and cookbook procedures, the best we can offer are the foundations of assessment and intervention design; knowledge of effective interventions and practices that are applicable to young children and the roles of caregivers; problem-solving methods; and the creative, sensitive, and careful implementation and evaluation of professional plans. Professional practices often involve approximations to various ideals, but still scientific methods can be applied. We have defined these by interrelated reflective and research-based strategies.

Reflective practice involves developing an understanding of a problem behavior in context. "In real-world practice, problems do not present themselves to the practitioner as givens. They must be constructed from . . . problematic situations which are puzzling, troubling, and uncertain" (Schön, 1983, p. 40). The most robust tools involve appraising child systems, problem behaviors, and objectives, and collaboratively involving caregivers in problem-solving steps. The most important safeguards include self-questioning of professional behaviors and actual tests of intervention plans.

Although limited, the research basis for intervention design that does exist is expanding rapidly. The most important facets are the identifications of interventions found in the literature that have established validity support and of functional assessments that lead to effective interventions for individual children.

Of increasing interest is the identification of empirically based syndromes or constellations of behaviors that may help define the adequacy of assessment and intervention plans (Achenbach, 1988) and help identify intervention research. This aspect of practice creates dilemmas. Applications of syndromal assessments to preschool populations remain tenuous and controversial. Lovaas, well known for his work with autistic children, wrote: "We have seen many parents who have spent an enormous amount of money and time trying to establish the 'correct' diagnosis for their child. In general, these parents usually become more confused because the more places they visit, the more diagnoses they receive (retarded, autistic, aphasic, brain damaged, emotionally disturbed, schizophrenic, psychotic, atypical development). . . . It is rare that the diagnosis really alters the treatment anyway, so it is pointless to seek all these fine and often imaginary classifications" (1981, p. 241).

On the other hand, without being guided by research literature on autistic behaviors of children, a practitioner may miss basic relevant interventions. Ironically, perhaps the most promising intervention research with children described as autistic has been reported by Lovaas (1987).

Reflective and research-based practices lead to *plans* for assessment and intervention design. The major criteria for the adequacy of plans are resulting changes in behaviors.

A useful concept is that of decision frames, which "refer to the decision-maker's conceptions of the acts, outcomes, and contingencies associated with a particular choice" (Tversky & Kahneman, 1984, p. 25). The adoption of a particular decision frame is "an ethically significant act" given a range of intervention alternatives and the risk status of children (p. 40). Therefore, the plans require evaluation of child and caregiver outcomes, including those that are unintended (Willems, 1977).

Legal and Ethical Issues

There are numerous reviews of the legal and ethical implications of educational and psychological intervention decisions. The field is quite complex and changing. The most significant changes are related to children's rights, dignity as a guiding construct, and reconfirmation of family (Hart, 1991; Melton, 1991). Certain legal foundations have been well established, including due process and equal protection. Here we review basic issues involved in designing and carrying out behavioral interventions.

Consent to Treatment

The major premise of consent to treatment is that clients are *informed* of all relevant aspects of the intervention that are required for making decisions. In other words, informed consent "refers to the clients' right to decide whether they want to participate in a proposed program, after they have been told what is going to be involved" (Stolz & Associates, 1978, p. 30). There are three especially significant elements of informed consent.

1. *Competence.* "Competence refers to the individual's ability to make a well-reasoned decision, to understand the nature of

the choice presented, and to give consent meaningfully" (Kazdin, 1984, p. 264).

2. *Knowledge.* "Knowledge . . . includes understanding the nature of treatment, the alternatives available, and the potential benefits and risks involved" (Kazdin, 1984, p. 264). The pros and cons of intervening versus not intervening should be established as firmly as possible. In reality, this requires difficult predictions, or a "prognosis" (Rekers, 1984) based on research in developmental psychopathology and behavioral interventions regarding behaviors, classes of behaviors, or syndromes. Also, individuals who are affected by the program must be given adequate notice and opportunity for a hearing. Of course, decisions that result from a hearing may subsequently be challenged.

3. *Volition.* "The client must agree to participate in treatment. Agreement to participate must not be given under duress" (Kazdin, 1984, p. 264). Voluntary consent means that the parent or guardian also has the right to withdraw consent without any condition or penalty. One potential danger is that the trappings of professional authority can be compelling, and thus the parents may feel considerable pressure to consent even though they may have questions or reservations about the intervention. The professional needs to be sensitive to this issue and should take proactive measures outlined in the subsequent section on intervention guidelines.

Determining competence to consent is quite difficult in some cases. In practice, we have frequently advised parents to bring trusted family or community members to assist in the process. Within the context of federal legislation, informed consent also means that requests are given in the parent or guardian's native language.

Although parents are typically placed in a position to make intervention decisions for children, a growing body of literature has raised questions about minors' so-called limited competence to consent, at least from elementary-age children upward. Many children can be involved in intervention planning to various degrees. Several authors have suggested a "bill of rights" for children in psychotherapy, including "the right to be told the truth," "the right to be treated as a person," "the right to be taken seriously," and "the right to participate in decision making" (Gelfand, Jenson, & Drew, 1982; Koocher, 1976; Ross, 1980). The findings of the American Psychological Association Commission on Behavior Modification suggest that professionals should consider obtaining consent from preschool children (Stolz & Associates, 1978). Recently, children's rights have been affirmed internationally (UN Convention on the Rights of the Child, 1991).

Sometimes, parents' and children's rights may conflict. Also, children's rights may take precedence over parents' rights when parental behaviors present risks to children (Martin, 1975). This situation is discussed in a subsequent section.

Controversial Treatments

Many forms of behavioral interventions have been attacked, primarily those involving aversive procedures such as punishment and time out, but also other interventions such as token economies. Corrao and Melton (1988) wrote: "In legal terms, these [interventions] have been regarded as issues of mistreatment, abuse, and neglect. . . . Though they constrain the behavior therapist's discretion slightly, the resulting rules probably do so little more than common sense would in most cases, while serving to protect the health, safety, and welfare of minors in behavior modification treatment programs" (p. 391).

Another class of situations falls under experimental therapy (Barlow, Hayes, & Nelson, 1984) when there are no known effective treatments. In these cases, informed consent and all the other protections are necessary. However, given the requirements of informed consent, under these circumstances it will be impossible to convey information to parents or guardians about an intervention in any "complete" sense, because information about an intervention or novel applications of interventions is lacking (Kazdin, 1984). In such situations, the *uncertainty* needs to be communicated to parents or guardians.

Many interventions that are widely disseminated lack

validity support. While this does not mean that they will be ineffective, it does mean that they cannot be used with great confidence since the outcomes are unknown. Examples include various parent training programs. Such programs are proliferating because of the family emphasis of recent preschool legislation. Sapon-Shevin (1982) provided an extensive review of ethical issues surrounding parent training programs.

Protections for the Professional. While the clients' rights have been clearly established, Griffith points out that many safeguards discussed in the present chapter help protect the change agent as well. "The issue of harm is as significant for the treating clinician as it is for the recipient client. An injured client, especially in situations where the treatment is questionable, has significant legal redress potential. If directed toward the clinician in the form of liability or malpractice litigation, the results are minimally professionally embarrassing, and quite possibly destructive in terms of liability" (1983, pp. 328–329).

Guidelines for Intervention Programs. As protection for the child and change agent, and for those responsible for administering services, one should adhere to general professional guidelines. Our review is based on guidelines developed by the Association for Advancement of Behavior Therapy (1977), the American Psychological Association (1981, 1990; Stolz & Associates, 1978), the Association for Behavior Analysis (Van Houten et al., 1988), in addition to many other sources. Martin (1975), Kazdin (1984), and Rekers (1984) have discussions of these issues within a context of broader social values. Lovaas and Favell (1987) provided an analysis of protections for aversive interventions. In Exhibit 12.1, ethical issues are addressed through a series of questions proposed by the Association for Advancement of Behavior Therapy. Exhibit 12.2 outlines a format developed for obtaining permission for intervention.

The fundamental principles are that selected intervention procedures are likely to be effective for the child and problem situation; that participants, parents, or guardians are fully aware of the intervention; and competent professionals are available to help carry out planned interventions. The end result logically

Exhibit 12.1. Ethical Issues for Human Services.

A. Have the goals of treatment been adequately considered?
  1. To insure that the goals are explicit, are they written?
  2. Has the client's understanding of the goals been assured by having the client restate them orally or in writing?
  3. Have the therapist and client agreed on the goals of therapy?
  4. Will serving the client's interests be contrary to the interests of other persons?
  5. Will serving the client's immediate interests be contrary to the client's long term interest?

B. Has the choice of treatment methods been adequately considered?
  1. Does the published literature show the procedure to be the best one available for that problem?
  2. If no literature exists regarding the treatment method, is the method consistent with generally accepted practice?
  3. Has the client been told of alternative procedures that might be preferred by the client on the basis of significant differences in discomfort, treatment time, cost, or degree of demonstrated effectiveness?
  4. If a treatment procedure is publicly, legally, or professionally controversial, has formal professional consultation been obtained, has the reaction of the affected segment of the public been adequately considered, and have the alternative treatment methods been more closely reexamined and reconsidered?

C. Is the client's participation voluntary?
  1. Have possible sources of coercion on the client's participation been considered?
  2. If treatment is legally mandated, has the available range of treatments and therapists been offered?
  3. Can the client withdraw from treatment without a penalty or financial loss that exceeds actual clinical costs?

D. When another person or an agency is empowered to arrange for therapy, have the interests of the subordinated client been sufficiently considered?
  1. Has the subordinated client been informed of the treatment objectives and participated in the choice of treatment procedures?
  2. Where the subordinated client's competence to decide is limited, have the client as well as the guardian participated in the treatment discussions to the extent that the client's abilities permit?
  3. If the interests of the subordinated person and the superordinate persons or agency conflict, have attempts been made to reduce the conflict by dealing with both interests?

E. Has the adequacy of treatment been evaluated?
  1. Have quantitative measures of the problem and its progress been obtained?
  2. Have the measures of the problem and its progress been made available to the client during treatment?

Exhibit 12.1. Ethical Issues for Human Services, Cont'd.

F.   Has the confidentiality of the treatment relationship been protected?
   1.   Has the client been told who has access to the records?
   2.   Are records available only to authorized persons?
G.   Does the therapist refer the clients to other therapists when necessary?
   1.   If treatment is unsuccessful, is the client referred to other therapists?
   2.   Has the client been told that if dissatisfied with the treatment, referral will be made?
H.   Is the therapist qualified to provide treatment?
   1.   Has the therapist had training or experience in treating problems like the client's?
   2.   If deficits exist in the therapist's qualifications, has the client been informed?
   3.   If the therapist is not adequately qualified, is the client referred to other therapists, or has supervision by a qualified therapist been provided? Is the client informed of the supervisory relation?
   4.   If the treatment is administered by mediators, have the mediators been adequately supervised by a qualified therapist?

Source: Azrin, N. H., Stuart, R. B., Risley, T. R., & Stolz, S. (1977). Ethical issues for human services. *Behavior Therapy, 8,* pp. v–vi. Copyright © 1977 by the Association for Advancement of Behavior Therapy. Reprinted with permission of the publisher and author.

may take the form of a contract where the conditions, goals, procedures, and roles are explicitly stated (Kazdin, 1984).

Define and clarify who is the client. The definition of "the client" is not always obvious. For example, a teacher may refer a child, but, based on the problem clarification, teacher behavior may be the focus of change efforts. Likewise, parents may refer children but most of the professional efforts may be on modifying parental behavior. More broadly, the client also may be defined as the institution or agency that employs the professional as a consultant. Institutions frequently have significant control over professional behavior. Ethical issues may arise when these relationships are not properly clarified. Defining the client is important, because the client needs to be actively involved in intervention planning.

Use collaboration in selecting target behavior. The result of consultation should be explicit written goals and methods to achieve those goals. An excellent device to test communication at key places is to have the caregivers restate the goals and other significant

**Exhibit 12.2. A Sample Permission
Format for Behavioral Interventions.**

I. Behavioral assessment

    A. Interviews are planned with the following persons.

        1.
        2.
        3.

    B. Observations will be conducted in the following settings.

        1.
        2.
        3.

II. Intervention decisions

    A. Pros and cons of intervening

    In deciding upon interventions, a prediction is made that there are risks involved in not intervening, and that likely gains will be made that affect current functioning, future functioning, or both.

    B. Pros and cons of the range of intervention alternatives

    Typically, there are several or more different interventions that may be used to help with problems of learning or adjustment. These may vary considerably according to the research foundation, potential costs, and acceptability. In some cases, there may not be an empirical basis for a proposed intervention, and the uncertainty of the procedure should be clarified with the parent or legal guardian.

    C. The agreed-upon intervention should be described in detail
        1. Describe the potential risks and benefits of the proposed intervention.
        2. Identify and describe the component strategies to be used.
        3. Identify the persons who will be conducting the intervention (behavior change agents).
        4. Define and describe the roles of all persons participating in the intervention (parent, teacher, behavior change agent).
        5. Present the plans for evaluation along with a suitable time line for accomplishing objectives.
        6. If aversive procedures are to be used, describe additional protections for the child.

Please initial the following after reviewing the above information.

[   ] The purpose, risks, and benefits of the intervention have been adequately explained to me.

[   ] All information that will be sought, and procedures that will be used have been identified verbally and in writing and have been adequately explained.

Exhibit 12.2. A Sample Permission
Format for Behavioral Interventions, Cont'd.

[   ]   I hereby give permission for the intervention.

[   ]   I hereby refuse permission for the intervention.

[   ]   If permission is granted, I understand that I have the right to withdraw
or revoke permission at any time.

Parent/Legal Guardian   Date

School Official Title (Teacher)   Date

School Official Title (Director of Agency)   Date

---

features of the intervention program in their own words. One
way to offer ethical protections and also to help decide on intervention strategies is to clarify potentially different "systems of
values and attitudes" that relate to a client's problems (Stolz &
Associates, 1978, p. 22).

    Use collaboration in intervention selection. In practice, inter-
vention design is guided by logical generalizations from research
and idiographic problem solving. In essence, the client has a
"right to an effective treatment"; the child should be receiving
the most reasonable intervention available for the problem behavior (Gelfand & Hartmann, 1984, p. 20). Other important
ethical considerations are those involving the least intrusive, restrictive, and aversive interventions. However, these last three
guidelines need to be balanced with considerations of potential
effectiveness. Thus, for self-injurious or other dangerous behaviors, at least some authorities currently think that aversive interventions may be the treatment of choice in specific instances,
as discussed earlier.

    One important ethical and practical consideration is the
possibility that the environment, and not children's behavior,

may need to be changed. For example, classroom-management practices have to be effective before individual behavior can be the focus of intervention. Likewise, family environments may be exacerbating problem behavior, or may not support the most promising intervention.

An important point of decisions involves the degree of research support for interventions, or the need for an experimental approach to intervention design. To help with the collaborative effort, and to help prevent sources of bias, professional roles include helping to enumerate and evaluate a range of intervention alternatives, including possible risks and benefits, and conducting a functional assessment.

Identify replicable procedures. The specific treatment components and steps should be described in detail. The practitioner reasons for this are at least twofold. First, it is an important element of informed consent. Second, it is basic to developing treatment-integrity measures.

Obtain written and verbal permissions from parent, agency, teacher (and perhaps child). Even though agreed-upon procedures are arrived at through parent and teacher consultation, they should also be obtained in writing. The intervention is described in a form of psychological report. Native-language considerations also are important. Another significant aspect of consent is to clarify who is to have access to the information. The professional and agency are guided by established rules and procedures for such record keeping and review.

Carefully select repeated measures to evaluate intended and potential unintended outcomes. Multiple measures over appropriate time periods are necessary for evaluating interventions. Data should be analyzed and shared with parents or guardians. Possible harmful outcomes for others (classmates, teachers) need to be evaluated. While all interventions need to be evaluated in this regard, group contingencies and aversives are especially vulnerable to unintended outcomes. Another example is that when using home–school contingencies, a child's unmet criteria may result in unplanned aversive consequences if the parents are abusive.

Plan for intervention modifications, failures, followup, and for transitions following intervention. Plans should include an agreed-upon time span for evaluating the intervention. Usually, this includes a brief trial period for the intervention, based on predictions made from research. If similar interventions for other children have had relatively immediate effects, it is important to consult with parents during the first few days of an intervention. Often, interventions need to be replanned or adjusted. Mutual agreement is necessary to replan an intervention or to refer the child, parent, or guardian to another professional or service agency if the intervention is unsuccessful. Planning for generalization is an explicit part of intervention design.

Use professional, agency, and public review. Accepted best practice dictates that professionals consult with others (supervisors, peers) about standards for practice and difficult or controversial situations. Memberships in relevant professional organizations are critical in this regard. Specific intervention decisions may affect the entire agency. Many agencies have functional teams and procedures to review service delivery to children, parents, and teachers. The goals of interventions and the interventions themselves should be open to such scrutiny.

Ensure professional competence. Two factors stand out. First, the behavior change agent should have experience or training in the procedures that will be used. Second, competent decisions need to be made on a case-by-case basis. Errors of professional judgment are relevant. One potential danger is treatment bias: "The clinician's conceptualization of problems and his knowledge of therapeutic techniques tend to influence him to listen selectively for problems that he can treat" (Kanfer & Grimm, 1977, p. 9). A different intervention bias is to apply a favored intervention for problem behaviors without sufficient regard to its appropriateness for individual cases. A safeguard is to establish a range of intervention alternatives that may fit a problem situation.

Determine an effective course when caregivers do not act in the best interest of the child. Caregivers may be unable or unwilling to act in the child's interests, for a number of reasons related to competence, motivation, stressors, health, or psychopathology. At the same time, a "physical and social environment that is safe, humane, and responsive to individual needs is a necessary prerequisite for effective treatment" (Van Houten et al., 1988,

p. 381). The professional cannot simply act as the agent of the parent (or school), but must determine how to best serve all those concerned in a situation. Gelfand and Hartmann wrote: "Therapists cannot respond automatically to requests to change a child's behavior but must independently assess their own ethical and legal responsibility in the matter" (1984, p. 16). Such situations are typically ambiguous, and peer review, consultation with other professionals, and supervisory relationships under more experienced professionals are essential.

Some parents or guardians present dangers to children through lack of supervision or through specific acts of violence or sexual or psychological abuse. In such cases, professionals must work within the context of best practices. In considering "best practices," guiding frameworks are legal requirements for reporting abuse and validity support for intervention effectiveness.

Use aversives and group contingencies with care. Aversives, punishment, and group contingencies require special consideration. Aversive techniques may be prevalent in the experiences of many children with severe learning and behavior problems, and their *ineffective use* (including reprimands, discipline, and time out) is an important point of parent and teacher consultation. Likewise, harmful group contingencies may be operating for children with special needs or problem behaviors.

There is general support for the proposition that positive approaches should be used before aversives. Possible exceptions were discussed by Axelrod (1990). The core issue is the use of the "least restrictive yet effective treatment" (Van Houten et al., 1988, p. 383). The situations for the use of punishment are tested by the question: "How urgent and important is it that a particular behavior cease?" (Axelrod, 1990, p. 63). Another important context is the analysis of positive features of the environment and nonaversive procedures for changing behavior (LaVigna & Donnellan, 1986). Specific permissions and agency review are recommended for all interventions.

Punishment. The following steps, procedures, and considerations are typically employed for treatments considered as punishing or aversive.

1. The decision-making steps and criteria should be clearly specified for all, in advance. The steps include establishing the need for intervention, determining the feasibility of carrying out an intervention within the present context or situation, evaluating prospective interventions and interdisciplinary team participation, and preparing a written plan, including goals, intervention components, and steps specified in detail. High-quality data useful for decision making are essential (Lovaas & Favell, 1987)

2. A functional assessment should be conducted to determine variables that are maintaining the problem behavior. Schrader and Gaylord-Ross (1990) recommend the following assessment areas: (a) stimulus and setting events that occur just before occurrences of the target behavior (antecedents); (b) situations where the target behavior is most and least likely to occur (referred to as *risk analysis*); (c) the consequences that maintain the target behavior and alternative behaviors, and the schedule that maintains the responses; (d) the behavioral repertoire of the client, including skill deficits, strengths, and "collateral behaviors"; and (e) the function of the target behavior (for example, communication) (p. 404).

3. "Insure the maximal amount of [positive] reinforcement possible in the environment" (Matson & DiLorenzo, 1984, p. 87). As Matson and DiLorenzo point out, time out, as an example, will not be effective unless the environment has attractive properties. Identifying and defining antecedent behaviors may be helpful for caregivers in "interrupting the sequence of behaviors" and directing the child to more positive tasks (p. 91). For autistic children, Smith (1990) recommends aversives as a last resort, in conjunction with positive approaches, and only with one or two behaviors during an intervention phase.

4. Although not appropriate for preschools, restrictive use of time out may be commonly used by parents. Focal points of parent consultation include the search for less aversive means of control or discipline, parental monitoring of behavior and safety issues, and the evaluation of intervention effectiveness.

The child should not be able to hurt himself or herself, either intentionally or unintentionally. The room should be devoid of potentially harmful objects, and parents should remain close by. In addition, potentially harmful objects in the child's possession may need to be removed. The procedures may be abused by being kept in effect too long, or by reducing the need to evaluate less aversive methods or positive intervention strategies (Axelrod, 1990).

5. If verbal prompts are used, as with time out, a "calm but firm voice" should be used (Matson & DiLorenzo, 1984, p. 88). Furthermore, the prompt should be a brief statement ("You are getting a time out now.") (p. 89).

6. Medical or physical problems should be taken into account before punishment or aversive procedures are used.

7. Agency regulations should be established and adhered to. Appropriate reviews help protect the rights of the client and staff members. Institutional interdisciplinary panels should review aversive procedures for adequacy, effectiveness, quality control, and constitutional rights of the clients. Institutional statements of policy are essential. Peer review by knowledgeable professionals, especially those with responsibilities that are independent of the program in question, can help determine the appropriateness of the intervention (Griffith, 1983).

8. The "least restrictive, or drastic" but effective intervention should be considered for use (Griffith, 1983; Van Houten et al., 1988). Support for the intervention's effectiveness with the behavior problem should be made available to those participating in the intervention decisions. Other safeguards should be in force to protect the client's rights. If the intervention is not successful, changes in the intervention or therapist may be necessary.

9. Staff training and supervision are essential (Lovaas & Favell, 1987). The person responsible for the intervention should

be appropriately qualified. Furthermore, since the use of aversives may focus caregivers' attention on inappropriate behaviors and noxious consequences, it is critical that skills in teaching alternatives to maladaptive behaviors receive primary emphasis. Lovaas and Favell wrote: "Thus, one should expect to see intensive and competent instructional and reinforcement procedures in place in any program in which aversive/restrictive procedures are also employed" (1987, p. 317).

Group Contingencies. The use of group contingencies discussed in earlier chapters merits additional considerations and safeguards. (Also, some of the concerns may apply to sibling interventions discussed in Chapter Eight.)

First, target children may become scapegoats if the intervention program is unsuccessful. Second, peer pressure may be considerable and may result in coercion, and thus unintended and potentially harmful outcomes. It is especially important that all members of the group be able to perform at a sufficient level. Third, as peers gain control over behaviors, personal control and autonomy are diminished. Fourth, confidentiality may be breached when class members are able to identify individual performances. Fifth, intervention programs require informed consent and permissions from children who serve in roles as peer change agents.

To help with these concerns, practices should include all the protections mentioned above. As with other interventions, group contingencies require expanded observations to detect undesirable outcomes. Cooper, Heron, and Heward stated: "If the practitioner is unable to observe the behavior of individuals within the group periodically to determine whether the desired effect is produced, the group-oriented contingency should probably not be used" (1987, p. 502).

Confidentiality

In designing and evaluating interventions, communications are required among many people. As an element of informed consent, professionals who will be consulted and individuals who will participate in the intervention should be made known to the parent or guardian.

Although there are some exceptions, basically parents or guardians have the right to control access to educational and psychological records and information. The exceptions to this generally involve other school-based professionals who have legitimate educational interest in the information or in situations of potential harm to the child or others. Still, it is important to clarify parental rights and share the process of record and information control with parents.

Right to Education and Treatment

Although we have not discussed early intervention within the context of special services defined by federal law (PL 99-457; PL 101-476), the realities are that many interventions will take place as an element of an Individualized Family Services Plan for infants and toddlers, or an Individual Educational Plan (IEP) for older children, as required by law for children with disabilities. We have presented the intervention issues in the context of alternative service delivery, and thus have deliberately avoided the categorical implications of the legislation. However, many of the general intervention principles and procedures that have been discussed have been applied to children described as handicapped or with disabilities.

We have not found any convincing discussions of how to identify preschool children with traditionally termed high-incidence handicapping or disabling conditions, or "developmental delays," given the considerations associated with decision reliability and validity. Regardless, children most often referred are those with learning or behavior problems; these children are viewed as hard to teach, parent, or befriend. Given the controversies, we think that the basic principles of parent and teacher consultation and intervention design should guide the process.

References

Abeson, A., Burgdorf, R. L., Jr., Casey, P. J., Kunz, J. W., & McNeil, W. (1975). Access to opportunity. In N. Hobbs (Ed.), *Issues in the classification of children* (Vol. 2, pp. 270–292). San Francisco: Jossey-Bass.

Abidin, R. (1986). *Parenting stress index* (2nd ed.). Richmond, VA: Pediatric Psychology Press.

Abidin, R. (1990). Special issue on the stresses of parenting. *Journal of Clinical Child Psychology, 19.*

Achenbach, T. M. (1982). *Developmental psychopathology* (2nd ed.). New York: Wiley.

Achenbach, T. M. (1988). Integrating assessment and taxonomy. In M. Rutter, A. H. Tuma, & I. S. Lann (Eds.), *Assessment and diagnosis in child psychopathology* (pp. 300–343). New York: Guilford.

Achenbach, T. M., & Edelbrock, C. (1983). *Manual for the Child Behavior Checklist and Revised Child Behavior Profile.* Burlington, VT: University of Vermont.

Achenbach, T. M., Edelbrock, C., & Howell, C. T. (1987). Empirically based assessment of the behavioral/emotional problems of 2- and 3-year old children. *Journal of Abnormal Child Psychology, 15,* 629–650.

Achenbach, T. M., & McConaughy, S. H. (1987). *Empirically based assessment of child and adolescent psychopathology: Practical applications.* Newbury Park, CA: Sage.

Achenbach, T. M., McConaughy, S. H., & Howell, C. T. (1987). Child/adolescent behavioral and emotional problems: Implications of cross-informant correlations for situational specificity. *Psychological Bulletin, 101,* 213–232.

AERA, APA, & NCME (American Educational Research Association, American Psychological Association, and National Council on Measurement in Education). (1985). *Standards for educational and psychological testing.* Washington, DC: Author.

Alessi, G. J. (1980). Behavioral observation for the school psychologist: Responsive-discrepancy model. *School Psychology Review, 9,* 31–45.

Alessi, G. J. (1988). Direct observation methods for emotional/behavior problems. In E. S. Shapiro & T. R. Kratochwill (Eds.), *Behavioral assessment in schools: Conceptual foundations and practical applications* (pp. 14–75). New York: Guilford.

Alessi, G. J., & Kaye, J. H. (1983). *Behavioral assessment for school psychologists.* Washington, DC: National Association of School Psychologists.

Alig-Cybriwsky, C. A., Wolery, M., & Gast, D. L. (1990). Use of constant time delay procedure in teaching preschoolers in a group format. *Journal of Early Intervention, 14,* 99–116.

Allen, K. E., Hart, B., Buell, J. S., Harris, F. R., & Wolf, M. M. (1964). Effects of social reinforcement on isolate behavior of a nursery school child. *Child Development, 35,* 511–518.

Allen, K. E., Turner, K. D., & Everett, P. M. (1970). A behavior modification classroom for Head Start children with behavior problems. *Exceptional Children, 37,* 119–127.

Alpert, C. L., & Rogers-Warren, A. K. (1985). Communication in autistic persons: Characteristics and intervention. In S. F. Warren & A. K. Rogers-Warren (Eds.), *Teaching functional language: Generalization and maintenance of language skills* (pp. 123–155). Austin, TX: Pro-ed.

American Psychiatric Association. (1987). *Diagnostic and statistical manual of mental disorders: DSM-III-R* (3rd ed. rev.). Washington, DC: Author.

American Psychological Association. (1981). Ethical principles of psychologists. *American Psychologist, 36,* 633–638.

American Psychological Association. (1990). Ethical principles of psychologists. *American Psychologist, 45,* 390–395.

Anastopoulos, A., & Barkley, R. A. (1990). Counseling and training parents. In R. A. Barkley, *Attention-deficit hyperactivity disorder: A handbook for diagnosis and treatment* (pp. 397–431). New York: Guilford.

Anderson-Inman, L. (1981). Transenvironmental programming: Promoting success in the regular class by maximizing the effect of resource room assistance. *Journal of Special Education Technology, 4,* 3–12.

Association for Advancement of Behavior Therapy. (1977). Ethical issues for human services. *Behavior Therapy, 8,* v–vi.

Atkeson, B. M., & Forehand, R. (1979). Home-based reinforcement programs designed to modify classroom behavior: A review and methodological evaluation. *Psychological Bulletin, 86,* 1298–1308.

Atwater, J. B., Carta, J. J., & Schwartz, I. S. (1989). *Assessment code/checklist for the evaluation of survival skills: ACCESS.* Kansas City, KS: Juniper Garden Children's Project, Bureau of Child Research, University of Kansas.

Atwater, J. B., & Morris, E. K. (1988). Teachers' instructions and children's compliance in preschool classrooms: A descriptive analysis. *Journal of Applied Behavior Analysis, 21,* 157–167.

Axelrod, S. (1990). Myths that (mis)guide our profession. In A. C. Repp & N. N. Singh (Eds.), *Perspectives on the use of nonaversive and aversive interventions for persons with developmental disabilities* (pp. 59–72). Sycamore, IL: Sycamore Publishing.

Ayllon, T., & Azrin, N. (1968). *The token economy: A motivational system for therapy and rehabilitation.* New York: Appleton-Century-Crofts.

Azar, S. T., Fantuzzo, J. W., & Twentyman, C. T. (1984). An applied behavioral approach to child maltreatment: Back to basics. *Advances in Behavioral Research and Therapy, 6,* 3–11.

Azar, S. T., & Wolfe, D. A. (1989). Child abuse and neglect. In E. J. Mash & R. A. Barkley (Eds.), *Treatment of childhood disorders* (pp. 451–489). New York: Guilford.

Azrin, N. H., & Besalel, V. A. (1979). *A parent's guide to bedwetting control: A step-by-step method.* New York: Simon & Schuster.

Azrin, N. H., & Foxx, R. M. (1974). *Toilet training in less than a day.* New York: Simon & Schuster.

Azrin, N. H., Nunn, R. G., & Frantz-Renshaw, S. (1980). Habit reversal treatment of thumbsucking. *Behavior Research and Therapy, 18,* 395–399.

Azrin, N. H., Stuart, R. B., Risley, T. R., & Stolz, S. B. (1977). Ethical issues for human services. *Behavior Therapy, 8,* v–vi.

Baer, D. M., & Fowler, S. A. (1984). How should we measure the potential of self-control procedures for generalized educational outcomes. In W. L. Heward, T. E. Heron, D. S. Hill, & J. Trap-Porter (Eds.), *Focus on behavior analysis in education* (pp. 145–161). Columbus, OH: Merrill.

Baer, D. M., & Wolf, M. M. (1970). The entry into natural communities of reinforcement. In R. Ulrich, T. Stachnik, & J. Mabry (Eds.), *Control of human behavior: Vol. 11. From cure to prevention* (pp. 319–324). Glenview, IL: Scott, Foresman.

Baer, R. A., Osnes, P. G., & Stokes, T. F. (1983). Training generalized correspondence between verbal behavior at school and nonverbal behavior at home. *Education and Treatment of Children, 6,* 379–388.

Baer, R. A., Williams, J. A., Osnes, P. G., & Stokes, T. F. (1985). Generalized verbal control and correspondence training. *Behavior Modification, 9,* 477–489.

Bagnato, S. J., & Neisworth, J. T. (1990). *SPECS: System to guide early childhood services.* Circle Pines, MN: American Guidance Service.

Bailey, D. B., Jr. (1984). Effects of lines of progress and semi-logarithmic charts on ratings of charted data. *Journal of Applied Behavior Analysis, 17,* 359–365.

Bailey, D. B., Jr. (1989). Assessing environments. In D. B. Bailey, Jr., & M. Wolery, *Asessing infants and preschoolers with handicaps* (pp. 97–118). New York: Merrill.

Bailey, D. B., Jr., & Simeonsson, R. J. (1988). *Family assessment in early intervention.* Columbus, OH: Merrill.

Bailey, D. B., Jr., & Wolery, M. (1984). *Teaching infants and preschoolers with handicaps.* Columbus, OH: Merrill.

Bailey, D. B., Jr., & Wolery, M. (1989). *Assessing infants and preschoolers with handicaps.* Columbus, OH: Merrill.

Bakeman, R., & Gottman, J. M. (1986). *Observing interaction: An introduction to sequential analysis.* New York: Cambridge University Press.

Bandura, A. (1969). *Behavior modification.* Englewood Cliffs, NJ: Prentice-Hall.

Bandura, A. (1977). *Social learning theory.* Englewood Cliffs, NJ: Prentice-Hall.

Bandura, A. (1978). The self-system in reciprocal determinism. *American Psychologist, 33,* 344–358.

Bandura, A. (1981). Self-referent thought: A developmental analysis of self-efficacy. In J. H. Flavell & L. Ross (Eds.), *Social cognitive development: Frontiers and possible futures* (pp. 200–239). New York: Cambridge University Press.

Bandura, A. (1985). Model of causality in human learning. In M. J. Mahoney & A. Freeman (Eds.), *Cognition and psychotherapy* (pp. 81–99). New York: Plenum.

Bandura, A. (1986). *The social foundations of thought and action: A social cognitive theory.* Englewood Cliffs, NJ: Prentice-Hall.

Bandura, A., Grusec, J. E., & Menlove, F. L. (1967). Vicarious extinction of avoidance behavior. *Journal of Personality and Social Psychology, 5*(1), 16–23.

Barkley, R. A. (1981). *Hyperactive children: A handbook for diagnosis and treatment.* New York: Guilford.

Barkley, R. A. (1987). *Defiant children: A clinician's manual for parent training.* New York: Guilford.

Barkley, R. A. (1989). Attention-deficit-hyperactive disorder. In E. J. Mash & R. A. Barkley (Eds.), *Treatment of childhood disorders* (pp. 39–72). New York: Guilford.

Barkley, R. A. (1990). *Attention-deficit hyperactivity disorder: A handbook for diagnosis and treatment.* New York: Guilford.

Barlow, D. H., Hayes, S. C., & Nelson, R. O. (1984). *The scientist-practitioner: Research and accountability in clinical and educational settings.* New York: Pergamon.

Barnard, J. D., Christophersen, E. R., & Wolf, M. M. (1977). Teaching children appropriate shopping behavior through parent training in the supermarket setting. *Journal of Applied Behavior Analysis, 10,* 49–59.

Barnett, D. W. (1983). *Nondiscriminatory multifactored assessment: A sourcebook.* New York: Human Sciences Press.

Barnett, D. W., Faust, J. A., & Sarmir, M. A. (1988). A validity study of two preschool instruments: The LAP-D and DIAL-R. *Contemporary Educational Psychology, 13,* 26–31.

Barnett, D. W., & Macmann, G. M. (in press). Decision reliability and validity: Contributions and limitations of alternative assessment strategies. *Journal of Special Education.*

Barnett, D. W., Silverstein, B., & Miller, R. (1988). *In vivo language intervention: A case study replication.* Unpublished manuscript, University of Cincinnati.

Barnett, D. W., Zins, J. E., & Wise, L. (1984). An analysis of parental participation as a means of reducing bias in the education of handicapped children. *Special Services in the Schools, 1,* 71–84.

Barnett, D. W., & Zucker, K. B. (1990). *The personal and social assessment of children: An analysis of current status and professional practice issues.* Needham Heights, MA: Allyn & Bacon.

Barnett, W. S., & Escobar, C. M. (1988). The economics of early intervention for handicapped children: What do we really know? *Journal of the Division for Early Childhood, 12,* 169–181.

Barnett, W. S., & Escobar, C. M. (1990). Economic costs and benefits of early intervention. In S. J. Meisels & J. P. Shonkoff (Eds.), *Handbook of early childhood intervention* (pp. 560–582). New York: Cambridge University Press.

Barone, V. J., Greene, B. F., & Lutzker, J. R. (1986). Home safety with families being treated for child abuse and neglect. *Behavior Modification, 10,* 93–114.

Barrios, B., & Hartmann, D. P. (1986). The contributions of traditional assessment: Concepts, issues, and methodologies. In R. O. Nelson & S. C. Hayes (Eds.), *Conceptual foundations of behavioral assessment* (pp. 81–110). New York: Guilford.

Barton, E. J. (1981). Developing sharing: An analysis of modeling and other behavioral techniques. *Behavior Modification, 5,* 386–398.

Barton, E. J. (1986). Modification of children's prosocial behavior. In P. S. Strain, M. J. Guralnick, & H. M. Walker (Eds.), *Children's social behavior: Development, assessment and modification* (pp. 331–372). Orlando, FL: Academic Press.

Barton, E. J., & Ascione, F. R. (1979). Sharing in preschool children: Facilitation, stimulus generalization, response generalization, and maintenance. *Journal of Applied Behavior Analysis, 12,* 417–430.

Barton, E. J., & Bevirt, J. (1981). Generalization of sharing across groups: Assessment of group composition with preschool children. *Behavior Modification, 5,* 503–522.

Barton, E. J., & Osborne, J. G. (1978). The development of classroom sharing by a teacher using positive practice. *Behavior Modification, 2,* 231–250.

Barton, L. E., Brulle, A. R., & Repp, A. C. (1986). Maintenance of therapeutic change by momentary DRO. *Journal of Applied Behavior Analysis, 19,* 277–282.

Bauman, K. E., Reiss, M. L., Rogers, R. W., & Bailey, J. S. (1983). Dining out with children: Effectiveness of a parent advice package on pre-meal inappropriate behavior. *Journal of Applied Behavior Analysis, 16,* 55–68.

Bem, D. J. (1982). Assessing situations by assessing persons. In D. Magnussen (Ed.), *Toward a psychology of situations: An interactional perspective* (pp. 245–257). Hillsdale, NJ: Erlbaum.

Bennett, C. W., (1973). A four-and-a-half year old as a teacher of her hearing-impaired sister: A case study. *Journal of Communication Disorders, 6,* 67–75.

Bereiter, C., & Englemann, S. (1966). *Teaching the disadvantaged child in the preschool.* Englewood Cliffs, NJ: Prentice-Hall.

Bergan, J. R., Feld, J. K., & Swarner, J. C. (1988). Behavioral consultation: Macroconsultation for instructional management. In J. C. Witt, S. N. Elliott, & F. M. Gresham (Eds.), *Handbook of behavior therapy in education* (pp. 245–273). New York: Plenum.

Berreuta-Clement, J., Schweinhart, L., Barnett, W., Epstein, A., & Weikart, D. (1984). *Changed lives.* Ypsilanti, MI: High/Scope Press.

Bierman, L. K. (1983). Cognitive development and clinical interviews with children. In B. Lahey & A. E. Kazdin (Eds.), *Advances in clinical psychology* (pp. 217–250). New York: Plenum.

Bijou, S. W. (1975). Development in the preschool years: A functional analysis. *American Psychologist, 30,* 829–837.

Bijou, S. W., Peterson, R. F., & Ault, M. H. (1968). A method to integrate descriptive and experimental field studies at the level of data and empirical concepts. *Journal of Applied Behavior Analysis, 1,* 175–191.

Bijou, S. W., Peterson, R. F., Harris, F. R., Allen, K. E., & Johnston, M. S. (1969). Methodology for experimental studies of young children in natural settings. *The Psychological Record, 19,* 177–210.

Billings, D. C., & Wasik, B. H. (1985). Self-instructional training with preschoolers: An attempt to replicate. *Journal of Applied Behavior Analysis, 18,* 61–67.

Bloom, M., & Fischer, J. (1982). *Evaluating practice: Guidelines for the accountable professional.* Englewood Cliffs, NJ: Prentice-Hall.

Boehm, A. E. (1986). *Boehm Test of Basic Concepts — Revised.* San Antonio, TX: Psychological Corporation.

Boer, A. P., & Sipprelle, C. N. (1970). Elimination of avoidance behavior in the clinic and its transfer to the normal environment. *Journal of Behavior Therapy and Experimental Psychiatry, 1,* 169–174.

Bornstein, P. H. (1985). Self-instructional training: A commentary and state-of-the-art. *Journal of Applied Behavior Analysis, 18,* 69–72.

Bornstein, P. H., & Kazdin, A. E. (Eds.). (1985). *Handbook of clinical behavior therapy with children.* Homewood, IL: Dorsey.

Bowers, K. S., & Meichenbaum, D. (Eds.). (1984). *The unconscious reconsidered.* New York: Wiley.

Bracken, B. A. (1984). *Bracken Basic Concept Scale.* Columbus, OH: Merrill.

Bracken, B. A., & Myers, D. K. (1986). *Bracken Concept Development program.* San Antonio, TX: The Psychological Corporation.

Bradley-Johnson, S., Sunderman, P., & Johnson, C. M. (1983). Comparison of delayed prompting and fading for teaching preschoolers easily confused letters and numbers. *Journal of School Psychology, 21,* 327–335.

Bramlett, R. K. (1990). *The development of a preschool observation code: Preliminary technical characteristics.* Unpublished doctoral dissertation, University of Cincinnati.

Brassard, M. R., & Gelardo, M. S. (1987). Psychological maltreatment: The unifying construct in child abuse and neglect. *School Psychology Review, 2,* 127–136.

Brassard, M. R., & Hart, S. N. (1987). (Mini-series editors). Psychological maltreatment of children. *School Psychology Review, 2.*

Breiner, J., & Beck, S. (1984). Parents as change agents in the management of their developmentally delayed children's noncompliant behaviors: A critical review. *Applied Research in Mental Retardation, 5,* 259–278.

Bricker, D. D. (1986). *Early education of at-risk and handicapped infants, toddlers, and preschool children.* Boston: Little, Brown.

Bricker, D. (1989, August). *Evaluation and programming system: For infants and young children.* Eugene, OR: Center on Human Development, University of Oregon.

Brinckerhoff, J. L., & Vincent, L. J. (1986). Increasing parental decision-making at the individualized educational program meeting. *Journal of the Division for Early Childhood, 11,* 46–58.

Brown, J. H., Cunningham, G., & Birkimer, J. C. (1983). A telephone home survey to identify parent-child problems and maintaining conditions. *Child & Family Behavior Therapy, 5,* 85–92.

Brown, L., Nietupski, J., & Hamre-Nietupski, S. (1976). The criterion of ultimate functioning and public school services for severely handicapped students. In M. A. Thomas (Ed.), *Hey, don't forget about me: New directions for serving the severely handicapped* (pp. 2–15). Reston, VA: Council for Exceptional Children.

Brown, W. H., Ragland, E. U., & Bishop, N. (1989). *A socialization curriculum for preschool programs that integrate children with handicaps.* Nashville, TN: John F. Kennedy Center for Research on Education and Human Development, Peabody College, Vanderbilt University.

Browning, M. (1991). Attention deficit . . . Your attention please. *The Dolphin.* Cincinnati, OH: Southwestern Ohio Special Education Regional Resource Center Publication.

Bruner, J. (1978). On prelinguistic prerequisites of speech. In N. Campbell & P. T. Smith (Eds.), *Recent advances in the psychology of language: Language development and mother-child interactions* (volume III4a, pp. 199–214). New York: Plenum.

Bryant, D. M., & Ramey, C. T. (1987). An analysis of the effectiveness of early intervention programs for environmentally at-risk children. In M. J. Guralnick & F. C. Bennett (Eds.), *The effectiveness of early intervention for at-risk and handicapped children* (pp. 33–78). San Diego, CA: Academic Press.

Bryant, L. E., & Budd, K. S. (1982). Self-instructional training to increase independent work performance in preschoolers. *Journal of Applied Behavior Analysis, 15,* 259–271.

Bryant, L. E., & Budd, K. S. (1984). Teaching behaviorally handicapped preschool children to share. *Journal of Applied Behavior Analysis, 17,* 45–52.

Budd, K. S., Green, D. R., & Baer, D. M. (1976). An analysis of multiple misplaced parental social contingencies. *Journal of Applied Behavior Analysis, 9,* 459–470.

Budd, K. S., Leibowitz, J. M., Riner, L. S., Mindell, C., & Goldfarb, A. L. (1981). Home-based treatment of severe disruptive behaviors: A reinforcement package for preschool and kindergarten children. *Behavior Modification, 5,* 273–298.

Burstein, N. D. (1986). The effects of classroom organization on mainstreamed preschool children. *Exceptional Children, 52,* 425–434.

Buysse, V., & Bailey, D. B. (in preparation). *Mainstreamed versus specialized settings: Behavioral and developmental effects on young children with handicaps.*

Cairns, R. B., & Green, J. A. (1979). How to assess personality and social patterns: Observations or ratings? In R. B. Cairns (Ed.), *The analysis of social interactions: Methods, issues, and illustrations* (pp. 209–266). Hillsdale, NJ: Erlbaum.

Caldwell, B. E., & Bradley, R. H. (1979). *Home observation for measurement of the environment.* Little Rock, AK: University of Arkansas.

Calhoun, J., & Koenig, K. P. (1973). Classroom modification of elective mutism. *Behavior Therapy, 4,* 700–702.

Calvert, S. C., & McMahon, R. J. (1987). The treatment acceptability of a parent training program and its components. *Behavior Therapy, 2,* 165–179.

Campbell, D. T., & Fiske, D. W. (1959). Convergent and discriminant validity by the multitrait-multimethod matrix. *Psychological Bulletin, 56,* 81–105.

Carden Smith, L. K., & Fowler, S. A. (1984). Positive peer pressure: The effects of peer monitoring on children's disruptive behavior. *Journal of Applied Behavior Analysis, 17,* 213–227.

Carey, K. T. (1989). *The treatment utility potential of two methods of assessing stressful relationships in families: A study of practitioner utlization.* Unpublished doctoral dissertation, University of Cincinnati.

Carlson, C. L., & Lahey, B. B. (1988). Conduct and attention deficit disorders. In J. Witt, S. N. Elliott, & F. M. Gresham (Eds.), *Handbook of behavior therapy in education* (pp. 653–677). New York: Plenum.

Carr, E. G., & Durand, V. M. (1985). Reducing behavior problems through functional communication training. *Journal of Applied Behavior Analysis, 18,* 111–126.

Carr, E. G., Robinson, S., & Palumbo, L. W. (1990). The wrong issues: Aversive vs. nonaversive treatment. The right issue: Functional vs. nonfunctional treatment. In A. C. Repp & N. N. Singh (Eds.), *Perspectives on the use of nonaversive and aversive interventions for persons with developmental disabilities* (pp. 361–379). Sycamore, IL: Sycamore Publishing.

Carstens, C. (1982). Application of a work penalty threat in the treatment of a case of juvenile firesetting. *Journal of Behavior Therapy and Experimental Psychiatry, 13,* 159–161.

Carta, J. J., Greenwood, C. R., & Atwater, J. B. (1985). *Ecobehavioral system for the complex assessment of preschool environments: ESCAPE.* Kansas City, KS: Juniper Gardens Children's Project, Bureau of Child Research, University of Kansas. (ERIC Document Reproduction Service Nos. ED 288 268, EC 200 587).

Carta, J. J., Sainato, D. M., & Greenwood, C. R. (1988). Advances in the ecological assessment of classroom instruction for young children with handicaps. In S. L. Odom & M. B. Karnes (Eds.), *Early intervention for infants and children with handicaps* (pp. 217–239). Baltimore: Paul Brookes.

Carta, J. J., Schwartz, I. S., Atwater, J. B., & McConnell, S. R. (1991). Developmentally appropriate practice: Appraising its usefulness for young children with disabilities. *Topics in Early Childhood Special Education, 11,* 1–20.

Cash, W. M., & Evans, I. M. (1975). Training preschool children to modify their retarded siblings' behavior. *Journal of Behavioral Therapy and Experimental Psychiatry, 6,* 13–16.

Chamberlain, P., & Reid, J. B. (1987). Parent observation and report of child symptoms. *Behavioral Assessment, 9,* 97–109.

Christensen, A. P., & Sanders, M. R. (1987). Habit reversal and differential reinforcement of other behaviour in the treatment of thumb-sucking: An analysis of generalization and side-effects. *Journal of Child Psychology and Psychiatry, 28,* 281–295.

Christophersen, E. R. (1989). Health intervention research. *Education and Treatment of Children, 12,* 391–404.

Christophersen, E. R., Arnold, C. M., Hill, D. W., & Quilitch, H. R. (1972). The home point system: Token reinforcement procedures for application by parents of children with behavior problems. *Journal of Applied Behavior Analysis, 5,* 485–497.

Clark, H. B., Greene, B. F., Macrae, J. W., McNees, M. P., Davis, J. L., & Risley, T. R. (1977). A parent advice package for family shopping trips: Development and evaluation. *Journal of Applied Behavior Analysis, 10,* 605–624.

Clark, H. B., McManmon, L., Smith-Tuten, J. K., & Smith, J. (1985). *The Family Mealtime Game: Advice for parents* (#102). Tampa, FL: Florida Mental Health Institute Publication Series. (Available from FMHI Publications, Florida Mental Health Institute, University of South Florida, Tampa, FL 33612).

Colletti, G., & Harris, S. L. (1977). Behavior modification in the home: Siblings as behavior modifiers, parents as observers. *Journal of Abnormal Child Psychology, 5,* 21–30.

Cone, J. D. (1978). The behavioral assessment grid (BAG): A conceptual framework and taxonomy. *Behavior Therapy, 9,* 882–888.

Cone, J. D., & Hoier, T. S. (1986). Assessing children: The radical behavior perspective. In R. Prinz (Ed.), *Advances in behavioral assessment of children and families* (Vol. 2, pp. 1–27). Greenwich, CT: JAI Press.

Conger, R. D., & Lahey, B. B. (1982). Behavioral intervention for child abuse. *The Behavior Therapist, 5,* 49–53.

Consortium for Longitudinal Studies. (1983). *As the twig is bent . . . : Lasting effects of preschool programs.* Hillsdale, NJ: Erlbaum.

Cooper, J. O., Heron, T. E., & Heward, W. L. (1987). *Applied behavior analysis.* Columbus, OH: Merrill.

Corrao, J., & Melton, G. B. (1988). Legal issues in school-based behavior therapy. In J. C. Witt, S. N. Elliott, & F. M. Gresham (Eds.), *Handbook of behavior therapy in education* (pp. 377–399). New York: Plenum.

Croghan, L., & Musante, G. J. (1975). The elimination of a boy's high building phobia by in vivo desensitization and game playing. *Journal of Behavior Therapy and Experimental Psychiatry, 6,* 87–88.

Crowley, C. P., & Armstrong, P. M. (1977). Positive practice, overcorrection and behavioral rehearsal in the treatment of three cases of encopreses. *Journal of Behavior Therapy and Experimental Psychiatry, 8,* 411–416.

Crozier, J., & Katz, R. C. (1979). Social learning treatment of child abuse. *Journal of Behavior Therapy and Experimental Psychiatry, 18,* 212–220.

Cunningham, C. E. (1990). A family systems approach to family training. In R. A. Barkley, *Attention-deficit hyperactivity disorder: A handbook for diagnosis and treatment* (pp. 432–461). New York: Guilford.

Cunningham, C. E., Cataldo, M. F., Mallion, C., & Keyes, J. B. (1983). A review and controlled single case evaluation of behavioral approaches to the management of elective mutism. *Child & Family Behavior Therapy, 5,* 25–49.

Curtis, M. J., & Watson, K. (1980). Changes in consultee problem clarification skills following consultation. *Journal of School Psychology, 18,* 210–221.

Deitz, D. E. D., & Repp, A. C. (1983). Reducing behavior through reinforcement. *Exceptional Education Quarterly, 3,* 34–46.

Deitz, S. M. (1977). An analysis of programming DRL schedules in educational settings. *Behavior Research and Therapy, 15,* 103–111.

Dishion, T., Gardner, K., Patterson, G., Reid, J., Spyrou, S., & Thibodeaux, S. (1984). *The Family Process Code: A multidimensional system for observing family interaction.* Eugene, OR: Oregon Social Learning Center.

Doleys, D. M. (1979). Assessment and treatment of childhood enuresis. In A. J. Finch & P. C. Kendall (Eds.), *Clinical treatment and research in childhood psychopathology* (pp. 207–233). New York: Spectrum.

Donnellan, A. M., & LaVigna, G. W. (1990). Myths about punishment. In A. C. Repp & N. N. Singh (Eds.), *Perspectives on the use of nonaversive and aversive interventions for persons with developmental disabilities* (pp. 35–57). Sycamore, IL: Sycamore Publishing.

Dowrick, P. W., & Hood, M. (1978). Transfer of talking behaviors across settings using fake films. In E. L. Glynn & S. S. McNaughton (Eds.), *Proceedings of the New Zealand Conference for Research in Applied Behavior Analysis*. Auckland: University of Auckland Press.

Drotar, D., & Crawford, P. (1987). Using home observation in the clinical assessment of children. *Journal of Clinical Child Psychology, 16,* 342–349.

Dunlap, G., Johnson, L. F., & Robbins, F. R. (1990). Preventing serious behavior problems through skill development and early interventions. In A. C. Repp & N. N. Singh (Eds.), *Perspectives on the use of nonaversive and aversive interventions for persons with developmental disabilities* (pp. 273–286). Sycamore, IL: Sycamore Publishing.

Dunst, C. J., Leet, H. E., & Trivette, C. M. (1988). Family resources, personal well-being, and early intervention. *Journal of Special Education, 22,* 108–116.

Dunst, C. J., McWilliam, R. A., & Holbert, K. (1986). Assessment of preschool classroom environments. *Diagnostique, 11,* 212–232.

Dunst, C. J., Snyder, S. W., & Mankinen, M. (1989). Efficacy of early intervention. In M. C. Wang, M. C. Reynolds, & H. J. Walberg (Eds.), *Handbook of special education: Research and practice, Volume 3: Low incidence conditions* (pp. 259–294). Elmsford, NY: Pergamon.

Dunst, C. J., & Trivette, C. M. (1987). Enabling and empowering families: Conceptual and intervention issues. *School Psychology Review, 16,* 443–456.

Dunst, C. J., Trivette, C. M., & Deal, A. (1988). *Enabling and empowering families: Principles and guidelines for practice.* Cambridge, MA: Brookline.

Dupaul, G. J., & Barkley, R. A. (1990). Medication therapy. In R. A. Barkley, *Attention-deficit hyperactivity disorder: A handbook for diagnosis and treatment* (pp. 573–612). New York: Guilford.

Durand, V. M., & Mindell, J. A. (1990). Behavioral treatment of multiple childhood sleep disorders: Effects on child and family. *Behavior Modification, 14,* 37–49.

Esposito, B. G. (1987). The effects of preschool integration on the development of nonhandicapped children. *Journal of the Division of Early Childhood, 12,* 31–46.

Etzel, B. C., LeBlanc, J. M., Schilmoeller, K. J., & Stella, M. E. (1981). Stimulus control procedures in the education of young children. In S. W. Bijou & R. Ruiz (Eds.), *Behavior modification: Contribution to education* (pp. 3–37). Hillsdale, NJ: Erlbaum.

Evans, I. M. (1986). Response structure and the triple-response-mode concept. In R. O. Nelson & S. C. Hayes (Eds.), *Conceptual foundations of behavioral assessment* (pp. 131–155). New York: Guilford.

Evans, I. M., & Meyer, L. H. (1985). *An educative approach to behavior problems: A practical decision model for interventions with severely handicapped learners.* Baltimore: Brookes.

Evans, I. M., & Nelson, R. O. (1986). Assessment of children. In A. R. Ciminero, K. S. Calhoun, & H. E. Adams (Eds.), *Handbook of behavioral assessment* (2nd ed., pp. 601–630). New York: Wiley.

Farran, D. C. (1990). Effects of intervention with disadvantaged and disabled children: A decade review. In S. J. Meisels & J. P. Shonkoff (Eds.), *Handbook of early intervention* (pp. 501–539). New York: Cambridge University Press.

Fawcett, S. B., Mathews, R. M., & Fletcher, R. K. (1980). Some promising dimensions for behavioral community technology. *Journal of Applied Behavior Analysis, 13,* 505–518.

Federal Emergency Management Agency. (1988). *Preadolescent firesetter handbook: Ages 0–7.* Washington, DC: US Fire Administration, US Government Printing Office.

Ferber, R. (1985). *Solve your child's sleep problems.* New York: Simon & Schuster.

Field, T. (1984). Play behaviors of handicapped children who have friends. In T. Field, J. L. Roopnarine, & M. Segal (Eds.), *Friendships in normal and handicapped children* (pp. 153–162). Norwood, NJ: Ablex.

Firestone, P. (1976). The effects and side effects of timeout on an aggressive nursery school child. *Journal of Behavior Therapy and Experimental Psychiatry, 6,* 79–81.

Fiske, D. W. (1982). Convergent-discriminant validation in measurements and research strategies. In D. Brinberg & L. Kidder (Eds.), *Forms of validity in research* (pp. 77–92). San Francisco: Jossey-Bass.

Flanagan, S., Adams, H. E., & Forehand, R. (1979). A comparison of four instructional techniques for teaching parents to use time-out. *Behavior Therapy, 10,* 94–102.

Fleiss, J. L. (1981). *Statistical methods for rates and proportions* (2nd ed.). New York: Wiley.

Forehand, R., & McMahon, R. J. (1981). *Helping the noncompliant child: A clinician's guide to parent training.* New York: Guilford.

Forsythe, W. I., & Redmond, A. (1974). Enuresis and spontaneous cure rate: Study of 1129 enuretics. *Archives of Disease in Childhood, 49,* 259–263.

Foster, S. L., & Cone, J. D. (1986). Design and use of direct observation. In A. R. Ciminero, K. S. Calhoun, & H. E. Adams (Eds.), *Handbook of behavioral assessment* (2nd ed., pp. 253–354). New York: Wiley.

Fowler, S. A. (1986). Peer-monitoring and self-monitoring: Alternatives to traditional teacher management. *Exceptional Children, 52,* 573–581.

Fowler, S. A., & Baer, D. M. (1981). "Do I have to be good all day?" The timing of delayed reinforcement as a factor in generalization. *Journal of Applied Behavior Analysis, 14,* 13–24.

Fox, J., Shores, R., Lindeman, D., & Strain, P. (1986). Maintaining social initiations of withdrawn handicapped and non-handicapped preschoolers through a response-dependent fading tactic. *Journal of Abnormal Child Psychology, 14,* 387–396.

Foxx, R. M., & Azrin, N. H. (1973). *Toilet training the retarded: A rapid program for day and nighttime independent toileting.* Champaign, IL: Research Press.

Foxx, R. M., & Shapiro, S. T. (1978). The timeout ribbon: A nonexclusionary timeout procedure. *Journal of Applied Behavior Analysis, 11,* 125–143.

Frankel, F., & Weiner, H. (1990). The Child Conflict Index: Factor analysis, reliability, and validity for clinic-referred and non-referred children. *Journal of Clinical Child Psychology, 19,* 239–248.

Freeman, B. J., Roy, R. R., & Hemmick, S. (1976). Extinction of a phobia of physical examination in a seven-year-old mentally retarded boy—A case study. *Behaviour Research and Therapy, 14,* 63–64.

Frentz, C., & Kelley, M. L. (1986). Parents' acceptance of reductive treatment methods: The influence of problem severity and perception of child behavior. *Behavior Therapy, 17,* 75–81.

Friedlander, S., Weiss, D. S., & Traylor, J. (1986). Assessing the influence of maternal depression on the validity of the child behavior checklist. *Journal of Abnormal Child Psychology, 14,* 123–133.

Fuchs, L. S., & Fuchs, D. (1986). Linking assessment to instructional interventions: An overview. *School Psychology Review, 15,* 318–323.

Furlong, M. J., & Wampold, B. E. (1982). Intervention effects and relative variation as dimensions in experts' use of visual inference. *Journal of Applied Behavior Analysis, 15,* 415–421.

Galagan, J. E. (1985). Psychoeducational testing: Turn out the lights, the party's over. *Exceptional Children, 52,* 288–299.

Gallagher, J. J., & Ramey, C. T. (Eds.). (1987). *The malleability of children.* Baltimore: Brookes.

Garbarino, J., & Stott, F. M. (1989). *What children can tell us.* San Francisco: Jossey-Bass.

Garbarino, J., & Whittaker, J. (Eds.). (1982). *Children & families in the social environment.* New York: Aldine.

Garmezy, N. (1985). Stress-resistant children: The search for protective factors. In J. E. Stevenson (Ed.), *Recent research in developmental psychopathology* (pp. 213–233). New York: Pergamon.

Garvey, W. P., & Hegrenes, J. R. (1966). Desensitization techniques in the treatment of school phobia. *American Journal of Orthopsychiatry, 36,* 147–152.

Gelfand, D. M., & Hartmann, D. P. (1984). *Child behavior analysis and therapy* (2nd ed.). New York: Pergamon.

Gelfand, D. M., Jenson, W. R., & Drew, C. J. (1982). *Understanding child behavior disorders.* New York: Holt, Rinehart, & Winston.

Gerber, M. M., & Semmel, M. I. (1984). Teacher as imperfect test: Reconceptualizing the referral process. *Educational Psychologist, 19,* 137–148.

Gersten, R., Carnine, D., & White, W. A. T. (1984). The pursuit of clarity: Direct instruction and applied behavioral analysis. In W. L. Heward, T. E. Heron, & J. Trap-Porter (Eds.), *Focus on behavioral analysis in education* (pp. 38–57). Columbus, OH: Merrill.

Gibbs, J. T., & Huang, L. N. (1989). *Children of color: Psychological interventions with minority youth.* San Francisco: Jossey-Bass.

Giebenhain, J. E., & O'Dell, S. L. (1984). Evaluation of a parent-training manual for reducing children's fear of the dark. *Journal of Applied Behavior Analysis, 17,* 121–125.

Gottman, J. (1977). The effects of a modeling film on social isolation in preschool children: A methodological investigation. *Journal of Abnormal Child Psychology, 5,* 69–78.

Gottman, J. M. (1986). Merging social cognition and social behavior. *Monographs of the Society for Research in Child Development.* Serial no. 213, *51*(22).

Graden, J. L., Zins, J. E., & Curtis, M. J. (Eds.) (1988). *Alternative educational delivery systems: Enhancing instructional options for all students.* Washington, DC: National Association of School Psychologists.

Graziano, A. M., & Mooney, K. C. (1980). Family self-control instruction for children's nighttime fear reduction. *Journal of Consulting and Clinical Psychology, 48*(2), 206–213.

Graziano, A. M., & Mooney, K. C. (1982). Behavioral treatment of "night fears" in children: Maintenance of improvement at 2½- to 3-year follow-up. *Journal of Consulting and Clinical Psychology, 50*(4), 598–599.

Graziano, A. M., Mooney, K. C., Huber, C., & Ignasiak, D. (1979). Self-control instruction for children's fear reduction. *Journal of Behavior Therapy and Experimental Psychiatry, 10,* 221–227.

Green, R. B., Hardison, W. L., & Greene, B. F. (1984). Turning the table on advice programs for parents: Using placemats to enhance family interaction at restaurants. *Journal of Applied Behavior Analysis, 17,* 497–508.

Greene, B. F., Clark, H. B., & Risley, T. R. (1977). *Shopping with children: Advice for parents.* Novato, CA: Academic Therapy Publications. (Available from FMHI Publications, Florida Mental Health Institute, University of South Florida, Tampa, FL 33612.)

Greenwood, C. R., Delquadri, J. C., & Hall, V. R. (1984). Opportunities to respond and student academic performance. In W. L. Heward, T. E. Heron, D. S. Hill, & J. Trap-Porter (Eds.), *Focus on behavior analysis in education* (pp. 58–88). Columbus, OH: Merrill.

Greenwood, C. R., Hops, H., Todd, N. M., & Walker, H. M. (1982). Behavior change targets in the assessment and treatment of socially withdrawn preschool children. *Behavioral Assessment, 4,* 273–297.

Greenwood, C. R., Walker, H. M., Todd, N. M., & Hops, H. (1981). Normative and descriptive analysis of preschool free play social interaction rates. *Journal of Pediatric Psychology, 6,* 343–367.

Greenwood, K. M., & Matyas, T. A. (1990). Problems with the application of interrupted time series analysis for brief single subject data. *Behavioral Assessment, 12,* 355–370.

Gresham, F. M. (1989). Assessment of treatment integrity in school consultation/prereferral intervention. *School Psychology Review, 18,* 37–50.

Gresham, F. M. (1991). Conceptualizing behavior disorders in terms of resistance to intervention. *School Psychology Review, 20,* 23–36.

Gresham, F. M., & Gresham, G. N. (1982). Interdependent, dependent, and independent group contingencies for controlling disruptive behavior. *The Journal of Special Education, 16,* 101–110.

Griest, D. L., Forehand, R., Rogers, T., Breiner, J., Furey, W., & Williams, C. A. (1982). Effects of parent enhancement therapy on the treatment outcome and generalization of a parent training program. *Behavior Research and Therapy, 20,* 429–436.

Griffith, R. G. (1983). The administrative issues: An ethical and legal perspective. In S. Axelrod & J. Apsche (Eds.), *The effects of punishment on human behavior* (pp. 317–338). San Diego, CA: Academic Press.

Grigg, N. C., Snell, M. E., & Loyd, B. (1989). Visual analysis of student data: A qualitative analysis of teacher decision making. *Journal of the Association for Persons with Severe Handicaps, 14,* 23–32.

Guralnick, M. J. (1981). Programmatic factors affecting child–child social interactions in mainstreamed preschool programs. *Exceptional Education Quarterly, 1,* 71–91.

Guralnick, M. J. (1986). The peer relationships of young handicapped and nonhandicapped children. In P. S. Strain, M. J. Guralnick, & H. M. Walker (Eds.), *Children's social behavior: Development, assessment, and modification* (pp. 93–140). San Diego, CA: Academic Press.

Guralnick, M. J., & Groom, J. M. (1987). The peer relations of mildly delayed and nonhandicapped preschool children in mainstreamed playgroups. *Child Development, 58,* 1556–1572.

Guralnick, M. J., & Groom, J. M. (1988). Friendships of preschool children in mainstreamed playgroups. *Developmental Psychology, 24,* 595–604.

Gutkin, T. B., & Curtis, M. J. (1982). School-based consultation: Theory and techniques. In C. R. Reynolds & T. B. Gutkin (Eds.), *Handbook of School Psychology* (pp. 796–828). New York: Wiley.

Gutkin, T. B., & Curtis, M. J. (1990). School-based consultation: Theory, techniques, and research. In C. R. Reynolds & T. B. Gutkin (Eds.), *Handbook of School Psychology* (pp. 577–611). New York: Wiley.

Hall, J. D., & Barnett, D. W. (1991). Classification of risk status in preschool screening: A comparison of alternative measures. *Journal of Psychoeducational Assessment, 9,* 152–159.

Hall, R. V., & Hall, M. C. (1980a). *How to use systematic attention and approval.* Austin, TX: Pro-ed.

Hall, R. V., & Hall, M. C. (1980b). *How to use planned ignoring.* Austin, TX: Pro-ed.

Hall, R. V., & Hall, M. C. (1980c). *How to select reinforcers.* Austin, TX: Pro-ed.

Hall, R. V., & Van Houten, R. (1983). *Managing behavior Part 1. Behavior modification: The measurement of behavior.* Austin, TX: Pro-ed.

Halle, J. W., Alpert, C. L., & Anderson, S. R. (1984). Natural environment language assessment and intervention with severely impaired preschoolers. *Topics in Early Childhood Special Education, 4,* 36–56.

Halle, J. W., Baer, D. M., & Spradlin, J. E. (1981). Teachers' generalized use of delay as a stimulus control procedure to increase language use in handicapped children. *Journal of Applied Behavior Analysis, 14,* 389–409.

Hamilton, S. B., & MacQuiddy, S. L. (1984). Self-administered behavioral parent training: Enhancement of treatment efficacy using a time-out signal seat. *Journal of Clinical Child Psychology, 13,* 61–69.

Hampel, N. T. (1991). *A teacher interview as a screening tool for a preschool population.* Unpublished dissertation, University of Cincinnati.

Haring, N. G. (Ed.). (1988). *Generalization for students with severe handicaps: Strategies and solutions.* Seattle, WA: University of Washington Press.

Haring, N. G., Liberty, K. A., & White, O. R. (1980). Rules for data-based strategy decisions in instructional programs. In W. Sailor, B. Wilcox, & L. Brown (Eds.), *Methods of instruction for severely handicapped students* (pp. 159–192). Baltimore: Brookes.

Harms, T., & Clifford, R. C. (1980). *Early childhood environment rating scale.* New York: Teachers College Press.

Harris, K. R. (1985). Definitional, parametric, and procedural considerations in timeout interventions and research. *Exceptional Children, 51,* 279–288.

Hart, B. (1985). Naturalistic language training techniques. In S. F. Warren & A. Rogers-Warren (Eds.), *Teaching functional language* (pp. 63–85). Austin, TX: Pro-Ed.

Hart, B., & Risley, T. R. (1975). Incidental teaching of language in the preschool. *Journal of Applied Behavior Analysis, 8,* 411-420.

Hart, B., & Risley, T. R. (1980). In vivo language interventions: Unanticipated general effects. *Journal of Applied Behavior Analysis, 13,* 407–432.

Hart, B., & Risley, T. R. (1982). *How to use incidental teaching for elaborating language.* Austin, TX: Pro-ed.

Hart, S. N. (1991). From property to person status: Historical perspective on children's rights. *American Psychologist, 46,* 53–59.

Hartman, A. (1978, October). Diagrammatic assessment of family relationships. *Social Casework,* pp. 465–476.

Hartmann, D. P. (1984). Assessment strategies. In D. H. Barlow & M. Hersen (Eds.), *Single case experimental designs: Strategies for studying behavior change* (2nd ed., pp. 107–139). New York: Pergamon.

Harvey, P., Forehand, R., Brown, C., & Holmes, T. (1988). The prevention of sexual abuse: Examination of the effectiveness of a program with kindergarten-age children. *Behavior Therapy, 19,* 429–435.

Hawkins, R. P. (1986). Selection of target behaviors. In R. O. Nelson & S. C. Hayes (Eds.), *Conceptual foundations of behavioral assessment* (pp. 331–385). New York: Guilford.

Hay, L. R., Nelson, R. O., & Hay, W. M. (1980). Methodological problems in the use of participant observers. *Journal of Applied Behavior Analysis, 13,* 501–504.

Hayes, L. A. (1976). The use of group contingencies for behavioral control: A review. *Psychological Bulletin, 83,* 628–648.

Hayes, S. C. (1981). Single case experimental designs and empirical clinical practice. *Journal of Consulting and Clinical Psychology, 49,* 193–211.

Hayes, S. C., & Nelson, R. O. (1986). Assessing the effects of therapeutic interventions. In R. O. Nelson & S. C. Hayes (Eds.), *Conceptual foundations of behavioral assessment* (pp. 430–460). New York: Guilford.

Hayes, S. C., Nelson, R. O., & Jarrett, R. B. (1986). Evaluating the quality of behavioral assessment. In R. O. Nelson & S. C. Hayes (Eds.), *Conceptual foundations of behavioral assessment* (pp. 461–503). New York: Guilford.

Hayes, S. C., Nelson, R. O., & Jarrett, R. B. (1987). The treatment utility of assessment: A functional approach to evaluating assessment quality. *American Psychologist, 42,* 963–974.

Haynes, S. N. (1986). The design of intervention programs. In R. O. Nelson & S. C. Hayes (Eds.), *Conceptual foundations of behavioral assessment* (pp. 386–429). New York: Guilford.

Head Start Evaluation, Synthesis, and Utilization Project. (1983). Report No. (OHDS) 83–31184. Washington, DC: U.S. Department of Health and Human Services, Office of Human Development, Administration for Children, Youth and Families.

Hecimovic, A., Fox, J. J., Shores, R. E., & Strain, P. S. (1985). An analysis of developmentally integrated and segregated free play settings and the generalization of newly acquired social behaviors of socially withdrawn preschoolers. *Behavioral Assessment, 7,* 367–388.

Hendrickson, J. M., Strain, P. S., Tremblay, A., & Shores, R. E. (1982). Interactions of behaviorally handicapped children: Functional effects of peer social initiations. *Behavior Modification, 6,* 323–353.

Herrnstein, R. J. (1970). On the law of effect. *Journal of the Experimental Analysis of Behavior, 13,* 243–266.

Hindley, C. B., & Owen, C. F. (1978). The extent of individual changes in I.Q. for ages 6 months and 17 years in a British longitudinal sample. *Journal of Child Psychology and Psychiatry, 19,* 329–350.

Hobbs, N. (1966). Helping disturbed children: Psychological and ecological strategies. *American Psychologist, 21,* 1105–1115.

Hoge, R. D., Meginbir, L., Khan, Y., & Weatherall, D. (1985). A multitrait-multimethod analysis of the Preschool Behavior Questionnaire. *Journal of Abnormal Child Psychology, 13,* 119–127.

Honzik, M. P., Macfarlane, J. W., & Allen, L. (1948). The stability of mental test performance between two and eighteen years. *Journal of Experimental Education,* 309–324.

Hopkins, B. L., & Hermann, J. A. (1976). Evaluating interobserver reliability of interval data. *Journal of Applied Behavior Analysis, 10,* 121–126.

Hops, H., Fleischman, D., Guild, J., Paine, S., Street, A., Walker, H. M., & Greenwood, C. R. (1978). *Procedures for etablishing effective relationships skills (PEERS).* Eugene, OR: Center at Oregon for Research in the Behavioral Education of the Handicapped, University of Oregon.

Horner, R. D., & Baer, D. M. (1978). Multiple probe technique: A variation of the multiple baseline design. *Journal of Applied Behavior Analysis, 11,* 189–196.

Horner, R. H., Dunlap, G., & Koegel, R. L. (Eds.). (1988). *Generalization and maintenance: Life style changes in applied settings.* Baltimore: Brookes.

Hresko, W. P., Reid, D. K., Hammill, D. D., Ginsburg, H. P., & Baroody, A. J. (1988). *SCREEN: Screening Children for Early Educational Needs.* Austin, TX: Pro-ed.

Humphreys, L., Forehand, R., McMahon, R., & Roberts, M. (1978). Parental behavioral training to modify child compliance: Effects on untreated siblings. *Behavior Therapy and Experimental Psychiatry, 9,* 235–238.

Isaacs, C. D. (1982). Treatment of child abuse: A review of the behavioral interventions. *Journal of Applied Behavior Analysis, 15,* 273–294.

Iwata, B. A., Vollmer, T. R., & Zarcone, J. R. (1990). The experimental (functional) analysis of behavior disorders: Methodology, applications, and limitations. In A. C. Repp & N. N. Singh (Eds.), *Perspective on the use of nonaversive and aversive interventions for persons with developmental disabilities* (pp. 301–330). Sycamore, IL: Sycamore Publishing.

Jackson, H. J., & King, N. J. (1981). The emotive imagery treatment of a child's trauma-induced phobia. *Journal of Behavior Therapy and Experimental Psychiatry, 12,* 325–328.

Jacobson, J. M., Bushell, D., Jr. & Risley, T. (1969). Switching requirements in a Head Start classroom. *Journal of Applied Behavior Analysis, 2,* 43–47.

James, S. D., & Egel, A. L. (1986). A direct prompting strategy for increasing reciprocal interactions between handicapped and nonhandicapped siblings. *Journal of Applied Behavior Analysis, 19,* 173–186.

Jersild, A. T., & Holmes, F. B. (1935). Methods of overcoming children's fears. *Journal of Psychology, 1,* 75–104.

Jewett, J., & Clark, H. B. (1979). Teaching preschoolers to use appropriate dinnertime conversation: An analysis of generalization from school to home. *Behavior Therapy, 10,* 589–605.

Johnson, J. E., Christie, J. F., & Yawkey, T. D. (1987). *Play and early childhood development.* Glenview, IL: Scott, Foresman.

Johnson-Martin, N. M., Attermeier, S. M., & Hacker, B. (1990). *The Carolina Curriculum for Preschoolers with Special Needs.* Baltimore: Brookes.

Johnston, J. M., & Pennypacker, H. S. (1980). *Strategies and tactics of human behavioral research.* Hillsdale, NJ: Erlbaum.

Jones, R. T., & Kazdin, A. E. (1980). Teaching children how and when to make emergency telephone calls. *Behavior Therapy, 11,* 509–521.

Kanfer, F. H. (1985). Target selection for clinical change programs. *Behavioral Assessment, 7,* 7–20.

Kanfer, F. H., & Gaelick, L. (1986). Self-management methods. In F. H. Kanfer & A. P. Goldstein (Eds.), *Helping people change: A textbook of methods* (3rd ed., pp. 283–345). New York: Pergamon.

Kanfer, F. H., & Grimm, L. G. (1977). Behavior analysis: Selecting target behaviors in the interview. *Behavior Modification, 1,* 7–28.

Kanfer, F. H., & Karoly, P. (1982). The psychology of self-management: Abiding issues and tentative directions. In P. Karoly & F. H. Kanfer (Eds.), *Self-management and behavior change: From theory to practice* (pp. 571–599). New York: Pergamon.

Kanfer, F. H., Karoly, P., & Newman, A. (1975). Reduction of children's fears of the dark by competence-related and situational threat-related verbal cues. *Journal of Consulting and Clinical Psychology, 43*(2), 251–258.

Kazdin, A. E. (1977). Assessing the clinical or applied significance of behavior change through social validation. *Behavior Modification, 1,* 427–452.

Kazdin, A. E. (1980). Acceptability of alternative treatments for deviant child behavior. *Journal of Applied Behavior Analysis, 13,* 259–273.

Kazdin, A. E. (1982). The token economy: A decade later. *Journal of Applied Behavior Analysis, 15,* 431–445.

Kazdin, A. E. (1984). *Behavior modification in applied settings* (3rd ed.). Homewood, IL: Dorsey.

Kazdin, A. E. (1985). Selection of target behaviors: The relationship of treatment focus to clinical dysfunction. *Behavior Assessment, 7,* 33–47.

Kazdin, A. E., & Mascitelli, S. (1980). The opportunity to earn oneself off a token system as a reinforcer for attentive behavior. *Behavior Therapy, 11,* 68–78.

Keenan, P. A., & Lachar, D. (1988). Screening preschoolers

with special problems: Use of the Personality Inventory for Children (PIC). *Journal of School Psychology, 26,* 1–11.

Kelley, M. L. (1990). *School-home notes: Promoting children's classroom success.* New York: Guilford.

Kelley, M. L., & Carper, L. B. (1988). Home-based reinforcement procedures. In J. Witt, S. N. Elliott, & F. M. Gresham (Eds.), *Handbook of behavior therapy in education* (pp. 419–438). New York: Plenum.

Kelly, G. A. (1955). *The psychology of personal constructs* (Vols. I & II). New York: Basic Books.

Kerr, M. M., & Nelson, C. M. (1983). *Strategies for managing behavior problems in the classroom.* Columbus, OH: Merrill.

Klorman, R., Hilpert, P. L., Michael, R., LaGana, C., & Sveen, O. D. (1980). Effects of coping and mastery modeling on experienced and inexperienced pedodontic patients' disruptiveness. *Behavior Therapy, 11,* 156–168.

Koegel, R. L., & Koegel, L. K. (1988). Generalized responsivity and pivotal behaviors. In R. H. Horner, G. Dunlap, & R. L. Koegel (Eds.), *Generalization and maintenance* (pp. 41–66). Baltimore: Brookes.

Koenig, C. H. (1972). *Charting the future course of behavior.* Unpublished doctoral dissertation, University of Kansas.

Kohler, F. W., & Fowler, S. A. (1985). Training prosocial behaviors to young children: An analysis of reciprocity with untrained peers. *Journal of Applied Behavior Analysis, 18,* 187–200.

Kolko, D. J. (1983). Multicomponent parental treatment of firesetting in a six year old boy. *Journal of Behavior Therapy and Experimental Psychiatry, 14,* 349–353.

Kolko, D. J., & Kazdin, A. E. (1989a). Assessment of dimensions of childhood firesetting among patients and nonpatients: The firesetting risk interview. *Journal of Abnormal Child Psychology, 17,* 157–176.

Kolko, D. J., & Kazdin, A. E. (1989b). The children's firesetting interview with psychiatrically referred and nonreferred children. *Journal of Abnormal Child Psychology, 17,* 609–624.

Konarski, E. A., Jr., Johnson, M. R., Crowell, C. R., & Whitman, T. L. (1980). Response deprivation and reinforcement in applied settings: A preliminary analysis. *Journal of Applied Behavior Analysis, 13,* 595–609.

Konarski, E. A., Jr., Johnson, M. R., Crowell, C. R., & Whitman, T. L. (1981). An alternative approach to reinforcement for applied researchers: Response deprivation. *Behavior Therapy, 12,* 653–666.

Koocher, G. P. (1976), *Children's rights and the mental health professions.* New York: Wiley.

Krantz, P. J., & Risley, T. R. (1977). Behavioral ecology in the classroom. In K. D. O'Leary & S. G. O'Leary (Eds.), *Classroom management: The successful use of behavior modification* (pp. 349–366). New York: Pergamon.

Kratochwill, T. R. (1977). N = 1: An alternative research strategy for school psychologists. *Journal of School Psychology, 15,* 239–249.

Kratochwill, T. R. (1978). Foundations of time series research. In T. R. Kratochwill (Ed.), *Single subject research: Strategies for evaluating change* (pp. 1–100). San Diego, CA: Academic Press.

Kratochwill, T. R. (1981). *Selective mutism: Implications for research and treatment.* Hillsdale, NJ: Erlbaum.

Kratochwill, T. R. (1985). Selection of target behaviors in behavioral consultation. *Behavioral Assessment, 7,* 49–61.

Kratochwill, T. R., & Bergan, J. R. (1990). *Behavioral consultation in applied settings: An individual guide.* New York: Plenum.

Kratochwill, T. R., & Morris, R. J. (Eds.). (1991). *The practice of child therapy* (2nd ed.). New York: Pergamon Press.

Krauss, M. W., & Jacobs, F. (1990). Family assessment: Purposes and techniques. In S. J. Meisels & J. P. Shonkoff (Eds.), *Handbook of early intervention* (pp. 303–325). New York: Cambridge University Press.

Kubany, E. S., Weiss, L. E., & Sloggett, B. B. (1971). The good behavior clock: A reinforcement/timeout procedure for reducing disruptive classroom behavior. *Journal of Behavior Therapy and Experimental Psychiatry, 1,* 173–179.

Labbe, E. E., & Williamson, D. A. (1984). Behavioral treatment of elective mutism: A review of the literature. *Clinical Psychology Review, 4,* 273–292.

La Greca, A. M., & Stark, P. (1986). Naturalistic observations of children's social behavior. In P. S. Strain, M. J. Guralnick, & H. M. Walker (Eds.), *Children's social behavior: Development, assessment, and modification* (pp. 181–213). San Diego, CA: Academic Press.

Lahey, B. B., Gendrich, J. G., Gendrich, S. I., Schnelle, J. F., Gant, D. S., & McNees, M. P. (1977). An evaluation of daily report cards with minimal teacher and parent contacts as an efficient method of classroom intervention. *Behavior Modification, 1,* 381–394.

Laosa, L. M., & Sigel, I. E. (Eds.). (1982). *Families as learning environments for children.* New York: Plenum.

LaVigna, G. W., & Donnellan, A. M. (1986). *Alternatives to punishment: Solving behavior problems with non-aversive strategies.* New York: Irvington.

Lazarus, A. A., & Abramovitz, A. (1962). The use of "emotive imagery" in the treatment of children's phobias. *Journal of Mental Science, 108,* 191–195.

LeBlanc, J. M., Etzel, B. C., & Domash, M. A. (1978). A functional curriculum for early intervention. In K. E. Allen, V. A. Holm, & R. L. Schiefelbusch (Eds.), *Early intervention — A team approach* (pp. 331–381). Baltimore: University Park Press.

Lefebvre, D., & Strain, P. S. (1989). Effects of a group contingency on the frequency of social interactions among autistic and nonhandicapped preschool children: Making LRE efficacious. *Journal of Early Intervention, 13,* 329–341.

Leitenberg, H., & Callahan, E. J. (1973). Reinforced practice and reduction of different kinds of fears in adults and children. *Behaviour Research and Therapy, 11,* 19–30.

LeLaurin, K., & Risley, T. R. (1972). The organization of day-care environments: "Zone" versus "man-to-man" staff assignments. *Journal of Applied Behavior Analysis, 5,* 225–232.

LeMay, D., Griffin, P., & Sunford, A. (1981). *Learning Accomplishment Profile: Diagnostic Edition* (rev). Wintson-Salem, NC: Kaplaw School Supply.

Lentz, F. E. (1988). Reductive procedures. In J. C. Witt, S. N. Elliott, & F. M. Gresham (Eds.), *Handbook of behavior therapy in education* (pp. 439–468). New York: Plenum.

Liberty, K. (1988). Characteristics and foundations of decision rules. In N. G. Haring (Ed.), *Generalization for students with severe handicaps: Strategies and solutions* (pp. 53–72). Seattle, WA: University of Washington Press.

Linehan, M. M. (1980). Content validity: Its relevance to behavioral assessment. *Behavioral Assessment, 2,* 147–159.

Lipton, H. (1980). Rapid reinstatement of speech using stimulus fading with a selectively mute child. *Journal of Behavior Therapy and Experimental Psychiatry, 11,* 147–149.

Litow, L., & Pumroy, D. K. (1975). A review of classroom group-oriented contingencies. *Journal of Applied Behavior Analysis, 8,* 341–347.

Lovaas, O. I. (1981). *Teaching developmentally disabled children: The me book.* Austin, TX: Pro-ed.

Lovaas, O. I. (1987). Behavioral treatment and normal educational and intellectual functioning in young autistic children. *Journal of Consulting and Clinical Psychology, 55,* 3–9.

Lovaas, O. I., & Favell, J. E. (1987). Protection for clients undergoing aversive/restrictive interventions. *Education and Treatment of Children, 10,* 311–325.

McCall, R. B., Appelbaum, M. I., & Hogarty, P. S. (1973). Developmental changes in mental performance. *Monographs of the Society for Research in Child Development, 38* (3, Whole No. 150).

MacDonald, J. D. (1985). Language through conversation: A model for intervention with language-delayed persons. In S. F. Warren & A. K. Rogers-Warren (Eds.), *Teaching functional language: Generalization and maintenance of language skills* (pp. 89–122). Austin, TX: Pro-ed.

McDonnell, A., & Hardman, M. (1988). A synthesis of "best practice" guidelines for early childhood services. *Journal of the Division for Early Childhood, 12,* 328–341.

McDowell, J. J. (1982). The importance of Herrnstein's mathematical statement of the law of effect for behavior therapy. *American Psychologist, 37,* 771–779.

Mace, F. C., Hock, M. L., Lalli, J. S., West, B. J., Belfiore, P., Pinter, E., & Brown, D. K. (1988). Behavioral momentum in the treatment of noncompliance. *Journal of Applied Behavior Analysis, 21,* 123–141.

Mace, F. C., & Kratochwill, T. R. (1988). Self-monitoring.

In J. C. Witt, S. N. Elliott, & F. M. Gresham (Eds.), *Handbook of behavior therapy in education* (pp. 489–522). New York: Plenum.

Mace, F. C., Page, T. J., Ivancic, M. T., & O'Brien, S. (1986). Effectiveness of brief time-out with and without contingent delay: A comparative analysis. *Journal of Applied Behavior Analysis, 19,* 79–86.

McEvoy, M. A. (1990). The organization of caregiving environments: Critical issues and suggestions for future research. *Education and Treatment of Children, 13,* 269–273.

McEvoy, M. A., Nordquist, V. M., Twardosz, S., Heckman, K. A., Wehby, J. H., & Denny, R. K. (1988). Promoting autistic children's peer interaction in an integrated early childhood setting using affection activities. *Journal of Applied Behavior Analysis, 21,* 193–200.

McEvoy, M. A., Twardosz, S., & Bishop, N. (1990). Affection activities: Procedures for encouraging young children with handicaps to interact with their peers. *Education and Treatment of Children, 13,* 159–167.

McGee, R., Williams, S., & Silva, P. A. (1984). Background characteristics of aggressive, hyperactive, and aggressive-hyperactive boys. *Journal of the American Academy of Child Psychiatry, 23,* 280–284.

McGillicuddy-DeLisi, A. V. (1985). The relationship between parental beliefs and children's cognitive level. In I. E. Sigel (Ed.), *Parental belief systems: The psychological consequences for children* (pp. 7–24). New York: Plenum.

McGinnis, E., & Goldstein, A. P. (1990). *Skill-streaming in early childhood: Teaching prosocial skills to the preschool and kindergarten child.* Champaign, IL: Research Press.

McGrath, P., Marshall, P. G., & Prior, K. (1979). A comprehensive treatment program for a fire setting child. *Journal of Behavior Therapy and Experimental Psychiatry, 10,* 69–72.

McLaughlin, T. F., & Williams, R. L. (1988). The token economy. In J. C. Witt, S. N. Elliott, & F. M. Gresham (Eds.), *Handbook of behavior therapy in education* (pp. 469–487). New York: Plenum.

McLean, M., & Odom, S. (1988). *Least restrictive environment and social integration.* Reston, VA: Division of Early Childhood, Council for Exceptional Children.

McMahon, R. J. (1987). Some current issues in the behavioral assessment of conduct disordered children and their families. *Behavioral Assessment, 9,* 235–252.

McMahon, R. J., & Wells, K. C. (1989). Conduct disorders. In E. J. Mash & R. A. Barkley (Eds.), *Treatment of childhood disorders* (pp. 73–132). New York: Guilford.

Macmann, G., & Barnett, D. (1984). The validity of two measures of adaptive behavior. *Journal of Psychoeducational Assessment, 2,* 239–247.

Macmann, G. M., & Barnett, D. W. (1985). Discrepancy score analysis: A computer simulation of stability. *Journal of Psychoeducational Assessment, 3,* 363–375.

Macmann, G. M., Barnett, D. W., Burd, S. A., Jones, T., LeBuffe, P. A., O'Malley, D., Shade, D. B., & Wright, A. (in press). The construct validity of the Child Behavior Checklist: Effects of item overlap on second order factor structure. *Psychological Assessment: A Journal of Consulting and Clinical Psychology.*

Macmann, G. M., Barnett, D. W., Sharpe, M., Lombard, T. J., & Belton-Kocher, E. (1989). On the actuarial classification of children: Fundamental studies of classification agreement. *The Journal of Special Education, 23,* 127–149.

MacPhee, D., Ramey, C. T., & Yeates, K. O. (1984). Home environment and early cognitive development: Implications for intervention. In A. W. Gottfried (Ed.), *Home environment and early cognitive development: Longitudinal research* (pp. 343–369). San Diego, CA: Academic Press.

Mardell-Czudnowski, C. D., & Goldenberg, D. S. (1990). *Developmental Indicators for the Assessment of Learning-Revised (DIAL-R).* Circle Pines, MN: American Guidance Service.

Marks, I. M. (1969). *Fears and phobias.* San Diego, CA: Academic Press.

Martens, B. K., Halperin, S., Rummel, J. E., & Kilpatrick, D. (1990). Matching theory applied to contingent teacher attention. *Behavioral Assessment, 12,* 139–155.

Martin, J. A. (1989). Personal and interpersonal components

of responsiveness. In M. H. Bornstein (Ed.), *Maternal respon-siveness: Characteristics and consequences* (pp. 5–14). San Francisco: Jossey-Bass.

Martin, R. (1975). *Legal challenges to behavior modification: Trends in schools, mental health, and corrections.* Champaign, IL: Research Press.

Martin, R. (1979). *Educating handicapped children: The legal mandate.* Champaign, IL: Research Press.

Mash, E. J., & Barkley, R. A. (Eds.). (1989). *Treatment of childhood disorders.* New York: Guilford.

Mash, E. J., & Terdal, L. G. (1988). *Behavioral assessment of childhood disorders* (2nd ed.). New York: Guilford.

Mason, S. A., McGee, G. G., Farmer-Dougan, V., & Risley, T. (1989). A practical strategy for ongoing reinforcer assessment. *Journal of Applied Behavior Analysis, 22,* 171–179.

Matson, J. L., & DiLorenzo, T. M. (1984). *Punishment and its alternatives: A new perspective for behavior modification.* New York: Springer.

Matson, J. L., & Ollendick, T. H. (1976). Elimination of low frequency biting. *Behavior Therapy, 7,* 410–412.

Meichenbaum, D., & Goodman, J. (1971). Training impulsive children to talk to themselves: A means of developing self-control. *Journal of Abnormal Psychology, 77,* 115–126.

Meisels, S. J., & Shonkoff, J. P. (Eds.). (1990). *Handbook of early childhood intervention.* New York: Cambridge University Press.

Melamed, B., Hawes, R. R., Heiby, E., & Glick, J. (1975). Use of filmed modeling to reduce uncooperative behavior of children during dental treatment. *Journal of Dental Research, 54,* 797–801.

Melamed, B. G., & Siegel, L. J. (1975). Reduction of anxiety in children facing hospitalization and surgery by use of filmed modeling. *Journal of Consulting and Clinical Psychology, 43*(4), 511–521.

Melton, G. B. (1991). Socialization in the global community: Respect for the dignity of children. *American Psychologist, 46,* 66–71.

Messick, S. (1989). Validity. In R. L. Linn (Ed.), *Educational measurement* (3rd ed., pp. 13–103). New York: Macmillan.

Miller, L. C., Barrett, C. L., & Hampe, E. (1974). Phobias in children in a prescientific era. In A. Davids (Ed.), *Child personality and psychopathology: Current topics* (Vol. I). New York: Wiley.

Miller, N. B., & Cantwell, D. P. (1976). Siblings as therapists: A behavioral approach. *American Journal of Psychiatry, 133*(4), 447–450.

Miltenberger, R. G., & Thiesse-Duffy, E. (1988). Evaluation of home-based programs for teaching personal safety skills to children. *Journal of Applied Behavior Analysis, 21,* 8–87.

Mischel, W. (1981). A cognitive-social learning approach to assessment. In T. V. Merluzzi, C. R. Glass, & M. Genest (Eds.), *Cognitive assessment* (pp. 479–502). New York: Guilford.

Mischel, W. (1984). Convergences and challenges in the search for consistency. *American Psychologist, 39,* 351–364.

Mitchell, A., Seligson, M., & Marx, F. (1989). *Early childhood programs and the public schools: Between promise and practice.* Dover, MA: Auburn House.

Mori, L., & Peterson, L. (1986). Training preschoolers in safety skills to prevent inadvertent injury. *Journal of Clinical Child Psychology, 15,* 106–114.

Morin, C., Ladouceur, R., & Cloutier, R. (1982). Reinforcement procedure in the treatment of reluctant speech. *Journal of Behavior Therapy and Experimental Psychiatry, 13,* 145–147.

Morris, R. J., & Kratochwill, T. R. (1983). *Treating children's fears and phobias: A behavioral approach.* New York: Pergamon.

Morris, R. J., Kratochwill, T. R., & Aldridge, K. (1988). Fears and phobias. In J. C. Witt, S. N. Elliott, & F. M. Gresham (Eds.), *Handbook of behavior therapy in education* (pp. 679–717). New York: Plenum.

Morrow, L. M., & Rand, M. K. (1991). Promoting literacy during play by designing early childhood classroom environments. *The Reading Teacher, 44,* 396–402.

Musselwhite, C. R. (1986). *Adaptive play for special needs children: Strategies to enhance communication and learning.* San Diego, CA: College-Hill Press.

Nash, R. T., Thorpe, H. W., Andrews, M. M., & Davis, K. (1979). A management program for elective mutism. *Psychology in the Schools, 16*(2), 246–253.

National Association for the Education of Young Children. (1986, September). Position statement on developmentally appropriate practice in early childhood programs serving children from birth through age 8. *Young Children,* 4–16.

National Association of School Psychologists. (1987). *Position statement on early intervention in the schools.* Washington, DC: Author.

National Safety Council. (1983). *Accident facts.* Chicago, IL: Author.

Nelson, C. M., & Rutherford, R. B. (1983, February). Timeout revisited: Guidelines for its use in special education. *Exceptional Education Quarterly,* 56–67.

Nelson, R. O., Hay, L. R., Devany, J., & Koslow-Green, L. (1980). The reactivity and accuracy of children's self-monitoring: Three experiments. *Child Behavior Therapy, 2,* 1–24.

Nelson, R. O., & Hayes, S. C. (1986). The nature of behavioral assessment. In R. O. Nelson & S. C. Hayes (Eds.), *Conceptual foundations of behavior assessment* (pp. 1–40). New York: Guilford.

Neuman, S. B., & Roskos, K. (1990). Play, print, and purpose: Enriching play environments for literacy development. *The Reading Teacher, 44,* 214–221.

Nevin, J. A., Mandell, C., & Atak, J. R. (1983). The analysis of behavioral momentum. *Journal of the Experimental Analysis of Behavior, 39,* 49–59.

Niemeyer, J. A., & Fox, J. (1990). Reducing aggressive behavior during car riding through parent-implemented DRO and fading procedures. *Education and Treatment of Children, 13,* 21–35.

Nordquist, V. M., & Twardosz, S. (1990). Preventing behavior problems in early childhood special education classrooms through environmental organization. *Education and Treatment of Children, 13,* 274–287.

Nordquist, V. M., Twardosz, S., & McEvoy, M. A. (1991). Effects of environmental reorganization in classrooms for children with autism. *Journal of Early Intervention, 15,* 135–152.

Nunnally, J. (1978). *Psychometric theory* (2nd ed.). New York: McGraw-Hill.

Obler, M., & Terwilliger, R. F. (1970). Pilot study on the effectiveness of systematic desensitization with neurologically impaired children with phobic disorders. *Journal of Consulting and Clinical Psychology, 34,* 314–318.

O'Connor, R. D. (1969). Modification of social withdrawal through symbolic modeling. *Journal of Applied Behavior Analysis, 2,* 15–22.

O'Connor, R. D. (1972). Relative efficacy of modeling, shaping, and the combined procedures for modification of social withdrawal. *Journal of Abnormal Psychology, 79*(3), 327–334.

Odom, S. L., Bender, M. K., Stein, M. L., Doran, L. P., Houden, P. M., McInnes, M., Gilbert, M. M., Deklyen, M., Speltz, M. L., & Jenkins, J. R. (1988). *The integrated preschool curriculum: Procedures for socially integrating young handicapped and normally developing children.* Seattle: University of Washington Press.

Odom, S. L., Hoyson, M., Jamieson, B., & Strain, P. S. (1985). Increasing handicapped preschoolers' peer social interactions: Cross-setting and component analysis. *Journal of Applied Behavior Analysis, 18*(1), 3–16.

Odom, S. L., & Karnes, M. B. (Eds.). (1988). *Early intervention for infants and children with handicaps: An empirical base.* Baltimore: Brookes.

Odom, S. L., & McEvoy, M. A. (1988). Integration of young children with handicaps and normally developing children. In S. L. Odom & M. B. Karnes (Eds.), *Early intervention for infants and children with handicaps: An empirical base* (pp. 241–267). Baltimore: Brookes.

Odom, S. L., & Strain, P. S. (1984). Peer-mediated approaches to promoting children's social interaction: A review. *Journal of Orthopsychiatry, 54,* 544–557.

Ollendick, T. H., & Francis, G. (1988). Behavioral assessment and treatment of childhood phobias. *Behavior Modification, 12*(2), 165–204.

O'Neill, R. E., Horner, R. H., Albin, R. W., Storey, K., & Sprague, J. R. (1990). *Functional analysis of behavior: A practical assessment guide.* Sycamore, IL: Sycamore Publishing.

Osnes, P. G., Guevremont, D. C., & Stokes, T. F. (1986). If I say I'll talk more, then I will: Correspondence training to increase peer-directed talk by socially withdrawn children. *Behavior Modification, 10,* 287–299.

Pace, G. M., Ivancic, M. T., Edwards, G. L., Iwata, B. A., & Page, T. J. (1985). Assessment of stimulus preference and reinforcer value with profoundly retarded individuals. *Journal of Applied Behavior Analysis, 18,* 249–255.

Page, T. J., & Iwata, B. A. (1986). Interobserver agreement: History, theory, and current methods. In A. Poling & R. W. Fuqua (Eds.), *Research methods in applied behavior analysis* (pp. 99–126). New York: Plenum.

Paine, S. C., Radicchi, J., Rosellini, L. C., Deutchman, L., & Darch, C. B. (1983). *Structuring your classroom for academic success.* Champaign, IL: Research Press.

Panaccione, V. F., & Wahler, R. G. (1986). Child behavior, maternal depression, and social coercion as factors in the quality of child care. *Journal of Abnormal Child Psychology, 14,* 263–278.

Panyan, M. (1980). *How to use shaping.* Austin, TX: Pro-Ed.

Parpal, M., & Maccoby, E. E. (1985). Maternal responsiveness and subsequent child compliance. *Child Development, 56,* 1326–1334.

Parsonson, B. S., & Baer, D. M. (1978). The analysis and presentation of graphic data. In T. R. Kratochwill (Ed.), *Single subject research: Strategies for evaluating change* (pp. 101–165). San Diego, CA: Academic Press.

Parsonson, B. S., & Baer, D. M. (1986). The graphic analysis of data. In A. Poling & W. R. Fuqua (Eds.), *Research methods in applied behavior analysis* (pp. 157–186). New York: Plenum.

Patterson, G. R. (1975). *Professional guide for families and living with children.* Champaign, IL: Research Press.

Patterson, G. R., & Bank, L. (1986). Bootstrapping your way in the nomological thicket. *Behavioral Assessment, 8,* 49–73.

Patterson, G. R., Reid, J. B., Jones, R. R., & Conger, R. E. (1975). *A social learning approach to family intervention* (Vol. 1). Eugene, OR: Castalia.

Pazulinec, R., Meyerrose, M., & Sajwaj, T. (1983). Punishment via response cost. In S. Axelrod & J. Apsche (Eds.), *The effects of punishment on human behavior* (pp. 71–86). San Diego, CA: Academic Press.

Peterson, D. R. (1968). *The clinical study of social behavior.* New York: Appleton-Century-Crofts.

Peterson, L. (1984a). The "Safe at Home" Game: Training comprehensive prevention skills in latchkey children. *Behavior Modification, 8,* 474–494.

Peterson, L. (1984b). Teaching home safety and survival skills to latch-key children: A comparison of two manuals and methods. *Journal of Applied Behavior Analysis, 17,* 279–293.

Peterson, L. (1988). Preventing the leading killer of children: The role of the school psychologist in injury prevention. *School Psychology Review, 17,* 593–600.

Piazza, C. C., & Fisher, W. (1991). A faded bedtime with response cost protocol for treatment of multiple sleep problems in children. *Journal of Applied Behavior Analysis, 24,* 129–140.

Pinkston, E. M., Reese, N. M., LeBlanc, J. M., & Baer, D. M. (1973). Independent control of a preschool child's aggression and peer interaction by contingent teacher attention. *Journal of Applied Behavior Analysis, 6,* 115–124.

Poche, C., Brouwer, R., & Swearingen, M. (1981). Teaching self-protection to young children. *Journal of Applied Behavior Analysis, 14,* 169–176.

Poche, C., Yoder, P., & Miltenberger, R. (1988). Teaching self-protection to children using television techniques. *Journal of Applied Behavior Analysis, 21,* 253–261.

Poling, A., & Ryan, C. (1982). Differential reinforcement-of-other-behavior schedules: Therapeutic applications. *Behavior Modification, 6,* 3–21.

Pomerantz, P. B., Peterson, N. T., Marholin, D., & Stern, S. (1977). The in vivo elimination of a child's water phobia by a paraprofessional at home. *Journal of Behavior Therapy and Experimental Psychiatry, 8,* 417–421.

Porterfield, J. K., Herbert-Jackson, E., & Risley, T. R. (1976). Contingent observation: An effective and acceptable procedure for reducing disruptive behavior of young children in a group setting. *Journal of Applied Behavior Analysis, 9,* 55–64.

Poth, R. L., & Barnett, D. W. (1983). Reduction of a behavioral tic with a preschooler using relaxation and self-control techniques across settings. *School Psychology Review, 12,* 472–475.

Poth, R. L., & Barnett, D. W. (1988). Establishing the limits of interpretive confidence: A validity study of two preschool developmental scales. *School Psychology Review, 17,* 322–330.

Powell, T. H., & Ogle, P. A. (1985). *Brothers and sisters — A special part of exceptional families.* Baltimore: Brookes.

Powers, M. D. (1984). Syndromal diagnosis and the behavioral assessment of childhood disorders. *Child & Family Behavior Therapy, 6,* 1–15.

Premack, D. (1959). Toward empirical behavior laws: Volume I: Positive reinforcement. *Psychological Review, 66,* 219–233.

Project Sunrise. (1989). *Preschool assessment of the classroom environment — Revised.* Morganton, NC: Family, Infant, and Preschool Program, Western Carolina Center.

Prutting, C. A. (1982). Pragmatics as social competence. *Journal of Speech and Hearing Disorders, 47,* 123–134.

Ramey, C. T., & Campbell, F. A. (1987). The Carolina Abedecarian project: An educational experiment. In J. J. Gallagher & C. T. Ramey (Eds.), *The malleability of children* (pp. 127–139): Baltimore: Brookes.

Rao, N., Moely, B. E., & Lockman, J. L. (1987). Increasing social participation in preschool isolates. *Journal of Clinical Child Psychology, 16,* 178–183.

Redmon, W. K., & Farris, H. E. (1987). Application of basic research to the treatment of children with autistic and severely handicapped repertoires. *Education and Treatment of Children, 10,* 326–337.

Reid, J. B. (Ed.). (1978). *A social learning approach to family intervention: Volume 2: Observation in home settings.* Eugene, OR: Castalia.

Reid, J. B. (1985). Behavioral approaches to intervention and assessment with child abusive families. In P. H. Bornstein & A. E. Kazdin (Eds.), *Handbook of clinical behavior therapy with children* (pp. 772–812). Homewood, IL: Dorsey.

Reimers, T., Wacker, D., & Koeppl, G. (1987). Acceptability of behavioral interventions: A review of the literature. *School Psychology Review, 16,* 212–227.

Rekers, G. A. (1984). Ethical issues in child behavior assessment. In T. H. Ollendick & M. Hersen (Eds.), *Child behavior assessment: Principles and procedures* (pp. 244–262). New York: Pergamon.

Repp, A. C., Nieminen, G. S., Olinger, E., & Brusca, R. (1988). Direct observation: Factors affecting the accuracy of observers. *Exceptional Children, 55,* 29–36.

Repp, A. C., & Singh, N. N. (Eds.). (1990). *Perspectives on the use of nonaversive and aversive interventions for persons with developmental disabilities.* Sycamore, IL: Sycamore Publishing.

Rimmerman, A. (1989). Provision of respite care for children with developmental disabilities: Changes in maternal coping and stress over time. *Mental Retardation, 27,* 99–103.

Risley, T. (1972). Spontaneous language and the preschool environment. In J. C. Stanley (Ed.), *Preschool programs for the disadvantaged: Five experimental approaches to early childhood education* (pp. 92–110). Baltimore: Johns Hopkins Press.

Risley, T. R., & Hart, B. H. (1968). Developing correspondence between the non-verbal and verbal behavior of preschool children. *Journal of Applied Behavior Analysis, 1,* 267–281.

Roberts, M. C., & Layfield, D. A. (1987). Promoting child passenger safety: A comparison of two positive methods. *Journal of Pediatric Psychology, 12,* 257–271.

Roberts, M. W. (1982). The effects of warned versus unwarned time out procedures on child noncompliance. *Child & Family Behavior Therapy, 4,* 37–53.

Roberts, M. W. (1985). Praising child compliance: Reinforcement or ritual? *Journal of Abnormal Child Psychology, 13,* 611–629.

Roberts, M. W. (1988). Enforcing chair timeouts with room timeouts. *Behavior Modification, 12*(3), 353–370.

Roberts, M. W., Hatzenbuehler, L. C., & Bean, A. W. (1981). The effects of differential attention and time out on child noncompliance. *Behavior Therapy, 12,* 93–99.

Roberts, M. W., & Powers, S. W. (1988). The Compliance Test. *Behavior Assessment, 10,* 375–398.

Robins, L. N. (1986). Changes in conduct disorder over time. In D. C. Farran & J. D. McKinney (Eds.), *Risk in intellectual and psychosocial development* (pp. 227–259). San Diego, CA: Academic Press.

Rogers-Warren, A. K. (1982). Behavior ecology in classrooms for young, handicapped children. *Topics in Early Childhood Special Education, 2,* 21–32.

Rogers-Warren, A., & Baer, D. M. (1976). Correspondence between saying and doing: Teaching children to share and praise. *Journal of Applied Behavior Analysis, 9,* 335–354.

Rogers-Warren, A., & Warren, S. F. (1980). Mands for verbalization: Facilitating the display of newly trained language in children. *Behavior Modification, 4,* 361–382.

Rolider, A., & Van Houten, R. (1984). The effects of DRO alone and DRO plus reprimands on the undesirable behavior of three children in home settings. *Education and Treatment of Children, 7,* 17–31.

Rolider, A., & Van Houten, R. (1990). The role of reinforcement in reducing inappropriate behavior: Some myths and misconceptions. In A. C. Repp & N. N. Singh (Eds.), *Perspectives on the use of nonaversive and aversive interventions for persons with developmental disabilities* (pp. 119–127). Sycamore, IL: Sycamore Publishing.

Rosen, C. E. (1974). The effects of sociodramatic play on problem-solving behavior among culturally disadvantaged preschool children. *Child Development, 45,* 920–927.

Rosenbaum, M. S., Creedon, D. L., & Drabman, R. S. (1981). Training preschool children to identify emergency situations and make emergency phone calls. *Behavior Therapy, 12,* 425–435.

Rosenfarb, I., & Hayes, S. C. (1984). Social standard setting: The Achilles heel of informational accounts of therapeutic change. *Behavior Therapy, 15,* 515–528.

Rosentiel, A. K., & Scott, D. S. (1977). Four considerations in using imagery techniques with children. *Behavior Therapy and Experimental Psychiatry, 8,* 287–290.

Ross, A. O. (1980). *Psychosocial disorders of children* (2nd ed.). New York: McGraw-Hill.

Rowbury, T. G., Baer, A. M., & Baer, D. M. (1976). Interactions between teacher guidance and contingent access to play in developing preacademic skills of deviant preschool children. *Journal of Applied Behavior Analysis, 9,* 85–104.

Russo, D. C., & Koegel, R. L. (1977). A method for integrating an autistic child into a normal public-school classroom. *Journal of Applied Behavior Analysis, 10,* 579–590.

Rutter, M. (1981). Stress, coping, and development: Some issues and some questions. *Journal of Child Psychology and Psychiatry, 22,* 323–356.

Rutter, M. (1984). Continuities and discontinuities in socio-emotional development: Empirical and conceptual perspectives. In R. M. Emde & J. R. Harmon (Eds.), *Continuities and discontinuities in development* (pp. 41–68). New York: Plenum.

Rutter, M. (1987). Psychosocial resilience and protective mechanisms. *American Journal of Orthopsychiatry, 57,* 316–331.

Sackett, G. P. (1978). Measurement in observational research. In G. P. Sackett (Ed.), *Observing behavior: Volume II: Data collection and analysis methods* (pp. 25–43). Baltimore: University Park Press.

Sainato, D. M., & Lyon, S. R. (1989). Promoting successful mainstreaming transitions for handicapped preschool children. *Journal of Early Intervention, 13,* 305–314.

Sainato, D. M., Maheady, L., & Shook, G. L. (1986). The effects of a classroom manager role on the social interaction patterns and social status of withdrawn kindergarten students. *Journal of Applied Behavior Analysis, 19,* 187–195.

Sainato, D. M., Strain, P. S., Lefebvre, D., & Rapp, N. (1987). Facilitating transition times with handicapped preschool children: A comparison between peer-mediated and antecedent prompt procedures. *Journal of Applied Behavior Analysis, 20,* 285–291.

Sainato, D. M., Strain, P. S., Lefebvre, D., & Rapp, N. (1990). Effects of self-evaluation on the independent work skills of preschool children with disabilities. *Exceptional Children, 56,* 540–549.

Sainato, D. M., Strain, P. S., & Lyon, S. R. (1987). Increasing academic responding of handicapped preschool children during group instruction. *Journal of the Division for Early Childhood, 12,* 23–30.

Saltz, E., Dixon, D., & Johnson, J. (1977). Training disadvantaged preschoolers on various fantasy activities: Effects on cognitive functioning and impulse control. *Child Development, 48,* 367–380.

Saltz, E., & Johnson, J. (1974). Training for thematic-fantasy play in culturally disadvantaged children: Preliminary results. *Journal of Educational Psychology, 66,* 623–630.

Sanders, M. R., & Christensen, A. P. (1985). A comparison of the effects of child management and planned activities training in five parenting environments. *Journal of Abnormal Child Psychology, 13,* 101–117.

Sanders, M. R., & Dadds, M. R. (1982). The effects of planned activities and child management procedures in parent training: An analysis of setting generality. *Behavior Therapy, 13,* 452–461.

Sanders, M. R., & Glynn, T. (1981). Training parents in behavioral self-management: An analysis of generalization and maintenance. *Journal of Applied Behavior Analysis, 14,* 223–237.

Sanders, M. R., & Plant, K. (1989). Programming for generalization to high and low risk parenting situations in families with oppositional developmentally disabled preschoolers. *Behavior Modification, 13,* 283–305.

Sapon-Shevin, M. (1982). Ethical issues in parent training programs. *The Journal of Special Education, 16,* 341–357.

Sattler, J. M. (1988). *Assessment of children* (3rd ed.). San Diego, CA: Author.

Saudargas, R. A. (1980). *The State-Event Classroom Observation System.* Knoxville, TN: University of Tennessee.

Savage, J. E., & Adair, A. V. (1980). Testing minorities: Developing more culturally relevant assessment systems. In R. L. Jones (Ed.), *Black Psychology* (2nd ed.). New York: HarperCollins.

Scarr, S., & Arnett, J. (1987). Malleability: Lessons from intervention and family studies. In J. J. Gallagher & C. T. Ramey (Eds.), *The malleability of children* (pp. 71–84): Baltimore: Brookes.

Schön, D. A. (1983). *The reflective practitioner: How professionals think in action.* New York: Basic Books.

Schrader, C., & Gaylord-Ross, R. (1990). The eclipse of aversive technology: A triadic approach to assessment and treatment. In A. C. Repp & N. N. Singh (Eds.), *Perspectives on the use of nonaversive and aversive interventions for persons with developmental disabilities* (pp. 403–417). Sycamore, IL: Sycamore Publishing.

Schreibman, L., O'Neill, R. E., & Koegel, R. L. (1983). Behavioral training for siblings of autistic children. *Journal of Applied Behavior Analysis, 16,* 129–138.

Schulte, A. C., & Borich, G. D. (1988). False confidence in intervals: Inaccuracies in reporting confidence intervals. *Psychology in the Schools, 25,* 405–412.

Schuster, J. W., & Griffin, A. K. (1990). Using time delay with task analysis. *Teaching Exceptional Children, 22,* 49–53.

Schwebel, M., & Maher, C. A. (Eds.). (1986). *Facilitating cognitive development: International perspectives, programs, and practices.* New York: Haworth Press.

Schweinhart, L. J., Weikart, D. P., & Larner, M. B. (1986). Consequences of three preschool curriculum models through age 15. *Early Childhood Research Quarterly, 1,* 15–45.

Sechrest, L. (1963). Incremental validity: A recommendation. *Educational and Psychological Measurement, 23,* 153–158.

Sechrest, L., West, S. G., Phillips, M. A., Redner, R., & Yeaton, W. (1979). Some neglected problems in evaluation research: Strength and integrity of treatments. In L. Sechrest, S. G. West, M. A. Phillips, R. Redner, & W. Yeaton (Eds.), *Evaluation studies annual review* (pp. 15–35). Newbury Park, CA: Sage.

Seymour, F. W. (1987). Parent management of sleep difficulties in young children. *Behaviour Change, 4,* 39–48.

Shapiro, E. S. (1979). Restitution and positive practice overcorrection in reducing aggressive-disruptive behavior: A long-term follow-up. *Journal of Behavior Therapy and Experimental Psychiatry, 10,* 131–134.

Shearer, D. E., & Shearer, M. S. (1976). The Portage Project: A model for early intervention. In T. D. Tjossen (Ed.), *Intervention strategies for high risk infants and young children* (pp. 335–350). Baltimore: University Park Press.

Shearer, M. S., & Shearer, D. E. (1972, November). The Portage Project: A model for early childhood education. *Exceptional Children,* 210–217.

Shelton, T., & Barkley, R. A. (1990). Clinical, developmental, and biopsychosocial considerations. In R. A. Barkley, *Attention-deficit hyperactivity disorder: A handbook for diagnosis and treatment* (pp. 209–231). New York: Guilford.

Sherburne, S., Utley, B., McConnell, S., & Gannon, J. (1988). Decreasing violent or aggressive theme play among preschool children with behavior disorders. *Exceptional Children, 55,* 166–172.

Sigel, I. E. (1982). The relationship between parental distancing strategies and the child's cognitive behavior. In L. M. Laosa & I. E. Sigel (Eds.), *Families as learning environments for children* (pp. 47–86). New York: Plenum.

Sigel, I. E. (Ed.). (1985). *Parental belief systems: The psychological consequences for children.* Hillsdale, NJ: Erlbaum.

Skinner, B. F. (1953). *Science and human behavior.* New York: Free Press.

Skinner, B. F. (1957). *Verbal behavior.* Englewood Cliffs, NJ: Prentice-Hall.

Smilansky, S. (1968). *The effects of sociodramatic play on disadvantaged children: Preschool children.* New York: Wiley.

Smith, T. (1990). When and when not to consider the use of aversive interventions in the behavioral treatment of autistic children. In A. C. Repp & N. N. Singh (Eds.), *Perspectives on the use of nonaversive and aversive interventions for persons with developmental disabilities* (pp. 287–297). Sycamore, IL: Sycamore Publishing.

Snow, C. E. (1977). Mother's speech research: From input to interaction. In C. E. Snow & C. A. Furgeson (Eds.), *Talking to children: Language input and acquisition.* New York: Cambridge University Press.

Snyder-McLean, L., & McLean, J. E. (1987). Effectiveness of early intervention for children with language and communication disorders. In M. J. Guralnick & F. C. Bennett (Eds.), *The effectiveness of early intervention for at-risk and handicapped children* (pp. 213–274). San Diego, CA: Academic Press.

Solomons, H. C., & Elardo, R. (1989). Bite injuries at a day care center. *Early Childhood Research Quarterly, 4,* 89–96.

Sowers-Hoag, K. M., Thyer, B. A., & Bailey, J. S. (1987). Promoting automobile safety belt use by young children. *Journal of Applied Behavior Analysis, 20,* 133–138.

Spiegler, M. D. (1983). *Contemporary behavioral therapy.* Palo Alto, CA: Mayfield.

Spradley, J. P. (1980). *Participant observation.* Troy, MO: Holt, Rinehart, & Winston.

Sroufe, L. A., & Rutter, M. (1984). The domain of developmental psychopathology. *Child Development, 55,* 17–29.

Stableford, W. (1979). Parental treatment of a child's noise phobia. *Journal of Behavior Therapy and Experimental Psychiatry, 10,* 159–160.

Stokes, T. F., & Baer, D. M. (1977). An implicit technology of generalization. *Journal of Applied Behavior Analysis, 19,* 349–367.

Stokes, T. F., Fowler, S. A., & Baer, D. M. (1978). Training preschool children to recruit natural communities of reinforcement. *Journal of Applied Behavior Analysis, 11,* 285–303.

Stokes, T. F., & Osnes, P. G. (1986). Programming the generalization of children's social behavior. In P. S. Strain, M. J. Guralnick, & H. M. Walker (Eds.), *Children's social behavior: Development, assessment, and modification* (pp. 407–443). San Diego, CA: Academic Press.

Stokes, T. F., & Osnes, P. G. (1988). The developing applied technology of generalization and maintenance. In R. H. Horner, G. Dunlap, & R. L. Koegel (Eds.), *Generalization and maintenance: Life-style changes in applied settings* (pp. 5–19). Baltimore: Brookes.

Stokes, T. F., & Osnes, P. G. (1989). An operant pursuit of generalization. *Behavior Therapy, 20,* 337–355.

Stolz, S. B., & Associates. (1978). *Ethical principles in behavior modification.* San Francisco: Jossey-Bass.

Strain, P. S. (1985a). Programmatic research on peers as intervention agents for socially isolate classmates. *Pointer, 29,* 22–29.

Strain, P. S. (1985b). Social and nonsocial determinants of acceptability in handicapped preschool children. *Topics in Early Childhood Special Education, 4,* 47–58.

Strain, P. S. (1988). *Early intervention.* Workshop presented at the National Association of School Psychologists.

Strain, P. S., Hoyson, M., & Jamieson, B. (Spring, 1985). Normally developing preschoolers as intervention agents for autistic-like children: Effects on class deportment and social interaction. *Journal of the Division for Early Childhood,* 105–115.

Strain, P. S., Lambert, D. L., Kerr, M. M., Stagg, V., & Lenkner, D. A. (1983). Naturalistic assessment of children's compliance to teachers' requests and consequences for compliance. *Journal of Applied Behavior Analysis, 16,* 243–249.

Strain, P. S., & Odom, S. L. (1986). Peer social initiations: Effective intervention for social skills development of exceptional children. *Exceptional Children, 52,* 543–551.

Strayhorn, J. M., & Strain, P. S. (1986). Social and language skills for preventative mental health: What, how, who, and when. In P. S. Strain, M. J. Guralnick, & H. M. Walker (Eds.), *Children's social behavior: Development, assessment, and modification* (pp. 287–330). San Diego, CA: Academic Press.

Striefel, S. (1981). *How to teach through modeling and imitation.* Austin, TX: Pro-Ed.

Strosahl, K. D., & Linehan, M. M. (1986). Basic issues in behavioral assessment. In A. R. Ciminero, K. S. Calhoun, & H. E. Adams (Eds.), *Handbook of behavioral assessment* (2nd ed., pp. 12–46). New York: Wiley.

Suen, H. K., & Ary, D. (1989). *Analyzing quantitative behavioral observation data.* Hillsdale, NJ: Erlbaum.

Sulzer-Azaroff, B., & Mayer, G. R. (1991). *Behavior analysis for lasting change.* Troy, MO: Holt, Rinehart, & Winston.

Tarpley, B. S., & Saudargas, R. A. (1981). An intervention for a withdrawn child based on teacher recorded levels of social interaction. *School Psychology Review, 10,* 409–412.

Taylor, E. (1988). Attention deficit and conduct disorder syndromes. In M. Rutter, A. H. Tuma, & I. S. Lann (Eds.), *Assessment and diagnosis in child psychopathology* (pp. 377–407). New York: Guilford.

Tertinger, D. A., Greene, B. F., & Lutzker, J. R. (1984). Home safety: Development and validation of one component of an ecobehavioral treatment program for abused and neglected children. *Journal of Applied Behavior Analysis, 17,* 159–174.

Thibodeaux, S., Gardner, K., Forgatch, M., & Reid, J. (1984). *Observer training.* Eugene, OR: Oregon Social Learning Center.

Thomson, C., Holmberg, M., & Baer, D. M. (1974). A brief report on a comparison of time-sampling procedures. *Journal of Applied Behavior Analysis, 7,* 623–626.

Thorndike, R. L., & Hagen, E. P. (1961). *Measurement and evaluation in psychology and education.* New York: Wiley.

Thyer, B. A., & Sowers-Hoag, K. M. (1988). Behavior therapy for separation anxiety disorder. *Behavior Modification, 12,* 205–233.

Timberlake, W., & Allison, J. (1974). Response deprivation: An empirical approach to instrumental performance. *Psychological Review, 81,* 146–164.

Touchette, P. E., & Howard, J. S. (1984). Errorless learning: Reinforcement contingencies and stimulus control transfer in delayed prompting. *Journal of Applied Behavior Analysis, 17,* 175–188.

Tremblay, A., Strain, P. S., Hendrickson, J. M., & Shores, R. E. (1981). Social interactions of normal preschool children: Using normative data for subject and target behavior selection. *Behavior Modification, 5,* 237–253.

Tryon, W. W. (1983). Further implications of Herrnstein's Law of Effect. *American Psychologist, 38,* 613–614.

Turnbull, A. P., & Turnbull, H. R. III (1986). *Families, professionals, and exceptionality: A special partnership.* Columbus, OH: Merrill.

Tversky, A., & Kahneman, D. (1984). The framing of decisions and the psychology of choice. In G. Wright (Ed.), *Behavioral decision making* (pp. 25–41). New York: Plenum.

Twardosz, S., Nordquist, V. M., Simon, R., & Bodkin, D. (1983). The effect of group affection activities on the interaction of socially isolate children. *Analysis and Intervention in Developmental Disabilities, 3,* 311–338.

Tyroler, M. J., & Lahey, B. B. (1980). Effects of contingent observation on the disruptive behavior of a toddler in a group setting. *Child Care Quarterly, 9,* 265–274.

Ultee, C. A., Griffioen, D., & Schellekens, J. (1981). The reduction of anxiety in children: A comparison of the effects of systematic desensitization in vitro and systematic desensitization in vivo. *Behaviour Research and Therapy, 20,* 61–67.

UN Convention on the rights of the child. (1991). *American Psychologist, 46,* 50–52.

Vandell, D. L., Anderson, L. D., Ehrhardt, G., & Wilson, K. S. (1982). Integrating hearing and deaf preschoolers: An attempt to enhance hearing children's interactions with deaf peers. *Child Development, 53,* 1354–1363.

Van Houten, R. (1980). *How to use reprimands.* Austin, TX: Pro-ed.

Van Houten, R. (1984). Setting up performance feedback systems in the classroom. In W. L. Heward, T. E. Heron, D. S. Hill, & J. Trapp-Porter (Eds.), *Focus on behavior analysis in education* (pp. 114–125). Columbus, OH: Merrill.

Van Houten, R., Axelrod, S., Bailey, J. S., Favell, J. E., Foxx, R. M., Iwata, B. A., & Lovaas, O. I. (1988). The right to effective behavioral treatment. *Journal of Applied Behavior Analysis, 21,* 381–384.

Vedder-Dubocq, S. A. (1990). *An investigation of the utility of the Parenting Stress Index for intervention decisions.* Unpublished doctoral dissertation, University of Cincinnati.

Vincent, L. J., Salisbury, C. L., Strain, P., McCormick, C., & Tessier, A. (1990). A behavioral-ecological approach to early intervention: Focus on cultural diversity. In S. J. Meisels & J. P. Shonkoff (Eds.), *Handbook of early childhood intervention* (pp. 173–195). New York: Cambridge University Press.

Vincent, L. J., Salisbury, C., Walter, G., Brown, P., Gruenewald, L. J., & Powers, M. (1980). Program evaluation and curriculum development in early childhood/special education: Criteria of the next environment. In W. Sailor, B. Wilcox, & L. Brown (Eds.), *Methods of instruction for severely handicapped students* (pp. 303–328). Baltimore: Brookes.

Vygotsky, L. S. (1978). *Mind in society: The development of higher psychological processes* (Cole, M., John-Steiner, V., Scribner, S., & Souberman, E., Eds.). Cambridge, MA: Harvard University Press.

Wahler, R. G. (1980). The insular mother: Her problems in parent-child treatment. *Journal of Applied Behavior Analysis, 13,* 207–219.

Wahler, R. G., & Afton, A. D. (1980). Attentional processes in insular and noninsular mothers: Some differences in their summary reports about child problem behaviors. *Child Behavior Therapy, 2,* 25–41.

Wahler, R. G., & Cormier, W. H. (1970). The ecological interview: A first step in outpatient child behavior therapy. *Journal of Behavior Therapy and Experimental Psychiatry, 1,* 279–289.

Wahler, R. G., & Dumas, J. E. (1986). "A chip off the old block": Some interpersonal characteristics of coercive children across generations. In P. S. Strain, M. J. Guralnick, & H. M. Walker (Eds.), *Children's social behavior: Development, assess-*

ment, and modification (pp. 49–91). San Diego, CA: Academic Press.

Wahler, R. G., & Fox, J. J. (1980). Solitary toy play and time out: A family treatment package for children with aggressive and oppositional behavior. *Journal of Applied Behavior Analysis, 13,* 23–39.

Wahler, R. G., & Hann, D. M. (1984). The communication patterns of troubled mothers: In search of a keystone in the generalization of parenting skills. *Education and Treatment of Children, 7,* 335–350.

Wahler, R. G., House, A. E., & Stambaugh, E. E. (1976). *Ecological assessment of child problem behavior.* New York: Pergamon.

Walker, C. E., Kenning, M., & Faust-Campanile, J. (1989). Enuresis and encopresis. In E. J. Mash & R. A. Barkley (Eds.), *Treatment of childhood disorders* (pp. 423–448). New York: Guilford.

Walker, H. M. (1983, February). Applications of response cost in school settings: Outcomes, issues and recommendations. *Exceptional Education Quarterly,* 47–55.

Walker, H. M., & Hops, H. (1976). Use of normative peer data as a standard for evaluating classroom treatment effects. *Journal of Applied Behavior Analysis, 9,* 159–168.

Walker, H. M., & Rankin, R. (1983). Assessing the behavioral expectations and demands of less restrictive settings. *School Psychology Review, 12,* 274–284.

Walker, H. M., Severson, H., & Haring, N. (1986). *Standardized screening and identification of behavior disordered pupils in the elementary age range: Rationale, procedures, and guidelines.* Unpublished manuscript.

Walle, D. L., Hobbs, S. A., & Caldwell, H. S. (1984). Sequencing of parent training procedures: Effects on child noncompliance and treatment acceptability. *Behavior Modification, 8,* 540–552.

Warren, S. F., & Gazdag, G. (1990). Facilitating early language development with milieu intervention procedures. *Journal of Early Intervention, 14,* 62–86.

Warren, S. F., & Kaiser, A. P. (1986). Incidental language teaching: A critical review. *Journal of Speech and Hearing Disorders, 51,* 291–299.

Watson, D. L., & Tharp, R. G. (1989). *Self-directed behavior: Self-modification for personal adjustment.* Pacific Grove, CA: Brooks/Cole.

Waye, M. F. (1979). Behavioral treatment of a child displaying comic-book mediated fear of hand shrinking: A case study. *Journal of Pediatric Psychology, 4,* 43–47.

Webster-Stratton, C. (1981a). Modification of a mothers' behaviors and attitudes through a videotape modeling group discussion program. *Behavior Therapy, 12,* 634–642.

Webster-Stratton, C. (1981b). Videotape modeling: A method of parent education. *Journal of Clinical Child Psychology,* 93–97.

Webster-Stratton, C. (1982). The long-term effects of a videotape modeling parent-training program: Comparison of immediate and 1-year follow-up results. *Behavior Therapy, 13,* 702–714.

Webster-Stratton, C., & Hammond, M. (1988). Maternal depression and its relationship to life stress, perceptions of child behavior problems, parenting behaviors, and child conduct problems. *Journal of Abnormal Child Psychology, 16,* 299–315.

Webster-Stratton, C., Hollingsworth, T., & Kolpacoff, M. (1989). The long-term effectiveness and clinical significance of three cost-effective programs for families with conduct-problem children. *Journal of Consulting and Clinical Psychology, 57,* 550–553.

Weinrott, M. R. (1974). A training program in behavior modification for siblings of the retarded. *American Journal of Orthopsychiatry, 44*(3), 362–375.

Weintraub, S., Winters, K. C., & Neale, J. M. (1986). Competence and vulnerability in children with an affectively disordered parent. In M. Rutter, C. E. Izard, & P. B. Read (Eds.), *Depression in young children: Developmental and clinical perspectives* (pp. 205–220). New York: Guilford.

Weitzman, J. (1985). Engaging the severely dysfunctional family in treatment: Basic considerations. *Family Process, 24,* 473–485.

Wenar, C. (1982). Developmental psychopathology: Its nature and models. *Journal of Clinical Child Psychology, 11,* 192–201.

Weninger, J. M., & Baer, R. A. (1990). Correspondence training with time delay: A comparison of reinforcement of compliance. *Education and Treatment of Children, 13,* 36–44.

Werner, E. E. (1986). A longitudinal study of perinatal risk. In D. C. Farran & J. D. McKinney (Eds.), *Risk in intellectual and psychosocial development* (pp. 3–27). San Diego, CA: Academic Press.

Werner, E. E., & Smith, R. S. (1982). *Vulnerable but invincible: A study of resilient children.* New York: McGraw-Hill.

Whalen, C. K. (1989). Attention deficit and hyperactivity disorders. In T. H. Ollendick & M. Hersen (Eds.), *Handbook of child psychopathology* (2nd ed., pp. 131–169). New York: Plenum.

White, B. L., Kaban, B. T., & Attanucci, J. S. (1979). *The origins of human competence.* Lexington, MA: Heath.

White, K. R. (1985–86). Efficacy of early intervention. *Journal of Special Education, 19,* 401–416.

White, O. R. (1974). *The "split-middle"—a "quickie" method of trend estimation.* Seattle, WA: Experimental Education Unit. Child Development and Mental Retardation Center, University of Washington.

White, O. R., & Haring, N. G. (1980). *Exceptional teaching* (2nd ed.). Columbus, OH: Merrill.

White, W. C., & Davis, M. T. (1974). Vicarious extinction of phobia behavior in early childhood. *Journal of Abnormal Child Psychology, 2,* 25–37.

Wilkins, R. (1985). A comparison of elective mutism and emotional disorders in children. *British Journal of Psychiatry, 146,* 198–203.

Willems, E. P. (1977). Steps toward an ecobehavioral technology. In A. Rogers-Warren & S. F. Warren (Eds.), *Ecological perspectives in behavior analysis* (pp. 39–61). Baltimore: University Park Press.

Williamson, D. A., Sanders, S. H., Sewell, W. R., Haney, J. N., & White, D. (1977). The behavioral treatment of elective mutism: Two case studies. *Journal of Behavior Therapy and Experimental Psychiatry, 8,* 143–149.

Willoughby-Herb, S. J., & Neisworth, J. T. (1982). *HICOMP preschool curriculum.* Columbus, OH: Merrill.

Wilson, F. E., & Evans, I. M. (1983). The reliability of target-behavior selection in behavioral assessment. *Behavioral Assessment, 5,* 15–32.

Witt, J. C., & Elliott, S. N. (1985). Acceptability of classroom management strategies. In T. R. Kratochwill (Ed.), *Advances in school psychology* (vol. 4, pp. 251–288). Hillsdale, NJ: Erlbaum.

Witt, J. C., & Martens, B. K. (1988). Problems with problem-solving consultation: A re-analysis of assumptions, methods, and goals. *School Psychology Review, 17,* 211–226.

Witt, J. C., Martens, B. K., & Elliott, S. N. (1984). Factors affecting teachers' judgments of the acceptability of behavioral interventions: Time involvement, behavior problem severity, and type of intervention. *Behavior Therapy, 15,* 204–209.

Wohlwill, J. F. (1980). Cognitive development in childhood. In O. G. Brim, Jr., & J. Kagan (Eds.), *Constancy and change in human development* (pp. 359–444). Cambridge, MA: Harvard University Press.

Wolery, M. (1989). Using direct observation in assessment. In D. B. Bailey, Jr., & M. Wolery (Eds.), *Assessing infants and preschoolers with handicaps* (pp. 64–96). Columbus, OH: Merrill.

Wolery, M. (1991). Instruction in early childhood special education: "Seeing through a glass darkly . . . knowing part." *Exceptional Children, 58,* 127–135.

Wolery, M., Bailey, D. B., & Sugai, G. M. (1988). *Effective teaching: Principles and procedures of applied behavior analysis with exceptional students.* Needham Heights, MA: Allyn & Bacon.

Wolery, M., & Gast, D. L. (1990). Re-framing the debate: Finding middle ground and defining the role of social validity. In A. C. Repp & N. N. Singh (Eds.), *Perspectives on the use of nonaversive and aversive interventions for persons with developmental disabilities* (pp. 129–143). Sycamore, IL: Sycamore Publishing.

Wolf, M. M. (1978). Social validity: The case for subjective measurement or how applied behavior analysis is finding its heart. *Journal of Applied Behavior Analysis, 11,* 203–214.

Wolfe, D. A. (1987). *Child abuse: Implications for child development and psychopathology.* Newbury Park, CA: Sage.

Wolfe, D. A., & Bourdeau, P. A. (1987). Current issues in the assessment of parent-child conflict. *Behavioral Assessment, 9,* 271–290.

Wolfe, D. A., Edwards, B., Manion, I., & Koverola, C. (1988).

Early identification for parents at risk of child abuse and neglect: A preliminary investigation. *Journal of Consulting and Clinical Psychology, 56,* 40–47.

Wolfe, D. A., Sandler, J., & Kaufman, K. (1981). A competency-based parent training program for abusive parents. *Journal of Consulting and Clinical Psychology, 49,* 633–640.

Wolfe, D. A., & Wolfe, V. (1988). The sexually abused child. In E. J. Mash & L. G. Terdal (Eds.), *Behavioral assessment of childhood disorders* (2nd ed., pp. 670–716). New York: Guilford.

Wolfensberger, W. (1972). *The principle of normalization in human services.* Toronto: National Institute on Mental Retardation.

Wolpe, J. (1962). The experimental foundations of some new psychotherapeutic methods. In A. J. Bachrach (Ed.), *Experimental foundations of clinical psychology* (pp. 554–575). New York: Basic Books.

Wright, H. F. (1967). *Recording and analyzing child behavior.* New York: HarperCollins.

Wurtele, S. K., & Drabman, R. S. (1984). "Beat the Buzzer" for classroom dawdling: A one-year trial. *Behavior Therapy, 15,* 403–409.

Yarrow, L. J. (1960). Interviewing children. In P. H. Mussen (Ed.), *Handbook of research methods in child development* (pp. 561–602). New York: Wiley.

Yeaton, W. H., & Bailey, J. S. (1978). Teaching pedestrian safety skills to young children: An analysis and one-year follow up. *Journal of Applied Behavior Analysis, 11,* 315–329.

Yeaton, W. H., & Bailey, J. S. (1983). Utilization analysis of a pedestrian safety training program. *Journal of Applied Behavior Analysis, 16,* 203–216.

Zangwill, W. M. (1984). An evaluation of a parent training program. *Child & Family Behavior Therapy, 5,* 1–16.

Zigler, E., & Valentine, J. (Eds.). (1979). *Project Head Start: A legacy of the war on poverty.* New York: Free Press.

Zwick, R. (1988). Another look at interrater agreement. *Psychological Bulletin, 103,* 374–378.

Name Index ❧❧❧❧❧❧❧

Subject Index

replicated, 107–127; research-based, 10–13, 107, 109, 143–213; resistance to, 111–112; resources for, 109, 120; risks of, 18–19; school-based, 293–367; scripts for, 226–227; self-mediated, 112–113, 194–197; self-monitoring, 88–89, 237–242; side effects of, 115–116; training for, 114, 121, 227; validity of, 36, 124, 135; withdrawal of, 125. *See also* Naturalistic interventions

Interviews: with children, 55–56; and observations, 61–62, 64; technical adequacy of, 59–62; techniques for, 56–59; by telephone, 58–60. *See also* Ecobehavioral interviews; Problem-solving interviews; Waking day and sleep

IQ tests, and cognitive change, 15–16

J

Judgment. *See* Professional judgment

K

K-ABC, 34

Kappa, 43

Keystone behavior: compliance as, 257; self-observation as, 86–87; self-regulation as, 194; and target behaviors, 103–104

L

Labeling and classification, 19, 35, 102, 112

Lag sequential analysis, for observations, 85–86

Language: and brief time delay, 156–157; and correspondence training, 198; developing, 153; early interventions for, 159–160; incidental teaching of, 156–159; mand-model for, 155–156; naturalistic interventions for, 6–7, 153–159; pragmatic, 154–155;

shaping of, 172; skills, 153–160; spontaneous, 172

LAP-D, 36

Learning: for dining, 233–236; errorless, 307–309; in family system, 227–242; natural strategies for, 147–153; observational, processes of, 151–152; power of, 146–147; by shopping, 228–233; and sibling interventions, 237–242; social, 258–259, 289–290

Legal and ethical issues: aspects of, 42–43, 375–389; of aversive procedures, 162, 385–388; of confidentiality, 388–389; of consent, 375–377, 381–383; of controversial treatments, 377–388; and right to education and treatment, 389

Legislation, and early intervention, 1, 389

Loose training. *See* Generalization

M

McCarthy Scales, 34

Macroconsultation, and curriculum-based interventions, 303–304

Mainstreaming, reverse, 325. *See also* Integration

Mands, in language model, 155–156. *See also* Language

Mediation, in learning experiences, 145–146

Mediators, functional, 119–120

Medical problems, screening of, 100

Medications, and attention deficits, 276, 277

Micronorms, and recording, 81–83

Milwaukee Project, and IQ change, 16

"Minimum 'celeration lines," 136, 137

Modeling: for fears, 245; learning from, 150–152, 164, 169, 174; and observational learning, 150–152; for social withdrawal, 346; symbolic, 245. *See also* Social cognitive theory